What readers are saying about *Prototype and script.aculo.us*

I use Prototype and script.aculo.us all day in my work, yet I learned a lot reading this book. I frequently dive back into it to find information I can't find anywhere else. This is a helpful book written by an experienced teacher that will help anybody who wants to easily add some JavaScript features to their application.

▶ **Stéphane Akkaoui**
   Ruby on Rails developer, Feedback 2.0

If you are thinking about learning a JavaScript framework (or would like your team to...), this book is a step-by-step guide to painless Prototype and script.aculo.us. From the basics to advanced code, this book is written in the cleanest style. You'll be amazed to find out all that JavaScript can do.

▶ **Arnaud Berthomier**
   Web developer, Weborama

This is a book that every Prototype and script.aculo.us developer should have. It's more than a reference book; you will find everything you need to know about these two frameworks, and you'll learn good JavaScript practices. I have learned great tips about script.aculo.us and have discovered Prototype functions to make my code more concise and more readable while improving performance. Thanks for this book!

▶ **Sébastien Gruhier**
   Founder and CTO, Xilinus

Tired of waiting around for a page to reload, again and again? Well, if you're like me, you're looking for a smart and elegant way to inject pieces of Ajax into your application. Well, you'll find in this book all you need to know about Prototype and script.aculo.us. This book will show you the best practices without forgetting the fun!

▶ **Amir Jaballah**
   Technical Leader, Fastconnect

At Relevance, we use Prototype and Scriptaculous for all of our web projects. When we train other developers, we always get the same two questions: Where can I get more information on the libraries? and Where can I learn to program JavaScript in a modern, functional style?

Prototype and script.aculo.us answers *both* of these questions. Christophe demonstrates the power and the beauty of these libraries, and of the idiomatic JavaScript style they employ. And he doesn't just skim the surface—his intro chapter shows more advanced Java-Script usage than some entire books on the subject. Even after years of using Prototype and Scripty, I learned new things in every chapter. Thanks, Christophe!

▶ **Stuart Halloway**
CEO, Relevance, Inc.
www.thinkrelevance.com

Prototype and script.aculo.us

You Never Knew JavaScript Could Do This!

Prototype and script.aculo.us
You Never Knew JavaScript Could Do This!

Christophe Porteneuve

The Pragmatic Bookshelf
Raleigh, North Carolina   Dallas, Texas

Many of the designations used by manufacturers and sellers to distinguish their products are claimed as trademarks. Where those designations appear in this book, and The Pragmatic Programmers, LLC was aware of a trademark claim, the designations have been printed in initial capital letters or in all capitals. The Pragmatic Starter Kit, The Pragmatic Programmer, Pragmatic Programming, Pragmatic Bookshelf and the linking *g* device are trademarks of The Pragmatic Programmers, LLC.

Every precaution was taken in the preparation of this book. However, the publisher assumes no responsibility for errors or omissions, or for damages that may result from the use of information (including program listings) contained herein.

Our Pragmatic courses, workshops, and other products can help you and your team create better software and have more fun. For more information, as well as the latest Pragmatic titles, please visit us at

http://www.pragprog.com

ISBN-10: 1-934356-01-8

ISBN-13: 978-1-934356-01-2

Printed on acid-free paper with 50% recycled, 15% post-consumer content.

First printing, November 2007

Version: 2007-11-19

To Élodie, my love, ever supportive.
You're my true home.

Contents

Preface

Prototype began its life in early 2005 at a time when the name "Java-Script" still evoked images of pop-up ads, blinking text, and copied-and-pasted <script> tags in most developers' minds. Even though web applications such as Gmail and Google Suggest were showing the world that JavaScript (and this new thing called "Ajax") could actually be used to improve the user experience, implementing these new techniques in your own apps proved to be painful and frustrating. Each web browser had its own quirks to work around, and most existing code wasn't designed to take advantage of JavaScript's object-oriented nature or powerful closure capabilities.

Inspired by the expressiveness of dynamic languages such as Ruby, we set out to build a browser programming environment that we could actually look forward to using. We started with a small set of tools that let us work with classes and functions. Then we extracted common Ajax and DOM manipulation operations from our existing applications. In March 2005, we released Prototype 1.0 as part of the Ruby on Rails framework. Prototype has grown a lot since then, but it remains focused on providing the best possible environment for JavaScript developers.

As for script.aculo.us, or "Scripty" as it's affectionately known by the Core team, it started out as a short section of code in Prototype that implemented the now-ubiquitous "yellow fade technique." With a desire to make web applications more user-friendly—and provide eye candy that's really useful to boot—it quickly grew into a complete real-time DOM-based effects engine, drag-and-drop framework, and controls library. Version 1.0 was released in June 2005.

You should understand that script.aculo.us is distinct from many other UI libraries in that it does not try to shield the developer from the DOM but rather extends and improves the DOM so that developers and designers can capitalize on their existing knowledge.

Combined with Prototype, it's engineered for building your own widgets, controls, and basically any artsy awesomeness in less time than it takes to configure heavier, widget-based frameworks.

To paraphrase the motto of Ruby, the language whose design has heavily influenced our libraries: Prototype and script.aculo.us are "a web programmer's best friends." According to the feedback we've received, we're not the only ones who feel that way.

Two-and-a-half years after the initial release, Prototype and script.aculo.us are in use on many of the web's most popular websites and power all sorts of innovative web applications.

This rapid popular uptake has been possible only through the efforts of the Prototype Core team, consisting of Seth Dillingham, Andrew Dupont, Mislav Marohnić, Justin Palmer, Christophe Porteneuve, Tobie Langel, Scott Raymond, and Dan Webb; the thousands of hours of work by hundreds of contributors from the Prototype and script.aculo.us community; and, of course, Christophe, for providing this very book.

Big thanks to all of them and to you.

Sam Stephenson (Creator of Prototype)
October 15, 2007

Thomas Fuchs (Creator of script.aculo.us)
October 15, 2007

Chapter 1

Introduction

Prototype is a wonderful JavaScript library aimed at easing dynamic web application development. Its close friend, script.aculo.us, provides a lot of user interface–oriented features with a high wow factor (still), such as drag and drop, autocompletion, mouse-driven element sorting, awesome visual effects, and in-place editing. It's all at your fingertips, with only a couple lines of script.

The close relation between the two lies in that they both originated in the Ruby on Rails universe, as Rails "spin-offs." They are provided with Rails but can be obtained separately on their official web sites and are actually backend-agnostic: you can use them over PHP, .NET, J2EE, Python, Delphi, or anything else that helps you produce dynamic web pages. And indeed, thousands of developers do just that every day. Also, script.aculo.us relies on Prototype, and both libraries are written in a consistent style.

These libraries will, quite simply, rock your world. You will discover, as I and countless others have, that client-side web page development does not need to be gruesome, kludgy, or even dull. It can be expressive, productive, efficient, clean, portable, and intellectually pleasing. It can call to our technical sense of aesthetics, and most important, it can be a huge amount of fun.

1.1 It's About Time

Prototype and script.aculo.us have been around for quite some time now. According to an Ajaxian.com survey in September 2006,[1] they

---

1. http://ajaxian.com/archives/ajaxiancom-2006-survey-results

are by far the two most popular JavaScript frameworks, with whopping 43% and 33% adoption rates, way more than the third contender, Dojo. With the advent of Prototype's new official site and comprehensive online reference documentation in January 2007, it will likely have an even higher adoption rate by the time this book hits the shelves.

Still, a year ago, both frameworks already were extremely popular. And what did shelves have to say about it? Nothing. In November 2006, Scott Raymond and Sergio Pereira produced a 30-page Prototype quick reference in O'Reilly's Short Cuts series, but that's it. The script.aculo.us wiki is a good starting point but uses a fairly inconsistent style and is way out-of-date. As for Prototype, most addicts started out with Sergio's unofficial page and then had to dive into the source code to try to figure out all the neat tricks.

And some source code it is. Both frameworks squeeze all the power they can get out of JavaScript and are written in a fairly advanced style. The unfortunate result is that those diving into the code without serious JavaScript knowledge could very easily become lost, dazzled, confused, or all of these at once. Although accurate, timely, and polite answers could be found on the Google Group,[2] all users agreed that some production-quality, official documentation was in order. It is now available, at least for Prototype, at its official website.[3]

"This is all well and good," you might say, "but then what the heck do I need this book for?" Well, there are several reasons why reading this book is a good idea:

- This book goes far beyond the documentation available online. It includes a lot more examples, goes further into details, and provides a lot more besides the actual reference material: a full-on tutorial; real-world scenarios and their solutions; and plenty of extra tips, tricks, best practices, and all-around advice.

- You may well want to leverage passive offline time to learn. This is about reading on the bus, in the subway, or in the passenger seat in a carpool highway lane.

- Even active offline time needs a book, such as when you're working on your laptop in a train or plane.

---

2. http://groups.google.com/group/rubyonrails-spinoffs
3. http://prototypejs.org

- Like many people, you may just like having the physical copy of the book close at hand. It just is nicer to the eye than on-screen text, you know?

I discovered Prototype and script.aculo.us in late 2005 and dived into them for real around June 2006 (since my early perusal had made me fall in love with them) when I was writing my first book, *Bien développer pour le Web 2.0*, which featured rather detailed coverage of them through dedicated chapters. I loved the code I saw, I loved the code I could write, and I started contributing heavily to the Google Group and then the official documentation site. So if you find examples in this book that also appear online, this is no accident. I may well have written the online page. And at any rate, when you have a very good example available, you just use it.

1.2 What's in This Book, and How Is It Organized?

The book is organized in three parts: the case-study tutorial, the Prototype reference, and the script.aculo.us reference. These are not references in the usual sense of the term, which generally implies a rather dry series of object and method descriptions sprinkled with laconic snippets of code. These references are written like books unto themselves, arranged by topics, and they devote plenty of time and effort to providing background, explaining concepts, detailing the architecture, and helping you grasp the big picture as well as the details.

Both reference parts open with an introductory chapter; these are Chapter 2, *Discovering Prototype*, on page 9 and Chapter 13, *Discovering script.aculo.us*, on page 245. They're here to help you dip your foot and test the waters. Then they tackle the library by topic, in roughly prioritized order, with the most critical appearing first. This is actually not a straight rule; for instance, in script.aculo.us, features are orthogonal, so you can study them in any order. I decided to go first with what seems most useful and perhaps brings the most fun.

This book is, quite simply, the *comprehensive reference* for these two libraries, with enough extra stuff to help you actually master them, be able to extend them for your own needs, or even contribute to them. This is the single book you need to become a Rails spin-offs guru. Doesn't that sound good? Of course it does.

Some Things This Book Doesn't Specifically Address

Although Prototype helps and encourages best practices such as unobtrusive JavaScript, better accessibility, and so on, it does not guarantee it at all: it's a tool, not a process.

I am personally very fond of JavaScript accessibility and the narrower subject of Ajax accessibility. I discussed them at length in my previous book, *Bien développer pour le Web 2.0*, which is, however, not available in English so far. . . . But the focus of this book is Prototype and script.-aculo.us, which makes it a sizeable book as it is. To stay focused and avoid straying too far afield, I won't cover the details of such general matters, which can be tackled and honored with any set of tools, as long as your development process embraces the right constraints.

Who Is This Book For?

This book is essentially for any JavaScript developer interested in fully leveraging the power of these two wonderful libraries: Prototype and script.aculo.us. I expect that you have at least a decent understanding of JavaScript (although you may not master its tricky details) and (X)HTML, as well as basic knowledge of the DOM and CSS. That's all you'll need, really! Whenever we tread in deeper waters, I'll try to help you wade through by explaining whatever details are relevant.

1.3 Acknowledgments

Writing a book is no walk in the park. It takes time, effort, dedication, steadfastness, and a tremendous amount of help and support.

I cannot thank Pragmatic Programmers enough. These guys take you through a book-writing journey that leaves you loathe to write for anybody else. As publishing goes, they're the bleeding edge and a real magnet for technical writers with a soft spot for efficiency and cool tool chains. My heartfelt thanks especially to Dave Thomas, Andy Hunt, and Daniel H. Steinberg. You're putting the word *editor* into a whole new perspective and a wonderful one at that.

I would also like to express my undying gratitude to my copy editor, Kim Wimpsett, who did a wonderful job with enormous insight and attention to detail; to my indexer, Sara Lynn Eastler, who produced the outstanding, Pragmatic-Bookshelf-quality index at the end of this book; and to my typesetter, Steve Peter, who provided all the final touches that make it all look so prim.

Before all this started, I asked Justin Palmer if I could step in his shoes and write this book for Pragmatic Programmers. Not only was he very gracious about it, but he got me on board with the Prototype documentation effort and later with Prototype Core. It has been an amazing ride so far. Thanks a bunch, Justin.

This book would be an order of magnitude less pleasant to read if it were not for the keen eyes and minds of its reviewers, both "live" and at the final draft stage. I am deeply in the debt of Stéphane Akkaoui, Arnaud Berthomier, Craig Castelaz, Seth Dillingham (Prototype Core), Tom Gregory (a prominent voice on the official mailing list), Sébastien Gruhier (of Prototype Window Class fame), Amir Jaballah, Tobie Langel (Prototype Core), Justin Palmer (again), and Sunny Ripert. Many readers also got onto the bandwagon at the beta stage and went so far as to report a number of typos, errata, and the like. Among those, I'm especially grateful to Steve Erbach, Brandon Kelly, and "DarkRat" (whose real name I'm sorry not to know), who've been particularly helpful.

Sam Stephenson (creator of Prototype) and Thomas Fuchs (creator of script.aculo.us) first deserve the highest accolade for having churned out those two libraries. The groundbreaking nature of their work cannot be emphasized enough, and the immense satisfaction they have brought to countless web developers commands respect. When it comes to this particular book—the first ever focusing in depth on their babies! —they not only revised the final draft but also agreed to write the preface, for which I cannot help but feel honored. Working with them is a privilege and a very fun ride, and I take this opportunity to thank them thrice over: for the libraries, for the review, and for the preface.

Élodie Jaubert, my fiancée, took admirably well to this second book-writing endeavor, barely four months after the previous one ended. She showed wonderful patience and support through the eight months it took to write and edit this one, bearing with quite a few late evenings and afternoons I spent writing at my desk, pushing me ahead, and giving me strength and love at all turns. I could not dream of more. This book is for her.

Part I

Prototype

Furious activity is no substitute for understanding.
  ▶ H. H. Williams

Chapter 2

Discovering Prototype

This part provides in-depth coverage of Prototype, which is the Java-Script library at the core of this book. Prototype is a very *dense* library: although rather small (at about 120KB raw, less than 30KB gzipped, it is no huge framework), it is replete with features, helper objects, and nifty tools, arranged in a reasonably consistent set.

But before we go ahead, we need to answer a few questions and tackle the more involved subjects with a clear mind and proper expectations. For example, what's Prototype exactly? What should we expect it to do for us? What kind of lingo may we need to learn? And apparently it relies on...well, prototypes, so what *are* JavaScript prototypes in the first place? So, I'll start with explaining all this quickly; you will then be armed with everything necessary to fully leverage the following chapters.

2.1 What Is Prototype, and What Is It Not?

Prototype is a JavaScript *library* designed to improve the browser's JavaScript environment; it extends DOM elements and built-in types with useful methods, has built-in support for class-style OOP (including inheritance), advanced support for event management, and powerful Ajax features.

Prototype is *not* a complete application development framework: it does not provide widgets or a full set of standard algorithms, I/O systems, or what have you. It stands in this middle ground between down-and-dirty manual coding of everything and full-fledged frameworks with their countless objects. Most massive frameworks do indeed use Prototype internally and build upon it.

Note, however, that there is a more visual-oriented library working closely with Prototype called script.aculo.us; we'll explore it in the second part of this book.

Although inspired by the Ruby programming language, Prototype is *not* attached to any server-side technology. True, it stems from the Ruby on Rails universe, but it is a stand-alone spin-off. It is indeed very easy to use Prototype when coding with Ruby on Rails, but the library can be used with no difficulty over any back end, such as PHP, J2EE, or ASP.NET. It is very successfully used in production for projects with all these technologies and more.

Prototype is distributed as a single file called prototype.js, currently weighing about 120KB (before any sort of packing or gzipping). Despite this relative litheness, it provides a large set of features, most of which interoperate in an intuitive way.

2.2 Using Prototype in Our Project

So, how do we go about enabling Prototype in a web page? It is really quite simple: we just need to load prototype.js, and loading it first will let us leverage its power in any other scripts we have. This loading is best done with a simple <*script*> element in the <*head*> of our page:

```
<head>
  ...
  <script type="text/javascript" src=".../prototype.js"></script>
  ...
</head>
```

Where Can We Get Prototype?

The official website is the authoritative source for the latest public version of Prototype and also provides detailed, up-to-date API documentation with plenty of examples, tutorial-style articles, and a blog updated by the Prototype Core team. It's located at http://prototypejs.org.

2.3 What Does Our JavaScript Look Like When Using Prototype?

Good question. To make a long story short, it looks *darn good*. It looks nifty. It looks smart. It looks Rubyesque. JavaScript is fun again. But don't take my word for it—see for yourself. Let's look at a simple example and then at a more involved, combined demo that will help you understand just how easy Prototype coding is.

A Note About Versions

This book covers Prototype 1.6. To understand how Prototype evolved, and where it's headed, it's worth looking at a short history.

The release of version 1.5, on January 18, 2007, was a major event for people using only the public versions. They had been stuck with 1.4 for a year, and 1.5 brought about a tremendous amount of improvements and new features.

These days, Prototype is rapidly pacing ahead, moving in swifter, shorter steps. Version 1.5.1 was released in April 2007 and brought a few new features and significant refactoring and cleanup of the code base. Version 1.5.1.1, a bugfix release with a few nice surgical improvements to boot, was released in June. With a first release candidate in early August 2007 and a final release scheduled in October 2007, version 1.6 is a major step ahead. It introduces a complete overhaul of the event system, the first improvements on subclassing, and many more new features. Prototype Core is considering a later 1.6.1 release with yet more event- and class-related improvements, and then we'll be done with the 1.x branch. The next steps will take us to 2.0. And we're hard at work on it already!

The information in this book is current at the time we're about to go to press. This means by the time this book is out, you're at worst one or two months behind; in other words, you're up-to-date on 95% of the library and have only to peruse the recent items in the change log to be on the very top of things.

You can get additional information on later releases and feature updates on the book's website and blog at: thebungeebook.net.

An important note: the code in the following two examples is intention-
ally heavy on Prototype "magic," which means it might use advanced
syntaxes and concepts that you may not—yet—be familiar with. Fear
not, however: this was done to let you feel the might of properly leveraging what Prototype has to offer you, and we'll dive together, in detail,
into these capabilities and syntaxes in the following chapters. If some of
the code is unclear as you go through this chapter, I'm confident you'll
be able to come back and squeeze every ounce of meaning out of it once
you're through the Prototype part of the book. In the meantime, I did
try to lace the text with enough explanations that you can grab the idea
and general dynamics of the code.

A Simple Example: Playing with People

Er, this sounds like an invitation to use pyramid scams on unsuspect-
ing strangers. Actually, I just suggest we put together a simple class
representing a person, then start spawning a few people with it, and
finally fiddle with the resulting population to extract a few pieces of
information. We'll do all of it the Prototype way.

I bet you could use some code before deciding whether what I just said
made any sense. So, let's create an empty folder, put Prototype's proto-
type.js in it (version 1.5.1 or later), and write the following bench page
for us to play in:

`prototype/intro/basic/index.html`

```
<!DOCTYPE html PUBLIC "-//W3C//DTD XHTML 1.0 Strict//EN"
  "http://www.w3.org/TR/xhtml1/DTD/xhtml1-strict.dtd">
<html xmlns="http://www.w3.org/1999/xhtml" lang="en-US" xml:lang="en-US">
<head>
    <meta http-equiv="Content-Type" content="text/html; charset=utf-8" />
    <title>A basic demo of Prototype at work</title>
    <link rel="stylesheet" type="text/css" href="basic.css" />
    <script type="text/javascript" src="prototype.js"></script>
    <script type="text/javascript" src="basic.js"></script>
</head>
<body>

<h1>A basic demo of Prototype at work</h1>

<div id="result"></div>

</body>
</html>
```

The *<div>* with id="result" is just a placeholder for our upcoming script
to spew HTML into.

Now, let's create this basic.js we referenced and write a Person class. In Prototype, we would do it this way:

`prototype/intro/basic/basic.js`

```
Line 1  var Person = Class.create({
          initialize: function(first, last, city, country) {
            this.first = first;
            this.last = last;
    5       this.city = city;
            this.country = country;
          },

          getFullName: function() {
   10         return (this.first + ' ' + this.last).strip();
          },

          getDisplayName: function() {
            var result = this.getFullName();
   15       if (this.city || this.country) {
              result += ' (';
              if (this.city) {
                result += this.city;
                if (this.country) result += ', ';
   20         }
              result += (this.country || '');
              result += ')';
            }
            return result;
   25     }
        });
```

This first fragment deserves some explanation:

- The Class.create() call on line 1 produces a Prototype class. For the JavaScript gurus among you, yes, that is a function object.

- When using Prototype classes, initialization is taken care of via a initialize() method, here on line 2, which receives all the arguments passed at construction time.

- Finally, our getDisplayName() method, starting on line 13, builds a variable-form string representation of the person, with the first name and/or last name and possibly city/country information between parentheses, all of it properly formatted and adjusted.

Being defined at the prototype level, all of these methods are basically *instance methods*. We'll add a *class method* (or *static method*) that provides a comparator between two people.

Just to make our code more "Prototypish" and to demonstrate neat JavaScript usage, we'll make it conform to the following usage syntax:

```
Person.compare([criterion = 'first',] p1, p2) → (-1|0|1)
```

Now, that's unusual—optional arguments appearing first! It's actually easy to deal with once you regard your arguments as just an array of values, much like Ruby would allow. Here is the code:

prototype/intro/basic/basic.js

```
Line 1   Person.compare = function() {
             var prop = 'first', args = $A(arguments);
             if (args.length == 3 && typeof args[0] == 'string')
                 prop = args.shift();
     5       var c1 = args[0][prop], c2 = args[1][prop];
             return (c1 < c2 ? -1 : (c2 < c1 ? 1 : 0));
         };
```

As you may know, functions in JavaScript get an automatic arguments variable that holds their arguments. It's not an array properly speaking, but it looks like one (in other words, it features a [] operator and a length property), so we can readily convert it to an actual array with Prototype's $A() utility function, as shown on line 2.

Prototype-enhanced arrays are mighty to say the least, but in this particular occasion all we need is their native shift() method, which will take the first element out and return it.

By simply checking whether there are three arguments instead of two, with a String-typed first one, we know we've been called with an explicit field name as the comparison criterion. So, we override our prop variable with the first argument, which we take out of the argument list at the same time.

Now that we have the name of the field we're going to use for comparison, we need to dynamically access it for each of the two people we're about to compare. This is trivially done in JavaScript with the square brackets operator, [], which we use on line 5. When used on an object, it takes an expression that evaluates to the name of a property in the object, and it returns the value of that property.

Finally, using nested ternary operators (?:), we return -1 if the first object looks lesser, 1 if it looks greater, and zero otherwise.

It's time we spawn a whole series of people to tinker with:

`prototype/intro/basic/basic.js`

```
var people = [
  new Person('Jes "Canllaith"', 'Hall', 'Wellington', 'NZ'),
  new Person('Sebastien', 'Gruhier', 'Carquefou', 'FR'),
  new Person('Clotile', 'Michel'),
  new Person('Stéphane', 'Akkaoui', 'Paris'),
  new Person('Elodie', 'Jaubert', 'Paris')
];
```

Notice how we do not need to pass all the arguments every time and how the objects are constructed: through the traditional **new** keyword.

OK, we're all set. We can now start playing with Prototype-induced power. For instance, let's say we need to get a sorted list of all the first names for these people, with no risk of duplicates:

`prototype/intro/basic/basic.js`

```
people.pluck('first').sort().uniq().join(', ')
// => 'Clotilde, Elodie, Jes "Canllaith", Sebastien, Stéphane'
```

Doesn't this rock? The pluck() method fetches a given property from all the objects in the series and returns an array of the resulting values. uniq() strips out duplicates. This is rather concise, don't you think?

How about getting full information on all people with a defined country, sorted by ascending country code:

`prototype/intro/basic/basic.js`

```
people.findAll(function(n) { return n.country; })
  .sort(Person.compare.bind(Person, 'country')).invoke('getDisplayName')
// => [ 'Sebastien Gruhier (Carquefou, FR)',
//       'Jes "Canllaith" Hall (Wellington, NZ)' ]
```

The findAll() method takes a predicate (a function taking an element and returning a boolean about it) and returns all the elements that passed it. Here, our predicate just returns each person's country property, whose value may very well be **undefined**. If it holds a nonempty string, it will be deemed **true**, so the predicate will pass. Otherwise, the predicate will fail.

Perhaps you come from a programming background with languages that do not have *higher-order functions*, meaning you can use functions as regular values to be assigned, passed around as arguments to other functions, returned as result values, and so on.

JavaScript, like many dynamic languages, has that important feature, so we can indeed pass a function around without having to resort to "ancient" tricks such as method pointers.

In the code we just saw, we're passing a function as an argument to the sort() method. This is one aspect of higher-order functions. The function we're passing is actually the result of calling bind() on the original Person.compare() method, which means this bind() thing, which I'll explain shortly in a moment, actually *returns* a function. This is another aspect of the language's support for higher-order functions.

In this code, we would like to use our comparator function, except we need to pass it with the first argument (the criterion one) prefilled. Prototype's bind() method on functions lets us do this, among other things (and we'll discuss it in depth in Section 4.2, *Proper Function Binding*, on page 47).

Finally, the invoke() method lets us call a given method on each element in the series returned by sort() (possibly with arguments, although we don't need any here) and returns an array of the resulting values. JavaScript places no restrictions on where you can use the dot (.) operator; as long as its left side is an object, you're in the clear. If that side is a method call, all you need is that method call to return an object; this lets you chain calls easily to any length you may need.

Finally, on page creation, once it is loaded and the DOM is all ready, we want to dynamically inject a bulleted list of all the people we have by ascending natural order (since the default value for the criterion is the first name, we'll get first-name ordering).

Manually creating all the required DOM nodes would be fastidious, so we elect to build valid XHTML text and inject it safely into the proper container. Here's the code:

```
prototype/intro/basic/basic.js
Line 1  document.observe('dom:loaded.', function() {
   -       html = '<ul>\n'
   -          + people.sort(Person.compare).map(function(p) {
   -             return '\t<li>' + p.getDisplayName().escapeHTML() + '</li>';
   5          }).join('\n')
   -          + '</ul>';
   -       $('result').update(html);
   -       $$('#result li:nth-child(2n)').invoke('addClassName', 'alternate');
   -    });
```

Look at the map() call on line 3; this is the all-purpose transformation method (pluck() and invoke() are special-purpose optimizations of it). We get an array of <li>...</li> text with our "display" names inside, then join them with line delimiters, and finally wrap the whole thing in a <ul>...</ul>. To guard us against weird characters in the people data, we use escapeHTML() on the resulting strings, effectively "defanging" any markup in there.

This is all just markup. To safely inject it into the DOM, we need to grab the element with id="result", which is gracefully done with $(). This method also makes sure the element we get back is equipped with the countless DOM extensions Prototype provides, including the mighty update() method, that we use to inject our markup into the element's DOM fragment.

Notice that our whole anonymous method is passed to document. observe(), which is part of Prototype's unified API to event handling (if you've ever played with events with your bare hands, you noticed, for instance, that Internet Explorer superbly ignores most of the official W3C specifications about it). Our method will be run when the document's DOM has finished loading, which is just what we need.

Finally, the killer call is on line 8. You know these fancy CSS 3 selectors we just can't use because they're not all that well supported yet? Well, we sure can use them with Prototype's $$()[1] to select any set of elements in the DOM! Then Prototype comes with CSS-tweaking methods, such as addClassName(), that take an extra CSS class name argument, but such methods are designed to work on the element we're calling them on. How can we use it on all the elements $$() returned? That's what invoke() is for, and using it lets us alter all matching elements concisely. The matching CSS is very short:

`prototype/intro/basic/basic.css`

```
#result li.alternate { font-weight: bold; color: green; }
```

Once loaded, our page looks like Figure 2.1, on the next page.

That's it for a first run. Excited? I hope so. Take some time to breathe. If you're on Firefox, why not bring up a Firebug[2] console and play with this script interactively? Or take a stroll. Go enjoy the company's free coffee. Check out the blogs.

---

1. Blazing fast since 1.5.1.
2. http://getfirebug.com

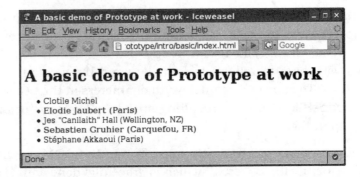

Figure 2.1: OUR DYNAMIC, CUSTOM-STYLED CONTENT

Ready to move ahead with something more involved? Here we go.

One Good-Looking Script: A Table Sorter

To let you feel how using Prototype can lead to neat, cool JavaScript code, we'll build a simple table sorter. As long as our (X)HTML tables properly feature a *<thead>* and a *<tbody>*, our sorter object will be able to sort it.

The idea is to unobtrusively bind sorter objects to *<table>* elements so that the user can click the column heading and have the table sort accordingly. Clicking a second time on the current sort heading switches to a descending sort. We'll also use a few CSS class names so that styling can be applied to express the current sorting status.

Our table sorter system is "simpler" insofar as it does not deal with data types; it treats every cell as text. On the other hand, it does grab the cell's whole text, regardless of internal markup.

The full source code is available online. For this example, we'll focus on the neat parts, but there's very little we're leaving out anyway: support for CSS rules, status toggling for the sort, and extra *<table>* elements.

Laying the Groundwork

OK, so we need an HTML page with a couple tables on it (just to show the sorting capability is neatly wrapped into an object and we can reuse it multiple times on the same page).

We can put together such a page with tables like the following one:

`prototype/intro/table_sorter/index.html`

```html
<table id="todo">
    <thead>
        <tr>
            <th>What?</th>
            <th>When?</th>
            <th>Location</th>
        </tr>
    </thead>
    <tbody>
        <tr>
            <td>Paris Web 2007</td>
            <td>2007-11-15</td>
            <td>IBM La Défense / INSIA</td>
        </tr>
        <tr class="alternate">
            <td>Paris On Rails 2007</td>
            <td>2007-12-10</td>
            <td>Cité des Sciences</td>
        </tr>
        <tr>
            <td>Burger Quiz party</td>
            <td>2007-04-14</td>
            <td>Volta</td>
        </tr>
    </tbody>
</table>
```

We also need a pinch of styling to make this look presentable. A few rules are important to our purposes: the *alternate* class so that lines alternate background colors, the decoration that will let the user see which column is being used for sorting, and whether we use ascending or descending order. These rules are as follows:

`prototype/intro/table_sorter/sorter.css`

```css
thead th.sort-asc, thead th.sort-desc {
  background: #aaf url('sort-asc.png') no-repeat right center;
}

thead th.sort-desc { background-image: url('sort-desc.png'); }

tr.alternate * {
  background-color: #ddd;
}
```

When loaded, our page looks like Figure 2.2, on the following page.

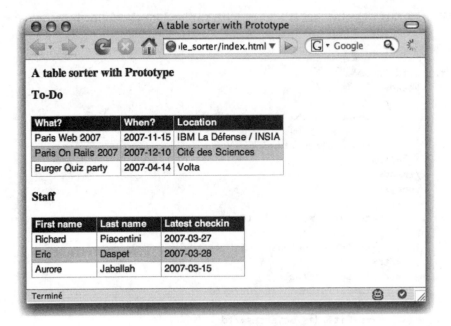

Figure 2.2: OUR INITIAL TABLES

And Now for the Scripting Part

First we'll create an object dedicated to handling the sorting of a given
<table> element; we'll call it TableSorter. In the best Prototype fashion,
the idea is to make it trivial to add sorting capabilities to a *<table>*
element.

We'd like to be able to do that with this simple code:

```
new TableSorter('tableId')
```

Here's the start of our object definition and its *constructor* function:

`prototype/intro/table_sorter/sorter.js`

```
Line 1   var TableSorter = Class.create({
     -     initialize: function(element) {
     -       this.element = $(element);
     -       this.sortIndex = -1;
     5       this.sortOrder = 'asc';
     -       this.initDOMReferences();
     -       this.initEventHandlers();
     -     }, // initialize
     -
```

```
10   initDOMReferences: function() {
-      var head = this.element.down('thead');
-      var body = this.element.down('tbody');
-      if (!head || !body)
-        throw 'Table must have a head and a body to be sortable.';
15     this.headers = head.down('tr').childElements();
-      this.headers.each(function(e, i) {
-        e._colIndex = i;
-      });
-      this.body = body;
20   }, // initDOMReferences
-
-    initEventHandlers: function() {
-      this.handler = this.handleHeaderClick.bind(this);
-      this.element.observe('click', this.handler);
25   }, // initEventHandlers
```

Types obtained through the Class.create() system use as a constructor
an initialize() method. There are a few interesting things to note in this
constructor:

- Notice the calls to methods such as down() and childElements(),
  as on line 15, and how they ease the task of walking through the
  DOM element hierarchy. They're part of a treasure trove of DOM
  extensions guaranteed through the $() call.

- Relying on $() also lets us pass in either an element ID or the
  element itself (that is, its DOM reference).

- The each() method on line 16 is just one example of how built-in
  iteration methods let us do away with manual numerical loops. It
  comes from the wonderful Enumerable module, which is one of the
  Rubyesque features offered by Prototype.

- If you ever tried using a method reference as an event handler, you
  may have noticed you lost its binding on the way (when its code
  relied on the **this** reference, it would use the wrong object for it).
  Calling bind(), on line 23, spares us that frequent nightmare.

So, we have this handleHeaderClick() method that will get called on
every click anywhere on our table. Its job is to make sure the click
actually happened on a heading (a <th> element within <thead>) and,
when so, to trigger sorting.

Here it goes:

`prototype/intro/table_sorter/sorter.js`

```
Line 1  handleHeaderClick: function(e) {
   -      var element = e.element();
   -      if (!('_colIndex' in element)) {
   -        element = element.ancestors().find(function(elt) {
   5          return '_colIndex' in elt;
   -        });
   -        if (!((element) && '_colIndex' in element))
   -          return;
   -      }
  10      this.sort(element._colIndex);
   -    }, // handleHeaderClick
```

Because at construction time we endowed every proper heading cell with a custom property named _colIndex,[3] checking for a valid heading is as easy as looking for that property. Note, however, how easy it is to walk the element chain from our clicked element outward until we find such a heading cell (if indeed we clicked somewhere in one). As shown on line 4, we just need to use find() over the ancestors() list.

This leaves us with the core sorting method, pragmatically named sort(). We'll leave the visual adjustments to another method, named adjust-SortMarkers(), which will also do the bookkeeping on our sortIndex and sortOrder properties. This is rather plain code, with no real Prototyp-ish flavor. But the sorting code, and its application to the actual DOM, gives our code a few opportunities to shine.

`prototype/intro/table_sorter/sorter.js`

```
Line 1    adjustSortMarkers: function(index) {
   -        if (this.sortIndex != -1)
   -          this.headers[this.sortIndex].removeClassName('sort-' +
   -            this.sortOrder);
   5        if (this.sortIndex != index) {
   -          this.sortOrder = 'asc';
   -          this.sortIndex = index;
   -        } else
   -          this.sortOrder = ('asc' == this.sortOrder ? 'desc' : 'asc');
  10        this.headers[index].addClassName('sort-' + this.sortOrder);
   -      }, // adjustSortMarkers
   -
   -      sort: function(index) {
   -        this.adjustSortMarkers(index);
  15        var rows = this.body.childElements();
```

---

3. In scripting parlance, we call such custom additions *expando properties*.

```
     rows = rows.sortBy(function(row) {
       return row.childElements()[this.sortIndex].collectTextNodes();
     }.bind(this));
     if ('desc' == this.sortOrder)
20     rows.reverse();
     rows.reverse().each(function(row, index) {
       if (index > 0)
         this.body.insertBefore(row, rows[index - 1]);
     }.bind(this));
25   rows.reverse().each(function(row, index) {
       row[(1 == index % 2 ? 'add' : 'remove') + 'ClassName']('alternate');
     });
   } // sort
 }); // TableSorter
```

1. First, as shown on line 16, we rely on the sortBy() method, which lets us provide a custom key for the rows to sort. We'll use that row's proper cell and this cell's full textual contents. To do this, we borrow the collectTextNodes() method, on line 17, that currently sits in script.aculo.us, not Prototype (this might well change soon, though). You can see the code for this method, which I pasted into the script, in the next code snippet.

2. Now that our local array holds the DOM references in the proper order, we need to mirror it in the document's DOM. A concise way to do this, starting on line 21, is to iterate through the sorted list in reverse order, inserting elements according to it. Because the DOM method insertBefore() will remove the row from its current position prior to reinserting it, it's just a one-call trick.

   Notice how we bind the anonymous function to the current Table-Sorter object, so it can use this.body to address the property we defined in the constructor (with no bind, **this** would be the current window object).

3. It's now time to update the zebra striping of our rows. The order was changed, so the same rows don't necessarily stripe the same way. It's not sorting *per se*, and I should have put that in its own function, but it's a nice example of Prototypish code, so I wanted it in this short snippet.

   The call on line 26 dynamically selects between the addClass-Name() and removeClassName() methods, both being extensions provided by Prototype. It then passes the proper class name to the selected method.

As mentioned earlier, we do need to use the collectTextNodes() method for proper sorting, and this would currently require script.aculo.us, which would be a bit overkill here. So, we can paste the corresponding code at the beginning of our script:

`prototype/intro/table_sorter/sorter.js`

```
// Borrowed from script.aculo.us' effects.js...
Element.addMethods({
  collectTextNodes: function(element) {
    return $A($(element).childNodes).collect( function(node) {
      return (node.nodeType==3 ? node.nodeValue :
        (node.hasChildNodes() ? Element.collectTextNodes(node) : ''));
    }).flatten().join('');
  }
});
```

There! We have this nice little object available, so how do we dynamically apply it to all *<table>* elements in the document? With very few lines and the wonderful $$() selector, this is how:

`prototype/intro/table_sorter/sorter.js`

```
document.observe('dom:loaded', function() {
  $$('table').each(function(table) { new TableSorter(table); });
});
```
Line 1

When the DOM is done loading, our anonymous function gets called, and its single line (line 2) uses the ubiquitous $$() function to select all tables in the document and then creates a TableSorter object over each. We'll dive more into the astounding powers of $$() in Section 3.4, *$$ Searches with Style*, on page 34.

OK, now let's refresh our page and try it. After a few clicks on headings, you could obtain something like Figure 2.3, on the facing page.

And that's it for our second, fuller example. All in all, our TableSorter object is about 70 lines of code, which is admittedly low for such a feature set. If you need advanced capabilities, such as support for data types, merged rows and columns, and more, check out the Table Sorting with Prototype library by Andrew Tetlaw,[4] a Prototype fan from Down Under. It's likely to have all the features you need and more.

---

4. http://tetlaw.id.au/view/blog/table-sorting-with-prototype/

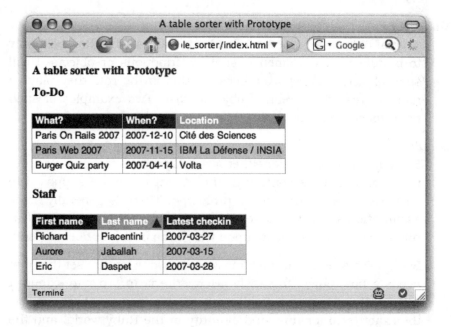

Figure 2.3: SORTED TABLES AFTER A FEW CLICKS

2.4 Prototype Jargon and Concepts

Prototype comes with a handful of specific notions that will come up time and again in this reference. To keep things nice and concise, I will provide names for these notions. As with any domain, knowing the lingo will help you grasp things more readily and avoid potential mistakes.

Objects, Namespaces, and Modules

Prototype objects fall into three categories, which I'll use when describing an object. This categorization lets you immediately understand how a given object is to be used. There are three categories: class, namespace, and module.

Class

> Such objects are intended for regular use: construction with the **new** operator, properties being stored in instance fields, and so on. Regular objects include ObjectRange, Ajax.Request, and PeriodicalExecuter, for instance.

Namespace

Several objects are not intended for instantiation. They exist only to bundle related elements, such as functions or objects. I call such objects *namespaces*, because this is the role they play—a named area where related objects exist. Two examples of such namespaces are Ajax and Event.

Module

Sometimes an object is neither a regular namespace nor a proper namespace. It does contain methods, but these are supposed to be *mixed in* another object's prototype. There is generally some assumption about this other object; it is usually supposed to feature one or more methods, upon which the mixed-in ones depend.

Such objects represent an almost stand-alone feature set that just needs a host object to satisfy a few criteria in order to extend it with all those features. I call such objects *modules,* because it is the exact term for this kind of entity in the Ruby world, and the word sounds nice. Prototype's most famous module is Enumerable, which is mixed in by numerous objects, such as Array.

Iterators

For brevity's sake, I use *iterators* for all callback functions that are passed to methods that, internally, iterate over a collection. Such callback functions are called in sequence over part or all of the iterated elements. The quintessential iteration function is Enumerable.each, which most functions from Enumerable rely upon internally.

Extended Elements

Prototype features an awesome DOM extension mechanism, described at great length in Chapter 7, *Playing with the DOM Is Finally Fun!*, on page 119. When I refer to *extended elements* (which happens fairly often), I mean a DOM element that went through DOM extension, one way or another. This essentially means all element-related methods can be invoked straight on it, which is good. elt.hide() feels much more object-oriented than Element.hide(elt), don't you think?

Aliases

Sometimes, a given feature is well-known under multiple names. For instance, consider a method that iterates through a sequence to find the first occurrence that matches a criterion. Depending on the technical environment you're used to, you may think of it as detect() or find().

Prototype provides many such methods, which are commonly referred to by at least two names. When that happens, Prototype uses a form of aliasing. I then refer to these methods as *aliases*; if one name clearly dominates or is deemed preferable for one reason or another, I may label its other name only as being an alias.

2.5 What Are Prototypes Anyway?

Most people are used to regular object-oriented programming where types are defined by classes, which are usually closed (you cannot change them dynamically), and where they serve as blueprints for all instances of the class. Classes can organize themselves in a hierarchy, where every child class inherits all the attributes of its ancestor classes.

JavaScript works in an entirely different way. Everything is an object, and every object is defined by a constructor function and this constructor's prototype. A *prototype* is basically a repository of things (mostly methods) that all objects produced by the constructor function share.

This all sounds a bit quirky, so let's look at some simple example code:

`prototype/intro/prototypes.js`

```
Line 1  function Person(lastName, firstName) {
   -      this.lastName = lastName;
   -      this.firstName = firstName;
   -    }
   5
   -    Person.prototype = {
   -      getFullName: function() {
   -        return this.firstName + ' ' + this.lastName;
   -      }
  10    }
   -
   -    var sam = new Person('Stephenson', 'Sam');
   -    var thomas = new Person('Fuchs', 'Thomas');
   -
  15    sam.getFullName()
   -    // -> 'Sam Stephenson'
   -    thomas.getFullName()
   -    // -> 'Thomas Fuchs'
```

On line 1, you can see a classic *constructor function*, which is simply a function that is intended to be used with the **new** operator and that manipulates the **this** reference to work with instance members (such as instance fields). You can see a call to the constructor on line 12.

Starting on line 6, we define what is in our constructor's *prototype*. Here, it's only a single method, called getFullName(), which uses a simple version of the full-name algorithm. The important point here is that this method's definition is shared by all instances of the Person class. It is defined only once and used from then on. We use it indifferently on both instances, as you can see from line 15.

This is very much preferable to "old-school" code that you still find in too many tutorials, which goes something like this:

```
prototype/intro/bad_function_definition.js
function Person(lastName, firstName) {
  this.lastName = lastName;
  this.firstName = firstName;
  this.getFullName = function() { // DON'T DO THIS!
    return this.firstName + ' ' + this.lastName;
  }
}
```

In such code, every single time an instance is created, it gets its own *singleton method* (a method that exists specifically on this object; its definition is not shared by any other instance). This is entirely wasteful, because the function's definition does not change over time and does not need lexical closure from the constructor's code, since it uses data obtained only from the **this** reference. The prototype-based approach is a much cleaner solution (and is how JavaScript is supposed to be used anyway).

Note that the syntax we use to express the prototype from line 6 onward is pure-vanilla JavaScript. The {...} block is a regular object literal, with a comma-delimited list of *key: value* pairs.

Now for the salient points. First, prototypes are open. You can alter them at any point, and this retroactively alters all the instances based on this prototype. So, for instance, adding a method to String.prototype makes it available to all String objects, whether they were created prior to or after the addition! This is a way of "monkey patching"[5] classes, much like you would do on Ruby classes and modules.

---

5. In scripting parlance, *monkey patching* is the practice of patching existing objects (classes, functions, and so on) at run time, not in their actual source code. Dynamic languages, which generally leave their types "open," are a prime candidate for this kind of approach.

Second, there is no inheritance *per se*. You cannot make a prototype inherit from another, at least not in the regular sense. But the syntaxes provided by Prototype let you emulate "classical" inheritance for just about all intents and purposes.

If you need to get further details on how Prototype uses constructor functions and prototype manipulation to implement classes and modules, look at Appendix A, on page 385. It explains all this and outlines all you need to know in order to extend Prototype for your own needs or even contribute to the framework itself.

2.6 Running Prototype Code Samples in This Book

Most of the functions, methods, and objects in this part of the book are documented through small code snippets. The files are available online, but in order to execute them, you'll often need to run the code in the context of a web page with Prototype loaded. The easiest way to try them is to set up a small web page, load it in your browser, and then copy/paste the snippets in your JavaScript console or, better yet, your Firebug console (if you're using Firebug on Firefox, which *you should be*, indeed). The page itself can be minimal to the point of Zenhood:

`prototype/bench.html`
```
<!DOCTYPE html PUBLIC "-//W3C//DTD XHTML 1.0 Strict//EN"
  "http://www.w3.org/TR/xhtml1/DTD/xhtml1-strict.dtd">
<html xmlns="http://www.w3.org/1999/xhtml" xml:lang="en" lang="en">
<head>
    <title>My Prototype test bench</title>
    <script type="text/javascript" src="prototype.js"></script>
</head>
<body>
    <h1>A simple page to test Prototype</h1>
</body>
</html>
```

Of course, you'd need to put Prototype's library file in the same directory for things to work smoothly. A few snippets here and there assume your page contains this or that element (for example, "a simple *<div>* element with an id= attribute set to *navbar*"). Just add whatever is necessary to your test page. In the long run, it will look something like Prototype's unit test pages (that is, it will feature a haphazard assortment of utterly unrelated elements that seem, at first glance, to have been thrown in there with no rhyme or reason). That's OK. It's a test bench! It should smell of sawdust, fresh paint, and hot iron.

Chapter 3

Quick Help with the Dollars

3.1 Shortcuts Should Be Short

There are little bits of code that you use all the time. For example, how often do you type document.getElementById? There are many such examples, and Prototype provides convenient shortcuts for the most common ones.

But shortcuts should live up to their name; they should actually be *short*. They should also be instantly recognizable as shortcuts. This is why Prototype uses the "dollar convention" to name shortcuts by using two characters: the dollar sign and an extra letter or sign.

Such shortcuts are referred to as *utility functions* in Prototype, and they are, indeed, very useful. This chapter will take you through them all, which will be quick enough but immeasurably useful; you'll be able to express in a very few characters of code what used to be boringly verbose or even dauntingly complex: ID- or even CSS-based DOM extractions, flexible array conversions, and more!

3.2 Quick Fetching of Smart Elements with $

The $() function is by far the most useful (and indeed, the most used) function in Prototype. Its goal is twofold:

- It lets you fetch a DOM element by its ID in the most concise syntax possible. Because of this, for example, if ($('foo')) is the preferred way of quickly verifying that an element exists. . . .

- It provides a guaranteed way of getting an *extended element*. Remember those? As discussed in Section 2.4, *Extended Elements*, on page 26, an extended element is a DOM element object that became endowed with all the additional methods provided by Prototype's DOM extension mechanism. It's a DOM element with superpowers, so to speak.

Having the guarantee that the resulting element is extended makes $() not only much more concise than its traditional pure-DOM counterpart (document.getElementById) but also superior from a usage standpoint. Since the resulting elements feature all the extended methods, you can make your code both shorter and more object-oriented. In short, you can make it more expressive:

`prototype/utility/dollar.js`

```
// Vanilla DOM
document.getElementById('navBar').style.display = 'none';

// Prototype's way - because of DOM extension!
$('navBar').hide();

// And if $ did not guarantee extended elements...
Element.hide('navBar');
```

Another key point is that you can pass $() either an ID string (such as 'navbar') or an actual DOM element reference. Either way, you'll get the extended version of the element (if this element was already extended, it is basically untouched). This behavior is used by every single method in Prototype that takes "an element" as an argument, always allowing you to pass either the element's ID or its actual reference.

A final feature is that you can grab many elements at once by passing multiple arguments (each of which has the same flexibility we just described), in which case you'll get an array of extended elements back. This can be very useful:

`prototype/utility/dollar-multiple.js`

```
// "I haven't read the whole doc on $()"
var items = [];
items[0] = $('navbar');
items[1] = $('adbar');
items[2] = $('footer');

// "I sure did!"
var items = $('navbar', 'adbar', 'footer');
```

To summarize, the following syntaxes are supported:

```
$(ID) → extendedElement
$(element) → extendedElement
$(ID|element...) → [ extendedElement, ... ]
```

In syntax blocks such as the previous summary, the | (referred to as the *pipe character*) describes an alternative, which remains local when applied to an argument. In the third syntax, you should not read, as you would on a regular expression, "an ID, or an element and an ID, or a series of elements." Instead, you should read "an ID or an element, followed by one or more arguments that each can also be an ID or an element, individually." As for the square brackets and dots on the return type, this reads "an array of extended elements," which does not imply anything about the size of returned arrays; they might contain any number of items, including 0 or 1.

Hey, who doesn't like having dollars around anyway?

3.3 $w, Because Array Literals Are Boring

Sometimes, typing string array literals can seem like a study in rigor; getting all the quotes and commas right seems like a burden to some, especially if there are numerous elements. Perl developers have long used the qw() function, and Rubyists are fond of %w. Prototype gives you $w(), which is slightly different from both these venerable precedents in that it requires you to pass it an actual string, which will be split based on whitespace:

```
prototype/utility/dollar-w.js
// The hard way
var fruits = ['raspberries', 'pears', 'peaches', 'kiwis'];

// The easy way
var fruits = $w('raspberries pears peaches kiwis');
```

Because it splits on whitespace, you cannot, obviously, use it when you have individual elements that contain whitespace. Also, if the passed string is nothing but whitespace (or is plain empty), you'll get an empty array back.

3.4 $$ Searches with Style

This one is quite the power tool. It lets you harvest your DOM and get elements based on *CSS selectors*—not just CSS class names, either. You can use advanced selectors, because $$() features almost the whole complement specified by CSS 3. Here are a few examples:

```
prototype/utility/dollar-dollar.js
```

```
$$('div')
// -> all DIVs in the document.  Similar to
//    document.getElementsByTagName('div'), although returning a non-live
//    Array of extended (as in $'d) elements, instead of a live NodeList
//    of (possibly unextended) elements.

$$('#contents')
// -> same as $('contents'), only it returns an array anyway.

$$('li.faux')
// -> all LI elements with class 'faux'

$$('#contents a[rel]')
// -> all links inside the element of ID "contents" with a rel attribute

$$('a[href="#"]')
// -> all links with a href attribute of value "#" (eyeew!)

$$('#navbar li', '#sidebar li')
// -> all list items within the elements of ID "navbar" or "sidebar"

$$('a:not([rel~=nofollow])');
// -> all links, excluding those whose rel attribute contains the word
//    "nofollow"

$$('table tbody > tr:nth-child(even)');
// -> all even rows within all table bodies

$$('div:empty');
// -> all DIVs without content (i.e., whitespace-only)
```

Supported CSS Selectors

To avoid browser compatibility hassles, Prototype has its own CSS parser code, which means it may well differ from the regular CSS selector set your browser originally provides. Version 1.6 supports the following selectors:

Type
    Tag names, as in div.

Descendant

   Whitespace between other selectors, as in #a li.

Attribute

   The full CSS 3 set is available:

   [attr] Is present.

   [attr=value] Has a specific value.

   [attr~=value] Has a whitespace-separated list containing a value.
      Think class= values.

   [attr|=value] Has a specific value or starts with it followed by a
      hyphen (-). Think language codes.

   [attr!=value] Does not have a specific value (note it's not standard
      CSS 3; it's just there for convenience).

   [attr^=value] Starts with a specific value.

   [attr$=value] Ends with a specific value.

   [attr*=value] Contains, anywhere, a specific value.

   If the value you're matching against includes a space, be sure to
   enclose the value in quotes, as in [title="Hello world!"].

Class

   CSS class names, as in .highlighted or .example.wrong.

Child

   As in #item1 > a.

Sibling

   As in #item1 + p.

Adjacent

   As in #item1 ~ p.

:not(. . .)

   As in *:not(.critical) or a:not([rel~=nofollow]).

:nth-*

   As in tbody > tr:nth-child(even), #dialog > p:nth-child(3n+1), or #intro
   > p:nth-of-type(2).

:first-*

   As in #intro > h1:first-of-type or #footer > *:first-child.

:last-*
>   As in ul > li:last-child or #article p:last-of-type.

:empty
>   As in p:empty.

:enabled, :disabled, and :checked
>   As in input:enabled or input:checked.

Naturally, you can combine these selectors and use multiple combinations as well, as shown in the previous large code example. This can actually get pretty complex, with stuff like this:

```
$$('#items td.controls > input[type!="submit"]:not(:disabled)')
```

However, try to optimize your markup so your CSS-based selections are as simple as can be. When you find yourself reaching for every ounce of syntax power in there, you're probably using something too complex for your actual needs. . . .

For further details on the exact semantics of these selectors, look up the W3C Recommendation for CSS 3 Selectors.[1] Oh, and in case you were wondering, the elements are, naturally enough, returned in document order (and with no duplicates).

3.5 $A, the Collection Unifier

This function is a kind of universal converter that turns just about anything roughly collection-like (or, if you prefer, "array-compatible") into an actual Array object.

When would you need to do that? Well, the occasions are plenty. When scripting a web page, you often find yourself getting some collection back from the DOM, usually an implementation of NodeList or HTMLCollection. Or perhaps you're dynamically exploring the arguments passed to your function, through JavaScript's predefined arguments variable. All of these are not actual arrays (as in, they are not instances of Array), but they "look like one." They feature an integer length property, and they have integer-indexed properties ranging between 0 and length - 1, accessible through the [] operator. You could say such objects are *iterable*.

---

1. http://www.w3.org/TR/css3-selectors/

OK, so we have several common cases when what we manipulate are not actual arrays but are iterable. What's the big deal? Well, you see, Prototype extends Array. A lot. You can get all the juicy details in Section 4.6, *Arrays*, on page 64, after which it should be abundantly clear to you just how badly Array trumps any other collection type in town.

To get the feel of it, just look at the following before/after examples:

`prototype/utility/dollar-a.js`

```javascript
// Using the regular types
var paras = document.getElementsByTagName('p');
for (var index = 0; index < paras.length; ++index)
  Element.hide(paras.item(index));
Element.update(paras.item(paras.length - 1), 'Jeez that is verbose');

// The Prototype way (nonextending version, though)
var paras = $A(document.getElementsByTagName('p'));
paras.each(Element.hide);
Element.update(paras.last(), 'This looks better');
```

Note that if we didn't mind extending fetched elements as we went, we could actually change the two lines fetching our paragraphs to hide them so they become this:

```javascript
var paras = $$('p');
paras.invoke('hide');
```

But hey, we were working on $A(), right? Here's another example with JavaScript's automatic `arguments` local variable in functions:

`prototype/utility/dollar-a-2.js`

```javascript
// Using the regular types
function showArgs() {
  alert(Array.prototype.join.call(arguments, ', '));
}

// The Prototype way
function showArgs() {
  alert($A(arguments).join(', '));
}
```

So, how does $A() go about converting stuff to an actual Array? It's quite simple really:

1. **null**, **undefined**, and **false** become an empty array.

2. If the object features a toArray() method, we delegate to it.

3. Otherwise, we assume the object is "iterable." We then iterate over it in the usual way to build our actual array.

The nifty thing about this reliance on toArray() is that all objects that mix in the Enumerable module have one, which makes for cool tricks. In the following code, we'll use the $R() function, which we'll discuss shortly in Section 3.8, *Handling Ranges with $R*, on the next page, that represents a range of values and constitutes a valid Enumerable. This lets you see a concrete conversion:

```
prototype/utility/dollar-a-tricks.js
```
```
$A($R(1, 10))
// -> [1, 2, 3, 4, 5, 6, 7, 8, 9, 10]

// OK, playing with the cool kids now...

var names = ['Amir', 'Arnaud', 'Stéphane', 'Sunny', 'Tobie'];
$A($R(1, names.length)).zip(names, function(a) { return a.join('. '); })
// -> ['1. Amir', '2. Arnaud', '3. Stéphane', '4. Sunny', '5. Tobie']
```

"A" as in "Amazing!"

3.6 $F Is a Field Expert

```
$F(fieldElt) → value | [ value, ... ]
```

$F() takes a form field (or its ID) and returns the field's value. Careful: it takes the *ID*, not the *name* (the value of the name= attribute).

Getting the value from a form field sounds like an easy task, but it isn't so simple actually. If you're dealing with a textual field (such as a *<input>* with type="text" or a *<textarea>*), you're pretty much in the clear. But radio buttons and checkboxes should yield a value only when they're checked, and listboxes rely on a list of options, where multiple options might be selected. Even when properly detecting the selected ones, the relevant *<option>* tags may not have a defined value= attribute, in which case you should use the text within the opening and closing tags.

As you can see, the complexity of the algorithm to guarantee you get the proper value quickly escalates. There are a few discrepancies, too, between browsers (for instance, Internet Explorer doesn't observe this latest rule for listbox options with no value= attribute).

To spare you the trouble of dealing with values in multiple ways or of having to work around these inconsistencies, $F() handles it all and returns the properly extracted value:

- For multiple-selection listboxes, you'll get an array of values, one for each selected option. For anything else, you'll get a single value.

- For unchecked radio buttons or checkboxes, you'll get **null**.

- For anything else, you'll get a single value.

All actual values are returned as strings, and for listbox options, if the value= attribute is missing, you get the option's text.

3.7 $H Makes a Hash of Things

Prototype provides a new kind of object, called *hashes*, through the Hash type. We will explore it in Section 10.1, *Storing Values in a Hash*, on page 215. Once you start working with hashes, it can get pretty addictive, so you might find yourself quite often writing new Hash(...). The $H() function is a convenience shortcut for this.

3.8 Handling Ranges with $R

This is probably a slightly underused function, simply because the object it relies on (see Section 10.2, *Expressing Ranges of... Well, Anything You Want!*, on page 220) is itself underused. This is simply a convenience alias over the ObjectRange constructor. No fancy fluff, no extra features or safeguard. A plain alias. Its most common use is, of course, for integer ranges:

`prototype/utility/dollar-r.js`

```
$R(1,5).each(function(n) {
  // Gets invoked 5 times, with n from 1 to 5
});

$A($R(1, 7))
// -> [1, 2, 3, 4, 5, 6, 7]

$R(1, 10).findAll(function(n) {
  return 0 != n % 2;
})
// -> [1, 3, 5, 7, 9]
```

Ranges can be very useful things in the appropriate context. You'll learn more about them in their dedicated sections.

And that's it! Those are Prototype's utility functions. You'll find yourself using them over and over again. They're pretty much ubiquitous, both in the library's source code and in real-world user code. And although $() and $A() are by far the most popular ones, do not pass over the other ones; they're all here for a reason, and they're all idiomatic Prototype.

Let's Review What We Learned

Prototype offers a series of *utility functions*, which are so commonly used that their names were made as short as reasonably possible: just two characters (a dollar sign and a letter).

- $() is all over the place, grabbing DOM elements by their id= and extending them on the fly if need be. It is the key to tapping the power of Prototype's countless DOM extensions and does away with the oh-so-verbose document.getElementById.

- $A() turns just about anything remotely array-compatible into a bona fide Array, complete with its scores of extended methods (which we'll detail in the next chapter). As a special shortcut to creating an array of no-space strings, $w() splits a single string into an array of "words."

- $$() lets us extract parts of our DOM using all the might of CSS 3 selectors, regardless of our browser's actual CSS support.

Those are the core ones. In addition, Prototype provides more targeted functions:

- $F() extracts the current value, however complex, of a form field. Remember that it uses the field's id=, *not* its name=.

- $H() is the short way of creating hashes, which are slightly enhanced associative arrays.

- Finally, $R() creates ranges, which come in handy to iterate over sequences of values, be they integers, characters, and so on.

Regular JavaScript on Steroids

Prototype goes to great lengths to make JavaScript development feel better. Prototype Core loves Ruby. (Who doesn't? Honestly, give it a serious try.) That's why Prototype tries to make JavaScript feel more like Ruby—so that most common tasks become a breeze and are eminently readable. Dealing with collections of items (be it for simple iteration, filtering, transforming, or whatnot), exploring object properties, manipulating strings, or even finally passing methods around without losing their binding along the way—all of this (and much more!) becomes easy as pie when using Prototype.

4.1 Generic Object Manipulation

In JavaScript, just about everything is an object: strings, numbers, functions, arrays, regular expressions. . . . And there is a basic inheritance that makes all objects descend from the fundamental Object type. Prototype carefully avoids adding anything in Object.prototype, because this would percolate into every single object, effectively breaking every legitimate use of the for...in construct. However, Prototype does add a few methods in the Object namespace that are mainly geared toward object introspection.

A Fresh Look at for...in

Misconception alert: for...in is *not* intended to iterate over an array. That it works (and works only as long as you leave Array's prototype untouched) is a mere side effect. Its actual purpose is fairly different. It is intended to iterate over *all the iterable properties and methods of an object*.

Native methods (and many native properties) usually do not appear in a for...in loop because JavaScript does not mark them as iterable. In an array, for example, only the numerical indices of its cells are iterable, which creates the illusion that you can use for...in to iterate over its contents. Unfortunately, our own code cannot mark properties or methods as "not iterable." Everything we augment native types with will show up on such a loop. Because Prototype relies a lot on extending native types with custom methods, using for...in when it's not exactly appropriate starts yielding weird values.

`prototype/steroids/for_in.js`

```
var arr = ['hello', 'world'];
var props = [];
for (var prop in arr)
  props.push(prop);

// Without extensions to Array.prototype:
// -> ['0', '1']

// With Prototype's extensions:
// -> ['0', '1', 'each', 'eachSlice', 'all', ..., 'clone'] (38 items)
```

Before throwing a vase at Sam Stephenson, remember that just about every common use case for iteration is covered in a very concise way by the methods Array gains, either directly or through mixing in the Enumerable module. Just look at Section 4.6, *Arrays*, on page 64.

In short, you just need to remember this: *for...in is not actually intended for array iteration. It iterates over all the properties of an object, including its methods.*

If you're looking for a pure-JavaScript, efficient array iteration, there's only one true way:

```
for (var index = 0, l = array.length; index < l; ++index)
        // your code using index here
```

This is usually regarded as optimum code; it uses local variables, caches array length (which is useful when, for some reason, the Java-Script runtime doesn't), and uses the prefix ++ operator to avoid the potential cost of uselessly saving the index's pre-incrementation value. You can't go much faster than that, I guess. Yes, it's a bit more verbose than the tricks wrapped around it by libraries. But it's fast, and it's *correct*. It won't get foiled by extensions to Array.prototype, because it's doing exactly what you need. It iterates on the array's integer-indexed properties, not *all* its properties.

Introspecting Objects

```
Object.inspect(obj) → String
Object.isArray(obj) → Boolean
Object.isElement(obj) → Boolean
Object.isFunction(obj) → Boolean
Object.isHash(obj) → Boolean
Object.isNumber(obj) → Boolean
Object.isString(obj) → Boolean
Object.isUndefined(obj) → Boolean
Object.keys(obj) → [ String, ... ]
Object.values(obj) → [ value, ... ]
Object.toQueryString(obj) → String
```

The keys() and values() methods let you treat any object like a basic hash (or associative array, if you will). They provide an array of property names or of these properties' values, respectively. The actual order of the array is not guaranteed, because this implementation relies on for...in internally, for which the JavaScript specification does not mandate any particular order. Still, because of this dependence, you will get all the extensions Prototype provides to the object, as in the second case in the previous code sample.

Version 1.6 introduces a series of type detection methods all starting with *is*. Most of them rely on the **typeof** operator (isFunction(), isNumber(), isString(), and isUndefined()). One is a convenience shortcut over an **instanceof** call (isHash()). Finally, two are a bit more advanced: isArray() checks the object's constructor against Array, and isElement() verifies the object's nodeType property value (expecting 1, which is the ELEMENT type). These methods are used extensively in Prototype to help make the code more expressive (that is, more concise and yet more readable at the same time); be sure to use them in your own code to reap the same benefit!

The inspect() method enjoys a loftier status, because it has a wider impact on the Prototype library. The idea for this method is to provide the developer with better string representations of objects, mostly for debugging purposes. The reason behind this is that the default string representations JavaScript provides are not very useful in quite a few cases.

For instance, take **null** or **undefined**; in many cases, they will amount to the empty string (such as when passed as arguments or when being items in arrays), which certainly will not give the developer enough clues. Arrays will be rendered without their square-bracket delimiters. Strings also appear without delimiters. This can cause confusion when

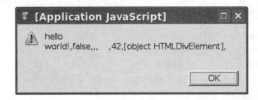

Figure 4.1: TOSTRING() MAKES FOR UNHELPFUL DISPLAYS.

---

you want to display something that contains, say, carriage returns or newline characters, or even just spaces. DOM objects usually get rendered as their interface name (for example, HTMLFormElement). Consider the following code:

`prototype/steroids/toString.js`

```
// Assuming a <div> with ID 'navbar' and a 'nonPrint' CSS class...
var data = ["hello\nworld!", false, null, , " ", 42, $('navBar'), "\n"];
alert(data);
```

On Firefox 2, for instance, this will display as in Figure 4.1.

That's not very helpful, is it? What Object.inspect() does is this:

1. It renders **null** and **undefined** properly (using their names).

2. If the object passed as an argument features an inspect() method, it delegates to it.

3. Otherwise, it reverts to the bare-bones toString() method (which all objects have).

The thing is, Prototype provides nice inspect() methods for several types, both native and custom, namely, String, Array, Enumerable, and Hash. The inspect() method is also added to extended DOM elements, letting you obtain a regular XML tag representation with its id and class attributes, if any. Because inspect() implementations for containers recursively call Object.inspect() on their items, you get as good a representation as possible.

Converting the previous code to inspect() results in the following listing:

`prototype/steroids/inspect.js`

```
// Assuming a <div> with ID 'navbar' and a 'nonPrint' CSS class...
var data = ["hello\nworld!", false, null, , " ", 42, $('navBar'), "\n"];
alert(Object.inspect(data));
```

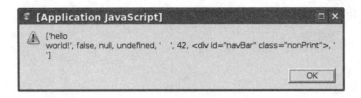

Figure 4.2: THE WONDERS OF OBJECT.INSPECT()

This produces a much more usable display, as you can see in Figure 4.2.

I find such output much more helpful from a debugging standpoint. Of course, you do not have to use such a kludge as the good ol' alert(). Depending on your installed browser or extensions, you may have nicer mechanisms at hand. I, for one, am a big fan of the Firebug[1] extension to Firefox and tend to use its console.log() method (and other debug-oriented methods in the same object) for such purposes.

Finally, version 1.6.0 added the toQueryString() method for use cases when you have any regular object and want to serialize it in the URL-encoded way. This used to be a static method of the Hash class but didn't quite make sense there. It's actually based on its instance-level namesake in Hash, though.

Cloning and Extending Objects

```
Object.clone(obj) → newObject
Object.extend(dest, source) → dest
```

Prototype devotes two methods to the (somewhat technical) task of cloning objects. By *cloning*, I mean "producing an object with a shallow copy of the original object's property set." In short, we start with an empty object and iterate over all the properties in the original one, copying them to the new one. This is *shallow copying*, which means the properties do not get cloned. We just share references. This is no issue for simple values, such as strings and numbers, but can be surprising when properties are themselves custom objects, arrays, and the like.

---

1. http://getfirebug.com

Let me illustrate:

```
prototype/steroids/clone.js
var o = {
  name: 'Prototype',
  version: 1.5,
  authors: ['sam', 'contributors']
};
var o2 = Object.clone(o); // Apparently cloning...

o2.version = '1.5 weird';
o2.authors.pop(); // Watch out!  Shared reference inside!

o.version
// -> 1.5

o2.version
// -> '1.5 weird'

o.authors
// -> ['sam'] // Ouch!  Shallow copy ended up with a shared array!
```

Therefore, tread carefully with clone(). Also note that several custom objects in Prototype provide their own clone() method, as does Array, but this is usually for performance or consistency purposes and does not involve deep copy.

The last method Prototype puts in the Object namespace is extend(), which is at the heart of how Prototype extends built-in objects. We will explore its usage in more depth in Appendix A, on page 385, but for now, know this: Object.extend() basically simulates a sort of *static inheritance* through a one-time copy of all properties (including methods, remember?) from the source (or *parent*) object to the destination (or *child*) object.

This is used extensively inside Prototype itself to mix in modules, extend namespaces, and so forth. Actually, Object.clone() is easily defined thanks to Object.extend():

```
prototype/steroids/extend.js
...
  clone: function(object) {
    return Object.extend({}, object);
  }
...
```

An important note: do not mistake this method with Element.extend(), which is much more intricate and is at the heart of Prototype's DOM extension machinery. We will explore this one in Chapter 7, *Playing with the DOM Is Finally Fun!*, on page 119, but just remember this for now: Object.extend() simply takes two objects and grafts the second one's properties onto the first one. On the other hand, Element.extend() takes a DOM element (not just any object) that it augments, if necessary, with all the extensions Prototype provides depending on its actual type (or tag name, if you prefer).

Miscellanea

```
Object.toHTML(obj)  →  String
RegExp.escape(touchyText)  →  String
```

The Object.toHTML() method will use the parameter's toHTML() method if it exists; otherwise, it will rely on String's interpret() (which produces an empty string for **null** or **undefined** and relies on native String conversion otherwise). It is mostly used internally for content insertion and replacement in the DOM extensions, but I mention it here for the sake of completeness.

As another utility function, RegExp.escape() lets you "defang" text that you want to use inside a regular expression, with no risk of its contents altering the expression semantics. Every character in the text that has meaning in a regex context will be escaped, so you can safely include it. For instance, RegExp.escape('Hi. [1] Anyone there?') yields 'Hi\. \[1\] Anyone there\?'.

4.2 Proper Function Binding

JavaScript has this particular notion called *function binding*. The binding of a function is, essentially, the object to which its **this** reference is bound when the function *executes*. It is a dynamic concept; it is not statically resolved when the function is defined. It all depends on the actual execution flow of your code—which chain of function calls and which objects these functions were called on (be it through the obj.method() notation or through more advanced JavaScript tricks, such as the apply() or call() methods), leading to your function eventually being called.

By default, a function defined outside any explicit object is bound to the current window object, accessible through the predefined window variable.

You can see this with the following code:

```
prototype/steroids/binding-window.js
function getName() {
  return this.name
}

getName()
// -> ''

window.name = 'Demo';
getName()
// -> 'Demo'
```

Functions defined in a specific object (which I will refer to as *methods* from now on) have, quite unsurprisingly, a default binding on their container object. It just so happens that JavaScript lets you drop the window object reference; it's implicit. So, defining what looks like a "global" is actually defining in the scope of the window object. This object *is* the global scope, in JavaScript.

This is all well and good, but there is one critical gotcha: *if the function invocation does not use its specific object, you lose the binding.* The most common case for this is when you pass a method as an argument to be invoked later. It then reverts to the default window binding. Just look at the following code:

```
prototype/steroids/binding-method.js
var CoolObj = {
  name: 'Joe the cool object',

  getName: function() {
    return this.name;
  }
};
window.name = '';

CoolObj.getName()
// -> 'Joe the cool object'

function callFx(fx) {
  return fx();
}

callFx(CoolObj.getName)
// -> ''

window.name = 'The window';
callFx(CoolObj.getName)
```

```
// -> 'The window'
```

Now that's a serious issue. Passing methods around is frequent, especially in Prototype, where just about every other method accepts an iterator argument (just look at Enumerable!). To fix this, Prototype gives Function some love with two new methods (yes, methods on functions; bear with me here):

```
bind(thisRef [, arg... ]) → boundFunction
bindAsEventListener(thisRef [, arg... ]) → boundFunction
```

Let us focus on bind() first. The most common usage scenario involves only the mandatory first argument, which is the object you want to be bound, at execution time, to the **this** reference. For instance, using a variant of our previous example, we get this:

prototype/steroids/bind.js

```
var CoolObj = {
  name: 'Joe the cool object',

  getName: function() {
    return this.name;
  }
};

CoolObj.getName()
// -> 'Joe the cool object'

function callFx(fx) {
  return fx();
}

callFx(CoolObj.getName.bind(CoolObj))
// -> 'Joe the cool object'
```

Of course, we do not need to call bind() every time. If we use the bound version quite a lot (or quite often, as in a loop), it would be wasteful to do so, too. We'll be better off binding once and for all and keeping the bound version on hand for later uses:

prototype/steroids/bind-saved.js

```
var CoolObj = {
  name: 'Joe the cool object',

  getName: function() {
    return this.name;
  }
};

CoolObj.getName()
```

```
// -> 'Joe the cool object'

function callFx(fx) {
  return fx();
}

// WRONG: creates a new bound function on each iteration!
for (var index = 1; index <= 42; ++index)
  callFx(CoolObj.getName.bind(CoolObj));

// RIGHT: caches the bound version
var boundGetName = CoolObj.getName.bind(CoolObj);
for (var index = 1; index <= 42; ++index)
  callFx(boundGetName);
```

Prefilling Arguments with bind

Here's a little-used, albeit cool, extra trick: bind() also lets you prepend the actual call with specific arguments; whatever arguments will be provided to the bound version will get appended to the predefined call. This is technically referred to as *partial function application*:

prototype/steroids/bind-args.js

```
var CoolObj = {
  name: 'Joe',

  getCallDef: function() {
    var call = 'getCallDef("' + this.name + '"';
    var extraArgs = arguments.length > 0
      ? ', ' + $A(arguments).join(', ')
      : '';
    return call + extraArgs + ')';
  }
};

CoolObj.getCallDef()
// -> 'getCallDef("Joe")'

var boundCall = CoolObj.getCallDef.bind(CoolObj, 1, 2, 3);

function callFx(fx) {
  return fx(4, 5);
}

callFx(boundCall)
// -> 'getCallDef("Joe", 1, 2, 3, 4, 5)'
```

This is pretty useful when you want to pass your method around, pre-filled with a few arguments. For instance, maybe you have this generic method that takes a behavior mode string and then one or more elements to process; you would then want to pass it *with a prefilled mode argument* to another part of your script, which would call it only with the elements to process. Using bind() with the mode value produces such a "prepared" method wrapper.

That's it for bind(). By now you're probably wondering what bindAsEventListener() is about. Well, Prototype provides a unified management of events in your browser window, which is great. As we'll see in much detail in Section 6.1, *The Art of Observing Events*, on page 101, properly registered event handler methods take the current event object as their first argument. But maybe you realized several handlers were very similar and refactored them in a single one, which now just needs an extra parameter or two so it can adjust its behavior slightly. And still you'd need the event parameter being passed first, as it usually is. That's what bindAsEventListener() is for, essentially. It works like bind(), but it preserves the current event as the first argument. For more examples and details, look at Section 6.1, *Methods as Listeners: Careful with the Binding!*, on page 103.

As a final note, know that failing to pass an argument to bind() makes it moot (it returns the original function). This behavior was added in Prototype 1.6 to facilitate generic code (that may or may not bind a passed function depending on whether a context argument was passed), such as in Enumerable.

4.3 Your Functions Actually Know More Tricks

Proper binding is key to a lot of object-oriented JavaScript code techniques, but Prototype offers even more nifty tools since version 1.6.

Prefilling Arguments

```
fx.curry(arg...) → Function
```

Often we find ourselves needing to pass a method around, but we need to prefill one or more arguments. For instance, we have a split() method handy, but we'd like to pass it prefilled with ':' as a delimiter.

Typically, we'd find ourselves doing something like this:

```
// WRONG: prefer curry :-)
String.prototype.splitOnColons = function() { return this.split(':'); }
// ...
'1:2:3:4'.splitOnColons()
// => ['1', '2', '3', '4']
```

That's really too verbose for the need. Enter curry(), whose name comes straight out of the functional programming world, where this feature has existed for a long time:

```
String.prototype.splitOnColons = String.prototype.split.curry(':');
```

No manual tricks with anonymous functions anymore. Oh, and should we fail to pass argument (who knows, rough night perhaps?), it will return the original function untouched, avoiding the cost of an anonymous wrapper function. But wait, there's more.

Executing Later

```
fx.delay(timeoutInSecs [, arg... ]) → timeoutHandle
fx.defer([arg... ]) → timeoutHandle
```

When dealing with events, DOM updates, or Ajax calls, we often need to execute a given function, only not just now but in a few moments. There are actually two use cases here:

- We're going to have to wait for some time to elapse. Perhaps we want to trigger some behavior only after a while, such as initiating a drag on a clickable element only when the mouse button stays down long enough (which it won't on a regular click) or delaying the appearance of a custom tooltip. That's what delay() is for.

- We just need the browser to take recent DOM updates into account, perhaps to actually display our indicator before running our Ajax call. All we need is to give the browser a little breathing time with no JavaScript load and then get back to our code. Typically, this is done with a tiny, 10-millisecond delayed execution. And this is exactly what defer() does.

Here are example calls:

```
function showQuestion(qId) {
  // Show question, move to next in 5 seconds.
  loadQuestion.delay(5, ++qId);
}

// Giving the browser time to breathe, and render DOM updates:
$('indicator').show();
postNewComment.defer();
```

As a cute side note, defer() is just a curried version of delay():

```
Function.prototype.defer = Function.prototype.delay.curry(0.01);
```

I told you curry() was nice. . . .

Note that on all JavaScript implementations that Prototype supports, a deferred (or delayed) call will execute only after the current function *completes*.

Wrapping and Playing with Arguments

```
fx.wrap(wrapper [, arg... ]) → Function
fx.argumentNames() → [ String, ... ]
```

Another cool tool is the ability to wrap a function in another *wrapper* function (if you're used to functional programming, that's a compose operation). This can spare us a few tricks with anonymous function and proper binding, too.

The biggest advantage here, probably, is the ability to modify the behavior of existing code, in a way akin to aspect-oriented programming (AOP), by wrapping the behavioral changes as a layer around the original code.

Here's a nice example that shows how to log all events by piggybacking on the event extension method (which equips all event objects with the event-related extended methods, as we'll see in Chapter 6, *Unified Event Handling*, on page 97):

```
if (Event.extend === Prototype.K) Event.extend = function(x){ return x };
Event.extend = Event.extend.wrap(function(proceed, event){
  proceed(event);
  if(event.type == 'mousemove') return; // That would slow us down too much
  console.log((event.eventName||event.type)+' on ' + event.target +
    ( event.target.id ? ' #'+event.target.id : '' ) +
    ' [' + event.pageX + '/' + event.pageY + ']');
});
```

The idea is to provide wrap() with your wrapper function (you call wrap() on the function *you want to wrap around*). The wrapper function will be passed, when called, the *original* function as its first argument, and "actual" arguments (those passed to your newly wrapped function later by user code) follow.

Prototype also finds it increasingly useful to examine the names of a function's arguments, especially in conjunction with wrapping (we use it to implement the new inheritance mechanism, for instance). argumentNames() provides a safe way to obtain a list of the argument names for the function we're calling it on, so we can implement, say, opt-in aspects based on specific argument names. Here's a simple example:

```
'hello'.gsub.argumentNames()
// => ['pattern', 'replacement']
```

"Methodizing": Functions Looking Like Methods

It often happens that existing features are provided in a traditional, function-based manner. You'd pass the object being processed as the first argument, with whatever parameters are needed as later arguments. In an object light, this is not very good form. We would prefer to be able to invoke the method on the object itself, passing only further arguments as necessary.

You can see such a duality at work in Prototype's DOM extensions, with most features being accessible as functions (for example, by passing your element, possibly unextended, to Element.update()) but are also available as methods on extended elements (so you would just call the element, the update() method). This recurring pattern is captured by the methodize() extension to functions:

```
fx.methodize([arg...]) → Function
```

This provides a new function that will, when called as a method on any given object, pass this object as the first argument to the original function. You can also prefill extra arguments by passing them to methodize().

As an example, consider some of the extensions to Number described in the next section. The abs(), ceil(), floor(), and round() methods are just "methodized" versions of their function counterparts in the native Math object. Here's the code for it:

```
$w('abs round ceil floor').each(function(method){
  Number.prototype[method] = Math[method].methodize()
});
```

Isn't that sweet?

4.4 Numbers

It often comes as a surprise to everyone except JavaScript gurus, but numbers are indeed *objects* in JavaScript. Hey, that's just like in Ruby!

For instance, ECMAScript-compliant numbers (as of the third edition, which is roughly JavaScript 1.5) feature, among other methods, toString() and toFixed().

What, you never used those?

```
prototype/steroids/numbers_ecma.js
Math.PI.toString()
// -> '3.141592653589793'

(42).toString(16)
// -> '2a'

parseInt('42', 11).toString(9)
// -> '51' (51 in base 9 is 42 in base 11)

Math.sqrt(2).toFixed(4)
// -> '1.4142'

(5 / 3).toFixed(6)
// -> '1.666667'

(3.141596).toString()
// -> '3.141596'
```

And there are more. Still, there are many common needs that still cry to
be addressed. Prototype goes ahead and answers several of them with
a slew of new methods:

```
abs() → Number
ceil() → Number
floor() → Number
round() → Number
succ() → Number
times(iterator) → sameNumber
toColorPart() → hexString
toPaddedString(length [, radix = 10]) → String
```

The four first ones are just convenience wrappers around their Math
counterparts, so instead of writing this:

```
Math.round(n)
Math.abs(n)
```

...we can do this:

```
n.round()
n.abs()
```

The second method, succ(), is there only to make Numbers compatible
with object ranges (n.succ() will return n + 1). We already had a peek
at them in Section 3.8, *Handling Ranges with $R*, on page 39, and we
will get deeper into them in Section 10.2, *Expressing Ranges of. . . Well,
Anything You Want!*, on page 220. But essentially, this means we can do
stuff like $R(1, 42), which is a range of numbers. In short, this method
is mostly for Prototype's internal use.

Prototype also sprinkles Number with Ruby-flavored powder by providing it with a times() method, which lets us do zero-based numerical loops in a rather straightforward and very legible way:

```
prototype/steroids/number_times.js
(5).times(function() { alert("Isn't this annoying?"); });

// With anything that is not a literal number, you don't need the extra
// parentheses:
var count = parseInt($F('soundCount'), 10);
count.times(playSound);
```

This is just so nice on the eyes.... Who would want to get back to vanilla **for** loops once this kind of syntax is available?

The fourth addition to Number is specifically geared toward CSS color string creation. As you probably know, CSS lets you specify colors in a variety of syntaxes, including reserved color names (such as white), six-digit hexadecimal color codes (such as #a0cf26), three-digit hexadecimal codes (for example, #dd0), and long-winded function-style definitions (something like rgb(220, 220, 0)).

I am fond of the three-digit form myself, which is the shorter syntax and also makes for "safer" colors (colors that have a better chance of being properly rendered on devices with less than 24-bit color resolution). The idea is that, essentially, #rgb is equivalent to #rrggbb. This decreases the amount of possibilities by a 2^{12} factor, leaving you with 4,096 colors.

Still, in order to provide maximum flexibility, toColorPart() goes for the six-digit game. The idea is that whenever you want to create a hexadecimal code for CSS color properties based on computed values in Java-Script, you have to struggle a bit or write the same boilerplate all over again. Even the native toString(radix) method doesn't help you much, because it will produce a single digit for values less than 16. So, toColorPart() provides a lowercase, two-digit hexadecimal representation of your number, which is assumed to be an integer in the valid range for a color component (red, green or blue): 0 to 255.

Therefore, you can deal quite easily with CSS color composition:

```
prototype/steroids/number_toColorPart.js
var rgb = [220, 110, 0];
'#' + rgb.invoke('toColorPart').join('')
// -> '#dc6e00'
```

Finally, there's a simple toPaddedString() method that lets you output a minimum-width, zero-padded representation of your number, in any radix (or *base*) you want:

```
prototype/steroids/number_toPaddedString.js
```
```
(5).toPaddedString(2)
// => '05'

(42).toPaddedString(4, 16)
// => '002a'
```

It can be useful, for instance, when formatting dates or times as strings, because numerical components usually mandate two characters.

4.5 Strings

Strings and arrays are probably the two richest types in native Java-Script; they come with tens of methods out of the box. But because they are so essential to just about any kind of processing, there is still plenty of room for useful improvement. Prototype endows them with numerous new methods, which I'll explain for you now, organized by theme.

Trimming the Fat: strip, stripTags, stripScripts, and truncate

Let's start with methods aimed at removing extra stuff in the string. All of these return the new version of the string:

```
strip() → String
stripScripts() → String
stripTags() → String
truncate([length = 30 [, truncation = '...']]) → String
```

For starters, strip() is the equivalent of the classic (but missing) trim(); it chops out leading and trailing whitespace. stripTags() purges any opening or closing tag but does not remove whatever lies between an opening tag and its closing match. stripScripts() is, in some regard, more surgical; it strips out any *<script>* element, with its contents and closing tag. Finally, truncate() chops text that is longer than its length argument, which will be used for the final length of the truncated version, including the truncation text. So if your text is, say, 35 characters long ending with "too bad really" and you're truncating to 30 characters, you'll end up with "too ba...".

Here is a combined example for these methods:

```
prototype/steroids/string_strips.js
var spacedOutText = '   Hello there!\n';
var markup = '<h1>This is marked up text</h1>\n' +
  '<p>See, there are <strong>tags</strong>.</p>';
var scriptMarkup = '<h1>Okay, still marked up</h1>\n' +
  '<p>But this time we have scripts as well.</p>\n' +
  '<script type="text/javascript">\n' +
  'window.location.href = "http://ooo-bad-sitey.com/scam_me";\n' +
  '</script>\n' +
  '<p>End of markup.</p>';
var longText = 'This text is sort of too long for my taste, you know.';


spacedOutText.strip()
// -> 'Hello there!'

markup.stripTags()
// -> 'This is marked up text\nSee, there are tags.'

scriptMarkup.stripTags()
// -> 'Okay, still marked up\nBut this time we have scripts as well.\n\n' +
//     'window.location.href = "http://ooo-bad-sitey.com/scam_me";\n\n' +
//     'End of markup.'

scriptMarkup.stripScripts()
// -> '<h1>Okay, still marked up</h1>\n' +
//     '<p>But this time we have scripts as well.</p>\n\n' +
//     '<p>End of markup.</p>'

longText.truncate()
// -> 'This text is sort of too lo...'

longText.truncate(42)
// -> 'This text is sort of too long for my ta...'

longText.truncate(42, '~')
// -> 'This text is sort of too long for my tast~'
```

Transformations: sub, gsub, escapeHTML, unescapeHTML, camelize, capitalize, underscore, dasherize, scan, and succ

Numerous extensions deal with string transformation, which can be sorted out among three categories: (un)escaping, part-based formatting, and search and replace.

```
succ() → String
```

The method succ() falls out of these three categories, however, because its primary use is to make strings range-compatible (make them usable with $R() and ObjectRange; for more about this, look at Section 10.2, *Expressing Ranges of... Well, Anything You Want!*, on page 220).

(Un)escaping HTML

```
escapeHTML() → String
unescapeHTML() → String
```

Prototype provides a bulletproof way of escaping HTML, based on using a DOM trick. Usage is simple: escapeHTML() "defangs" an HTML fragment by replacing whatever is needed in there (mostly opening and closing angle brackets) with the corresponding HTML entities. Conversely, unescapeHTML() turns an escaped HTML string into literal HTML.

Here are two demo calls:

`prototype/steroids/string_escaping.js`

```
'<h1>A nice title</h1>'.escapeHTML()
// -> '&lt;h1&gt;A nice title&lt;/h1&gt;'

'&lt;h1&gt;A nice title&lt;/h1&gt;'.unescapeHTML()
// -> '<h1>A nice title</h1>'
```

Part-Based Formatting

```
camelize()   → String
capitalize() → String
dasherize()  → String
underscore() → String
```

Prototype provides many methods taken straight out of Ruby's (or Rail's extension of) String class. These are mostly useful for turning part-based strings into suitable IDs, CSS class names, and the like.

camelize() turns a hyphenized string into an upper camel string (a string with no delimiters between parts, but each part starts with an uppercase letter). Note that only the first characters of each part are transformed; the rest is left untouched. It is very useful, for instance, to turn CSS property names into their DOM property names. A usual method as well is capitalize(), which quite simply capitalizes the first letter and puts the remainder in lowercase.

The story is more complex on underscore(), which does hail straight from Ruby on Rails shores and is capable of turning virtually any identifier name into an underscore-delimited lowercased string. This is more sophisticated than other methods, because it does not chop the string in parts based on a single delimiter character. It looks for hyphens (-) and case changes (from lowercase to uppercase, although it also handles uppercase sequences properly). It actually goes beyond that, dealing with double colons (which are replaced by slashes), but that is rather seldom useful in a web page context.

Finally, dasherize() is a simple conversion from underscores to hyphens. After explaining underscore(), it is a bit of an anticlimax, I'll give you that. But combining both lets us easily turn CSS-related DOM properties into their regular CSS names. Just a thought.

With all those details, I'm sure you'd love a nice dollop of examples. Here, my treat:

```
prototype/steroids/string_transfos.js
```

```
'border'.camelize()
// -> 'border'

'border-style'.camelize()
// -> 'borderStyle'

'border-sTYLE'.camelize()
// -> 'borderSTYLE' // See?  Leaving non-initials untouched.

'border-left-color'.camelize()
// -> 'borderLeftColor'

'borderLeftColor'.underscore()
// -> 'border_left_color'

'borderLeftColor'.underscore().dasherize()
// -> 'border-left-color'

'Draft-WHATWebForms1'.underscore()
// -> 'draft_what_web_forms1'

'cool stuff'.capitalize()
// -> 'Cool stuff'

'COOL STUFF'.capitalize()
// -> 'Cool stuff' // Lower-casing the remainder, too.
```

Advanced Replacing

```
gsub(pattern, replacement|iterator) → String
interpolate(scopeObject [, pattern]) → String
scan(pattern, iterator) → sameString
sub(pattern, replacement|iterator [, count = 1]) → String
```

This leaves us with the two more advanced methods: sub() and gsub(). They let us replace one or more occurrences of a given regular expression with either a template string or the result of calling an iterator function over the match description. This is a bit more advanced than what the native String.replace() method lets us do (plus, browsers such as Safari 1.*x* and early 2.*x* do not all fully implement replace() yet when it comes to replace functions).

To properly understand how to use these, you must know how regular expression matches are provided in JavaScript. Specifically, you do not get a String back; you get either **null** (no match) or a MatchData object. Suffice to say that such an object can be used like an array of matched groups, with index 0 (zero) being the whole match and indices from 1 up are groups within the match. Remember that in regular expressions, you can group fragments for later reference by enclosing them in parentheses.

A vanilla[2] example should help clarify this:

`prototype/steroids/string_match.js`

```
var md = 'Hey guys!'.match(/^(.)(\w+)/);
md[0] // -> 'Hey'
md[1] // -> 'H'
md[2] // -> 'ey'
```

You have two ways of specifying replacements in sub() and gsub()— either by using a template string or by providing an iterator function.

Template strings use Ruby's expansion syntax: #{...}, where you would specify the match object's property name between the curly braces (if you need more details right now about template processing, check out Section 10.4, *Templating Made Easy*, on page 223). Here, the properties amount to the numerical indices described earlier.

You can also specify a custom behavior by passing an iterator function, which will get called with the MatchData instance as an argument and whose return value will be used as a replacement.

Finally, know that the only difference between gsub() and sub() is that the former replaces all occurrences, while the latter can replace a specific amount, defaulting to only the first one.

Finally, there are cases when you just want to detect all occurrences of a pattern in a string, pass each match to an iterator, and still get

---

2. Well, maybe not *that* vanilla. Perhaps you're not too keen on regular expressions. If so, you should gain proficiency; they're powerful tools for text processing. Head over to a nice online tutorial, perhaps something like http://etext.lib.virginia.edu/services/helpsheets/unix/regex.html or http://jmason.org/software/sitescooper/tao_regexps.html.

the same string back (maybe to chain calls on other methods). In short, this is a particular use case for gsub(). Well, this is exactly what scan() does for you.

This certainly calls for a bunch of example invocations:

`prototype/steroids/string_subs.js`

```
// OK, emulating a String.replace on a global regex:
'Vowels are bad for you'.gsub(/[aeiouy]/, '-')
// -> 'V-w-ls -r- b-d f-r ---'

// Group-based replacement
'My name is Henry-James'.gsub(/[aeiouy]/, '[#{0}]')
// -> 'M[y] n[a]m[e] [i]s H[e]nr[y]-J[a]m[e]s'

// Escaping #
'Life is short'.sub(/\w+/, '\##{0}\#')
// -> '#Life# is short'

// Coming soon to a monitor near you...  String#replace could not
// work here on Safari 1.x and early 2.x.
'Die hard 4 (scripting is back with a vengeance)'.gsub(/\w+/,
  function(match) { return match[0].capitalize(); })
// -> 'Die Hard 4 (Scripting Is Back With A Vengeance)'

// How about bracketing the 3 first words?
'Poor sample string gets framed'.sub(/\w+/, '[#{0}]', 3)
// -> '[Poor] [sample] [string] gets framed'

// Let's count the 'o' sequence lengths...
var oCounts = []
'foo boo boz'.scan(/o+/, function(match) {
  oCounts.push(match[0].length);
});
oCounts
// -> [2, 2, 1]
```

The possibilities are limitless....

Version 1.6 also introduced the interpolate() method, which is just a convenience wrapper over the one-shot creation of a Template object based on the current string as its template text. See Section 10.4, *Templating Made Easy*, on page 223 for details.

Script Fragments: extractScripts and evalScripts

Prototype-enabled pages often deal with strings containing HTML markup, most often in Ajax responses. You may need to take scripts out of the markup, holding on to it for later evaluation.

Or you may just want to evaluate the scripts in an HTML fragment:

```
extractScripts() → [ JSString, ... ]
evalScripts() → [ resultValue, ... ]
```

If you need the scripts in a HTML fragment, just call extractScripts(). It returns an array of scripts (without their enclosing *<script>* tags, just pure JavaScript). If you want to eval() all the scripts in a fragment, go directly with evalScripts(). As a bonus, it will return an array of all the result values for said scripts (a script with no specific return value yields **undefined**). By the way, do not mistake extractScripts() with strip-Scripts() (which strips the scripts out of the fragment and returns the expurgated fragment).

Converting and Extracting: toQueryParams, parseQuery, toArray, and inspect

We'll end this exploration of String extensions with a few methods turning strings into some other representation of their contents:

```
inspect([useDoubleQuotes = false]) → String
parseQuery/toQueryParams([separator = '&']) → Object
toArray() → [ char, ... ]
```

We already heard about the inspect() method back in Section 4.1, *Intro-specting Objects*, on page 43. With strings, it takes an extra customization, letting you bracket its text with either single quotes (the default) or double quotes. It basically escapes backslashes, special characters such as tabulations and carriage returns, and the proper quote type within the string.

If you want to handle a String like an Array of characters, you can go with toArray() (and therefore, get concise with $A()).

Finally, Prototype provides String with a URL-related decoding method, aimed at turning the query string part of a URL (lengthy stuff like name=john&text=cool%20stuff&show=yes) into a set of properties. You can even use it on strings that are not quite query-string-like and use another delimiter than the ampersand (&) simply by passing an alternative delimiter (which can very well be longer than a single character). Also note this method is aliased, making it available under two names. Use whichever suits you best: parseQuery() or toQueryParams().

The result is an anonymous object whose properties mirror the parameters in the query string. If multiple parameters share the same name, there is only one property, and its value is an array of parameter values. Of course, proper decoding is done on both parameter names and parameter values, thanks to the native decodeURIComponent() method.

As a final usage note, be aware that an anchor (the trailing #... part, which usually refers to an id= or name= attribute within the document), if present, is ignored.

Here are a few example calls for these methods:

```
prototype/steroids/string_convs.js
'Sam Stephenson\nThomas \'madrobby\' Fuchs'.inspect()
// -> "'Sam Stephenson\\nThomas \\'madrobby\\' Fuchs'"

'Sam Stephenson\nThomas \'madrobby\' Fuchs'.inspect(true)
// -> "\"Sam Stephenson\\nThomas 'madrobby' Fuchs\""

'hello'.toArray()
// -> ['h', 'e', 'l', 'l', 'o']

$A('hello')
// -> ['h', 'e', 'l', 'l', 'o']

var query = '?login=tdd&age=29&country=FR';
query.parseQuery()
// -> { login: 'tdd', age: '29', country: 'FR' }
```

Searching for Contents: startsWith, endsWith, and include

These are three no-brainer methods that just let you do away with any roundabout use of indexOf():

```
endsWith(string) → Boolean
include(string) → Boolean
startsWith(string) → Boolean
```

Usage is pretty self-explanatory.... I don't think you need an example of those, do you?

4.6 Arrays

Arrays are already resourceful objects in native JavaScript. They are endowed with a fair amount of methods, the most common ones probably being push(), concat(), join(), pop(), and shift(). If your eyes are

> **Playing Nice to the Latest JavaScript**
>
> Prototype goes out of its way to smooth things over with recent JavaScript versions, starting with 1.6.
>
> - It homogenizes its API extensions to those proposed by official JavaScript (for example, it features aliases such as filter( ) and every( ) over array methods it originally calls select( ) and all( )).
>
> - It relies on native implementations of its features whenever possible for performance reasons (for example, the enumeration of arrays will use the native forEach( ) when present).

goggling just now, I advise you to take a look at Array again, such as at DevMo[3] or W3Schools.[4] Still, there is much room for improvement.

In Prototype, arrays are probably the richest objects of all. First, they mix in the Enumerable module, which brings in a host of great methods, as we will see in Chapter 5, *Advanced Collections with Enumerable*, on page 77. Second, they get an extra load of extensions, which we are going to discuss now. The net result is simple; arrays in Prototype are very much more powerful than you would expect. They do feel like they are on steroids!

As was the case for String, the sheer amount of new methods is better reviewed in categories. Do remember that this section alone does not account for all that Prototype brings to arrays. At the time of this writing, arrays have no less than 35 outward-facing[5] extra methods, either through Enumerable or specifically for Array, thanks to Prototype. Factor in the native methods described in JavaScript 1.5, and arrays feature a whopping 47 "public" methods. . . .

Enumerating an Array

As Array mixes Enumerable in, it obviously features its cornerstone each( ) method. I just want to make it perfectly clear (although it is fairly

---

3. http://developer.mozilla.org/en/docs/JavaScript
4. http://w3schools.com/js/js_obj_array.asp
5. That is, designed for public use, as opposed to internal use.

evident) that iteration happens in increasing numerical index order, from 0 (zero) to length - 1.

However, there is the question of sparse arrays. Sparse arrays are arrays where you manually assign values to nonadjacent indices, something like this:

```
var a = [];
a[0] = 'foo';
a[10] = 'bar';
```

Using a regular fast loop, you would iterate over the "missing" indices (1 to 9), with **undefined** values. But starting with version 1.6, Prototype leverages the native forEach() method in JavaScript arrays when it is available (recent enough JavaScript version), and this method will *not* iterate through undefined indices. You'll get index 0 for *foo* and index 1 for *bar*.

The thing is, using sparse arrays is using arrays instead of hashes (which, in JavaScript, are any literal object). Arrays are *designed* for sequential, integer-based indexing—not sparse population, which is what hashes are for. So when you find yourself playing with sparse arrays, either convert to a hash or explicitly define the missing indices. Here's the hash version, on which enumeration iterates only on the defined properties:

```
var a = {}; // Note the curly braces instead of square brackets
a[0] = 'foo';
a[10] = 'bar';
```

However, I should mention that property iteration order is undefined in JavaScript; it is essentially browser-dependent. One browser may go 0 and then 10, and another one may go 10 and then 0—there's no guarantee. It's usually no big deal, though. If worse comes to worst, you can grab the keys, sort them, and iterate on the sorted list.

As of Prototype 1.6, if the native JavaScript method forEach() is available on arrays, it is used instead of manual iteration.

Transformations: clear, compact, flatten, intersect, reverse, reduce, uniq, and without

Prototype introduces many methods to specifically alter the contents, or even the structure, of an array:

```
clear() → emptiedArray
compact() → newArray
flatten() → Array
```

```
intersect(Array) → Array
reduce() → Array | singleValue
reverse([inline = true]) → Array
uniq([sorted = false]) → Array
without(value...) → Array
```

Most of these methods are easy to understand and use. A few deal with removing unwanted elements: clear() removes them all, returning the original array, now empty; compact() returns a new version exempt of any **null** or **undefined** element; intersect() returns a new set of the elements that exist both in the current array and in the one passed as a parameter (using the === operator for comparisons);[6] uniq() returns a new version devoid of any duplicate, while retaining the original order; finally, without(value...) returns a new version purged of any of the passed arguments.

If you call uniq() on a large array that is already sorted, tell it so. It'll work in linear time instead of quadratic time, resulting in a significant performance boost.

A common operation when dealing with recursively built arrays is flatten(). As its name implies, it takes an arbitrarily nested array and turns it into its "flat" (linear) equivalence, using depth-first traversal; check the next example code for a demo. Another structural method is reduce(), which leaves multiple-element arrays untouched but turns single-element arrays into their unique element. Imagine gathering all the values for a given form field name; if you end up with only one value, as will most commonly be the case, you want to spare external code the need to index your result with [0]. You could use reduce() on the array of values you got from the initial collection process.

Finally, reverse() lets you reverse the contents of an array. Unless you explicitly pass **false** as its optional inline argument, it will reverse the array itself. Otherwise, it clones the original array and reverses the copy. In both cases, the reversed array is returned. As an interesting note, reverse() exists, strictly inline, as a native method for JavaScript arrays. Prototype replaces it with this version that lets you choose whether you want inline reversal, which delegates to the native one unless you need to leave the original array untouched.

---

6. Beware: it starts by using uniq() on the current array, which may have performance impacts as discussed in the next paragraph.

Theory is good but is no substitute for actual code:

prototype/steroids/array_transfos.js

```
var easy = [42, 'Hey', NaN, 'fellas', null, "What's up?"];
var harder = [42, ['Hey', [NaN], 'fellas'], null, [[["What's up?"]]]];

easy.reverse()
// easy: ["What's up?", null, 'fellas', NaN, 'Hey', 42]
easy.reverse(false)
// -> [42, 'Hey', NaN, 'fellas', null, "What's up?"]
// easy: ["What's up?", null, 'fellas', NaN, 'Hey', 42]

var easy2 = harder.flatten()
// -> [42, 'Hey', NaN, 'fellas', null, "What's up?"]

easy2 = easy2.without(NaN, 'fellas').compact()
// -> [42, 'Hey', NaN, "What's up?"] // Remember NaN != NaN...

easy2.clear()
// easy2: []

[].reduce()        // -> undefined
[1].reduce()       // -> 1
[1, 2, 3].reduce() // -> [1, 2, 3]

[1, 2, 3, 7, 2, 5, 7, 4, 8].uniq()
// -> [1, 2, 3, 7, 5, 4, 8]
```

Conversions: from and inspect

```
Array.from(iterable) → Array
inspect() → String
```

If you fail to see the difference between Array.from() and the $A() utility function, it is because there is none. These are aliases, and the latter form is simply the preferred one, thanks to its conciseness. See Section 3.5, *$A, the Collection Unifier*, on page 36 for full details on how Array.from() works.

We already discussed inspect() methods, particularly in Section 4.1, *Introspecting Objects*, on page 43. The Array version produces a string of the form *[item1, item2... itemN]*, using Object.inspect() on each item. Here are a few examples:

prototype/steroids/array_convs.js

```
Array.from === $A
// -> true

Array.from('hello')
// -> ['h', 'e', 'l', 'l', 'o']
```

```
$A({0: 'What kind', 1: 'of twisted', 2: 'example is this?', length: 3})
// [ 'What kind', 'of twisted', 'example is this?']

[42, 'hello', Number.POSITIVE_INFINITY, []].inspect()
// -> "[42, 'hello', Infinity, []]"
```

Extractions: first, last, and indexOf

Prototype provides a few extra methods to quickly get at specific elements in an array:

```
first() → value
indexOf(value) → position
lastIndexOf(value) → position
last() → value
```

We often need to get at the first, or last, element of an array. Although writing arr[0] is certainly easy enough, arr[arr.length - 1] leaves a bitter taste. This is why Prototype introduces first() and last(), whose names are self-explanatory. Note that on empty arrays, they yield **undefined**.

Another fairly common need is to determine whether an element exists in an array and where it is. Mere presence is better addressed by the include() method mixed in from Enumerable, but actual position can be obtained by indexOf(), which encapsulates the all-too-common numerical loop over a == operator. In the usual fashion, it returns -1 if the element is not found and otherwise returns the index of its first occurrence. Note that because it uses == instead of ===, you must be careful about equivalences, such as 0 == false == " and null == undefined. If a value may be present multiple times, you may want to differentiate between its first and last positions. Use lastIndexOf() for the latter case.

Here are a few quick lines to get the hang of these simple methods:

prototype/steroids/array_extracts.js

```
[].first()
// -> undefined

[1, 2, 3].first()
// -> 1

[].last()
// -> undefined

[1, 2, 3].last()
// -> 3

['Hey', 'fellas', "What's up?"].indexOf('fellas')
// -> 1
```

```
['Hey', 'fellas', "What's up?"].indexOf('Fellas')
// -> -1 (String == String is case-sensitive)

[0, 1, 2, 3].indexOf('')
// -> 0 (0 == '')
```

Optimizations: clone, size, and toArray

Sometimes code exists in a generic fashion that could be optimized locally for Array. Prototype usually takes the smart road and introduces local optimizations or type-specific variants.

```
clone/toArray() → newArray
size() → Number
```

The clone() method is not an override of a mixed-in method but provides a type-specific alternative to the slower Object.clone() method discussed in Section 4.1, *Cloning and Extending Objects*, on page 45. It basically relies on the native concat() method.

Aliasing toArray() over clone() does override the toArray() method mixed in from Enumerable, and this is a good thing: Enumerable's version is significantly slower, because it requires manually iterating over all the elements (because of its generic nature).

Finally, size() also overrides the mixed-in version, which required prior array conversion, something that would, on actual arrays, be utterly unnecessary, not to mention wasteful. It simply uses the array's native length property.

These methods are straightforward enough that I believe there is no need for example code here. If you insist on seeing code, just look at the generic versions of toArray() and size() in Chapter 5, *Advanced Collections with Enumerable*, on page 77.

The Case of Opera and concat

As an interesting note, by November 2006 Opera did not implement the native concat() method properly. This was noticed by Thomas Fuchs, who tweaked Prototype so that it now replaces (on Opera only) the native version with a "guaranteed" one.

4.7 Full-Spectrum JSON Support

Version 1.5.1 introduced full support for JSON, thanks to the tireless efforts of Tobie Langel.

> **⑂ Joe Asks. . .**
>
> **Hang on. . . What's This JSON Thingy?**
>
> JSON stands for JavaScript Object Notation. It's a simple representation of any object as text using only standard JavaScript syntax for literal values (objects, arrays, strings, numbers, booleans, and so on).
>
> It was formalized by Douglas Crockford, noted JavaScript guru. The specification is available at http://json.org.
>
> The major advantage of JSON is that it's trivial to produce *and* parse in JavaScript, no matter how rich and structured the information may be. This makes it a tasty format for exchanging complex information with a server through, say, Ajax. It's rapidly becoming prevalent over XML in this use case.

The resulting API is as follows:

```
Object.toJSON(obj) → String
array.toJSON() → String
date.toJSON() → String
hash.toJSON() → String
number.toJSON() → String
string.toJSON() → String
jsonString.evalJSON([sanitize = false]) → Object
```

Converting Any Object to JSON

The generic way of turning a JavaScript value into its JSON representation is to call Object.toJSON(), passing it the value. It honors the JSON serialization mechanism, which basically means the following:

- Functions, DOM elements, **undefined**, and exotic stuff[7] are ignored.
- **null** and booleans are represented literally.
- If the object features a toJSON() method, it is used; Prototype does equip all relevant types (see the API block in the prior section) with appropriate toJSON() methods. It even equips Date with one

---

7. For instance, in Internet Explorer, objects that are accessed across a COM+ bridge, which makes dear old Internet Explorer's **typeof** burp the nonstandard 'unknown' value.

serialization method, which uses a format akin to W3DTF (for example, 2007-04-29T22:53:49).

• Otherwise, the object is manually serialized, iterating over its properties and using Object.toJSON() on each one, in a recursive fashion.

Here's a small example:

`prototype/steroids/json_serializing.js`

```
var undef;
Object.toJSON(undef)
// => ''
Object.toJSON(null)
// => 'null'

var doudou = { first: 'Élodie', last: 'Jaubert',
  birthDate: new Date(1980, 9, 29), // 0 == January
  gang: [ 'Camille', 'Clotilde', 'Diane' ],
  getJob: function() { return 'Chef du monde' },
  blond: false
};
Object.toJSON(doudou);
// (single-line value, wrapped here, assuming we're GMT+1 in Fall)
// => '{"first": "Élodie", "last": "Jaubert",
//      "birthDate": "1980-10-28T23:00:00Z",
//      "gang": ["Camille", "Clotilde", "Diane"], "blond": false}'
```

Converting a JSON Representation to an Object

Turning a JSON text into actual JavaScript objects (an arbitrarily complex object, which can be regarded as a tree of objects, basically) is done through the new evalJSON() method added to String. This simply returns the resulting object, which you can then use as any vanilla JavaScript object.

Here's a bit for taste:

`prototype/steroids/json_deserializing.js`

```
'[1, 2, 3]'.evalJSON()
// => [1, 2, 3]

var doudou = '{"first": "Élodie", "last": "Jaubert"}'.evalJSON();
doudou.first
// => 'Élodie'
doudou.last
// => 'Jaubert'
```

JSON and Security

Prototype offers two features regarding JSON security.

The first one is JSON *sanitizing*. It will validate that the JSON text follows the accepted syntax and does not contain any attempt at tricking the JavaScript evaluator into undesirable processing (for example, disclosing sensitive information). You can enable it by passing **true** as an argument to the evalJSON() method. If you're using an Ajax requester or updater (see Chapter 9, *Ajax Has Never Been So Easy*, on page 177), there's a sanitizeJSON option that lets you request this for automatic JSON evaluation.

The second one lets you wrap JSON data with special "filter" text that aims to defeat *JavaScript hijacking*, a recently discovered security hole.[8] The default filter, represented by the Prototype.JSONFilter regular expression, has you start with /*-secure- and finish with */ (with allowed whitespace after that). Such a wrapper is automatically stripped by evalJSON().

Still, these are by no means silver bullets. They provide a rough security improvement, but as with any data format that can contain active code and can go through an eval()-like call, you should be extra careful about the reliability and security of your JSON exchanges.

So, What Did We Learn Here?

We sure covered a lot of ground in this chapter: Prototype's augmentation of native JavaScript capabilities and types is quite impressive. Let's take a minute to recap the main points we've gone through:

- The **for. . . in** loop is not intended to iterate over arrays; it iterates over an object's *properties*. We should not use it to go through an array's integer-indexed values and should rely on a regular loop or a prebaked enumeration instead.

- Most type detections (for example, whether something is an array, a string, a function. . .) are straightforwardly available as Object. is...() methods.

---

8. For all the details, read up on it at http://www.fortifysoftware.com/servlet/downloads/public/JavaScript_Hijacking.pdf.

- Numbers are actual objects, and they are replete with cool methods, either from native JavaScript (such as toFixed()) or thanks to Prototype extensions (such as ceil() and toPaddedString()).

- Strings gain a lot of mojo with Prototype, especially when content transformation is concerned. Stripping, replacing, splitting, and converting to and from syntaxes and URLs—it's all there for the taking!

- Arrays are even more powerful; already well-endowed by native JavaScript, they become über-collections thanks to Prototype, with close to 50 public-facing methods. Thanks to method chaining (calling a method straight from the result of another one), we can produce mighty transformations in a concise way.

- Function binding (what **this** refers to when the function actually runs) is an important issue often unknown to or misunderstood by web developers. Prototype provides a nifty bind() method that lets us not only guarantee context but also prefill arguments.

- When it comes to function tricks, we're actually well stocked. curry() provides *partial application* (prefilling part of the arguments of a function and producing a new function out of it); defer() and delay() let us schedule the execution of a method call for later; finally, wrap(), argumentNames(), and methodize() open up a large field of dynamic function analysis and usage.

- Prototype now has excellent support for JSON, the JavaScript Object Notation.

Neuron Workout

Here are a few questions to help you flex these fresh scripting muscles:

- What's the technical reason a **for**...**in** loop on an array will go berserk when you're using Prototype?

- What happens to **this** when you attempt to bind an already-bound function?

- When should you use curry() instead of bind()?

- When, at the earliest, will a delay()ed function run? Is this also true of defer() red calls? Why?

- What situations (outside of debugging) can you think of that would find argumentNames() very useful?

- Why can we write Math.PI.toFixed(4) but must add parentheses in (240).toColorPart()?

- After a call to stripTags(), do we still have the *contents* of <*script*>s in the string?

- What happens if we pass sub() a RegExp with a global flag (for example, /test/g)?

- How could we use without() to strip from an array *all the values from another one* without resorting to a form of loop?

"But Wait! There's More!"

At this point, you must be beginning to realize just how much improvement Prototype manages to pack into such a small library. Vastly improved strings and arrays, class-based element selection, properly bound functions, debug-oriented string representations. . . it is quite a feat, indeed. Yet there is much, much more to discover and marvel at. And the next step on this journey is about the *new* objects and modules Prototype brings to the mix.

By relieving the brain of all unnecessary work, a good notation sets it free to concentrate on more advanced problems.

▶ Alfred North Whitehead

Chapter 5

Advanced Collections with Enumerable

OK, this is it. This, dear reader, is *the mother lode*—one of the true cornerstones on which the power of Prototype is built. This is the module that provides many an object type with no less than *27 new methods*, which address just about any common collection manipulation need, from filtering to sorting to transforming to grouping to....

This method set is, most important, mixed into Array; with Prototype, all your arrays have these new methods. Of course, anything easily convertible to an array (through $A(), such as DOM NodeLists, for instance) also gets the prize. With Prototype, arrays become this super collection type that features just about everything you need.

Many other types also mix Enumerable in, but you'll use that aspect less often. I'll make sure to remind you of this mixing in when we hit those types in later chapters.

5.1 The Core Method: Iterating with each

```
each(iterator [, context]) → enumerable
```

At the heart of Enumerable lies each(), the fundamental iteration method. This is the one that actually relies on the host type providing an _each() method to implement the raw iteration algorithm (a technical detail we'll cover in Section 5.8, *Which Objects Can Mix Enumerable In?*, on page 94). So, what is the added value of each()?

Well, it takes care of all the extra fluff:

- It makes sure the iterator you pass gets invoked with two arguments: the current item and the current index in the iteration (starting at zero).

- It handles the special $break exception your iterator may use to short-circuit the iteration loop.

Indeed, whatever iterator you pass to each(), when invoked upon every iteration, gets not only the current item but also the numerical index for the current iteration (this lets you, for instance, distinguish between first item and later items). Just look at the following code:

```
prototype/new/enumerable_each.js
```
```javascript
// Alerts 'one', 'two', then 'three'
['one', 'two', 'three'].each(function(s) {
  alert(s);
});

// Alerts '0: hello' then '1: world'
[ 'hello', 'world'].each(function(s, index) {
  alert(index + ': ' + s);
})
```

We'll get to the context parameter in a moment, but there are a few things I'd like to explain first, which are generally more useful.

Short-Circuiting Enumerations

With vanilla loop constructs (such as **for** or **while**), you can use two short-circuit instructions: **continue** skips the remainder of the loop body and goes over to the next iteration (if any), while **break** terminates the loop altogether. Such instructions, or their equivalents, are found in many languages (such as C/C++, Java, C#, and Delphi).

What seems to be a problem here is that we *do not use vanilla loops*; we use each()! So, how can we obtain the same kind of functionality? Well, quite easily. We can skip the remainder of the current iteration by simply returning from the iterator function, using **return** as the Gods of Code intended us to use. However, there is no such straightforward substitute for **break**. That is why Prototype introduces a specific exception constant, named $break. Just throw it from your iterator, and each() will automatically catch it, cleanly terminate the loop, and return normally.

> ### Whatever Happened to $continue?
>
> Originally there were two exception constants related to iteration short-circuits: $break and $continue. However, the latter can be replaced by a simple **return**, which happens to yield much better performance.
>
> This is why, starting with version 1.5.1, $continue got kicked out of Prototype. Use **return** instead!

Here's a small code example for this:

`prototype/new/enumerable_shortCircuits.js`

```
// This could be done better with an accumulator using inject, but humor me
// here...
var result = [];
$R(1,10).each(function(n) {
  if (0 == n % 2)
    return;
  if (n > 6)
    throw $break;
  result.push(n);
});
// result -> [1, 3, 5]
```

each Underlies Most Other Enumerable Methods

Because each() is the fundamental iteration mechanism, it forms the basis of most other methods in Enumerable. Whatever need these address, they always need to iterate over some or all of the items in the collection. This means you can also use **return** and the $break exception in the iterators you pass to these methods (although you'd better know what you're doing, because short-circuiting predefined algorithms may yield results you hadn't expected).

Currently, the only methods not relying on each() are eachSlice() and inGroupsOf(), which makes sense, considering their job is to work with *groups* of items instead of single items.

Enumeration Context

Starting with Prototype 1.6, every Enumerable method has a new, final context parameter. This was introduced in order to mimic JavaScript

1.6+ behavior when necessary. This parameter is quite simply the binding to be used for the execution of your iterator functions. If the iterator you pass is already bound (using bind()), this last argument is useless. But if your iterator function is not specifically bound, you can ask it to be by passing its bound object (the object to which **this** will refer within the iterator function) as the context argument to your Enumerable method.

When the method you use is not provided directly by JavaScript 1.6+, it won't be any faster than manually binding the iterator. It may be a tad more concise, though:

```
items.all(function(item) { ... }.bind(obj))
// vs.
items.all(function(item) { ... }, obj)
```

When the method you use *is* a native one, using this argument will be much faster than manually binding the iterator (you'll save the cost of the wrapper anonymous function created by bind(), at every turn of the loop).

I will not repeat this final context argument on the signatures of each Enumerable method. That would be pretty verbose and likely to distract from each method's specific purpose. Just know it's there every time if you need it.

5.2 Getting General Information About Our Collection

The first set of methods we'll look at (each() doesn't count. Come on. A one-method *set*?) is about quickly checking simple facts about our elements, including whether any or all of them suit our needs, whether an element is there, or how many elements there are:

```
all/every([iterator = Prototype.K]) → Boolean
any/some([iterator = Prototype.K]) → Boolean
include/member(value) → Boolean
size() → Number
```

The all() and any() methods are more and more common in collection libraries. In Mozilla browsers, native JavaScript arrays actually feature them already, although under the names every() and some(). They're likely to be standardized in JavaScript 2.0 (ECMAScript, 4th edition, due in 2007). To help smooth over runtime differences, Prototype includes aliases for them when needed, starting with version 1.6. But because we need to support $break for now, we override with our

> ## Joe Asks. . .
> ### What Is This Prototype.K Thing?
>
> It's an *identity function*, which simply takes its first argument and returns it untouched. It's very useful to Enumerable, because it lets most methods make the iterator argument optional. Either you pass in your own element processing or it will use the raw elements, without having to use two separate algorithms internally.
>
> Prototype.K( ) is part of a few boilerplate functions described in Section 10.5, *Boilerplate Functions*, on page 228.

own versions for now. Anyway, these two methods let us verify that all, or at least one, of the elements satisfy a given condition, which we express in the iterator. The iterator function is then a *predicate*, that is, a function that returns a boolean information about its argument (for example, "no, this argument is not greater than 10").

It is possible *not* to pass iterators to these two methods, in which case they use the elements themselves as booleans. If you are fuzzy on Java-Script boolean equivalence, here it is: **null**, **undefined**, **false**, 0, NaN (Not a Number), and the empty string are all equivalent to **false**. Anything else is equivalent to **true**.

Here are a few example uses:

`prototype/new/enumerable_quickChecks.js`

```
// Are there only numbers in there?
[1, 2, 3, '4', 'hello'].all(function(item) {
  return 'number' == typeof item;
})
// -> false (ticks on '4', stops right there)

// Only higher percentiles?
[92, 97, 90, 98].all(function(grade) { return grade >= 90; })
// -> true (kick-ass class!)

var nodes = $('topBar', 'menuBar', 'navBar', 'footer');
// Found any of those?
if (nodes.any())
  // whatever...
```

Oh, and in case you're wondering, both methods obviously stop iterating internally as soon as possible: all() will not bother checking ahead once it encounters an item that fails the predicate, and any() is satisfied as soon as an item passes the test.

Then we have the aliased duo with include() and member(). As always with aliases, just pick whichever feels more natural to you. It's all about your comfort. The names are self-explanatory anyway. They just let you know whether a given value is among the elements. It relies on lenient comparison (that is, using == instead of ===), which can be surprising if you don't pay attention to details. Finally, size() obviously returns the number of elements in the collection.

Here's a final series of example calls to get things straight:

```
prototype/new/enumerable_quickChecks.js
```

```
$R(1, 20).include(12)
// -> true
$R(1, 20).include('20')
// -> true (20 == '20')
$A(document.childNodes).member(document.body)
// -> false (not so fast, son!)
$R(5, 20).size()
// -> 16
```

5.3 Finding Elements and Applying Filters

One of the most common usage patterns over a collection of elements is finding stuff, or filtering the contents to retain only the relevant items. In this area, Enumerable comes with a varied set of methods, catering to just about every common need:

```
detect/find(iterator) → firstElement | undefined
filter/findAll/select(iterator) → Array
grep(pattern [, iterator = Prototype.K]) → Array
partition([iterator = Prototype.K]) → [trueItems, falseItems]
reject(iterator) → Array
```

The find() method (and its detect() alias) searches for the first element that matches the criteria expressed by the iterator you provide. That is, it returns the first element in the collection for which your iterator returns **true**. If no element lives up to the test, it doesn't return anything, which means it returns **undefined**.

If you're interested in getting *all* the elements that match your iterator, use findAll() (or its select() alias) instead. It returns an array of results, which will be empty if no elements matched (I repeat: an empty array, not **undefined**). These can be pretty plain to illustrate, so I threw in an optimal[1] JavaScript prime detection, on the house:

`prototype/new/enumerable_finders.js`

```
// An optimal naive-class (i.e. not requiring a Math Ph.D. and 50+ lines of
// code) deterministic prime detection method, slightly compacted.
function isPrime(n) {
  if (2 > n) return false;
  if (0 == n % 2) return (2 == n);
  for (var index = 3; n / index > index; index += 2)
    if (0 == n % index) return false;
  return true;
} // isPrime

$R(10,15).find(isPrime)
// -> 11

['hello', 'world', 'this', 'is', 'nice'].find(function(s) {
  return s.length <= 3;
})
// -> 'is'

$R(1, 10).findAll(function(n) { return 0 == n % 2; })
// -> [2, 4, 6, 8, 10]

['hello', 'world', 'this', 'is', 'nice'].findAll(function(s) {
  return s.length >= 5;
})
// -> ['hello', 'world']
```

grep() is a rather specialized variant of findAll(). Before version 1.6, it matched the String representation of elements (the result of their toString() method) against a regular expression pattern. Since 1.6, it's much more flexible. It takes as a pattern (the first argument) any object that has a match() method and uses this method on each item in turn. All elements for which match() returns **true** (or something equivalent to **true**) are returned.

This opens the door to a lot of power. Prototype extends RegExp, so it features a match() method equivalent to its native test() on the item's toString() result, so we can use regular expressions, preserving backward compatibility.

---

1. Well, optimal in the naive class (essentially, a class of solutions not requiring a math PhD). If you're geeky enough, check out the AKS primality test, for instance.

But Selector (described in Section 7.3, *Selector*, on page 156), also features a match() method that will check that the element you pass to it does match its CSS 3 selection. And naturally, you can create your *own* objects with custom match() logic.

Just like findAll(), it returns all the matching elements in an array.

You can pass an iterator if you need to get a derived value based on the elements, instead of the elements themselves. Note that this is about transforming the values *being returned*, not altering the string representation being matched against the pattern.

An example should drive the point home on this:

`prototype/new/enumerable_grep.js`

```
// Get all strings with a repeated letter somewhere
['hello', 'world', 'this', 'is', 'cool'].grep(/(.)\1/)
// -> ['hello', 'cool']

// Get all numbers ending with 0 or 5!
$R(1,30).grep(/[05]$/)
// -> [5, 10, 15, 20, 25, 30]

// Those, minus 1
$R(1,30).grep(/[05]$/, function(n) { return n - 1; })
// -> [4, 9, 14, 19, 24, 29]
```

5.4 Grouping Elements and Pasting Collections Together

Sometimes, you want to cut collections into chunks, roughly equal-sized. Maybe you want to put them into multiple columns or some other stylish layout. Maybe you can pass only so many at a time to a backend processing layer (aaaah, those hard-coded, arbitrary limits in legacy software. . .). Maybe you just feel like it. That's what inGroupsOf() is for. As it was coded, it spawned eachSlice(), a nice group-based iterator.

Another grouping issue arises when you need to zip stuff together. Picture the fly on a pair of trousers: there's the left side, the right side, and zip! They're bound in pairs. Taking two collections and turning it into a collection of pairs is what zip() does:

```
eachSlice(size [, iterator = Prototype.K])  →  [ slice, ... ]
inGroupsOf(size [, filler = null])  →  [ group, ... ]
zip(sequence... [, iterator = Prototype.K])  →  Array
```

Don't Waste Time: findAll vs. partition vs. reject

The reject() method does exactly the opposite of findAll() (or select(), its alias). Instead of getting the elements that match the iterator, it gets those that *do not*. It's fairly simple.

Often enough, your code needs to extract both sets: the selectees and the rejectees. The dummy way of doing this is to call the two methods in sequence. This will iterate twice, calling the iterator twice as much when a single pass could suffice. So, the smart way in such a context lies with partition(). It sorts out the elements in two arrays: those that pass the iterator and those that fail it. Then it returns those two sets wrapped in another array (remember that JavaScript, like most languages, lets you return only one thing at a time).

Note that partition() doesn't require the iterator. Without it, it will use the elements' boolean equivalence to sort them apart.

Here is an example using it:

prototype/new/enumerable_partition.js

```
['hello', null, 42, false, true, , 17].partition()
// -> [['hello', 42, true, 17], [null, false, undefined]]

$R(1, 10).partition(function(n) {
  return 0 == n % 2;
})
// -> [[2, 4, 6, 8, 10], [1, 3, 5, 7, 9]]
```

So, let's play with inGroupsOf() for starters. It's actually fairly simple. It takes the full list of elements we have and arranges them in fixed-size groups. If there are not enough elements for the last group to be complete, it gets filled with either **null** or the second, optional argument. Naturally, groups are composed in iterating order.

This is actually a special case of generic grouping. You may well not want to fill up the last group, or you may want to do something altogether different to the groups as they're created, turning them into something else. This is why the actual slicing behavior resides in eachSlice(), which is then reused internally by inGroupsOf(). You pass the maximum size of each slice and an optional iterator that is used to transform each slice once they are all defined.

For instance, inGroupsOf() uses a simple iterator that fills the slice to size if needed and returns the updated slice.

I know, I know—that makes quite a few ideas to juggle around and picture in your head. How about seeing some code? Let's start by defining a series of students, with their first names (doesn't "Élodie" feel lovely?) and ages:

prototype/new/enumerable_slicing.js

```
var students = [
  { name: 'Sunny', age: 20 },  { name: 'Audrey', age: 21 },
  { name: 'Matt', age: 20 },   { name: 'Élodie', age: 26 },
  { name: 'Will', age: 21 },   { name: 'David', age: 23 },
  { name: 'Julien', age: 22 }, { name: 'Thomas', age: 21 },
  { name: 'Serpil', age: 22 }
];
```

Then we get our first eachSlice() out to produce groups of up to four students, with an iterator that will turn the original groups (arrays of student objects) into name-only groups (arrays of strings):

prototype/new/enumerable_slicing.js

```
students.eachSlice(4, function(toon) {
  return toon.pluck('name');
})
// -> [ ['Sunny', 'Audrey', 'Matt', 'Élodie'],
//      ['Will', 'David', 'Julien', 'Thomas'],
//      ['Serpil'] ]
```

We could actually do this more efficiently by "plucking" the whole set and then grouping, but, hey, humor me. We'll do that later with in-GroupsOf(), anyway.

Still with me? All right, on to the next one, which demonstrates a simple use with no iterator:

prototype/new/enumerable_slicing.js

```
students.eachSlice(2).first()
// -> [{ name: 'Sunny', age: 20 }, { name: 'Audrey', age: 21 }]
```

Prototype.K() leaves the groups intact, and we call first() on the resulting object to grab the first group only. The result is unsurprising (even more than you think).

Now, here comes the mammoth.

It actually does some heavy lifting here, so there is some code involved:

`prototype/new/enumerable_slicing.js`

```
Line 1  students.eachSlice(3, function(toon) {
          var maxAge = toon.max(function(s) { return s.age; });
          var leader = toon.findAll(function(s) { return s.age == maxAge })
            .sortBy(function(s) { return s.name; }).last();
     5    return { leader: leader.name, members: toon.pluck('name').sort() };
        })
        // -> [ { leader: 'Audrey', members: ['Audrey', 'Matt', 'Sunny'] },
        //      { leader: 'Élodie', members: ['David', 'Will', 'Élodie'] },
        //      { leader: 'Serpil', members: ['Julien', 'Serpil', 'Thomas' ] } ]
```

We use eachSlice() on line 1 to break the students in threes and then proceed to turn arrays of student objects into something more structured—an object with the name of the group leader and a list of the group members' names. Most of the code in the iterator has to do with how to appoint the leader. I decided, quite arbitrarily, that the oldest student should lead, and if many students are at that age, the last one in alphabetical order should get the job.

So, we start by getting the maximum age on line 2 and then get the students in the group who are at that age (using findAll() at line 3), and because there may be more than one, we sort the resulting array by name (here comes sortBy(), which we will describe later) and pick the last one. After that, it's a matter of turning the original group description into the new format we described in the previous paragraph.

We use pluck() again (described later) to restrict objects to a specific property of theirs and sort the result. Note that if Élodie ends up last in the members list of her group, it is because it's actually a lexicographical sort (based on the order of characters in the Unicode table) instead of a localized sort (in French, Élodie would turn up between David and Will).

Agreed, after such a hard-core iterator, the illustration of inGroupsOf() is rather anticlimactic:

`prototype/new/enumerable_slicing.js`

```
Line 1  students.pluck('name').inGroupsOf(4) {
        // -> [ ['Sunny', 'Audrey', 'Matt', 'Élodie'],
        //      ['Will', 'David', 'Julien', 'Thomas'],
        //      ['Serpil', null, null, null] ]
```

Just note how it fills up the groups to a fixed size, as opposed to a similar eachSlice() call, which we saw earlier. This makes it nicely suited to a variety of purposes, say, rendering elements into a full grid, such as a calendar.

What zip() does is another matter entirely. It takes one or more sequences and creates tuples made of one element per sequence (starting with the one you're invoking zip() on), walking the sequences in lockstep. When sequences passed in arguments are too short, we get **undefined** at the proper position in the tuple.

This is useful in many cases. For instance, say we need to assign numbers to items we have in a sequence:

prototype/new/enumerable_zip.js
```
$w('Prototype script.aculo.us Dojo DWR').zip($R(1, 4))
// -> [['Prototype', 1], ['script.aculo.us', 2], ['Dojo', 3], ['DWR', 4]]
```

The sequences in arguments can be longer than the one we're calling zip() on. Extra items will simply be ignored. Now remember, from the syntax blocks earlier, that zip() can take an iterator, which will transform the original tuple into whatever we need. We might want to turn the framework/rank tuples we just made into nice text:

prototype/new/enumerable_zip2.js
```
$w('Prototype script.aculo.us Dojo DWR').zip($R(1, 4), function(tuple) {
  return tuple.reverse().join('. ');
})
// -> ['1. Prototype', '2. script.aculo.us', '3. Dojo', '4. DWR']
```

5.5 Computing a Derived Collection or Value

There are many ways to transform a collection into something else. We can compute a global value or turn each element into something else derived from it.

Computing a Global Value

```
inject(accumulator, iterator) → value
```

Injection is a pretty well-known mechanism in functional languages but is less famous in the mainstream. The idea is simple; we start with an initial value for the accumulator, then iterate over the collection, and, for each element, call the iterator with the current accumulator value, the current element, and the index (this last bit is mostly Prototype,

since all iterations pass the index as the final argument of the iterator).
The iterator computes a new value for the iterator and returns it.

Since JavaScript passes object arguments by reference, you can use
complex objects as accumulators whose state evolves across the iteration. For instance, you can fill up an array like this, which is pretty
frequent within Prototype itself. As an example, the flatten() and uniq()
methods added to Array are both implemented using inject() over an
initially empty array, which *accumulates* values over time.

Injection is commonly used to create internal sums or products:

prototype/new/enumerable_inject1.js

```
$R(1,10).inject(0, function(acc, n) { return acc + n; })
// -> 55 (sum of 1 to 10)

$R(2,5).inject(1, function(acc, n) { return acc * n; })
// -> 120 (factorial 5)
```

However, we can use it, as I just said, to fill up resultsets (usually
expressed as arrays):

prototype/new/enumerable_inject2.js

```
['hello', 'world', 'this', 'is', 'nice'].inject([],
  function(array, value, index) {
    if (0 == index % 2)
      array.push(value);
    return array;
  })
// -> ['hello', 'this', 'nice']

// Note how we actually use references:

var array1 = [];
var array2 = [1, 2, 3].inject(array1, function(array, value) {
  array.push(value * value);
  return array;
});
array2
// -> [1, 4, 9]
array1
// -> [1, 4, 9]
array2.push(16);
array1
// -> [1, 4, 9, 16]
```

Turning Each Element into Something Else

This is actually the most common case. Most beginners at Prototype often commit the venial sin of overusing each() instead of leveraging these tailor-made methods.

```
collect/map(iterator) → Array
invoke(methodName [, arg...]) → Array
pluck(propertyName) → Array
```

The collect() method, and its more commonly used alias map(), let you turn each element into virtually anything! Here's how it goes: each element is passed to your iterator, which computes the value being stored in the resultset instead of the original element.

Here are a couple examples, using both method names:

```
prototype/new/enumerable_collect.js
['Hitch', "Hiker's", 'Guide', 'To', 'The', 'Galaxy'].collect(
  function(s) {
    return s.charAt(0).toUpperCase();
  }).join('')
// -> 'HHGTTG'

$R(1,5).map(function(n) {
  return n * n;
})
// -> [1, 4, 9, 16, 25]
```

A common use case for collect() is to either call the same method on each element, with the same arguments, or get the same property for each element. Then we use either the method call result or the property value instead of the original element. These two use cases make up, together, a significant share of collect()-like scenarios.

This is why Prototype provides two specific methods, which should be preferred over collect(). For the method-calling need, use invoke(). Just pass the name of the method and whichever arguments you would want it to get. Combined with the DOM extension mechanism, which equips all DOM elements with numerous cool methods, this is a potent tool. For the property-getting use case, go with pluck(), passing in the property name. pluck() has a gentle, delicate aura about it that fits perfectly with the efficient, minimalistic approach it takes, codewise, to performing its task.

> **Always Remember invoke and pluck**
>
> These two methods address two very common needs:
>
> - invoke() calls a specific method on each element and returns an array of the results.
> - pluck() gets a specific property from each element and returns an array of their values.
>
> When you're looking for one of these behaviors, you should forgo collect() and go with the specific method. I mean it. Why? Because not only does it make your code more concise and yet more readable, it also makes it more efficient.
>
> You see, collect() takes an iterator, which will then be invoked for each element, with the associated costs of function call and lexical closure. On the other hand, pluck() and invoke() do not need such iterators, avoiding all these extra costs. It's just better in all respects.

As always, examples help make it all click:

`prototype/new/enumerable_invokePluck.js`

```js
['hello', 'world', 'cool!'].invoke('toUpperCase')
// ['HELLO', 'WORLD', 'COOL!']

['hello', 'world', 'cool!'].invoke('substring', 0, 3)
// ['hel', 'wor', 'coo']

// Of course, this works on Prototype extensions (why shouldn't it?!)
$('navBar', 'adsBar', 'footer').invoke('hide')

['hello', 'world', 'this', 'is', 'nice'].pluck('length')
// -> [5, 5, 4, 3, 4]

$$('.cool').pluck('tagName').sort().uniq(true)
// -> sorted list of unique canonical tag names for elements with this
// specific CSS class...
```

5.6 Order Now: Getting Extreme Values and Using Custom Sorts

Naturally, Enumerable comes with a few methods about ordering and sorting:

```
max([iterator = Prototype.K])  →  value
min([iterator = Prototype.K])  →  value
sortBy(iterator)  →  Array
```

The names are self-explanatory. However, we need to shed some light on the semantics of these iterators. For min() and max(), passing an iterator lets you produce derived values on which to search for a minimum or maximum, instead of working on the raw elements.

You might, for instance, want to determine not the last string in lexicographical order, but the longest string. As for sortBy(), it requires an iterator, which computes a criterion value that is then used to sort the elements.

Here are examples of both methods, with both call modes:

`prototype/new/enumerable_minMax.js`

```
$R(1,10).min()
// -> 1

['hello', 'world', 'gizmo'].min()
// -> 'gizmo'

['hello', 'world', 'gizmo'].max()
// -> 'world'

function Person(name, age) {
  this.name = name;
  this.age = age;
}

var john = new Person('John', 20);
var mark = new Person('Mark', 35);
var daisy = new Person('Daisy', 22);

[john, mark, daisy].min(function(person) {
  return person.age;
})
// -> 20

[john, mark, daisy].max(function(person) {
  return person.age;
})
// -> 35
```

Note that Array natively features a sort() method, which can be passed a customized comparison function. So, you should use it, with no argument, when sorting on the "natural order" of the elements (that is, when relying on the native < operator between two raw elements). If you need custom sorting, using sortBy() lets you compute just a criterion, instead of recoding a complete, overflow-proof comparison method:

```
prototype/new/enumerable_sortBy.js
['hello', 'world', 'this', 'is', 'nice'].sortBy(function(s) {
  return s.length;
})
// -> 'is', 'this', 'nice', 'hello', 'world']

['hello', 'world', 'this', 'is', 'cool'].sortBy(function(s) {
  var md = s.match(/[aeiouy]/g);
  return null == md ? 0 : md.length;
  // 100% Prototypish: return (md || []).length;
})
// -> [ 'world', 'this', 'is', 'hello', 'cool'] (sorted by vowel count)
```

5.7 Turning Our Collection into an Array or Debugging String

We're almost done with Enumerable. The last methods we shall see are those that let us turn an Enumerable into an array (with no element transformation) or into a debug-oriented string:

```
entries/toArray() → Array
inspect() → String
```

We already mentioned entries() earlier, explaining that it is the main reason why collect() accepts being called with no iterator. It is actually an alias over the more generic toArray() method. Recall that toArray() provides compatibility with the $A() utility function, as we saw in Section 3.5, *$A, the Collection Unifier*, on page 36.

We also talked already about inspect() methods, which we introduced in Section 4.1, *Introspecting Objects*, on page 43. This version is rather generic and currently relies on its Array variant, surrounded by #<*Enumerable:* and >. Just wash it down with a few lines of code:

```
prototype/new/enumerable_converts.js
$R(1, 5).toArray()
// -> [1, 2, 3, 4, 5]

$R(1, 5).inspect()
// -> '#<Enumerable:[1, 2, 3, 4, 5]>'
```

5.8 Enumerable Is Actually a Module

So, this is a *module*.... If you remember what we explained in Section 2.4, *Objects, Namespaces, and Modules*, on page 25, this means Enumerable is not for direct instantiation; rather, it is supposed to be *mixed in* other object types, which are usually concrete types such as Array or Hash. From a technical standpoint, modules have no constructor function, so the **new** operator does not work with them. You will just get an error, something along the lines of "Enumerable is not a constructor."

Which Objects Can Mix Enumerable In?

Modules often make requirements on the objects they get mixed in, in order for the mix to work. Enumerable makes one specific demand on its "host objects"—that they provide the fundamental iteration mechanism through a method named _each(). It can be as simple as a vanilla numerical-index **for** loop (as it is for Array). Let your object feature this method, and it becomes, shall we say, "Enumerable-compatible."

This _each() method will be passed a single argument, which is a callback function. All it has to do is call it for each element in the iteration. Simple as Sunday (but not as SOAP).

As a real-world example, consider the implementation of _each() in Array (your favorite collection type):

```
prototype/new/array_each.js
_each: function(iterator) {
  for (var i = 0, length = this.length; i < length; i++)
    iterator(this[i]);
}
```

See? No big deal.

How to Mix Enumerable In?

That's easy. If your type was created using Class.create(), just use its addMethods() method with the module, like so:

```
YourObjectType.addMethods(Enumerable);
```

If it's a more custom type, go like this:

```
Object.extend(YourObjectType.prototype, Enumerable);
```

Be sure to do so *before* adding your own methods to your object type in order to make sure you can override generic methods from Enumerable if need be (for instance, Array defines optimized versions of size() and toArray(), to name but two).

For further details on Object.extend(), go to Section 4.1, *Cloning and Extending Objects*, on page 45.

What's Enumerable Already?

There are quite a few object types that mix Enumerable in, out of the box:

- Ajax.Responders

- Array

- Element.ClassNames (which is deprecated in 1.6, though)

- Hash

- ObjectRange

We mostly use Array, Hash, and ObjectRange, though.

What We Just Learned

Enumerable is quite something. Let's quickly go through the salient points:

- The core enumeration is each(), which relies on your enumerable container's own _each() implementation. All the more specific methods (for example, map() or inject()) end up using each() to do their jobs.

- To skip ahead to the next turn, just **return** from your iterator function. To short-circuit the enumeration, throw $break.

- There is likely a predefined method for just about every common need you might have.

- There's often a way to squeeze more performance out of Enumerable if you know it well. For instance, use pluck() or invoke() instead of the more generic map() whenever appropriate, or leverage partition() instead of calling both select() and reject().

- Method chaining (calling a method directly on the result of another method call) can quickly whip up complex processings in a rather concise way; however, because every call is an enumeration, you might sometimes turn out to run faster with fewer predefined calls and a more advanced custom iterator. . . .

- Although sortBy() looks more comfortable, it's usually less efficient than sort() with a custom iterator.

Neuron Workout

Think you got it all? Great! Then try this for size. . . .

- Which is faster when iterating over an array, a standard integer-based **for** loop or each()? Are there circumstances where one is preferable over the other?

- If you must check that all elements in an Enumerable meet a condition that can be expressed both positively and negatively, is all() the best choice?

- So, we've got items.max(function(i) { return i.size; }). Does it return the item with the biggest size or the biggest size itself?

- Use inject() to write a function that computes the product of all values of an array. Add your new function to the Array prototype.

- Do it again in a more concise way by leveraging curry() as well.

- Aside from strings with regular expressions and DOM elements with CSS selectors, what situations can you imagine where it would make sense to provide a match() method to become grep()-compatible?

- Ignoring the slight structural difference of the resulting elements, what's faster: a.zip(b).zip(c) or a.zip(b, c)? Why?

Pfew. There! We're all done with Enumerable! That was quite a handful. It is, indeed, one of the largest modules in Prototype. Time for lunch, dinner, a beer, or maybe just a nice cookie with a glass of milk. Suit yourself, and then come back and read ahead. The next chapter explores Prototype's delicious API for unified event handling. Those battling with Internet Explorer vs. W3C code will at long last find peace.

Unified Event Handling

This book is all about Prototype and script.aculo.us, the two libraries at the forefront of Web 2.0 application scripting the world over. We're surrounded by JavaScript, and our pages must react to events coming from a variety of sources: DOM events resulting from user interaction with elements on the page, wake-up calls by timers, UI notifications from the browser itself, custom events triggered by library objects.... It's an event-rich world our code lives in.

Until now, we could basically test whichever code sample was in this part of the book by simply opening a blank page in your browser that loaded Prototype, grabbing a JavaScript console (or better yet, Firebug's console on Firefox), and typing away. That sure was handy and allowed for easy experimentation, irb style.[1]

But now, we're going to get into more and more complex examples, which will require our code to react to events from many sources. To do that, we first need to get familiar with event objects, including their nature, their origins, their behavior, and what we can do with them.

6.1 Event

The fundamental object here is Event. Depending on your browser, such an object may already exist. In that case, Prototype will merely expand it. Otherwise, it creates it from scratch. Event provides an entry point for using event-related methods and constants (although, as we'll see, we can also access the key methods directly on DOM elements and documents).

---

1. irb is a command-line tool that provides an interactive Ruby shell.

> ### Version 1.6 Changed Everything!
>
> Prototype 1.6 was internally dubbed the "event overhaul" release. It brought about major changes in the API and provided many new, exciting, powerful features. This chapter attempts to systematically point out when a feature or syntax was changed or appeared in this release.

Internet Explorer vs. the Rest of the World

Events can be a pretty messy thing to play with, mostly because there is no unified support across major browsers. More specifically, there are two factions: Microsoft Internet Explorer, which just walks its own path, and everybody else, who follows W3C specifications. In this instance, the bible is DOM Level 2 Events.[2] And on just about every aspect of dealing with events, Internet Explorer superbly ignores it and does things its own way (which must be a persisting itch to the six Microsoft experts who helped with the specification, especially Chris Wilson, Mr. Internet Explorer).

Even Internet Explorer 7, with a fairly recent release, has not made an inch of progress on the JavaScript/DOM front (or too little progress to warrant mention). It focused on "security" and catching up a bit on CSS, which is certainly good but won't help us at all when it comes to event support and DOM manipulation.

Never fear, though, for you now use Prototype! And as you may have come to expect, it comes to the rescue in these areas, too.

Smooth Operator: A Unified Interface to Events

Indeed, Prototype provides a unified way of dealing with events. In the following sections, I will mention, for each feature, three syntaxes: Prototype, the W3C, and Internet Explorer. This should help those of you who are familiar with the W3C's or Internet Explorer's ways understand exactly how to migrate your code, and it provides an informal conversion table.

---

2. http://www.w3.org/TR/DOM-Level-2-Events/events.html

Registering an Event Listener

- Prototype: $(elt).observe(eventName, handler)

- W3C: elt.addEventListener(eventName, handler, useCapture)

- Internet Explorer: elt.attachEvent(onEventName, handler)

Internet Explorer parts from the W3C specs in that it does not use official event names (you need to use the *on* prefix) and does not support capture-style propagation[3] (which is why Prototype now ignores that aspect too, because it's not portable so far).

Unregistering an Event Listener

- Prototype: $(elt).stopObserving([eventName[, handler]])

- W3C: elt.removeEventListener(eventName, handler, useCapture)

- Internet Explorer: elt.detachEvent(onEventName, handler)

We get the same kinds of differences we had on registration.

Stopping Event Propagation

- Prototype: event.stopPropagation() or event.stop()

- W3C: event.stopPropagation()

- Internet Explorer: event.cancelBubble = true

Internet Explorer uses a custom property on the event object.

Preventing the Default Behavior

- Prototype: event.preventDefault() or event.stop()

- W3C: event.preventDefault()

- Internet Explorer: event.returnValue = false

Internet Explorer uses another custom property on the event object.

---

3. If you're unfamiliar with capture, don't fret. I'll explain the idea behind it in Section 6.1, *A Quick Primer on Event Propagation*, on page 106. Still, Prototype ditched it with version 1.6, so it's not that big of a deal.

Grabbing the Source Element

- Prototype: event.element()

- W3C: event.target

- Internet Explorer: event.srcElement

Internet Explorer uses yet another custom property on the event object. Note that the Prototype version returns the extended form of the element (more on the extension in the next chapter) and also guarantees you get an element back (not, say, a text node).

Getting Details on the Event

- Prototype: event.pointerX(), event.pointerY(), event.isLeftClick()...

- W3C: event.clientX, event.clientY, event.button...

- Internet Explorer: event.clientX, event.clientY, event.which...

Internet Explorer has some specific properties, mostly about mouse buttons and key codes.

Event-Related Methods Straight in the DOM

1.6

The three fundamental methods for event manipulation, observe(), stopObserving(), and fire(), do not need to be accessed through the Event namespace. As described in the syntax blocks of the previous sections, they are part of the DOM extensions Prototype performs for every element, plus the document object itself. See Section 7.2, *Handling Events*, on page 132 for details.

A Normalized Event Object

1.6

In the same spirit, Prototype 1.6 introduced event object normalization; most methods that used to be called from the Event namespace, such as element(), stop(), or isLeftClick(), can now be accessed directly on the event object passed to handlers. W3C methods that browsers such as Internet Explorer currently fail to provide (for example, stopPropagation()) are filled in when necessary. Finally, Prototype provides a few normalized properties (for example, target, relatedTarget, and pageX), as defined by the W3C, based on what the browser natively defines. Such normalization has a trimming effect on Prototype's code base and probably on yours, too! We will review and use them in the coming sections.

The Art of Observing Events

A lot of web developers these days are still using plenty of *obtrusive* JavaScript. That is, their HTML pages are laden with event-related attributes (think <body onload="...">) or inline *<script>* elements. But you see, this is increasingly regarded as *bad* because this mixes content and behavior, which is generally not the best thing to do (although I should mention it may yield a performance boost in specific cases or make it easier to provide tooling for script-based features). It also leads to inconsistent behaviors when Internet Explorer calls handlers attached this way.

You may object that your page-creation tools are the culprits and that you just can't make them do things in a better way. Well, first, check your vendor for upgrades; *unobtrusive JavaScript*, which aims to put all (or at least most) scripting outside the content file (in separate Java-Script files), is quickly becoming the widely accepted best practice.

The clean scenario is like this:

1. The DOM of the page loads, creating elements in source document order—the *<html>* node, the *<head>* node, and at some point the *<script>* nodes—which immediately load and process your scripts.

   Because the body of the page is not loaded yet, it is important to remember *not to register event listeners on page elements yet*. You'll have to wait for phase 2, or at worst phase 3, in this sequence.

2. The DOM is fully loaded; all elements described by the document are created in memory. External resources may not yet be loaded (for example, images, CSS files, embedded objects), but *their DOM elements exist*. From this point on, you can register event listeners on them. Prototype 1.6 introduces a normalized *DOMContent-* *Loaded* event (originally a custom event from Mozilla) so you can react at this phase. Just use the custom *dom:loaded* event on the document object.[4]   *1.6*

3. The page is fully loaded; all external resources were loaded in and processed. That's when the *load* event triggers on the window

---

4. Due credit: the code is inspired by the excellent works of Dan Webb, Mathias Miller, Dean Edwards, and John Resig. As Isaac Newton would have said, we stand on the shoulders of giants....

object. If your page is heavy on external resources, this may happen quite some time after the page's initial rendering. . . .

Events can start happening from phase 1 (but they are not user-related events, which start more at phase 2). Whenever an event happens, associated listeners get notified, and there is an event object representing everything there is to know about the current event.

How can we get this event object? Well, the W3C spec mandates that all listeners get passed this event object as their first argument. Natively, Internet Explorer does things differently if you're using inline event attributes in your markup (but not if you're attaching listeners through JavaScript). It doesn't pass the event as argument but makes it available through a global event object (technically available as the window.event property, but that's functionally equivalent to a global variable for your scripts).

Basic Scenario: Regular Functions as Listeners

```
element.observe(eventName, observer) → element
element.stopObserving([eventName [, observer]]) → element
```

This is quite simple:

```
prototype/events/basic.js
```

```
function checkForm(event) {
  var form = event.element();
  var formOK = true;
  // Generic form checking code...
  if (!formOK)
    event.stop();
}

$('signUpForm').observe('submit', checkForm);
```

If we were to remove this listener later (for some reason, this check is no longer necessary), we could do it simply with one line of code:

```
prototype/events/basic_unreg.js
```

```
$('signUpForm').stopObserving('submit', checkForm);
// Or $('signUpForm').stopObserving('submit')
// Or $('signUpForm').stopObserving()
```

Easy as pie.

1.6

Note that two important things changed in version 1.6:

- First, Prototype used to sport an extra, optional boolean argument on these two methods that let you request capturing instead of bubbling.[5] Because Internet Explorer (including version 7) doesn't support this, Prototype did away with the argument, which was misleading developers into thinking capture was emulated across browsers.

- Second, you don't need to provide the handler you registered anymore, or even the event name. Prototype will automatically unregister any handlers matching the partial request. So if you just provide an event name, you'll unregister all handlers for that event on this element. If you don't provide anything (something like element.stopObserving()), you'll unregister all handlers for this element, regardless of the event name.

Methods as Listeners: Careful with the Binding!

Before Prototype 1.6, event handlers did not get any automatic binding when you registered them as listeners. They were subjected to JavaScript's usual binding rules (which you can review at Section 4.2, *Proper Function Binding*, on page 47). Starting with 1.6, event handlers are automatically bound to the element they're registered on. In other words, within an event handler, **this** always refers to the equivalent of W3C's currentTarget property.

1.6

The thing is, your listeners are often methods that do rely on their containing object to perform their work. They need the **this** reference within these handlers to work properly. You may then be tempted to use bind(), as we saw in Section 4.2, *Proper Function Binding*, on page 47. This is not always enough, though. Just look at this:

```
prototype/events/methods_bind.js
var Displayer = {
  intro: 'Received click event: ',

  display: function(e) {
    alert(this.intro + e);
  }
};

document.observe('click', Displayer.display.bind(Displayer));
document.observe('click', Displayer.display.bind(Displayer, 42));
```

---

5. If you're unfamiliar with them, check out Section 6.1, *A Quick Primer on Event Propagation*, on page 106.

Clicking will first alert something like *Received click event: [object MouseEvent]*, which is right and proper. Then it will alert something more like *Received click event: 42*.

Huh?! What happened to the event object in the second case? I said Prototype took care of passing it as the first argument. . . . That's right, but bind() will fail to pass this first argument through if you provide specific arguments. They will be prepended, as usual. Let's change our display() method to show its complete argument list:

`prototype/events/methods_bind_list.js`

```
var Displayer = {
  intro: 'Received click event: ',

  display: function() {
    alert($A(arguments).inspect());
  }
};

document.observe('click', Displayer.display.bind(Displayer));
document.observe('click', Displayer.display.bind(Displayer, 42));

// Clicking on the doc will yield the two following alert strings
// in Firefox:
// 1. "[[object MouseEvent]]"
// 2. "[42, [object MouseEvent]]"
```

This is the kind of use case in which we should use bindAsEventListener(), which guarantees that the event object is first, then puts whatever arguments we provided it, and then adds the arguments passed when the event occurs. Here is our adapted code:

`prototype/events/methods_bAEL.js`

```
var Displayer = {
  display: function() {
    alert($A(arguments).inspect());
  }
};

document.observe('click',
  Displayer.display.bindAsEventListener(Displayer));
document.observe('click',
  Displayer.display.bindAsEventListener(Displayer, 42));

// Clicking on the doc will yield the two following alert strings
// in Firefox:
// 1. "[[object MouseEvent]]"
// 2. "[[object MouseEvent], 42]"
```

OK, that's better, but there is still another common pitfall that lies in ambush, ready to jump at your code and slice its throat when you least expect it. Consider this, where you decide to pass the handler argument to stopObserving(), for clarity's sake, and do it the following way:

prototype/events/bound_stop.js

```
var Displayer = {
  count: 0,

  display: function(e) {
    if (++this.count >= 3)
      document.stopObserving('click', this.display.bind(this));
    alert('Received click event: ' + e + ' (' + this.count + ')');
  }
};
```

```
document.observe('click', Displayer.display.bind(Displayer));
```

OK, run this, and then start clicking. Once, twice, a third time. . . . What happens on the fourth click? Damn! It still works! Did we fall victim to a fencepost error? Not so. We just called stopObserving() using *a different listener* from the one we had used when calling observe(). The thing is, to perform their magic, binding methods return a fresh anonymous method wrapping the original one. Every time you bind, you get a new method.

Depending on your situation, there are two solutions for this. If you want to unregister only that specific handler, you'll need to cache it before registering and then use the cached version on the second call too, like so:

prototype/events/bound_cached.js

```
var Displayer = {
  count: 0,

  _display: function(e) {
    if (++this.count >= 3)
      document.stopObserving('click', this.display);
    alert('Received click event: ' + e + ' (' + this.count + ')');
  }
};
```

```
Displayer.display = Displayer._display.bind(Displayer);
```

```
document.observe('click', Displayer.display);
```

On the other hand, if you can afford to unregister all handlers for this event on this element (say you got only one, which is the most common case), just do away with the second argument altogether.

Note that if Displayer was not a singleton but an actual type, which could be instantiated, we wouldn't have to define display() externally. For instance, here is a version using Prototype's class definition scheme:

```
prototype/events/prototypish.js
var Displayer = Class.create({
  count: 0,

  initialize: function() {
    this.display = this._display.bind(this);
  },

  _display: function(e) {
    if (++this.count >= 3)
      document.stopObserving('click', this.display);
    alert('Received click event: ' + e + ' (' + this.count + ')');
  }
});

document.observe('click', new Displayer().display);
```

Listener Caching and Internet Explorer Memory Leaks

Every time you register an event listener, the description of this registration (all the arguments you passed to observe()) goes into a repository. The reason for this is that Internet Explorer has been known to exhibit serious memory leaks when event listeners are not explicitly detached. Prototype makes it easy on the web developer by automatically reacting to page unloading (an event that happens when the tab or window is closed) to go through this repository and automatically call stopObserving() for each previous registration. This is a sort of ad hoc, Internet Explorer–only garbage collector.

A Quick Primer on Event Propagation

When an event fires up, it is triggered on the elements that registered a listener for it. That sounds simple, but it's incomplete and barely half the story anyway.

An event always remembers the actual element on which it happened. By "on," I mean *geographically on*. Keyboard events obviously happen on whichever visual component currently has the focus (most often an input field, but it could very well be a link, for instance), but mouse events are associated with whichever element was "on top" (appeared above any other) right under the mouse cursor. This is commonly referred to as the *source element*.

The W3C defines a target property for this, while Internet Explorer calls it srcElement (which, admittedly, is a rather fitting name).

Event Bubbling

Once it is first triggered, an event *propagates*. The default propagation mode, which is also the only one Internet Explorer supports,[6] is called *bubbling*. The idea is simple: listeners relevant to the event are triggered from the source element outward. Consider the following HTML document body:

```
prototype/events/propagation_doc.html
```

```html
<body>
  <h1>Event propagation</h1>

  <p>There are essentially two propagation modes:</p>

  <ul>
    <li id="bubbler"><em>Bubbling</em>: inside out</li>
    <li><em>Capture</em>: outside in (not supported by Internet
      Explorer)</li>
  </ul>
</body>
```

Let's now assume we have the following script in there:

```
prototype/events/bubbling.js
```

```javascript
function showEvent(e, reg) {
  alert(e.type + ' from ' + Event.element(e).tagName + ' (' + reg + ')');
}

document.observe('dom:loaded', function() {
  document.observe('click', showEvent.bindAsEventListener(this, 'doc'));
  $('bubbler').observe('click', showEvent.bindAsEventListener(this,
    'bubbler'));
});
```

If you click anywhere but inside the first list element, you'll get only one message. For instance, click the background of the page, and you'll get something like *click from HTML (doc)*. Click in the territory of the second list element, and you'll get *click from LI (doc)*, and so on. Although you are not clicking the document itself (it's not quite possible, because the whole surface is actually its child node, the HTML document node), the listener registered on the document gets invoked.

---

6. And can't be cleanly emulated, which is why Prototype 1.6 dropped the related API elements.

That's one consequence of bubbling, and it's very useful; it lets us define generic event listeners capable of dealing with the actual elements the event was triggered on, which helps avoid code duplication (and sometimes helps reduce the amount of listeners you're registering, which has a significant positive impact on your page's setup time).

Another important advantage of leveraging bubbling is that you can tweak the elements inside your container as much as you need, without having to re-register the handlers for them. You didn't register previous handlers on the elements you're replacing, removing, or adding to; you registered it on the container, which is still there and will be glad to grab the bubbling events originated from new or updated elements inside it.

Now click the first list element. You get two messages. First you get something like *click from LI (bubbler)* and then *click from LI (doc)*. The order in which you registered the listeners is irrelevant; it's where you click that counts. The first listener from the click target outward is the bubbler-registered one, and then the event bubbles up to the document level.

Note that you can stop this propagation at any level by calling the proper method on the event object. The unified Prototype way of doing this is event.stop().

The event will simply not bubble up (it will also cancel its default behavior; if you don't want it to, use event.stopPropagation() instead, which Prototype guarantees even on Internet Explorer). This is useful when your listener takes definitive action for the event and there is no need to let listeners higher up the document hierarchy pay attention to it.

Event Capture

Event capture is the second form propagation can take, and it lets you implement local censorship on events. Basically, whenever an event occurs, any listener registered in capture mode gets triggered in sequence, from the outside inward. Any listener that stops propagation effectively censors the event; it gets trumped, shot, chopped to bits, seasoned, and thrown to the dogs your browser keeps in a small pen next to the garbage collector.

This can be a powerful tool (for example, to implement "glass panes" over the whole UI, which could be nice for fake modal dialog boxes); alas, it is currently *not* supported by Internet Explorer, which essentially means nobody can risk using it on anything other than an intranet web app where they control what browser is used. That's why (again) Prototype 1.6 dropped support for it entirely, so as not to mislead developers into thinking it emulated such propagation on Internet Explorer. Some day perhaps. . . .

The Duality of event.stop

```
event.stop()
event.stopPropagation()
event.preventDefault()
```

There are two things you can do on an event that relate to what happens   *1.6*
next with it: you can stop its propagation, and you can prevent the browser from applying the default behavior for this event.

Many events have an associated default behavior. For instance, a *submit* event on a form triggers submission (ahem) of the form. A *click* event on a link navigates to the link's destination, and so on. Obviously, when you register a client-side form-checking method as a listener for a form's *submit* event, you want to inhibit the default behavior if your checks fail. So-called smart pop-ups unobtrusively listen to their link's *click* event to open it in a pop-up window, at which point navigation *should not* take place in the link's window. The DOM Level 2 Events specification endows event objects with a specific method for this: preventDefault(). As we saw earlier, Internet Explorer doesn't support it, but Prototype smooths that over and guarantees it's there.

Because these two behaviors—stopping propagation and preventing default behavior—are often indissociable, stop() does both. It calls the event's stopPropagation() and preventDefault() methods. It's a nifty little shortcut.

Getting Information About the Event

There's a whole world of information you might want to extract for the current event: what element it was triggered on, what the key being pressed or released was, what modifier keys are active, what are the coordinates of the mouse cursor, and so on. Not all of this is easy to grab in a cross-browser way, but some of it is.

Getting Elements for the Event

```
event.element() → HTMLElement
event.findElement(selector) → HTMLElement
event.relatedTarget
```

To get the source element, you can simply use Prototype's element() function, passing it the event object. As of Prototype 1.5.1.1, it will make sure the returned element is extended, too.

The W3C-compliant currentTarget property is not normalized, because you don't really need it. From version 1.6 on, your handler executes, by default, in the scope of the element you registered it on. **this** can be used in lieu of currentTarget. Let's go back to our previous bubbling example. We have two *click* listeners, one registered at the document level and one at the first list item's level (the one with id="bubbler"). Say you click the <em>Bubbling</em> element. For both listeners, element() will return the <em> element. But **this** will return the first list item for one and the document for the other.

However, most of the time you can get by with just retrieving, say, "the closest <p> ancestor of the source element." This is a breeze with Prototype with the findElement() method:

```
prototype/events/findElement.js
function hideSurroundingParagraph(e) {
  e.stop();
  var p = e.findElement('p');
  if (p)
    $(p).hide();
}
```

Starting with Prototype 1.5.1.1, this can take not just a simple tag name as its second argument but also a CSS selector expression just like what you'd use with Element.up() (which is now used internally), so the whole panoply of Selector-supported syntaxes is available.

1.6 Prototype now normalizes the W3C target property, which is the node that actually received the event, but you'll usually go through event. element() instead to guard against the few odd cases where target would return a text node and make sure the returned element is extended.

1.6 Finally, Prototype 1.6 normalizes Mozilla's custom relatedTarget property, which provides a secondary element for specific events, mostly the standard *mouseover* and *mouseout* events. When the primary element for these two are the element being entered and exited, respectively, relatedTarget works conversely. It provides, respectively, the element that was just exited or entered (entering an element usually means exiting another one, and conversely, at least from a visual standpoint).

Mouse Information

```
event.pointerX() → Number
event.pointerY() → Number
event.isLeftClick() → Boolean
event.isMiddleClick() → Boolean
event.isRightClick() → Boolean
```

Mouse coordinates are a complex thing. The official specification for DOM Level 2 Mouse Events defines two sets of coordinates: *client* and *screen*. That's fairly clear, but screen coordinates are mostly useless to the web app, and client ones (relative to the viewport) are far less useful than page coordinates (relative to the document itself, unaffected by scrolling).

Prototype provides two methods you can use, pointerX() and pointerY(), which do provide page coordinates. This makes nifty stuff like drag and drop or visual effects much easier to achieve. If you need client-based coordinates, the clientX and clientY properties of the event object are fairly portable.

Even something apparently as simple as the mouse button being pressed or released is tricky. W3C mandates a button property, theoretically ranging from zero (left) to 2 (right),[7] but Internet Explorer provides a generic which property, whose button-related values range from 1 to 3. There are many other issues surrounding mouse click, such as different events being fired for right-clicking and button emulation on single-button devices.

This quickly becomes a mess, so Prototype provides three methods: isLeftClick(), isMiddleClick(), and isRightClick().

Keyboard Information

Finally, you may need to retrieve keyboard information about the event. Prototype provides a standardized set of keyboard codes through KEY_*xxx* constants in the Event namespace.

The easy part first: looking up *modifier keys*. Traditionally, we consider only Ctrl, Alt, and Shift (although some keyboards provide a Meta key, which might be mapped to the Windows key or the Esc key). The state of these modifier keys can be rather reliably examined, whether on a mouse or a keyboard event, by using three event object properties: respectively ctrlKey, altKey, and shiftKey. These are booleans, set to **true**

---

7. Obviously, this is mirrored if the user's mouse is configured for the left-handed.

when the corresponding key is pressed. There is no portable way of determining laterality (all these keys usually exist on both sides of the keyboard), something DOM Level 3 Events will more than address with its future keyLocation field.

Now for the tough part: determining *which key* was pressed. It depends on no less than three contextual parameters:

- What your browser is (ouch!)

- Whether you're after a character key (for example, A or 6) or not (for example, PageDown or Esc).

- Whether you're listening to a key movement event (*keydown* or *keyup*) or a character-producing event (*keypress*).

If you're on Internet Explorer, are handling a key movement event, or are dealing with noncharacter keys, you're going to look at the event object's keyCode property, which holds the Unicode value for the key.

On the other hand, if you're *not* on Internet Explorer, are handling a character-producing event, and are interested in character keys, you'll look exclusively at the charCode property, which holds the Unicode value for the character. Both properties are *never* both set on the same event.

If you think carefully about this, there's a lesson to be learned: *never* rely on *keypress*, because this opens the gate to a browser-compatibility nightmare. Always use *keydown* and *keyup*, along with the event's keyCode property. That's portable.

Finally, here is the current set of keyCode constants provided by Prototype in the Event namespace: KEY_BACKSPACE, KEY_DELETE, KEY_DOWN, KEY_END, KEY_ESC, KEY_HOME, KEY_INSERT, KEY_LEFT, KEY_PAGEDOWN, KEY_PAGEUP, KEY_RETURN, KEY_RIGHT, KEY_TAB, and KEY_UP. This is by no means an exhaustive list (obviously!); this is just a list compiled from the needs of Prototype and script.aculo.us over time.

As an interesting side note, know that the future DOM Level 3 Events specification chooses a more generic way, equipping keyboard events with a keyIdentifier property, which is a normative string identifier for the key. The specification, currently at the working draft level, defines a comprehensive set of 196 key identifiers.

Firing Custom Events

Prototype 1.6 introduces *custom events*, which are events with a name-spaced name (that is, a name with two components separated by a colon delimiter, as in *widget:activated*) that you can fire on any DOM element, which bubble as regular DOM events and are equipped with the usual normalized properties and methods.

1.6

Prototype will soon bundle a series of built-in custom events to make several lifecycle maintenance tasks easier (for example, react to DOM fragments being updated or removed, react to drag and drops in better ways, and so on). So far, you can still use this facility for adding your own events to DOM elements.

```
element.fire(eventName [, memo = {}]) → Event
```

To fire a custom event on an element, simply call the fire() method on it, possibly passing any data object you want to attach to the event (it will be accessible through the event object's memo property). The event then triggers on the element and bubbles like any regular event. It is detected normally by registered observers, can be canceled, and so on.

To steal an example from the release notes, imagine you have a title element somewhere, and every time the title is changed, you'd like some visual behavior to happen (say, a highlight effect). You could define a custom event for this element (let's call it *title:changed*) and register the proper listener for it.

Assuming the following XHTML fragment:

```
<div id="container">
  <h1><span id="title">Release notes</span></h1>
  ...
</div>
```

...we'd use the following code to register a listener for our custom event:

```
$('container').observe('title:changed', function(event) {
  this.highlight({ duration: 0.5 });
});
```

As you can see, it is no different from our usual handlers. Now when some code, somewhere, changes that title (perhaps from a script in an Ajax response), it would just need to conclude its edit with the following line:

```
$('title').fire('title:changed');
```

That's it! If we wanted to make the highlight duration controllable, we could handle an option in the event's data object, something like this:

```
$('container').observe('title:changed', function(event) {
  this.highlight({ duration: event.memo.duration || 0.5 });
});
...
$('title').fire('title:changed', { duration: 2 });
```

6.2 The Events Hall of Fame

Here are a few choice events you'll very likely find extremely useful in real-world web applications.

load

Applicable mostly to window.

This triggers when the full contents of the document (including all external resources) are loaded. Often, though, this is a bit late for you to bind all required listeners to the DOM elements; you'll want to use custom DOM-specific load events for this, such as Prototype's custom *dom:loaded* event, described in Section 6.1, *The Art of Observing Events*, on page 101.

submit

Applicable to *<form>*.

This is triggered when the user, or the script, attempts to submit a form, whatever the means (for example, hitting the Return key while in a form field that does not capture it, clicking the submission button, or invoking the form element's submit() method). The event's source element is always the form itself. The default action submits the form; canceling it (for instance, because client-side checks of input data failed or because the form was quietly switched over to Ajax processing) prevents submission.

click

Applicable to most elements.

This is a sequence of *mousedown* + *mouseup* that happened over the element on which the event was registered (the mouse might have moved in the meantime). This is not specific to the left (or, more accurately, "primary") button. You can right-click or even middle-click. The default action is usually clear (the most common case is the click over a link, which normally navigates to this link; smart pop-ups disable this after having ensured the link was opened in a pop-up window).

mousedown and mouseup

Applicable to most elements.

A button of the mouse was pressed or released, respectively. A click will generate, in this order, the events *mousedown*, *mouseup*, and *click*.

mouseover, mousemove, and mouseout

Applicable to most elements.

The mouse cursor entered, hovered on, and exited the element's surface, respectively. Yes, *mouseover* is very poorly named. Remember that most "rollover" effects (that alter an element's aspect while the mouse cursor is over it) can be more efficiently achieved through judicious use of CSS. Also remember that *mouseover* and *mouseout* can leverage Prototype's guarantee for the event's relatedTarget property.

keydown and keyup

Applicable to most elements (through bubbling).

A key was pressed or released, respectively. This is where you use the event object's keyCode property. A great many keystrokes have default behaviors that are often browser-dependent.

change

Applicable to <input>, <select>, and <textarea>.

This one is a bit peculiar. It's supposed to trigger only when the element loses focus and its value has changed since it last gained the focus. This works pretty much that way on <input> and <textarea>, but things can be different for <select>, especially if it renders as a drop-down list (which is the default case, if you do not provide it with a size= attribute greater than 1).

In this latter context, this event may well trigger whenever you change the selected value, either through the keyboard or through the mouse. Because of this, triggering large content changes (such as page reloads) on this event goes against accessibility, because people relying on the keyboard or assistive technologies might not be able to select a distant option in one pass.

6.3 Reacting to Form-Related Content Changes

When working with Ajax, you often find yourself monitoring the changes on a form field or even the whole form. Whenever a field value changes, you whip up some Ajax stuff in reaction.

It is in fact a frequent need, and Prototype caters to it through two tailor-made classes, aptly named Form.EventObserver and Form.Element. EventObserver (because of the aliasing of Form.Element, this latter class can also be used as Field.EventObserver).

Form.EventObserver

new `Form.EventObserver(form, callback)`

This class lets you instantly react to any change-related event in a form that resulted in the form's overall data (the values of all its fields) having changed. It will then invoke the callback method you provided when you created the observer, passing it two arguments: the form and its serialized data.

Change-related events are determined on a per-field basis, as described in the next section. A Form.EventObserver essentially creates and manages Form.Element.EventObserver instances for all fields in the form at construction time. Note that this has an interesting consequence. Fields added dynamically to the form after the observer is created are *not* taken into account.

For details on how the data get serialized, see Section 8.3, *Serializing Fields and Whole Forms*, on page 169.

Form.Element.EventObserver

new `Form.Element.EventObserver(field, callback)`

This second class lets you instantly react when a field's value changes (based on the *click* event for radio buttons and checkboxes and on the *change* event for other field types). The callback then gets invoked with two arguments: the field and its value. For further details on how the value is represented (this can get interesting on fields such as multiple-selection listboxes), see Section 8.3, *Shape Shifters: The Changing Nature of Field Values*, on page 168.

What We Just Learned

Events are probably the most critical block of dynamic web apps, and Prototype has a *lot* to offer smoothing them out. The take-away points from this chapter are as follows:

- The whole event machinery lies in the Event namespace.

- The events world in web development is essentially split in two factions: on the one hand, Internet Explorer, and on the other hand, pretty much every other browser and the W3C. Prototype's unified API lets us write code for both sides only once.

- Prototype 1.6 overhauled the entire event system, addressing many long-standing requests and wish lists.

- All event objects are extended to feature the namespace's methods directly. You go e.stop() instead of Event.stop(e), for instance.

- The three key methods to manage behavior on elements and the document itself are observe( ), stopObserving( ), and fire( ).

- An event handler will run, by default, in the context of the element it was registered on (using observe( )). It's bound to it, and **this** will refer to that element. If the handler was already bound, it retains its original binding.

- Event handlers are always passed the event object as their first argument.

- In addition to regular browser and DOM events, Prototype lets you observe and fire custom events, which among other things helps to decouple your scripts.

- Prototype supports bubbling only, because it would not be able to cleanly emulate capture on Internet Explorer.

- The standard *load* event, on the window object, triggers late—only once all the resources in the page, including style sheets, images, Flash animations and scripts, have loaded. To quickly slap behavior onto your DOM, just wait for it to load (which is pretty fast) using the custom *dom:loaded* event on document.

Neuron Workout

Here are a few puzzlers to help you digest these new skills:

- Why do we need element() when our handler is bound to the element we called observe() on?

- What's the better alternative to doing individual observe() calls with the same handler on a series of similar elements?

- So, we've got element(). Why do we need findElement() then? If it weren't there, how could we easily emulate it?

- If we could use event capture in addition to bubbling, what scenarios would it be useful in?

- Can you find a use case where bindAsEventListener() is absolutely necessary (as in cannot be emulated in a reasonably concise way)?

- What's the best way to guarantee that a <form> won't be submitted to the server if our script decides it shouldn't?

Playing with the DOM Is *Finally* Fun!

When writing modern web applications, you find yourself doing a *lot* of DOM manipulation. Traversing the DOM, fetching elements, showing and hiding them, replacing fragments of the document with new (X)HTML contents, fiddling with CSS class names... this is what we web developers *do*.

Unfortunately, if we stick with the raw standards (such as DOM Level 2), we find ourselves tragically underequiped. The tools of the trade were judged and found wanting. It feels like building a skyscraper with cardboard and string.

But you're using Prototype now.

True to its aim, Prototype comes with plenty of nifty tools you can use to tweak the DOM. At the heart of it is the notion of *DOM extension*. The idea is simple: one way or another, you can get "extended" versions of the original DOM nodes, and these versions are *way* easier to play with than their bare-bones counterparts. At the time of this writing, there are 45+ extension-provided methods in there.

7.1 Extending DOM Elements

Let's first focus on the net result for the web developer: fetching an element through the $() function (which we saw in Section 3.2, *Quick Fetching of Smart Elements with $*, on page 31) *guarantees* that what you get is the extended version of the original DOM element.

An extended element is a DOM element that also features all the methods we will see in the next section (plus extra ones if it's a form or form field element, as we'll see in Chapter 8, *Form Management*, on page 163). It is not a fresh object, distinct from the original DOM node. It's the same node but augmented with Prototype's extensions.

I could discourse for pages about Prototype's extension mechanism, but this would be slightly beyond the scope of this book. So instead of entering into the nitty-gritty details of stuff like Element.Methods, Element.Methods.Simulated, or Element._attributeTranslations, let me answer the most common questions first.

Speed Cost

On browsers providing DOM element types with a prototype, the cost is close to zero. Prototype automatically extends the relevant prototypes at loading time, which is blazing fast. This is, most notably, the case of all Gecko-based browsers (and hence Firefox), Opera (at least from version 9), Konqueror, and Safari (although specific versions of Safari may handle this in a specific way, the particulars are addressed by Prototype, and the speed cost is roughly identical).

For browsers with no such support (for example, Internet Explorer), the element is extended on the fly the first time it is requested as an extended element (either through the $() function or through a direct call to Element.extend(), which your own code should never need to do). Such an extension request can very well happen inside Prototype's code, because numerous methods in Prototype return extended elements. The element is then marked as extended, and there will be no further cost associated with requesting it as an extended element.

However, on-the-fly element extension is not a trivial cost in itself, and when applied over a large number of elements (depending on your environment, this can be anywhere between 100 and 1,000 elements), the speed hit can be noticeable. So, you should refrain from needlessly relying on $() (or other methods that guarantee extended results) when working with very large sets of elements. All extended methods can be called indirectly on "raw" elements (but because they will use $() over the element internally, what may have been raw before is now extended anyway...).

What If These Methods Exist Natively?

Simple as Sunday: they're left as is. Prototype's method extensions apply only when there is no native version present in order to maximize execution speed.

7.2 Element, Your New Best Friend

Your gateway to DOM extension is the Element namespace. It contains the DOM extension machinery and the repositories for the extra methods (mostly Element.Methods).

Calling the Methods

All those methods can be used in two ways:

- As vanilla functions, which can be passed any DOM element (including, most important, nonextended ones) as their first argument. The easiest way is to call them through the Element namespace, like this:

```
Element.remove(elt);
Element.next(elt, 'li');
```

- As methods over extended elements, which certainly feels more like object-oriented programming:

```
$(elt).remove();
$(elt).next('li');
```

All *mutative* methods return their original element extended. A mutative method alters the element in some way. Methods returning elements (for example, fetching the descendant elements of the one passed as first argument) return extended elements, too. This makes method chaining easy:

```
$(elt).next('li').remove();
```

Building a Staff Manager

To get familiar with most methods provided through DOM extension, we'll build a complete example that heavily relies on it. The idea is to have a simple web page that lets us describe people and groups of people. Groups can be nested to an arbitrary depth.

Our page lets us see the whole staff using a tree representation, on the left, and lets us create new groups and people, as well as rename existing ones, through a small editor zone next to the tree. Naturally, all

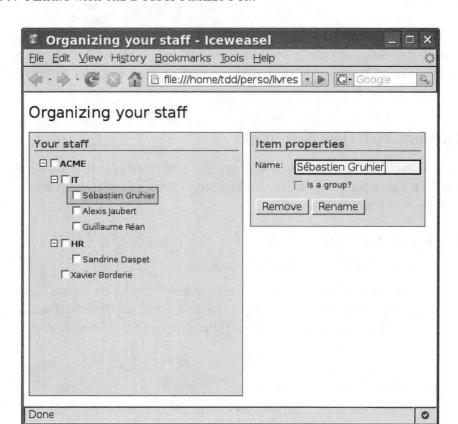

Figure 7.1: OUR FINISHED SCREEN

groups in the tree can be collapsed and expanded. All nodes can also be checked using a plain checkbox. This opens the door to further use of the data (for example, we could use this to select to whom to send an e-mail).

The completed screen looks like Figure 7.1. Note that we provide a highlighted representation of the selected node. To build this tool, we will need to follow several steps:

1. Create the HTML file for our screen.
2. Create a JavaScript representation of our data tree.
3. Write a function that takes the JavaScript representation of a person or group and inserts the corresponding DOM fragment in the document.

4. Handle clicks anywhere in the tree to deal with group togglers (those little +/- signs that let us expand or collapse groups) but also select (or deselect) nodes.

5. Maintain editor state depending on the currently selected node (buttons may be disabled or enabled, information needs to be pre-filled when a node gets selected).

6. Handle uses of the form on the right in order to deal with node creation, renaming, or removal.

Of course, we'll do all this with the proper double take of polish, making sure the user experience is as smooth as possible and trying to leverage Prototype's features as much as possible.

Because the primary goal of this chapter is to acquaint you with Prototype's DOM extensions, we will not add an extra layer of complexity by using Ajax to deal with server-side data. However, in a later chapter, we will come back to this example and turn it into an actual client/server application, using Ajax for a snappy user experience. Data will not reside only as JavaScript objects on the client side but be stored on the server side. This will let us tinker away with form serialization methods and most Ajax-related utilities.

Laying the Groundwork: Our HTML Page

The markup for our screen is fairly simple: a title, proper definition of charset, binding on the style sheets and scripts, and two zones (the tree and the editor form). Here you go:

`prototype/dom/people.html`

```html
<!DOCTYPE html PUBLIC "-//W3C//DTD XHTML 1.0 Strict//EN"
 "http://www.w3.org/TR/xhtml1/DTD/xhtml1-strict.dtd">
<html xmlns="http://www.w3.org/1999/xhtml" lang="en" xml:lang="en">
<head>
  <meta http-equiv="Content-Type" content="text/html; charset=utf-8" />
  <title>Organizing your staff</title>
  <link rel="stylesheet" type="text/css" href="people.css" />
  <script type="text/javascript" src="../../prototype.js"></script>
  <script type="text/javascript" src="people.js"></script>
</head>
<body>
  <h1>Organizing your staff</h1>

  <div id="tree">
    <h2>Your staff</h2>
    <form id="staff">
      <ul></ul>
    </form>
  </div>
```

```html
<div id="props">
  <h2>Item properties</h2>
  <form id="editor">
    <p>
      <label for="edtName" accesskey="N">Name:</label>
      <input type="text" id="edtName" />
    </p>
    <p>
      <input type="checkbox" id="chkIsGroup" />
      <label for="chkIsGroup" id="lblIsGroup"
       accesskey="G">Is a group?</label>
    </p>
    <p>
      <input type="button" id="btnRemove" value="Remove"
       accesskey="R" />
      <input type="button" id="btnAddChild" value="Add as child"
       accesskey="C" />
      <input type="submit" id="btnSubmit" value="Create" />
    </p>
  </form>
</div>
</body>
</html>
```

We use a *<form>* element in the tree because we're going to put check-boxes in there and strict HTML mandates that form fields be located in forms (which rather makes sense). We also nest a *<ul>* element because in our tree, all group-like levels (be it the root level, like here, or a regular group level) use a *<ul>* to contain their children.

This is because we're going to represent our tree with proper semantic markup: using nested lists. Since we have no specific ordering require-ments, we use *<ul>* instead of *<ol>*. Each item in such a list is a *<li>*, inside which all item contents (including sublists) are located.

The markup for our editor form is fairly short as well: a text field, a checkbox, and three buttons (two regular ones that need to be specifi-cally activated, which will trigger the removal of the currently selected element and the creation of a new node below this same element, re-spectively, and a submission button, which is activated whenever the user hits the [Return] key in the text field or the checkbox in addition to plain old clicking. . .). That submission button either creates an element at root level (when no element is selected) or renames the currently selected element. This makes for faster batch-oriented operation.

So far, with no styling, the page is a mess. Let's add some CSS magic:

`prototype/dom/people.css`

```
Line 1   body { font-family: sans-serif; font-size: small; }
    -    h1 { color: navy; font-size: x-large; font-weight: normal; }
    -    h2 {
    -      color: green; font-size: larger;
    5      border-bottom: 1px solid green; margin: 0 0 0.5em;
    -    }
    -    img { border: 0; }

    -    #tree {
   10      width: 25em; height: 30em; overflow: auto; float: left;
    -      border: 1px solid #444; background: #eee; padding: 0.5em;
    -      cursor: default;
    -    }

   15    #props {
    -      width: 25em; height: 10em; margin-left: 27em;
    -      border: 1px solid #444; background: #eee; padding: 0.5em;
    -    }

   20    #tree ul {
    -      list-style-type: none;
    -      margin: 0; padding: 0;
    -    }
    -    #tree ul ul { padding-left: 1.3em; }
   25    #tree li { padding-left: 0.1em; margin: 0.4em 0; }
    -    #tree span { padding: 5px; }

    -    span.group { font-weight: bold; }

   30    #tree span.person { font-weight: normal; margin-left: 16px; }

    -    #tree span.selected {
    -      border: 1px solid #004; padding: 4px; background: #ddf;
    -      color: navy;
   35    }

    -    #editor p { position: relative; height: 1.3em; }
    -    #edtName, #chkIsGroup { position: absolute; left: 4em; margin-left: 0; }
    -    #edtName { padding: 0 0.1em; right: 0; }
   40    #edtName:focus, #edtName:active { border: 2px solid black;
    -      background: #ffd; }
    -    #lblIsGroup { position: absolute; left: 6.3em; }
```

Some of this is not immediately useful, because it relates to elements that will be created dynamically by script to represent tree nodes (those are the lines 24 to 35). The rest is styling as usual. Our page is now ready for life to be breathed into it, thanks to scripting.

Representing the Staff: Our Staff Object

We'll put most of the functionality of staff management into a custom object, which we'll call, quite simply, Staff. Inside it, we'll put many methods, plus the actual data structure, tucked neatly in a nodes field. It is an array of "tree nodes," each of which is a simple object with at least two properties: id and name.

The id property matches the id= attribute of the *<li>* elements representing the tree node in the screen and is of the form *itemXXX*, where *XXX* is an incrementally generated integer. The name property holds the tree node's name, its visible label.

If a tree node is actually a group, it also features a children property, which is an array. Such an array holds tree node objects for anything inside the group, and so on and so forth, recursively.

Let us start by defining a default tree with data for the staff of an imaginary company, ACME.[1] This goes like this:

```
prototype/dom/fragments/people_1.js
```
```
var Staff = {
  nodes: [
    { id: 'item1', name: 'ACME',
      children: [
        { id: 'item11', name: 'IT',
          children: [
            { id: 'item111', name: 'Sébastien Gruhier' },
            { id: 'item112', name: 'Alexis Jaubert' },
            { id: 'item113', name: 'Guillaume Réan' }
          ] },
        { id: 'item12', name: 'HR',
          children: [
            { id: 'item121', name: 'Sandrine Daspet' }
          ] },
        { id: 'item13', name: 'Xavier Borderie' }
      ] },
  ]
}; // Staff
```

Here we are: our staff is represented in Staff.nodes. The next step is to turn this data into actual tree nodes on the screen. . . .

---

1. Boy, that's *groundbreaking*.

Walking Around: Moving Across the DOM

```
down([selector = '*']  [, index = 0])  →  HTMLElement
firstDescendant()  →  HTMLElement
next([selector = '*']  [, index = 0])  →  HTMLElement
previous([selector = '*']  [, index = 0])  →  HTMLElement
up([selector = '*']  [, index = 0])  →  HTMLElement
```

To build and manipulate DOM fragments based on this JavaScript data structure, we need to learn about two categories of methods in Element: those that let us walk the DOM easily and those that let us alter the contents of elements.

Bare-bones DOM walking is quite the nightmare: the properties provided by the W3C specification—firstChild, lastChild, childNodes, previousSibling, and nextSibling—work only at the node level, not at the element level. The immediate consequence of this low-level attitude is that we end up walking through empty text nodes produced by markup formatting (for example, line breaks and indentation), comment nodes, entity references, and so forth. This is indeed unfortunate, because in the vast majority of cases, we concern ourselves only with elements. Not only that, but we usually want to reach for a specific kind of element (for example, a <ul> or <a> element).

Prototype extends DOM elements with methods that let us do just that (it also lets us look at whole element chains in all directions, as we'll see in Section 7.2, *Meeting the Family: Ancestors, Children, Siblings...*, on page 149). These are named up(), down(), next(), and previous(), and all share they same signature:

- With no argument, they get you to the closest element in their direction.
- With a string argument, they interpret it as a CSS selector, relying on the amazing capabilities of the Selector class, which we will explore in greater depth on page 156. A common form of selector in this context is a simple tag name.
- With an integer argument, they get you to the *index*th element in their direction.
- With two arguments, a string and an integer, they get you to the *index*th element among those obtained by the selector, counting from the current element outward.

There is also an optimized method for a common use case, which just needs the first child element, with no additional requirement. It's covered by firstDescendant().

This makes for numerous possibilities, so let me illuminate this with a few examples. Let us assume the following document:

`prototype/dom/walking.html`

```html
<body>
  <h1 id="title">Johnny Walker</h1>
  <ul id="list">
    <li id="item1">Hey there</li>
    <li id="item2">
      <p id="p2_1">OK, so here I walk.</p>
      <p id="p2_2">And walk again&#8230;.</p>
    </li>
  </ul>
</body>
```

Here are a few calls and their results:

`prototype/dom/walking.js`

```
$('item1').up()            // => #list
$('item1').up(1)           // => body
$('item1').up().previous() // => #title
$('item1').next()          // => #item2
$('item1').previous()      // => undefined
$('item1').down()          // => undefined
$('item2').down()          // => #p2_1
$('list').down('p')        // => #p2_1
$('list').down('p', 1)     // => #p2_2
```

Note that when no element is found, you get **undefined**.

Replacing Contents and Removing Elements

```
cleanWhitespace() → HTMLElement
remove() → HTMLElement
replace(content) → HTMLElement
update(content) → HTMLElement
```

In order to create DOM fragments for our JavaScript "node" objects conveniently, we need another toolset focusing on altering the contents of DOM elements. When we limit ourselves with methods from the W3C DOM specifications, we need to build every tiny detail by hand, which is quickly cumbersome. True, script.aculo.us provides a Builder class, which can come in handy, but it can also be pretty verbose to use (although it's far nicer than raw DOM manipulation, as we will see in Chapter 17, *Building DOM Fragments the Easy Way: Builder*, on page 335).

What we have here are methods designed to work with multiple kinds of input for content:

An (X)HTML text
> You will most commonly have (X)HTML fragments as fodder for insertion or replacement. More often than not, you're getting them as responses from the server after an Ajax call. Their processing is described in the next section. Before version 1.6, only this form was acceptable.

An object featuring a toElement() method
> The result of calling this method is used instead of the original object. Such a method must return a DOM element or fragment.

A DOM element or fragment
> It is used directly.

An object featuring a toHTML() method
> The result of calling this method is used as direct XHTML text would be. We actually rely internally on Object.toHTML(), as outlined in Section 4.1, *Miscellanea*, on page 47, so if a code mistake ends up in passing something else, we get fallback behavior.

The fundamental methods are replace() and update(). The difference between the two is critical. replace() actually *replaces* the element you are calling it on, but update() replaces only its *contents*. For instance, consider the following DOM fragment:

```
<div id="container"><p>This is an example</p></div>
```

Here are two distinct calls and the resulting DOMs:

```
$('container').update('<h1>Don\'t cross the streams!</h1>');
// DOM: <div id="container"><h1>Don't cross the streams!</h1></div>
$('container').replace('<h1>Don\'t cross the streams!</h1>');
// DOM: <h1>Don't cross the streams!</h1>
```

Aside from these, we have a convenience remove() method, which simply takes the element out of the DOM, and a cleanWhitespace() method, which scours the element's DOM fragment to expunge any text node with only whitespace in it. This can be handy when you go from a HTML template with some indenting or line breaks and they end up messing with your styling.

OK, we're all set to bring this JavaScript tree to visual life! Let's first add a method to our Staff object that does produce a DOM fragment for any given node. To do this, we'll need to leverage the Template class we

will cover in Section 10.4, *Templating Made Easy*, on page 223, with
two templates: one for the people and one for the groups:

`prototype/dom/fragments/people_2.js`

```
Line 1   var Staff = {
           _templates: {
             person: new Template(
               '<span class="person">' +
       5       '<input type="checkbox" name="item[]" value="#{id}" />' +
               '<span>#{name}</span></span>'),
             group: new Template(
               '<span class="group">' +
               '<a href="" title="Click to collapse">' +
      10       '<img class="toggler" src="group_open.gif" alt="-" /></a>' +
               '<input type="checkbox" name="item[]" value="#{id}" />' +
               '<span>#{name}</span></span>' +
               '<ul></ul>')
           },
      15
           nodes: [
             // ...
           ],

      20   createDOMFragment: function(parentId, node) {
             var element = $(document.createElement('li'));
             element.id = node.id;
             var tpl = this._templates[node.children ? 'group' : 'person'];
             var escapedNode = { id: node.id, name: node.name.escapeHTML() };
      25     element.update(tpl.evaluate(escapedNode));
             $(parentId).down('ul').appendChild(element);
             element.down('input').checked = node.checked;
             return node;
           }
      30 }; // Staff
```

We start by putting two Template objects in a "private" field (as the initial
underscore convention implies). Both these fragments are intended to
be the whole initial contents of the *<li>* element for our new tree node.
Note the embedded *<span>* around the name part, which will make it
easier for us to rename the node later. We are going to create the *<li>*
element the regular way and use update() on it to fill it in.

That "regular" way appears in createDOMFragment(), on line 20. It's
a simple document.createElement('li'). We wrap it in a $() call to make
sure we get the extended version of the element.

Then we start leveraging the magic of Prototype:

1. Line 23 selects the appropriate Template object, depending on the
   node's nature. We already saw that a node representing a group

features a children property, which will otherwise be **undefined** (thereby boolean-equivalent to **false**).

2. On line 24, we produce a template-oriented version of the node, with just id and label, this latter field being HTML-escaped to prevent markup injection.

3. We can then evaluate the template around this object, on line 25, and inject the resulting HTML into the newly created *<li>* element. Notice it doesn't have to be present in the whole page's DOM at this point.

4. A little more walking lets us grab the parent node (which is either a *<li>* element or the root *<form>*), walk down to find its child-containing *<ul>*, and add our DOM fragment as its last child (that is, at the end of its existing contents).

5. Time for a walk: we need to update the status of the checkbox in the node, depending on the presence (and value) of a checked property in the JavaScript node, which is what we do on line 27. So far, none of our default nodes features such a property, which is equivalent to featuring one with a value of **false**. So, all our checkboxes here will be unchecked for the basic tree.

I'll bet you're dying to try this out, so let's add another little method, specifically designed to initialize our view with the default state of our nodes field:

```
prototype/dom/fragments/people_3.js
```

```
Line 1   var Staff = {
  -        // ...
  -
  -        createDOMFragment: function(parentId, node) {
  5          // ...
  -        },
  -
  -        init: function(id, nodes) {
  -          id = id || 'staff';
  10         nodes = nodes || this.nodes;
  -          nodes.each(function(n) {
  -            n.container = nodes;
  -            this.createDOMFragment(id, n);
  -            if (n.children)
  15             this.init(n.id, n.children);
  -          }.bind(this));
  -        }
  -      }; // Staff
```

The new init() method recursively injects our default node tree into our web page. There are a couple things to look at here:

- Notice the ‖ idiom at the beginning of the init() function (from line 9). It's a common way to provide default values for arguments where a **false**-equivalent value is invalid.[2] Either there is a valid value passed or the argument is missing, and we use the operand on the right as its value. These two lines make sure that calling init() with no arguments will start working at the root level of the tree (*staff* is the id= of our *<form>*, remember?), both in the view and in our JavaScript structure.

- You may be intrigued by this container property we're tweaking on line 12. This is because we want to make sure all JavaScript nodes keep a reference on their container node. We'll need that to properly handle node removal.

- There's also an important line here. Line 16 contains a call to bind(). Without it, our anonymous function would be *unbound* and could not find its methods (it uses this.createDOMFragments and this.init). Explicitly binding it to our **this** avoids such nasty surprises.

Rubber, meet road: save it all, refresh your web page in your browser of choice, fire up a JavaScript console (or better yet in Firefox, use *Firebug*'s console), and try it:

⇐ `Staff.init()`

If you got it all right, you should see the whole tree appear as if by magic! Figure 7.2, on the next page, illustrates this.

Handling Events

```
observe(eventName, handler) → HTMLElement
stopObserving([eventName [, handler]]) → HTMLElement
```

Well, our little staff project is moving along nicely. Still, that manual JavaScript call will not cut it with the HR people, I'm afraid.

We would need to make it automatically happen once the page is ready. And as long as we're binding event listeners here, now that we are equipped with the knowledge to create DOM fragments based on our JavaScript nodes, we could deal with form submission (as well as this Remove button, too).

---

2. Remember that zero is false-equivalent. If it's acceptable as an argument, you can't rely on this idiom.

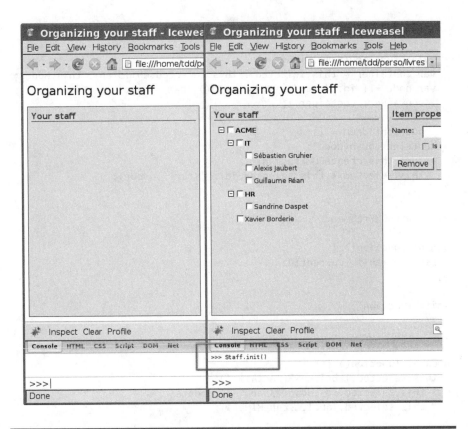

Figure 7.2: MANUALLY INJECTING OUR INITIAL TREE

So, let's start by equipping our Staff object with two methods to create a new node or rename the currently selected one and some ID-generating machinery. We also need to keep track of the currently selected node. For now, we have no way to select a node, but when we do, creating a node will add it as a child to the selected one.

`prototype/dom/fragments/people_4.js`

```
var Staff = {
  // _templates...

  _currentId: 1000,

  selected: null,
```

```
  // nodes...

  create: function(name, isGroup) {
    var container = this.selected ? this.selected.children : this.nodes;
    var node = { id: 'item' + this.genId(), name: name,
      container: container };
    if (isGroup)
      node.children = [];
    container.push(node);
    return this.createDOMFragment(
      this.selected ? this.selected.id : 'staff', node);
  },

  // createDOMFragment...

  genId: function() {
    return ++this._currentId;
  },

  init: function() {
    // ...
  },

  update: function() {
    this.selected.label = $F('edtName');
    $(this.selected.id).down('span', 1).update(
      this.selected.label.escapeHTML());
  }
}; // Staff
```

The create() code is quite simple. First, we determine what's the container for our new JavaScript node: either the root one or the selected node's children property (if we're creating a group, we also need to provide it with its own children container). Then, we create the node simply by initializing it as an anonymous object. ID generation is delegated to a tiny genId() routine in case we need to refactor it at some point. Finally, once the node is created and added to its container, we reuse our beloved createDOMFragment() to add it, either below the selected node or at the root level.

Update is much simpler, because we are just renaming the currently selected node (we decided not to let a person node become a group node or the other way around). The $F() function will give us the text field's value, which we can use to update the JavaScript node. Then, all that is left to do is update the contents of the name-wrapping <span>, which is the second, in document order, inside the <li> element (recall indices in DOM-walking methods start at zero).

Well, the data model is ready. Now let's bind this to our view:

`prototype/dom/fragments/people_5.js`

```
// Staff...

function processForm(e, addChild) {
  e.stop();
  if (Staff.selected && !addChild)
    Staff.update($F('edtName'));
  else
    Staff.create($F('edtName'), $('chkIsGroup').checked);
} // processForm

document.observe('dom:loaded', function() {
  Staff.init();
  $('editor').observe('submit', processForm);
  $('btnAddChild').observe('click',
    processForm.bindAsEventListener(this, true));
});
```

There are a few items of interest in this code. The idea is that process-Form() deals with both the submission button and the *Add as child* button. How to differentiate? We could use the event's source element and check its ID, but I thought this was a nice way to introduce a real-world example of bindAsEventListener().

Here's the deal: when the submission button is clicked, processForm() gets invoked with only its event object as an argument (this is automatically provided). Its addChild argument is **undefined** and therefore is equivalent to **false**. This submission button is intended to always be available (except when the text field is empty, but we'll get to that in due time).

On the other hand, when the *Add as child* button is clicked, process-Form() gets invoked with its event argument *and* a second argument (in our case, addChild set to **true**). This is what bindAsEventListener() is *for*, my friend.

So, we end up with the following use cases:

- No selected element: branching on **else**, creating a new element (which will, then, be added at the root level of the tree)
- Selected element, regular submission button (which we will soon make sure then reads *Rename*): branching on **if**, updating the element (which, as we saw, is just a renaming indeed)
- Selected element, *Add as child* button: branching on **else**, creating a new element (which will appear below the selected one)

Also note that we triggered the default tree injection, too. This whole event registration business happens when the page is loaded so as to make sure we have the whole basic DOM available to us and can bind event handlers without problems.

To move ahead, we need to be able to select elements, which requires us to dynamically alter the CSS class name set of elements. From then on, we'll be able to adjust the form's look and behavior depending on the selection state, and we'll also be ready to implement element removal.

Tweaking CSS Class Names

```
addClassName(className)    → HTMLElement
hasClassName(className)    → Boolean
removeClassName(className) → HTMLElement
toggleClassName(className) → HTMLElement
```

It's really no big deal, or so it seems—the set of CSS classes pertaining to an element is stored as a whitespace-separated list in its class= attribute, which is accessible through its className property in Java-Script.

The trick is that since it's a string concatenation and not some form of container, we keep having to pull some string-fu to work with it. That is why Prototype provides these tricks for you.[3]

The names are self-explanatory: addClassName() makes sure a given class name is in the set (without hurting any existing class name in there), removeClassName() makes sure it gets out, hasClassName() tests whether it's in, and toggleClassName() removes it if it's there or adds it if it's missing.

Knowing this, we can start dealing with clicks on our tree zone. Creating an individual handler for all items in there would be wasteful. We can leverage event bubbling and attach only one handler at the tree level, which will get all click events happening somewhere in it. However, we need to be careful about which clicks we're talking about:

- Clicks on checkboxes are left for the browser to deal with (they will toggle the checkbox status). We're not interfering with this.

---

3. Until version 1.6, it used to rely internally on a tiny Element.ClassNames class, which made for a rather heavy-handed execution of these CSS manipulations. It's now deprecated, along with the classNames() method, and these manipulations are implemented with optimized string manipulation.

- Clicks on the links surrounding the toggler images (which are, incidentally, the only links in the tree) will, later, actually toggle the relevant group's visibility. We don't know everything we have to know just yet in order to do that.

- Clicks anywhere else must fall either below the actual tree or somewhere in the screen space of a *<li>* element that represents an item. We then need to select this item.

This makes for quite a few code additions:

`prototype/dom/fragments/people_6.js`

```
Line 1   var Staff = {
           // templates, nodes, createDOMFragment...

           find: function(id, nodes) {
    5          nodes = nodes || this.nodes;
             var result;
             nodes.each(function(n) {
               result = n.id == id ? n : n.children && this.find(id, n.children);
               if (result)
   10            throw $break;
             }.bind(this));
             return result;
           },

   15      // genId, init...

           select: function(id) {
             if (this.selected)
               $(this.selected.id).down('span').removeClassName('selected');
   20        this.selected = (this.selected && this.selected.id == id
               ? null : this.find(id));
             if (this.selected) {
               var elt = $(id);
               elt.down('span').addClassName('selected');
   25        }
             this.updateEditor();
             return this.selected;
           },

   30      update: function() {
             // ...
           },

           updateEditor: function() {
   35        if (!this.selected) {
               $('edtName').value = '';
               $('chkIsGroup').enable().checked = false;
               $('btnSubmit').value = 'Create';
```

```
 -            $('btnRemove', 'btnAddChild', 'btnSubmit').invoke('disable');
40          } else {
 -            $('edtName').value = this.selected.name;
 -            var isGroup = this.selected.children;
 -            $('chkIsGroup').checked = isGroup;
 -            $('btnSubmit').value = 'Rename';
45            $('btnRemove').enable();
 -            $('btnAddChild', 'chkIsGroup').invoke(
 -              isGroup ? 'enable' : 'disable');
 -          }
 -          $('edtName').activate();
50        }
 -      }; // Staff
```

Finding a JavaScript node in our custom-made JavaScript tree is going to be a recurrent need. We address it with a find() method (starting on line 4), which recursively browses our data structure and returns either a node object or **undefined**. It's intended to be called with a simple ID.

Visually selecting a node requires us to do two things, so look at the code for select(), starting on line 17. We start by catering to the current selection, if any. We need to deselect it. This just means we'll remove *selected* from its CSS class name set. Then, we can find the JavaScript node for the new selection, assign it to the selected field, add *selected* to its classes, and update the state of the editor form on the right to reflect the new state of things.

The condition over calling find() provides a nice extra touch—clicking the current selection simply deselects it. This lets us add new nodes at root level any time, which is nice.

The updateEditor() function is pretty straightforward, although slightly bulky. If there is no selected node, we reset the form and disable all buttons (this is because the *Add as child* button would be redundant over *Create*, and this latter one will have to wait for the user to type a valid name in order to become enabled). On the other hand, a selected node will see its name and group quality reflected in the form; the submit button will be labeled *Rename*, and *Remove* will become enabled, as will *Add as child* if the selection is a group node. Note, however, that if the selection is a person node, it should not be possible to make it become a group, and we cannot add a group node as a child to it. Therefore, we disable the checkbox.

That's it for the staff logic, but we need to listen for clicks in the tree area now. That's what we do with the following handler, attached at page-loading time, as usual:

`prototype/dom/fragments/people_7.js`

```
Line 1   function handleTreeClick(e) {
  -        var elt = e.element();
  -        if (elt.tagName == 'INPUT')
  -          return;
  5        e.stop();
  -        if (elt.tagName == 'IMG')
  -          elt = elt.up('a');
  -        if (elt.tagName == 'A') {
  -          // Some toggle code, coming soon!
 10          return;
  -        }
  -        // Other click.  Let's select if we're on a valid item!
  -        if ('LI' != elt.tagName)
  -          elt = elt.up('li');
 15        if (!elt)
  -          return;
  -        Staff.select(elt.id);
  -      } // handleTreeClick
  -
 20      // processForm...
  -
  -      document.observe('dom:loaded', function() {
  -        Staff.init();
  ▶        Staff.updateEditor();
  2▶       $('tree').observe('click', handleTreeClick);
  -        $('editor').observe('submit', processForm);
  -        $('btnAddChild').observe('click',
  -          processForm.bindAsEventListener(this, true));
  ▶        new Field.Observer('edtName', 0.3, function() {
  3▶         $('btnSubmit').disabled = $F('edtName').blank();
  ▶        });
  -      });
```

We use the event's element() method to know *on what element* the click
occurred, wrapping it in a $() call to get the sweet candy of DOM exten-
sions. Clicking checkboxes should be left alone. We let go of *INPUT*-
related clicks. Otherwise, this click is ours to deal with. We start by
stopping the event so it won't bubble up and trigger further handlers.

If we clicked toggler images, we'll just go up the DOM toward their containing link. We can then deal with such clicks in a uniform manner
(which will be detailed later, when we have learned enough about playing with elements' visibility). Any other target element means we clicked
either somewhere nonspecial in a tree node (that is, in a *<li>* element's
area) or outside any tree node (for example, empty space in the tree
area). This is what the tests from line 13 take care of.

Eventually, if we reach the method's final line, we're on a valid item. We need to select it, which we delegate to our dear Staff.select(). Binding these event handlers requires a few extra lines in our page-load setup code. First, note we make sure our editor form starts out in a state consistent with our policy by calling Staff.updateEditor() up front. We then go ahead and bind our handler to click events in the tree zone.

As a final touch (remember how I mentioned polish?), we're going to leverage a small tool that we'll better explore later, Field.Observer, starting on line 29. This lets us watch out for changes of value in a given form field at regular intervals. We decide to keep an eye on the text field and adjust the submission button's state (enabled or disabled) based on it. If the value is blank (that is, if it contains only whitespace or is actually empty), the submission button is disabled. That's a simple UI rule: never let your users believe they can activate something only to tell them "no" when they do. To be responsive enough to typing, without hogging the browser with our checking, we go for a 0.3" interval; checking on the name three times a second sounds good enough, doesn't it?

OK, there you go: node selection, form maintenance, node creation, and node renaming! This is great, but removal sort of screams to be implemented here; can't you hear? And indeed, now that selection is implemented, there's no reason not to answer its plea. So off we go:

```
prototype/dom/fragments/people_8.js
```

```
var Staff = {
  // everything up to init...

  removeSelected: function() {
    if (!this.selected)
      throw 'No selection to remove';
    var container = this.selected.container;
    container = container.without(this.selected);
    var elt = $(this.selected.id);
    var previous = elt.previous('li');
    if (!previous)
      previous = elt.up('li');
    elt.remove();
    this.selected = null;
    if (previous)
      this.select(previous.id);
    else
      this.updateEditor();
  },

  // select, update...
}; // Staff
```

```
// ...

document.observe('dom:loaded', function() {
  // ...
  $('btnRemove').observe('click', Staff.removeSelected.bind(Staff));
  // ...
});
```

Our new Staff method, removeSelected(), needs no argument. It can grab the selected node from the selected field. Because it relies on a proper **this** reference, we must remember to properly bind it when making it an event listener. Because it doesn't care for the event object as its first argument, a simple bind() is sufficient.

This is where the few lines we added earlier to maintain a container property in all JavaScript nodes pay off. Thanks to that, we can update the container (it is the array containing our node) to avoid stray references that would wreak havoc in our application's behavior. Then there's some boilerplate algorithm to determine which element to select after the removal. It has to be the previous one, in a previous-and-up traversal. The usual stuff. Let's not forget to reset the selection at the proper moment and to update the editor explicitly if there was no new selection.

Well, my friend, that's some meaty JavaScript already! All that's left is the group toggling, letting us collapse and expand the group nodes in our tree. This is actually a rather light task, but to tackle it, we need to learn about playing with elements' visibility.

Peek-a-Boo: Hiding, Showing, and Checking Visibility

```
hide()    →  HTMLElement
show()    →  HTMLElement
toggle()  →  HTMLElement
visible() →  Boolean
```

Prototype provides elements with four methods to deal with their visibility. More exactly, these methods deal with the CSS display property. Hiding an element means setting this property to *none*. Showing it again is achieved by restoring the property to whatever it was before that. When dealing with these methods, you can be in one of two situations. If your element is in the normal flow and is visible, you don't have anything extra to do. However, if you plan on hiding an element that uses a specific value for its display property or if you need to hide the element from the start, you *must* specify the original property value in *an inline style* (a style= attribute on the HTML element).

\\//
°ʕ **Joe Asks...**
~   **display? Is That *All* You're Looking At?!**

Simply relying on the CSS display property can indeed seem sloppy. After all, for an element to *actually* be visible, a number of things need to be verified—not only display but also visibility, positioning, opacity, overflow control, and all of this recursively through the container chain....

You get the idea: it's a flippin' nightmare! To obtain an authoritative answer on whether our element is, indeed, visible, we would have to come up with some serious Java-Script/DOM mojo, which would be incredibly complex and likely inefficient, not to mention how we would have to battle against browser compatibility.

So yes, like many other libraries, Prototype checks only on display. And believe it or not, that's actually enough for most cases. Plus, that's super fast.

Yes, this is an intrusion of appearance in contents. This is a breach of the separation of concerns. This is lame. Yes. But this is a necessary evil, because there currently is no reliable, *cross-browser* way to grab the property's specified value, if it is not specified inline.

This is an issue most Prototype and script.aculo.us beginners stumble upon. If your element has anything other than the default value for its display property and you plan to use hide/show methods or effects on it, you must set its CSS display property through an inline style= attribute. Repeat after me: *inline attribute*. Let it sink in.

So, now that we know this, we can complete our staff management example application. It only needs its toggling capability to be wrapped up; let's get on with it:

`prototype/dom/fragments/people_9.js`

```
Line 1  var Staff = {
   -      // ...

   -      createDOMFragment: function(parentId, node) {
   5        // ...
   -        element.down('input').checked = node.checked;
```

```
         this.makeVisible(node.id);
         return node;
       },

       // find, genId, init

       makeVisible: function(id) {
         var elt = $(id);
         // Open all containing groups
         while (elt = elt.up('ul'))
           if (!elt.visible())
             this.toggle(elt.up('li').id);
       },

       // removeSelected

       select: function(id) {
         // ...
         if (this.selected) {
           var elt = $(id);
           elt.down('span').addClassName('selected');
           this.makeVisible(id);
         }
         // ...
       },

       toggle: function(id) {
         var elt = $(id);
         var group = elt.down('ul');
         var toggler = elt.down('img');
         var groupIsVisible = group.toggle().visible();
         toggler.src = 'group_' + (groupIsVisible ? 'open' : 'closed') +
           '.gif';
         toggler.alt = (groupIsVisible ? '-' : '+');
         toggler.up('a').title = 'Click to ' +
           (groupIsVisible ? 'collapse' : 'expand');
       },

       // update, updateEditor
     }; // Staff

     function handleTreeClick(e) {
       // ...
       if (elt.tagName == 'A') {
         Staff.toggle(elt.up('li').id);
         return;
       }
       // ...
     } // handleTreeClick

     // ...
```

Let's start with the toggle code. Our toggle() method starts on line 33. It goes like this: we get the *<li>* and grab the *<ul>* holding the group in it and the *<img>* used to display the plus or minus icon. We can toggle the group (the *<ul>*) and immediately check whether it's now visible. All that's left to do is adjust the image's source file and alternative text (let's think about accessibility here, you never know. . .), as well as the link's title (used, for instance, to display tooltips when the mouse hovers on the link's area for a short time).

Of course, our method is useless if we don't call it somewhere. This is what we do in our handleTreeClick() handler, as you can see on line 51.

Being able to toggle groups on and off raises questions about selection and node creation. Adding a node as a child of a collapsed group would be invisible, unless we make the node visible by expanding its parent group. More generally, creating a node (or selecting it) by code, which means it could be any node, at any depth within the tree, should make this node visible.

So, let's start by writing a simple makeVisible() method (starting on line 13) that recursively expands any parent group of the node passed to it. Then we just need to call it when a DOM fragment is created (on line 7), catering to programmatic node creation, and when a node is programmatically selected (on line 28).

We've been very brave. We're done with our (slightly long-winded, but, hey, doesn't this small page feel snappy?!) full example. There are still a host of features provided by DOM extension, though, so we'll quickly fly through them in the following pages.

Inserting New Contents

Inserting new contents in the DOM is a common need, especially when using Ajax. Here are a few scenarios that keep popping up when developing web apps:

- There's this Ajax processing you do that needs to have some place to put its error messages when something gets borked.
- The user adds an item by filling in a form, which is then submitted through Ajax. What comes back from the server is the polished XHTML fragment that now needs to find its place at the bottom of the item list (perhaps a shopping cart or a comments listing). A highlight effect would be nice, too, but we'll get to that later.

- You've got this cool web-based chat application (who said "Camp-fire?"), and as new dialogue comes in, it needs to be appended to the room transcript.
- Your message list displays incoming e-mail from most recent to oldest, conforming with the user's preferences. As you routinely check for new messages, you suddenly need to put the fresh ones at the top of the list.

You see? It's all over the place.

Lightweight DOM Element Creation

new Element(tagName *[, attributes]*) → HTMLElement

Version 1.6 introduces a lightweight DOM element creator, which is a trimmed-down version of script.aculo.us's Builder facility. It lets you create elements in a straightforward manner by simply invoking Element as a constructor, with at least a tag name (the case is irrelevant) and possibly a hash-like object containing the attributes. For instance:

```
var header = new Element('h1', { id: 'mainTitle', lang: 'fr' });
header.appendChild(document.createTextNode('La construction facile'));
```

You will get details on the syntax for the attributes argument in the description of the writeAttributes() method on page 155.

Replacing vs. Inserting

There are really two categories of contents alteration:

- Contents *replacement*: you want to replace an element's contents or the element itself. This is done through this element's update() and replace() methods, respectively, which were described in Section 7.2, *Replacing Contents and Removing Elements*, on page 128.
- Contents *insertion*: you need to squeeze new contents some place. This is what the insertion methods are about.

You could, of course, craft your own code by hand by using the DOM interfaces (those in DOM Level 2 Core and DOM Level 2 HTML, for instance), but you'll quickly find that cross-browser issues actually are legion. There is, naturally, a large set of problems with Internet Explorer, especially when playing inside *<table>* elements. But this is only a facet of the troubles you'll get in.

That is why Prototype takes care of all the cross-browser tricks for you, be it for contents replacement or contents insertion. Believe me, you're better off using the Prototype methods than embarking on a lonely crusade through such barren lands.

How Is Our XHTML Fragment Processed?

The same way hedgehogs mate: with great care (and a hearty spirit). The general idea (for both update()/replace() and the insertion methods) is as follows:

1. The fragment is stripped of its <script> elements, which are kept aside.

2. The stripped fragment is inserted, taking care of the cross-browser issues and potential pitfalls.

3. The scripts originally in the fragment get evaluated; at this point, the elements in the fragment are indeed part of the page's DOM, so they are accessible through regular scripting.

At this point, you may roar in outrage at the mere thought of inline <script> tags. But in an Ajax context, this is the only way[4] for the server to send both page contents and the companion scripting. A common use case is that of a new item to be appended to a list and then subjected to a highlight effect (you know, this yellow fade thing you keep seeing now and then), or you could make the new content draggable or otherwise script-enabled.

As a warning note, you should always use JavaScript <script> elements (that is, not some other scripting language, such as Internet Explorer's proprietary VBScript). This is because Prototype will extract the tags and evaluate only their contents (not the tag itself), assuming they are JavaScript.

So, How Do We Insert Stuff?

Version 1.6 provides two new methods that cater to the usual needs, replacing the now-deprecated Insertion object:

```
insert(content) → HTMLElement
insert({ pos: content [, ... ] }) → HTMLElement
wrap([wrapper = 'div'] [, attributes]) → WrapperHTMLElement
```

insert() inserts contents before, at the top of, at the bottom of (the default), or after the reference element. This is a replacement of the former Insertion namespace.

---

4. Well, not quite so, but other ways would have you pull some mean coding and configuration tricks, so I figure they're just not worth it, compared to how convenient the inline <script> approach is here....

There are two ways to invoke it. If you simply pass some content (with the same possible values as for replace() or update(), which we discussed in Section 7.2, *Replacing Contents and Removing Elements*, on page 128), it will get inserted at the bottom of the container, but if you pass an object with position-named properties, you can insert content at up to four positions all in one call. The properties of the object you pass are named before, top, bottom, and after, and their possible values were discussed in detail a few sections back.

wrap() wraps the current element with the passed one (the passed contents replaces the current element, which is then added as the contents' last child). You can specify the wrapper element as an existing element or a tag name, or you can leave it to the default (a new *<div>* element). You can also pass attributes for the wrapper element, using an attribute hash, which will be applied even when you specify an existing element as the wrapper. Note that you could pass just attributes, which would be applied to a new *<div>* (which I refrain from doing in the next example, for the sake of readability). Finally, note that wrap() returns the wrapper element, not the original one. Although this is not very consistent with the rest of the API, intensive real-world use showed this to be the more intuitive (and the more useful) way to go.

To better visualize the various insertion types, let's try them on a demo page. Our page body contains the reference element:

```
prototype/insertions/index.html
<!DOCTYPE html PUBLIC "-//W3C//DTD XHTML 1.0 Strict//EN"
 "http://www.w3.org/TR/xhtml11/DTD/xhtml11-strict.dtd">
<html xmlns="http://www.w3.org/1999/xhtml" lang="en-US" xml:lang="en-US">
<head>
    <meta http-equiv="Content-Type" content="text/html; charset=UTF-8" />
    <title>Insertion</title>
    <link rel="stylesheet" type="text/css" href="demo.css" />
    <script type="text/javascript" src="prototype.js"></script>
    <script type="text/javascript" src="demo.js"></script>
</head>
<body>

<h1>Insertion methods</h1>

<div id="ref">Reference element</div>

</body>
</html>
```

Then a small script will use all four insertions at page load time, using both invocation syntaxes. This also demonstrates inline scripts:

`prototype/insertions/demo.js`

```
Line 1  function demoAllInsertions() {
   -      // Default syntax
   -      $('ref').insert('<div class="element bottom">' +
   -        '<code>bottom</code></div>');
   5      // Advanced syntax
   -      $('ref').insert({
   -        before: '<div class="element before"><code>before</code></div>',
   -        top: '<div class="element top"><code>top</code></div>',
   -        after: '<div class="element after"><code>after</code></div>'
  10      });
   -      // A bit of inline scripting?
   -      $('ref').wrap('div', { className: 'element wrap' });
   -      $('ref').insert({ top:
   -        '<div class="element top" id="scripted">Such a nice book</div>' +
  15        '<script type="text/javascript">' +
   -        '$("scripted").update("Such a great book!")' +
   -        '<\/script>' });
   -    } // demoAllInsertions
   -
  20  document.observe('dom:loaded', demoAllInsertions);
```

Notice the escaping of </script> on line 17: this is because such a script would otherwise not be parsed properly if you used it in an inline <script> element (although it would work just fine using unobtrusive JavaScript).

Finally, a little bit of styling will make things stand out better:

`prototype/insertions/demo.css`

```
code, tt { font-size: 115%; color: green; }

#ref, .element {
  border: 1px solid gray;
  padding: 1ex; width: 30ex;
  background: #ffd;
  text-align: center;
}

.element { background: #dfd; width: 28ex; }
.element.top, .element.before { margin-bottom: 1ex; }
.element.bottom, .element.after { margin-top: 1ex; }
.element.wrap { background: #ddf; width: 32ex; }
```

The result, loading the page, looks like Figure 7.3, on the next page.

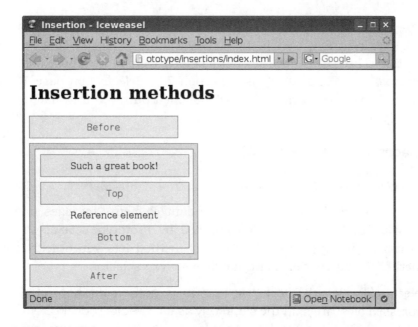

Figure 7.3: DEMONSTRATING THE INSERTION METHODS

Meeting the Family: Ancestors, Children, Siblings...

```
adjacent(expression...) → [ HTMLElement, ... ]
ancestors() → [ HTMLElement, ... ]
childElements() → [ HTMLElement, ... ]
descendantOf(ancestor) → Boolean
descendants() → [ HTMLElement, ... ]
empty() → Boolean
nextSiblings() → [ HTMLElement, ... ]
previousSiblings() → [ HTMLElement, ... ]
siblings() → [ HTMLElement, ... ]
```

Besides regular DOM walking (with methods such as up()), Prototype can gather entire node chains for you and deal with common lookup cases. It is important to note that *these focus on elements*. You won't get any text node, entity reference node, or whatnot.

The methods ancestors(), descendants(), previousSiblings(), and next-Siblings() fetch the whole chain of elements you get in the four usual directions: upward, downward, before, and after your node, respectively. A convenience siblings() shortcut returns the whole list of your sibling elements, in document order. Finally, childElements() is a one-level-down narrowing of descendants(), returning only elements that are direct children of your element.

More recently introduced, adjacent() lets you fetch all siblings (and their children) that match the CSS selectors you're passing as arguments. Technically, those selectors behave exactly like those passed to Selector#findChildElements() (see Section 7.3, *Selector*, on page 156 for details). The current node is, obviously, left out even if it matches; it's not adjacent to itself!

Selecting Elements with CSS

```
match(selector) → Boolean
select/getElementsBySelector(selector...) → [ HTMLElement, ... ]
```

These methods let you fetch descendant elements by class name or using a full CSS selector (as handled by Prototype's Selector class, discussed on page 156). The match() method lets you quickly check whether the current element matches a given selector.

Selectors for select() (formerly known as getElementsBySelector()) are expressed as strings, in the same way as for Selector.findChildElements(), which will be discussed later in this chapter. Note, however, that this method is not used much. Most of the time you'll find yourself going with the $$() utility function instead; it's just faster and more concise.

Tweaking Individual Style Properties

```
getStyle(propertyName) → value
setStyle({ name: value [,...] } | CSSPropertiesString) → HTMLElement
```

Prototype provides elements with a uniform access to style properties (DOM properties representing CSS properties), smoothing over many a browser compatibility issue (and trust me, in this specific area, compatibility issues are *legion*).

First, getStyle() retrieves the specified (or failing that, computed) value for a specific CSS property. You can use the CSS syntax (hyphen-separated, as in *border-width*) or the DOM syntax (camelized, as in *borderWidth*). Since the DOM syntax is the one ending up being used, providing it directly makes for faster processing. If the property cannot be retrieved or is set to *auto*, you'll get a **null**.

In a general manner, refrain from using CSS shorthand names for properties. Use detailed names as per the DOM Level 2 Style specification.

Second, setStyle() lets you set any number of style properties at once by simply passing a "hash" of properties as the first argument. Since version 1.6, the property names *must* be camel-cased (for example, *fontSize*, not *font-size*) when using the "hash" form, and you can use an

Not backward-compatible with 1.5.x!

alternate form as a regular CSS property set (exactly like what you would type in an inline style= attribute).

Here are examples of the two call forms:

```
elt.setStyle('font-size: 12px;');
elt.setStyle({ fontSize: '12px' });
elt.setStyle('font-size: 12px; color: #444');
elt.setStyle({ fontSize: '12px', color: '#444' });
```

As a very noticeable browser compatibility effort, both methods provide uniform access to the CSS *opacity* property, despite Internet Explorer 6 not supporting it. Prototype will work with Internet Explorer's proprietary filter capability to emulate it.

Positioning

Prototype extends DOM elements with many position-related methods that let you obtain an element's position (within a variety of coordinate systems) and play with the element's position-related aspects.

All of these methods are intensively used inside visual features such as the visual effects and drag-and-drop facilities in script.aculo.us, but this doesn't mean your own code will never need them. In case you do need them, I include them here.

Until Prototype 1.6, these methods were available through the Position namespace and suffered from inconsistent naming. A recent effort was made to clean this up.

In the following syntax, the PositionInfo type is basically a two-views object. For backward compatibility, it acts as a two-item array (with indices 0 and 1), holding the left and top coordinates, respectively. In the newer way, it also holds these data in two properties, named left and top. Also note that all coordinates are expressed as numbers, in pixels.

```
cumulativeOffset() → PositionInfo
cumulativeScrollOffset() → PositionInfo
positionedOffset() → PositionInfo
viewportOffset() → PositionInfo
getOffsetParent() → HTMLElement
absolutize() → HTMLElement
relativize() → HTMLElement
clonePosition(source [, options]) → PositionInfo
```

The whole set of methods ending with -Offset returns a coordinate set. Depending on the coordinate system you're interested in, you'll pick one or the other:

- cumulativeOffset() returns the position in the document's system (from the document's top-left corner, regardless of scrolling).

- cumulativeScrollOffset() provides the total scroll offsets of an element; that is, if this element's parent chain contains more than one scrolled container, we cumulate scroll offsets. So if our element is in a <form> that is in a scrolled <div> that is in the scrolled document, we'll take both the document's scrolling and the <div>'s scrolling into account to compute these offsets.

- positionedOffset() returns the position in the system of the positioning container system (see getOffsetParent() a few lines later).

- viewportOffset() returns the position in the viewport (the visible part of the document), which is useful to detect, say, that the element is getting over the visible edges of the document. Starting with version 1.6, Prototype provides nifty access to viewport dimensions through the document.viewport object. Check out Section 10.5, *Querying the Current Viewport*, on page 228 for further details.

getOffsetParent() returns the *positioning container* of the element. Every positioned element (be it relative or absolute positioning) has a positioning container, which is defined by a nontrivial set of rules in the CSS specification, as the "CSS-containing block."

Sometimes you need to take an element and start manipulating it like it is positioned in a certain way (usually relative or absolute). And perhaps it is not positioned that way yet. You can make it positioned according to your needs without changing its visible position (which would cause a rather troubling sudden movement) by using either absolutize() or relativize().

Finally, clonePosition() lets you apply the positioning of another element to yours. However, getting the same positioning may not be what you had in mind. You more likely want a derivative positioning, such as "just put me below it, with the same width and its original height" (this is what happens, for instance, with the list of suggestions in script.aculo.us's autocompletion feature).

> ### ∖╎⁄ Joe Asks...
> ### ᒐᔆ Positioning Container? What Are the Ground Rules Here?
>
> The full details are at http://www.w3.org/TR/CSS21/visudet.html# containing-block-details. To make a long story short and ignoring a few edge cases, it goes like this:
>
> - If you're relatively positioned, it's the content area of your nearest block-level ancestor.
>
> - If you're fixed, it's the viewport itself.
>
> - If you're absolutely positioned, it's usually the padding edge (that is, immediately inside the border) of your nearest positioned ancestor (regardless of its positioning being relative, fixed, or absolute).

So, the options argument lets you specify which properties you want to clone, using booleans named setLeft, setTop, setWidth, and setHeight. They all default to **true**. You can also specify an offset from your source element's position using the offsetLeft and offsetTop properties (they both default to zero).

For instance, script.aculo.us's Autocompleter.Base code does something like the following:

```
update.clonePosition(element, {
  setHeight: false,
  offsetTop: element.offsetHeight
});
```

This positions the suggestion list (update) right below the text field, with the same width as the text field but retaining its original height.

Figure 7.4, on the next page, attempts to convey the interrelations of the -Offset methods.

The source code archive for this book contains, in code/prototype/dom/ positioning, a live example that reproduces Figure 7.4 and lets you interactively play with scrolls. Hovering on the colored zones will update the results of all four offset methods in a top-right display.

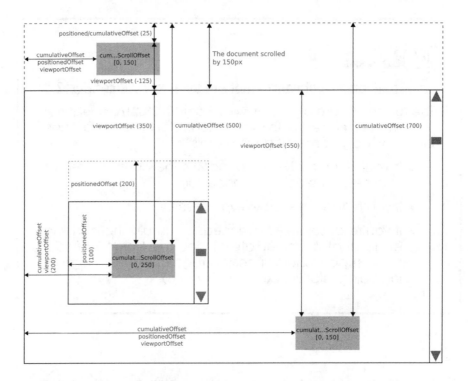

Figure 7.4: Positioning properties

More Visual Aspects

```
getDimensions() → { width: Number, height: Number }
getHeight() → Number
getWidth() → Number
makeClipping() → HTMLElement
makePositioned() → HTMLElement
scrollTo() → HTMLElement
undoClipping() → HTMLElement
undoPositioned() → HTMLElement
```

Those are a host of position-related methods. The most common ones are getDimensions(), which returns an object with both a width and a height property, plus getHeight() and getWidth(), when you need only one dimension. The others deal with making the element a *CSS-containing block* (makePositioned(), necessary to apply several visual effects) or restricting an element's rendering to a part of it.

Aside from this, the scrollTo() method is more humble. It simply has the viewport scroll so that the element appears at the top of it, much as if the user had clicked a link to this element's ID.

Miscellanea

```
hasAttribute(attrName) → Boolean
identify() → ElementID
inspect() → String
readAttribute(attrName) → String
writeAttribute(attrName [, attrValue = true]) → HTMLElement
writeAttribute({ attrName: attrValue [, ...] }) → HTMLElement
Node.xxx_NODE
```

Prototype provides a portable, reliable version of hasAttribute(), which is sometimes missing (case in point, Internet Explorer). There is also a readAttribute() method, extensively used by Prototype itself, which provides a portable way of accessing numerous DOM properties representing HTML attributes and dealing with naming or semantics discrepancies from one browser to the next (for example, when working with name= attributes). Both methods take an HTML attribute name.

Version 1.6 introduces the converse operation with writeAttribute() that takes either a single attribute's name and value or a hash-like object with properties for each attribute to set. It takes care of **false** and **null** values by removing the attribute altogether; conversely, **true** values, used to express the presence of a "flag" attribute (such as disabled= or selected=), follow XHTML guidelines by setting the attribute's value to its own name (for example, selected="selected"). Other attributes are set without value tweaking.

Do note the attribute names are HTML names, not DOM property names (for example, *class* instead of *className*, or *for* instead of *htmlFor*). *writeAttribute allows both, though.*

Also new in version 1.6, the identify() method makes sure the element has a unique ID. Either it already has an id= attribute and it is returned untouched or it lacks one, and a unique attribute, of the form *anonymous_element_X* (where *X* is a unique integer), is generated and assigned to the attribute. This is useful when you need to refer to the element later by its ID, say, through a generated script or something.

As another effort to help smooth over browser differences, Prototype 1.6 guarantees that the node type constants exist in the Node namespace (this is normally provided by the W3C DOM), so you get, for instance, Node.ELEMENT_NODE and Node.TEXT_NODE (and the ten other constants). We use this internally to avoid "magic numbers" in the Prototype code base, and if you ever dabble with node types, so should you!

We've already seen many inspect() methods. This one is actually pretty nice. It provides a markup representation of the element with its id=

and class= attributes, if any. For instance, a paragraph with an ID of *intro* and a CSS class name set of *hush* and *fancy* will render as <p id="intro" class="hush fancy"> (although the actual order of attributes may vary from one browser to the next).

My friend, you deserve a break. You've been through the humongous set of DOM extensions provided by Element and are still here to tell the tale. I salute you. But this chapter is not quite finished yet, though; here's the tasty Selector class to look at and a few nice debugging tips to learn.

7.3 Selector

Selector is the hidden power of $$(), which we covered extensively in Section 3.4, *$$ Searches with Style*, on page 34. What $$() actually does is simply call Selector.findChildElements() over the whole document, with its arguments as the selectors.

And indeed, in the vast (very vast!) majority of times, you'll just need to go with $$() instead of manually building Selector objects. It's the easier way, and you won't take a speed hit because you went for the convenience method. In fact, the only reason you would want to work with Selector directly is if you keep reusing the same selectors over and over again. Then you'll probably want to squeeze more performance out of your script by analyzing those selectors only once and keeping the resulting Selector objects close at hand.

Before plunging in, remember that all elements returned by a selector are guaranteed extended. Because good things should come in twos.

```
new Selector(expression) → Selector
sel.findElements([root = document]) → [ HTMLElement, ... ]
sel.inspect() → String
sel.match(element) → Boolean
sel.toString() → String
Selector.matchElements(elements, expression) → [ HTMLElement, ... ]
Selector.findElement(elements [, expression = '*'] [, index = 0]) → HTMLElement
Selector.findChildElements(element, expression...) → [ HTMLElement, ... ]
```

"Precompiling" a selector to tuck it away for later use is as simple as creating it. Just use **new**, and pass it a full CSS expression (not a rule with commas, though; that would require multiple selectors, which is what Selector.findChildElements() does). If the browser supports DOM Level 3 XPath, Selector will leverage it to achieve blazing speed. Otherwise, it will revert to an optimized DOM/JavaScript code base.

Using an existing Selector object for DOM queries is mostly done via its findElements() method, which you can contextualize by passing a specific element as the root for your search (otherwise you'll query the whole document). You can also check whether any given element in the DOM matches your selector by using the match() method.

There's also the usual duet of string representation methods: toString() returns the original CSS expression passed at construction time, and inspect() returns slightly more debug-oriented text—this same expression surrounded by #<*Selector:* and >.

When you have no Selector object handy, you can still have needs beyond a simple $$() call. Those needs are addressed by Selector. matchElements(), which filters an existing element set to return only those matching the passed expression, and Selector.findElement(), which goes one step further by extracting a specific element from such a resultset.

Astoundingly shrewd readers (yes, that's you, too) will have noticed that Selector.findElement() shares its second and third parameters with Element's DOM-walking methods, such as up(), which we saw in Section 7.2, *Walking Around: Moving Across the DOM*, on page 127. The reason is obvious: those methods all rely on Selector.findElement() when they get passed an expression argument, simply passing the proper element line as the first argument (for instance, up() uses ancestors()). It all comes together and makes some solid sense, wouldn't you say?

Also note, Selector.findChildElements() takes a root element ($$() passes it the whole document) and an array of expressions. It then returns the full set of nodes matching those expressions, *with no duplicates.*

7.4 Debugging Our DOM-Related Code

Debugging DOM-related code the traditional way feels like you're stumbling blindfolded in a large room full of echoes. There are basic steps you can take to see the light, or at least get a clearer picture of what you're dealing with.

Using Firebug

Let's start with the easiest way. If you're using Firefox (and you *should* develop on Firefox first and then test with other majors browsers!), use the DOM inspector (and other DOM-related features) in the Firebug[5] extension. This lets you see the actual DOM as nested markup, modify some of it on the fly, highlight corresponding elements in the rendered page, and explore DOM objects and all their properties.

The main tool for this is the HTML tab, which represents your document's DOM as markup source code, lets you expand and collapse it, select it, highlight in the web page whatever element you're mousing over in the source pane, see and tweak the current element's CSS properties (with a special view for its layout-related properties), and view its actual DOM object in detail.

Some of these features are illustrated in Figure 7.5 and in Figure 7.6, on the facing page.

Using DOM Inspectors

Most browsers feature some sort of a DOM inspector, either available directly or through some extra plug-in. Firefox has one out of the box (provided you select it at installation or, on Linux, install the proper package), which is reasonably good (see Figure 7.7, on page 160).

Internet Explorer has nothing to offer by itself, but the Internet Explorer Developer Toolbar, a browser add-on, provides a host of features targeting most web developer needs, including inspectors for the DOM, CSS style sheets, and more.

Safari 2 has a hidden Debug menu, which can easily be revealed:

1. Shut Safari down entirely (close all windows, and close the application menu).
2. Open a terminal.
3. Type defaults write com.apple.Safari IncludeDebugMenu 1.
4. There! Launch Safari again, and behold its gorgeous Debug menu.

And WebKit (which means, by extension, the upcoming Safari 3) comes with a full-blown, nicely polished debugger, plus a DOM inspector and a network monitor. (Now we're talking!)

Finally, Opera provides only a detailed, filter-capable message window, with no extra developer tools. When it comes to DOM debugging, you're pretty much on your own. However, Opera has excellent W3C DOM support. If your code works on Firefox and Safari, there is extremely little chance it would bork on Opera.

---

5. http://getfirebug.com

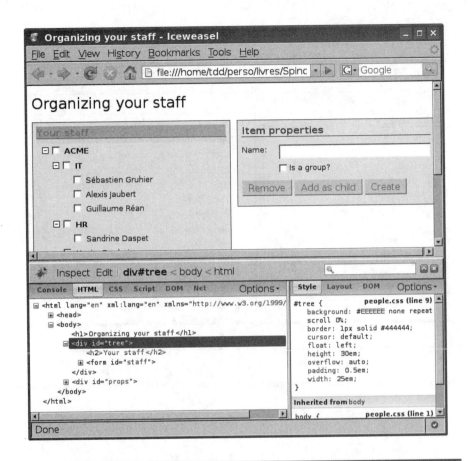

Figure 7.5: FIREBUG'S DOM INSPECTOR IN ACTION

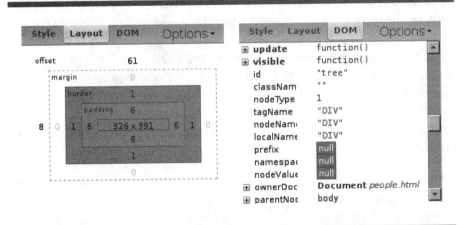

Figure 7.6: ALTERNATE VIEWS IN FIREBUG'S DOM INSPECTOR

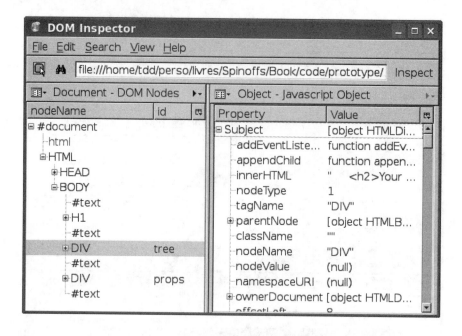

Figure 7.7: THE DOM INSPECTOR IN FIREFOX

Last-Resort Debugging

If you find yourself in such a tight spot as having to debug DOM issues with no developer tool whatsoever in your browser (what the heck are you doing!?), you can at least use Prototype's DOM abilities to construct DOM source representations and either alert() those (which can quickly become a nightmare) or log them into an ad hoc element on your web page (such as a <div> with a style along the lines of *position: absolute; width: 15em; height: 30em; right: 1em; top: 1em; border: 1px solid black; background: silver; opacity: 0.5; overflow: auto; font-family: monospace; padding: 0.2em;*).

You can then walk the DOM node using the methods we saw earlier on page 127 and on page 149, build small representations with inspect(), escape the whole thing using escapeHTML() on the String, and add the resulting text at the bottom of the log by wrapping it in a <p> and using an insertion (as we saw in Section 7.2, *Inserting New Contents*, on page 144).

What We Just Learned

There's a lot to grok in this chapter; DOM extension is at the heart of Prototype and is one of the major reasons why it's so nice to use. Let's quickly go over the central points we explored:

- DOM extension is the process of slapping extra methods on DOM elements to be used as any native DOM method. Prototype provides tons of such methods out of the box and a mechanism to add your own (Element.addMethods()).

- The speed cost of DOM extension is almost null (a few milliseconds at script load to update the prototypes for the DOM elements) on many browsers and slower on Internet Explorer (which doesn't feature prototypes for DOM interfaces). Still, it's very reasonable and has an excellent cost/benefit ratio (usually less than a millisecond to equip your element with many power tools).

- The extension *propagates*. The starting point is often a call to $(), which returns a guaranteed extended element. Every extended method, when returning one or more elements, guarantees their extension. And element-related methods in the event system also return the extended versions.

- All mutative methods (methods that alter the element) return the element itself, so you can chain-call (for example, like this: element.update('cool').highlight()).

- Areas where DOM extension radically shortens your code include DOM traversal, DOM extraction, DOM construction, CSS class processing, and positioning. And that's not even all....

- The Selector API, which is the basis for the well-loved $$() utility function, lets you extract DOM elements based on the full complement of CSS 3 selectors, regardless of your browser's actual support for CSS.

Chapter 8

Form Management

Although this is technically part of Prototype's DOM extensions, I feel that form manipulation is a topic unto itself. Prototype indeed equips forms, and form fields, with many extra methods in addition to the generic element extensions. Because forms are such an important part of web app development, I decided to cover these extensions in a specific chapter.

Form.Element vs. Field

First, note that the "official" namespace for methods grafted upon form elements is, quite unsurprisingly, Form.Element. However, as this is a somewhat long name, it is aliased to Field. I prefer this shorter version over the more verbose one. So in this book, I use Field in my code and examples. It's just more concise and no less expressive.

8.1 Toward a Better User Interface

Savvy web developers put increasing effort into the design of the forms in their apps. Proper markup (with an emphasis on semantics and accessibility) is a major step, as is proper styling, which lets us do things like highlight the focused field or clearly mark incorrect or incomplete fields. With a dollop of scripting, we can also provide timely, contextual help on field semantics.

This is all well and good, but two key aspects of form ergonomy need your sweet care, too: form navigation (that is, how the user can go from one field to the next or previous one) and proper management of field enablement.

Navigation is important not only for users with special needs or mouse-less devices. Users will automatically intuit navigation from the form's layout. They will form expectations on the order of navigation for your fields, and efficient ones will want to be able to use the keyboard to tab through your fields even if there is a mouse at hand. Failing to meet their navigational expectations can lead to a lot of frustration.

Management of field enablement has many ramifications, too. Whenever a field is enabled, it should be enabled for a good reason. Conversely, whenever a field should not be touched, make sure it *cannot* be touched. Disable it for the time being.

Properly disabling fields (including buttons) when they are irrelevant or inoperant is a *much* better way to go than just leaving them enabled and then responding to their activation with some "Not just now" message, or worse—doing nothing.

Dealing with Focus and Value Selection

Let's start with the fundamentals: giving a field the focus (making it the primary target of keyboard activity). Users may expect, at least for certain text fields, that they will automatically select their textual contents when focused. Maybe the optimal ergonomy for this particular app screen requires such a thing for massive, batch-mode use, for instance. Whenever there is a clearly dominant use case on a text field where preselecting the contents is nice, you should do it.

```
fieldElt.activate() → fieldElt
fieldElt.clear() → fieldElt
Field.focus(fieldElt) → fieldElt
fieldElt.present() → Boolean
Field.select(fieldElt) → fieldElt
```

Field elements already feature native focus() and select() methods. Those do not return the original field, however, which means you cannot easily call-chain:

```
// NONE OF THIS WILL WORK!
$('edtLogin').focus().setStyle({ backgroundColor: '#ffd' });
$('edtLogin').focus().select();
```

Call-chaining is a very nice card to have up your sleeve in order to write more concise code, which is why Prototype makes most of its DOM extensions call-chain-friendly and, in our specific case here, provides two "static" methods. This preserves the original methods and their semantics but still provides a chain-enabled variant:

```
Field.focus('edtLogin').select();
```

Because focusing a field, and then selecting its textual contents, is such a recurrent need, Prototype equips fields with a new method called acti-vate(). It first focuses the field, and then if it's an appropriate field type (for example, an *<input>* with type="input" or a *<textarea>*), it selects its contents.

As for the value itself, present() tests that it is not empty (a regular empty string), and clear(), well, clears the value.

As we discussed earlier, a clean, intuitive keyboard navigation path across form fields is important. This usually relies on proper document ordering and well-chosen tabindex= attribute values, but from a script-ing point of view, there is more to do.

```
formElt.findFirstElement()  →  fieldElt
formElt.focusFirstElement()  →  formElt
Form.reset(formElt)  →  form
```

A common best practice for most web app screens with a main form mandates that we focus this form's first element when the page is loaded so as to get the user in a position to immediately use it, without having to click the element or tab their way to it.

Of course, the concept of a "first" element is more complex than it sounds. Is it the first element in document order or the first one once the layout is applied? Or maybe the form layout obeys customs or legal requirements that make it have a few fields first that are generally left untouched and the first field that should get the focus appears fur-ther down? We'd usually mark this with a proper tabindex=, but then should "first" follow those attributes? And what about element enable-ment? Should we ignore disabled elements? What about visibility?

These are the kinds of questions you start asking yourself, and a few months later your loved ones will find you drooling and babbling in tongues, all rolled up in a fetal position in a dark corner under your desk. Allow me to rescue your endangered sanity by detailing how find-FirstElement(), which you call on the containing *<form>*, goes about it:

1. The method starts by getting all fields in the form that are nei-ther of a *hidden* type (not to be confused with styling, which we blissfully ignore[1]) nor disabled.

2. Then we look for the smallest value of the tabindex= attribute among the remaining elements.

---

1. As we discussed in the *Joe Asks...* on page 142, dealing with this would be practically infeasible.

3. If we find one, we use the resulting field.

4. Otherwise, we use the first *<input>*, *<select>*, or *<textarea>* we get, in document order.

In practice, this algorithm maps rather well to the intuitive notion of the "first" element.

Since most of the time we want to grab the first element to give it focus (and select its textual contents, if appropriate), Prototype rolls in a convenience method for this: focusFirstElement(), which is a neat combination of findFirstElement() and activate().

Finally, again for the sake of call-chaining, there is a "static" variant of the native reset() method for forms, which returns the original form element (something the native method may or may not do). Recall that resetting a form does not mean clearing it. It means resetting all fields to the values defined in the original markup.

Enabling and Disabling Elements

```
fieldElt.disable() → fieldElt
fieldElt.enable() → fieldElt
formElt.disable() → formElt
formElt.enable() → formElt
```

We discussed earlier how important it is to disable any UI element that is, in fact, useless at the moment. Maybe this is a Delete button for items in a list, where no items are currently selected. Or maybe this is a form submission button, and the form is currently being sent (either through Ajax or the regular way; that's irrelevant). Perhaps you're dealing with a Clear button for a shopping cart, which is indeed currently empty.

Whatever the business logic, if your UI element should not be used at this point in time, it should not be *usable*. Users will expect, and rightly so, that UI elements available to them should perform properly, instead of burping message dialogs with notifications such as "Sorry, can't do that now."

Prototype endows form fields with two methods, enable() and disable(), that alter the disabled DOM property. It makes certain that the element loses focus before being disabled, because this can be an issue in a few browsers.

Disabled? Let It Show!

A few browsers do not efficiently display disabled elements; for instance, Konqueror and Internet Explorer do not alter the font color of disabled drop-down listboxes or the background color of disabled flat listboxes or multiline text fields (and single-line too, on Internet Explorer). Opera does not alter the background color of checkboxes and radio buttons. Such lackings make it impossible for the user to understand at a glance that part of the UI is off-limits.

This can be fixed quickly with a bit of CSS styling. If you're targeting CSS 2–compatible browsers, just use something like this:

```
*[disabled] { background-color: #ccc; color: gray; }
```

(CSS 3 would even let us use *:disabled, but do you really want to exclude Internet Explorer for another decade?)

If you must support browsers that do not feature CSS 2 attribute selectors, you will need to equip your disabled elements with specific class names, too. This can be done easily with Prototype's magic:

```
$('myForm).select('*:disabled').invoke('addClassName',
  'disabled');
//...and later on, re-enabling...
$('myForm').select('.disabled').invoke('removeClassName',
  'disabled');
```

There is also a common use case where you need to disable an entire form (or enable it). Well, that's a piece of cake—just use the same methods over the form itself, instead of specific elements.

8.2 Looking at Form Fields

```
formElt.getElements() → [ fieldElt, ... ]
formElt.getInputs([typeName] [, name]) → [ fieldElt, ... ]
```

We often need to grab some or all of the elements in a specific form. Even inside Prototype, this is a common task: to disable or enable all the fields, to find the first one, or to serialize the form or determine whether anything has changed since the last time we looked. . . .

The catchall approach is to use getElements(), which returns all fields in the form, in document order. This includes *<input>* tags having type="hidden", disabled fields, and so on. However, *<button>* fields are omitted; only *<input>*, *<select>*, and *<textarea>* tags are taken into account.

If you need to be more surgical about it (which is a good thing), you can go with getInputs(). This one is designed specifically for those cases where you need to fetch *<input>* fields, usually with a specific type=, name=, or both.

For this second method to work properly, you'd better stick to lowercase (official XHTML) type names in your markup, your DOM generation code, and your getInputs() calls. In the same vein, name filtering is case-sensitive. If you need to filter on name but not on type, simply pass **null** as the first argument. Elements are returned in document order.

Here's a common use case: do you want to check whether any of the checkboxes with name="answer" is, indeed, checked? There you go:

```
if ($('myForm').getInputs('checkbox', 'answer').pluck('checked').any())
  // ...
```

However, if you need more advanced filtering, you'll have a simpler time using methods such as $$() or select(). For instance, assuming your required fields all have *Req* in their id= attributes, you could check (naively, because this relies on empty strings, not blank strings) that they're all filled in like this:

```
if ($('myForm').select('*[name*="Req"]').invoke('present').all())
  // Missing fields!
```

Whatever the method you used, all returned elements are extended for your DOM extension pleasure.

8.3 Submitting Forms Through Ajax

Indeed, Ajax-based form submission is at the heart of the new generation of web applications, so if you haven't got on board yet, it's about time. I'll help you in, don't worry. But before plunging into Ajax (something we'll do in detail in Chapter 9, *Ajax Has Never Been So Easy*, on page 177), we need to consider *what's in a form?*

Shape Shifters: The Changing Nature of Field Values

```
fieldElt.getValue() → value | [ value, ... ]
fieldElt.setValue(value | [ value, ... ]) → HTMLElement
```

Depending on the nature of a field, its value can take one of two forms: a single value (usually a string or, for checkboxes and radio buttons, a boolean) or an array of values. This second variant happens in only one situation: listboxes with multiple selections enabled (<select multiple=multiple">).

Now for those pesky details that you will wonder about at least once:

- Unchecked radio buttons and checkboxes yield the value **null**. Otherwise, they yield their value property, which is based on their value= attribute (you should *always* specify this attribute, which has no normalized default value).
- Other <*input*> elements yield their value property, based on user interaction (full text contents for text fields, for instance).
- Single-selection listboxes (drop-down or flat) yield the value of the selected option in a DOM-compliant way (Internet Explorer would otherwise fail to use the option's text if no value= attribute were specified).
- Multiple-selection listboxes yield an array of option values, obtained in a DOM-compliant way in the document order of the relevant <*option*> elements.

Version 1.6 introduces the reverse operation, setValue(), which lets you set a field's value using the same value syntax you'd get as a result of getValue(). It relies on the same internal mechanisms, so consistency is guaranteed. This comes in handy when you need to populate a form dynamically (perhaps from JSON data fetched through Ajax).

One last thing: remember the $F() utility function is actually an alias of getValue().

Serializing Fields and Whole Forms

Getting a single field's value in a unified way is nice enough, but most of the time you'll need to take some or all of the fields in a form, mash them together into some reliable string representation, and send that over to the server side.

How Can I Serialize Then?

To serialize, just use a nice method from Prototype, of course. And you have a few to choose from, depending on your use case:

```
fieldElt.serialize() → String
formElt.serialize([options]) → String | hashObj
Form.serializeElements(elements, [options]) → String | hashObj
```

Let's start simple, with the serialization of only one field. All fields feature a serialize() method, which either returns an empty string (if the

Joe Asks. . .
Why Should I Serialize?

You use serialization when you captured information thanks to a form field (or a whole form) and now need to send this data over the wire in some suitable format. And Prototype's serialization plays nicely with HTTP.

When a form is submitted the regular way, the browser takes care of this for you. When you take over, you're a bit more on your own. Serialization becomes your business, not the browser's anymore.

You can do this from an HTML page in two ways: with a GET request, using URL-encoded parameters right in the URL (as in /myapp/users/list?filter=john&details=yes), or with a POST request, using parameters in the request body. The default format for these is, indeed, the very same URL-encoding you would use in a GET request. It is the format attached to the MIME type *application/x-www-form-urlencoded*, which rules supreme on the Web.

That is why our serialization methods use that format. If you need something else (say, XML or JSON), you can easily grab the form fields you're interested in—which is what we learned to do in the previous section—and cook it up just to your taste (a pinch of basil would be nice). It can be as simple as this:

```
Object.toJSON($(ourForm).serialize(true))
```

Calling serialize(true) returns a hash-like object instead of the default serialized string. The generic Object.toJSON() mechanism will easily process this vanilla object. But for most cases, you should be happy with the default serialization. After all, this is what most server-side technologies natively work with.

field value is **undefined**, which should almost never happen except for files) or returns a *name=value* string, with its two parts properly URL-encoded.

Now, here's the nitty-gritty, which mostly boils down to regular HTML form serialization:

- Values are based on the getValue() method we discussed earlier.

- Fields with **null** values will be handled as if their value were an empty string.

- Fields with undefined values will be serialized with only their name as key (no = sign).

- Fields with array values (that is, multiple-selection listboxes) get serialized as if there were multiple fields with this same name, one per value.

The two other methods are closely related and deal with serializing part or all of a form. Calling serialize() on a form simply forwards to Form.serializeElements() using all elements in the form (except for type="submit" elements, where only one will be used, which is by default the first one).

Most of the time you're happy with a URL-encoded string representation, which is what you get by default. If you pass a hash option with the value **true**, you'll get the resulting hash object (not actually a Hash instance, just a vanilla JavaScript object) back, containing all field names and values, which you can then use to build your own serialization.

By default, if there are multiple type="submit" fields, only the first one in document order will be serialized. You can change that by specifying the value of the name= attribute for the submission field you want to serialize. Just specify it as the submit option.

For instance, the following call:

```
$('myForm').serialize({ hash: true, submit: 'delete' })
```

...will return a serialization hash (not a preencoded string), having used the name="delete" submit field instead of the first one in the form.

What About File Fields?

When a form contains a file field (<*input*> with type="file"), traditional serialization cannot happen anymore. Instead of using regular URL-style encoding, the form must be transmitted as *multipart/form-data* and encode the file bytes in a specific MIME part.

Manually creating this multipart encoding would not be difficult, but JavaScript security prevents it from accessing the contents of local files directly (unless you tinker with it, which is beyond most user's abilities or access rights). Because of this, Prototype cannot use actual Ajax for sending local files.

The usual workaround for this is to use a hidden <*iframe*> as the target for the <*form*> and submit the form the regular way. Once the <*iframe*> is done loading the result, we can access it through scripting. This is rather old-school and a bit ugly, but so far this is all we have.

Note than a later version of Prototype may autoswitch to such a technique when you're trying to Ajaxify a form with file fields. In the meantime, you can find detailed walk-throughs for this on many web pages, such as http://www.webtoolkit.info/ajax-file-upload.html (and a Google search on *Ajax file upload* will yield tons of other options).

Streamlining Ajax Forms with request

This chapter is about forms, not Ajax. We will dive into the details (and multiple options) of Ajax processing in Chapter 9, *Ajax Has Never Been So Easy*, on page 177. But there is a form-specific Ajax facility, which we'll look at quickly here. It appeared in Prototype 1.5.1 and aims at streamlining a very common use case: take a regular form, complete with method= and action=, and submit it over Ajax.

```
formElt.request([options]) → Ajax.Request
```

You'll have to refer to Section 9.2, *Options Common to All Ajax Objects*, on page 190 for all the details on the wealth of available options. Just know that this simple call (for example, $('myForm').request()) submits your form through Ajax, using its attributes to determine the HTTP verb

(GET or POST) and the target URL.[2] You can use this to unobtrusively turn your forms over to Ajax when JavaScript is enabled:

```
document.observe('contentloaded', function() {
  $$('form').invoke('observe', 'submit', function(e) {
    e.stop();
    $(Event.element(e)).request();
  });
});
```

This covers a common idiom but is certainly not sufficient for all situations. For more advanced needs, you will have to manually use Ajax. Request and its flock.

8.4 Keeping an Eye on Forms and Fields

In Section 6.3, *Reacting to Form-Related Content Changes*, on page 116, we discovered event-based observers for forms and fields. Whenever an event was triggered to herald a possible value change on a field (or somewhere in a form), these observers would verify that a change had indeed occurred and, if satisfied, would trigger a callback.

Such an approach is not always satisfactory: change-related events trigger late (usually when the field loses focus), too late for some uses (such as autocompletion or on-the-fly validation). Enter time-based observers:

```
new Form.Observer(formElt, interval, callback)
new Field.Observer(fieldElt, interval, callback)
observer.stop()
```

These observers work the same way, but they require an interval or period (expressed in seconds, with fractional numbers allowed), which determines how often they will check up on the data they're observing (field observers check up on a single field, and form observers check up on the whole set of values within the form, relying on serialization for it). Aside from this, the rules do not change. As soon as there actually is a new value (including, obviously, the first time it checks), the callback is triggered.

We used a time-based field observer in our consolidated example in Chapter 7, *Playing with the DOM Is Finally Fun!*, on page 119, in order to enable or disable buttons based on whether a text field was blank.

---

2. Starting with Prototype 1.6, if *<form>* features no action= attribute or an empty one, the current URL will be used.

Waiting for the field to lose its focus was inadequate. The user might click the enabled button only to find it suddenly disabled because by clicking, the text field would lose its focus. Visual feedback needed to take place earlier and be *live*. The resulting code was confoundingly simple:

```
new Field.Observer('edtName', 0.3, function() {
  $('btnSubmit').disabled = $F('edtName').blank();
});
```

Checking every 0.3" is definitely live enough (the user won't have to consciously wait after they type to see the UI get updated) but large enough an interval not to hog the processor.

1.6

Since Prototype 1.6, these observer classes descend from PeriodicalExecuter, so they inherit its stop() method, which lets you put the observer to rest.

What We Just Learned

Here are the main take-away points about Prototype's form-related features:

- The features operate at two levels: full forms (the Form namespace) and individual fields (the Field namespace, which is an alias of Form.Element).

- Most methods in these namespaces appear as additional extensions on the relevant DOM elements.

- Most of the API deals with value retrieval and setting, either individually through getValue() and setValue() or at the form's level through such methods as serialize().

- Prototype smooths over cross-browser inconsistencies in field value retrieval (on such issues as no-value-attribute list elements or elements that can be toggled) and provides a powerful value-setting mechanism that helps implement dynamic form filling.

- Form serialization is handy for Ajax submission of the data, but common cases can be automated one step further using the request() method.

- Interval-based observers let us react quickly to changes in a form or individual field to implement dynamic behavior (such as enabling or disabling parts of the UI based on the current form data).

Neuron Workout

- How would you implement an equivalent of Field.Observer using PeriodicalExecuter[3] directly? What about Form.Observer?

- Write a method that takes all the radio buttons with a given field name and toggles their availability (enables or disables them, depending on their state).

---

3. For details on this class, see Section 10.3, *Periodical Execution Without Risk of Reentrance*, on page 221.

Ajax Has Never Been So Easy

In another book, I might have to explain to you what Ajax is, why it is useful, and why it is not just a fad. But not here. This is a book about Prototype and script.aculo.us, which are *big* on Ajax. If you have this book, chances are extremely good you know what Ajax is well enough and have embraced the opportunities it offers. So in essence, you're sold on the idea of Ajax. If you have no idea what it is, you can catch up quickly on the Web, such as at http://en.wikipedia.org/wiki/AJAX or http://developer.mozilla.org/en/docs/AJAX.

But you're probably dying to know more about it and about how Prototype and script.aculo.us let you use it to best effect.

As for script.aculo.us, it does provide wonderful little Ajax-based controls, such as an autocompleted text field. Many common Ajax-related use cases (for example, sorting a list and persisting its new order server-side) will be best approached using script.aculo.us stuff, so we will delay such examples until a later chapter.

But when it comes to Prototype itself, there's a lot to have fun with. Because simply listing and explaining the classes, options, and callbacks would probably be a bit dry, I decided to lace this chapter with several core implementations of actual web app features you're likely to need on real-world projects. Those are the "Get It" sections in this chapter. They do their best to illustrate most of the API.

9.1 Before We Start...

Yes, you're giddy with anticipation. I know, I can't wait to show you this stuff, too. But before we get on with Prototype objects and let the magic flow, there are a few general issues I'd like to talk to you about.

Technical Limitations You Should Know About

There are essentially two constraints in Ajax: the SOP and the two-request limit.

The *Same Origin Policy* (SOP) essentially mandates that Ajax requests cannot access another fully qualified domain than the page from which they're running. You can't even access the same domain on another port. This makes a lot of sense, securitywise, because this would open a Pandora's box of cross-site scripting (XSS) attacks. Imagine a malevolent script running on a sensitive intranet page that could use its privileged position to access confidential data and then silently send those over to its author's cracking domain. . . . Not good.

The SOP is all about XSS (how's that for a geek phrase?) and also prescribes what other documents in the browser a given script is allowed to access (for example, explore or modify their DOM). Originated in Netscape Communicator 2.0, this approach is widely supported by modern browsers (although, as usual, Internet Explorer acts the lone wolf on this). You'll find a great description of the SOP, and links to more detailed resources, on the ever-useful Wikipedia: http://en.wikipedia. org/wiki/Same_origin_policy.

The second general issue you need to keep in mind when designing Ajax-based pages, especially if you intend to use Ajax heavily, is the infamous two-request limit. This is a recommendation in the defining standard for us kids: HTTP/1.1. It is described in RFC 2616, and section 8.1.4[1] clearly states that "a single-user client SHOULD NOT maintain more than 2 connections with any server or proxy. [. . .] This is intended to improve HTTP response time and avoid congestion."

Most modern browsers abide by this rule, including Internet Explorer. True, you can tweak this, but this requires manual client-side configuration (for Internet Explorer, you would have to tweak a registry key, and Firefox would have you tinker at internal options using about: config). In short, unless you have an absolute need for more simultaneous requests, have servers that can indeed handle the resulting load, and have enough control over the whole browser base (as in an intranet), you can forget using more than two connections at once.

This works for any request, incidentally. When the browser fetches external resources for your web page, such as images, CSS files, script

---

1. http://tools.ietf.org/html/rfc2616#section-8.1.4

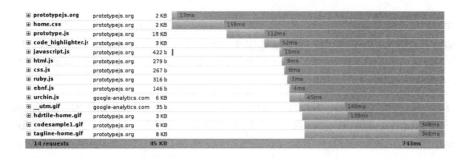

⊞ prototypejs.org	prototypejs.org	2 KB	17ms				
⊞ home.css	prototypejs.org	2 KB		159ms			
⊞ prototype.js	prototypejs.org	18 KB			112ms		
⊞ code_highlighter.js	prototypejs.org	3 KB			52ms		
⊞ javascript.js	prototypejs.org	422 b			10ms		
⊞ html.js	prototypejs.org	279 b			9ms		
⊞ css.js	prototypejs.org	267 b			6ms		
⊞ ruby.js	prototypejs.org	316 b			7ms		
⊞ ebnf.js	prototypejs.org	146 b			4ms		
⊞ urchin.js	google-analytics.com	6 KB				45ms	
⊞ __utm.gif	google-analytics.com	35 b				140ms	
⊞ hdrtile-home.gif	prototypejs.org	3 KB				138ms	
⊞ codesample1.gif	prototypejs.org	6 KB					348ms
⊞ tagline-home.gif	prototypejs.org	8 KB					346ms
14 requests		45 KB					743ms

Figure 9.1: THE TWO-REQUEST LIMIT IN ACTION AT PROTOTYPEJS.ORG

files, and the like, it follows this guideline as well. Have a look at Firebug's Net tab for the home page of Prototype's official site, shown in Figure 9.1. Notice how there are never more than two resources being loaded at any given time.

There are workarounds, of course, such as tinkering with *<iframe>* to create the illusion of multiple "users" (from a HTTP/1.1 standpoint), playing with server-side configuration and DNS mapping to alias multiple subdomains over the same server, and distributing requests across such domains (which brings quite a few issues, though, such as being careful with cookies and the SOP). Still, I believe 99.9% of the UI needs for web applications should be properly covered despite the two-request limit, especially with a fast server.

Under the Hood: A Quick XHR Primer

We're entering a critical topic, and I believe a bit of background wouldn't hurt, both on the path that led to today's situation and on the technical tidbits.

A Tiny Bit of History

Ajax is all about a small object named *XMLHttpRequest*.[2] And because good men put credit where it's due, I find it important to state that this one was invented by none other than Microsoft. It first appeared in Internet Explorer 5.0, all the way back in 1999. The first compatible implementation appeared in Mozilla 1.0 in 2002, and now every major

---

2. Well, technically, on some occasions you'll have to revert to ugly *<iframe>* tricks, but let's not split hairs!

browser (including Firefox, Safari, Opera, and Konqueror) plus a few smaller players (for example, iCab) feature it with a rather good compatibility. All those compatible implementations are exposed as a native JavaScript object.

Although originally a proprietary technology, XMLHttpRequest was deemed of sufficient interest to now be specified by a W3C recommendation,[3] which at the time of this writing is about to enter a second (!) *Last Call* phase and should become an official standard sometime before 2007 ends. This working draft is already used as the basis for interoperability by implementations in all the major browsers.

XMLHttpRequest was originally exposed to the script as an ActiveX control and remained so until Internet Explorer 7.0, which finally provides it as a native JavaScript object, thereby adopting a unified model with other browsers and making it available to security-conscious environments.

The Life and Works of XHR

In the rest of this book, we'll mostly use the shorter XHR abbreviation for it. An XHR object has the following life cycle (normative states appear in *italics*):

1. You create it. It's *uninitialized*.

2. You open a connection to the server side. It's *open*.

3. If necessary, you set request headers according to your needs.

4. You send the request (and any body contents for the HTTP request you may need to include). It becomes *sent*.

5. The server side starts responding. Your object is now *receiving*.

6. You're done getting all of the response. It is now *loaded*.

This is the official life cycle, but legacy implementations, which are still the most widespread ones, may differ slightly. As we'll see in Section 9.2, *Hooking Up Our Code: Ajax Callbacks*, on page 194, Prototype defines a series of callbacks for state changes and events mapping to the official states, plus a few ones. But not all those callbacks are "guaranteed." Some of them may not fire with the same semantics on all browsers or sometimes not fire at all; I even see occasional reports

---

3.   http://www.w3.org/TR/XMLHttpRequest/

of callbacks firing in a different order, although reproducing these oddities often proves challenging. Fortunately, the key ones (especially the completion-related ones) are safe.

Should We Reuse Our XHR Objects?

Although in Prototype this translates to "Should we reuse our Ajax.* objects?" the question is equally as valid. These are network connections that we are talking about. Such an object has a nontrivial creation and initialization cost, and we may want to reuse them in order to speed things up.

Well, let me give you some perspective.

First, from a technical standpoint, reuse is not free of issues, depending on the browser you're on, the way you manipulate the original methods of the XHR object, and a few other points. So, it's not as simple as simply keeping a reference on it and ending up calling open( ) and send( ) again and again.

Second, this is *UI* we're talking about. You're using Ajax to smooth things up, to make your UI snappier, to avoid full-page reload, and to interact more richly with the user. The time constraints we face here are *user time*, where a satisfactory response delay is of the order of one second. Plus, we're bound by this two-request limit anyway. Overusing XHR objects will end up delaying most of them, resulting in the opposite effect: increased latency.

For the overall scheme of things, the setup cost for an XHR object (and thus, for an Ajax.* object in Prototype) is fairly negligible. If your UI is properly designed (especially from an ergonomy perspective), you'll be well in the clear with creating such objects when you need them and discarding the references afterward.

Response Types: XHTML, XML, JS, JSON...

Yes, the *X* in Ajax stands for XML. That's right. That's also far from real use, as far as I can see when reading the 30-some daily posts on the official Prototype help list,[4] used by 4,000+ people.

The simple truth is this: most Ajax responses provide (X)HTML fragments, JavaScript, or both. This includes JavaScript Object Notation (JSON)[5] responses.

---

4. http://groups.google.com/group/rubyonrails-spinoffs
5. http://json.org

"Pure XML" (by which I mean not XHTML, but other XML dialects) responses are quite the rare thing. In my humble opinion, this is because the main reason for XML responses was structured data, and we get this in a far more convenient format with JSON. All we have to do is eval() it, and we get an immediately usable JavaScript object representing all our data! That sure beats the living crap out of DOM traversal.

Here are a few guidelines to help you decide what format to use, depending on your circumstances:

- You just dealt with creating or updating an item, which is part of a displayed list that needs to show the new or updated item? Use an item-level template to produce its XHTML fragment, and send it back for client-side insertion in the page. You can append a small inline script to it that will trigger some attention-getter effect (such as a highlight).

- You're being polled so the server keeps track of things? Rely on HTTP status codes and minimalistic contents for the response's text proper (perhaps a simple number or text or a more structured JSON representation).

- Your only response is JavaScript code (for example, effect triggering)? Instead of returning an HTML-typed response with a *<script>* tag, use a JavaScript MIME type (the most common one being *text/javascript*), and put the raw JavaScript code in the response body. It will be evaluated automatically by the requester object. This constitutes, by far, the easiest way to return dynamic behavior from the server side so your client page executes it.

- You have no idea what I'm talking about? Just read on and grab the examples.

JSON and Prototype: Like Peas in a Pod... Now

When Prototype 1.5.0 was released in January 2007, the help list began receiving a lot of buzz about issues people were having with their Ajax features being broken all of a sudden. As it turned out, Prototype's Ajax request header mechanism relied on JavaScript's **for...in** loop, which iterates over all the properties of an object. The object used here was a local anonymous one, which sounded safe enough.

Well, it is safe until some loaded script breaks the ground rules and starts expanding Object.prototype: then we get in trouble. That is what, unfortunately, the "official" JSON library, json.js, does. The thing is, when you get interested in JSON, you go to its official site, discover there's a library all waiting for you, and grab it! It's too bad it comes with this major misbehavior. Of course, this impacts users who rely on higher-level frameworks that provided the same (or same kind of) code, such as Rico. All in all, that's a lot of people.

Prototype 1.5.1 decided to retain the occasional **for...in** loop, which should never break when other scripts behave, but it implemented JSON support (and credit for that mostly goes to Tobie Langel). It introduced built-in, comprehensive JSON support, from JSON parsing to JSON building, all of which is described in Section 4.7, *Full-Spectrum JSON Support*, on page 70.

Prototype 1.6 also introduces a host of new JSON-related options for requests, plus the new Ajax.Response object, which do a terrific job simplifying JSON processing in an Ajax context. You have Tobie Langel to thank for that.

9.2 Hitting the Road: Ajax.Request

We're not going to dive into the details of raw XHR objects. There's just no point. With Prototype, you'll never need to touch these objects directly, at least not until they're done with the whole request/response thing. So, why bother? We're much better off focusing on the features and objects Prototype offers us.

Ajax.Request is the fundamental requester object. The other ones all depend on it. It's the heart of Prototype's Ajax support. Using it is fairly simple: just create the object with the proper arguments and options, and off it goes, querying your server side and dealing with the response! You usually won't even need to store the object reference (as we discussed in Section 9.1, *Should We Reuse Our XHR Objects?*, on page 181).

```
new Ajax.Request(url [, options])
```

I tried to make this as lively as possible, because there is a lot to discover and learn. So, we'll go through an actual application feature example first and then go through the common options and callbacks all Ajax.* objects share.

Get It: Geometry Persistence

Our first example will use Ajax to implement geometry persistence. In a less formal tone, we're trying to keep widgets tucked somewhere from one page view to the next, OK? Here's how it goes:

- The server side holds the "geometry" of each widget. To keep things simple and the code concise enough, we'll assume that they do have a default position and that the user can only move them, not resize them.

- The server side is used to produce the initial page view, which is necessary in order for page views to restore any previously persisted geometry.

- Whenever a widget is moved, we react to the move's ending by synchronizing the server-side storage. To do that, we use a simple Ajax request containing the geometry of all widgets.

We're going to use Ruby scripts to provide a server side for all our Ajax-enabled examples. You may panic a bit at this if you don't know a thing about Ruby or have never used it yourself before. As Douglas Adams would say, Don't Panic. It's a walk in the park. Head over to the few pages in Appendix C, on page 409, and then come back ready to play; it's quick and painless—it's even fun!

To keep things simple, there's no actual database here—only global variables storing both the widgets' contents (title and text) and their geometry. Here goes the server script:

`prototype/ajax/geometry/server.rb`

```ruby
Line 1   #! /usr/bin/env ruby

    -    require 'cgi'
    -    require 'erb'
    5    require 'webrick'
    -    include WEBrick

    -    template_text = File.read('index.rhtml')
    -    template = ERB.new(template_text)
   10
    -    server = HTTPServer.new(:Port => 8042)
    -    server.mount('/', HTTPServlet::FileHandler, '.')

    -    LABELS = [
   15      { :title => 'Some widget',
    -          :text => 'This is a widget' },
    -        { :title => 'Some other widget',
```

```
   -          :text => "This is another widget.\nIt's just bigger, you know." },
   -       { :title => 'Yet another widget',
  20          :text => 'This is a third widget.  It\'s actually quite small.' }
   -       ]
   -
   -    $geometry = [
   -       { :left => 20, :top => 100, :zIndex => 1},
  25       { :left => 220, :top => 160, :zIndex => 2},
   -       { :left => 400, :top => 130, :zIndex => 3}
   -       ]
   -
   -    server.mount_proc('/home') do |request, response|
  30      response['Content-Type'] = 'text/html'
   -      response.body = template.result(binding)
   -    end
   -
   -    server.mount_proc('/geometry') do |request, response|
  35      params = request.query
   -      $geometry.each_with_index do |pos, index|
   -        [:top, :left, :zIndex].each { |key|
   -          pos[key] = params[key.to_s + index.to_s].to_i
   -        }
  40      end
   -      response.body = 'OK.'
   -    end
   -
   -    trap('INT') { server.shutdown }
  45
   -    server.start
```

I use ERb, a prominent templating engine in Ruby, to deal with template text, which is the template for our whole page. Looking at the parameter analysis snippet starting at line 36, you can see that we expect a set of three parameters for each widget, with each parameter being suffixed with the widget's numerical index. Our client side will take care of building this parameter string properly. It could look something like this:

left0=100&top0=50&zIndex0=1&left1=224&top1=100&zIndex1=2...

The template for the whole page is fairly simple. It just uses a loop over LABELS to produce properly styled XHTML fragments with an adequate title and contents. It's nothing too fancy:

prototype/ajax/geometry/index.rhtml

```
<!DOCTYPE html PUBLIC "-//W3C//DTD XHTML 1.0 Strict//EN"
 "http://www.w3.org/TR/xhtml1/DTD/xhtml1-strict.dtd">
<html xmlns="http://www.w3.org/1999/xhtml" lang="en" xml:lang="en">
```

```
<head>
  <meta http-equiv="Content-Type" content="text/html; charset=utf-8" />
  <title>Drag it up!</title>
  <link rel="stylesheet" type="text/css" href="geometry.css" />
  <script type="text/javascript" src="prototype.js"></script>
  <script type="text/javascript"
   src="scriptaculous.js?load=effects,dragdrop"></script>
  <script type="text/javascript" src="geometry.js"></script>
</head>
<body>
  <h1>Drag it up!</h1>
<%
LABELS.each_with_index do |labels, index|
  pos = $geometry[index]
  style = "top: #{pos[:top]}px; left: #{pos[:left]}px; "
  style += "z-index: #{pos[:zIndex]};"
%>
<div id="win<%= index %>" class="widget" style="<%= style %>">
  <h2><%= labels[:title] %></h2>
  <% labels[:text].each_line do |line| %>
  <p><%= line %></p>
  <% end %>
</div>
<% end %>
</body>
</html>
```

Of course, this will require a dollop of CSS styling to look any good:

`prototype/ajax/geometry/geometry.css`

```css
.widget {
  position: absolute; top: 5em; width: 15em;
  border: 0.25em solid gray; background: silver;
  padding: 1em 0.5em 0.5em;
  overflow: auto;
}

.widget h2 {
  position: absolute;
  top: 0; left: 0; right: 0; height: 1.5em;
  font-size: inherit; line-height: 1.5em;
  margin: 0; padding: 0 0.2ex;
  background: gray; cursor: move;
}

#win0 {
  border-color: red; background: #fdd;
  height: 8em; left: 2em;
}

#win0 h2 { background: #f99; color: maroon; }
```

```
#win1 {
  border-color: green; background: #dfd;
  left: 20em; height: 10em;
}

#win1 h2 { background: #9f9; color: #080; }

#win2 {
  border-color: blue; background: #ddf;
  left: 38em; height: 6em;
}

#win2 h2 { background: #99f; color: #008; }
```

Well, before we start hurling some JavaScript-fu at this, we might as well check out the initial state to verify we set it up properly. Get a shell in this example's directory, and start your server:

```
$ ruby server.rb
[2007-03-09 23:19:49] INFO  WEBrick 1.3.1
[2007-03-09 23:19:49] INFO  ruby 1.8.5 (2006-08-25) [i486-linux]
[2007-03-09 23:19:55] INFO  WEBrick::HTTPServer#start: pid=24720 port=8042
```

OK, let's fire up our trusty browser and navigate to http://localhost:8042/ home (don't forget the *home* at the end, or you'll get no response or even a mistaken binary download attempt). We should get something like Figure 9.2, on the next page.

The XHTML fragment for our widgets looks like this:

```
<div id="win0" class="widget"
 style="top: 100px; left: 20px; z-index: 1;">
  <h2>Some widget</h2>
  <p>This is a widget</p>
</div>

<div id="win1" class="widget"
 style="top: 160px; left: 220px; z-index: 2;">
  <h2>Some other widget</h2>
  <p>This is another widget.  </p>
  <p>It's just bigger, you know.</p>
</div>

<div id="win2" class="widget"
 style="top: 130px; left: 400px; z-index: 3;">
  <h2>Yet another widget</h2>
  <p>This is a third widget.  It's actually quite small.</p>
</div>
```

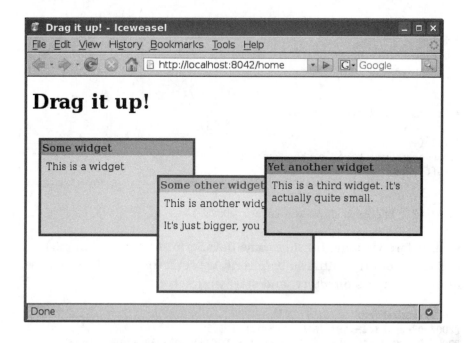

Figure 9.2: OUR INITIAL VIEW. LOOKING GOOD!

Now for the JavaScript. We'll resort to some script.aculo.us mojo to bring off the drag and drop. When the page is done loading, we create Draggable objects[6] over every widget, using its internal <h2> as a handle (dragging by the title bar is a natural UI reflex for most folks). We'll also register a global drag-and-drop observer to react to drags ending by firing up an Ajax request.

It doesn't even take 40 lines of JavaScript to cover the whole process:

`prototype/ajax/geometry/geometry.js`

```
function bindWidgets() {
  var widgets = $$('.widget');
  widgets.each(function(w) {
    var handle = w.down('h2');
    handle.observe('mousedown', function() {
      raiseWidget(widgets, w);
    });
    new Draggable(w, { handle: handle, zindex: false });
  });
} // bindWidgets
```

Line numbers: Line 1, -, -, -, 5, -, -, -, -, 10

---

6. We'll explore Draggable in detail later in this book, in Section 15.1, *Dragging Stuff Around*, on page 275.

```
     function raiseWidget(widgets, widget) {
       var widgetZIndex = widget.getStyle('zIndex');
       widgets.each(function(w) {
15       var zI = w.getStyle('zIndex');
         if (zI > widgetZIndex)
           w.setStyle({ zIndex: zI - 1 });
       });
       widget.setStyle({ zIndex: widgets.length });
20   } // raiseWidget

     function syncGeometryOnServer() {
       var widgets = $$('.widget');
       var params = {};
25     widgets.each(function(w, index) {
         var pos = Position.cumulativeOffset(w);
         params['left' + index] = pos[0];
         params['top' + index] = pos[1];
         params['zIndex' + index] = w.getStyle('zIndex');
30     });
       new Ajax.Request('/geometry', { parameters: params });
     } // syncGeometryOnServer

     Draggables.addObserver({ onEnd: syncGeometryOnServer });
35
     document.observe('dom:loaded', bindWidgets);
```

The bindWidgets() method iterates over our widgets (any element with class="widget"), isolates the *<h2>* in there, and does two things:

- It makes the widget draggable by creating a new Draggable object over it.

- It attaches an extra behavior to the handle's *mousedown* event: raiseWidget().

The raiseWidget() method is a nice touch we add to make widgets behave more like actual windows: the idea is to make sure the last one clicked or dragged is on top and stays there once the click or drag is over. The default Draggable behavior would temporarily raise the element's zIndex during the drag and restore it once dropped, which won't do. Plus, this would require an actual drag, and casual clicks would not bring the widget to the front.

So, what we do here is react to mouse buttons being pressed over a widget drag handle by rearranging zIndex properties so the current one comes naturally on top while preserving the remaining ordering. The algorithm for this is simple enough: take all "higher" widgets one notch down, and then get our own on top.

The actual Ajax magic happens on line 31. This is where we create an Ajax.Request object. Creating it will automatically trigger the request proper. Because this is our first example, the call is concise. Only the target URL (look at our server script to see it listens for /geometry requests in order to process updates) and the parameters for it. It will use default values for all other options, which especially means we're going POST on this one. The parameters will be transmitted as the request's body in the usual URL-encoded format.

The last trick is, of course, to *build* these parameters. To avoid tweaking URL-encoded stuff, we'll use the ability of the parameters option to take an object that it then uses as a hash of parameters. Building such an object is simple enough, as the code starting at line 25 demonstrates. For each widget, grab its absolute position, and then add the corresponding properties to the parameters object.

Let's drag our widgets a few times. Firebug's Ajax monitoring tells us about the requests that let the server side know what's going on, as you can see in Figure 9.3, on the next page.

Now just try refreshing the page. Or better: shut down your browser (but leave your server script running). Then fire it back up, and navigate again to the page (feel free to vacuum your cache before). You end up with a preserved layout! That's it! Persistent geometry!

Options Common to All Ajax Objects

Now that we went through a full, integrated example, I believe the time has come to take a look at the nice range of options you get with all Ajax requesters.

asynchronous

> Setting this to **false** results in synchronous requests, which are requests that will essentially freeze the script until a response has been fully received. That's rather bad form. Avoid it. I mean it.

> Defaults to **true**.

contentType

> This is the format of your request data. If you don't plan on using the default (which is what the browser would send for both POST and GET requests), change it accordingly so the server side doesn't have to guess. For instance, you may want to send your data as an XML document or as Base64-encoded binary data.

> Defaults to *application/x-www-form-urlencoded*.

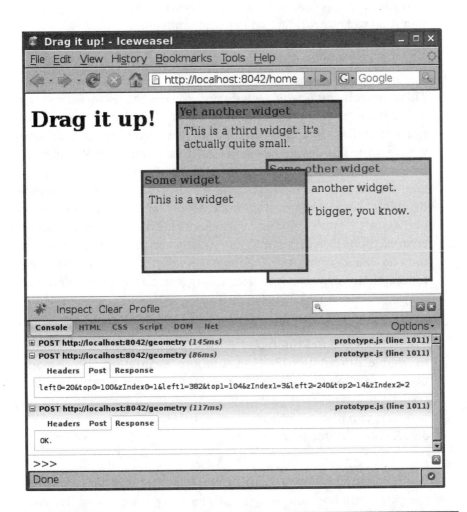

Figure 9.3: A FEW DRAGS AND THEIR TELLTALE AJAX REQUESTS

encoding

The character encoding for your request. This is best left untouched, unless you do run into weird encoding issues, but that would usually be because you haven't gone UTF-8 the whole way. And mark my words: sooner or later, you'll have to do so. So, you might as well start now and get some mileage.

Defaults to *UTF-8*.

1.6   evalJS

This controls *automatic JavaScript evaluation*. Before Prototype 1.6, whenever you got a response with a JavaScript content type (we'll describe that later in this chapter), your response's body was regarded as JavaScript and eval'd automatically. We now provide some control over that through this new option. It defaults to **true**, which preserves usual behavior. But you can set it to **false**, disabling JavaScript evaluation entirely, or you can go berserk and set it to 'force', asking for JavaScript evaluation *regardless of content type*. This latter mode is mostly for the poor guys among us who use a server-side technology so bad it won't let them customize their response handlers (I suggest a minute of silence for them).

1.6   evalJSON

Also introduced in Prototype 1.6, this new option controls whether to enable automatic JSON evaluation, evaluating the response body as JSON and storing the resulting object in the response object's responseJSON property. It defaults to **true**, and just like evalJS, it can also be **false** or 'force', with the same semantics. The JSON content type is *application/json*. Also see sanitizeJSON.

method

The HTTP method used. Current implementations guarantee only the two methods allowed by HTML forms: *get* and *post*. The W3C recommendation for XMLHttpRequest, however, acknowledging the ever-growing interest of REST, mandates that compatible implementations support all six methods defined by HTTP/1.1, including for instance *put* and *delete*. Currently, using such values (that is, anything but *get* or *post*) will trigger one of the very few Rails-specific behaviors of Prototype. It will actually use *post* and will include a _method parameter in the data, with the original value. This circumvents the fact that browsers such as Safari and Internet Explorer do not yet accept these HTTP methods for XMLHttpRequest.

Defaults to *post*.

parameters

The parameters to be sent by the request, specified either as a hash-like object (quite the convenient way and the one we used in our geometry persistence example) or as a predigested, URL-encoded string.

Defaults to the empty string.

postBody

The request body data if you're using the *post* method. Because not providing it will use parameters instead and because it does not allow using a hash-like object but requires a properly URL-encoded query string, I advise you to use parameters whenever you don't need another representation for your data.

No default value.

requestHeaders

The headers sent with your request. It is best to pass a hash-like object. For backward compatibility, you can also pass an array of values, with even indices for header names and odd indices for header values. However, support for this might be discontinued in later releases, and it's also a more cryptic way to go, so I advise you to go the hash-object way. The default set contains the following headers:

- X-Requested-With: *XMLHttpRequest*
- X-Prototype-Version: Whatever version you're using (for example, *1.6.0*)
- Accept: *text/javascript, text/html, application/xml, text/xml, and */**
- Content-Type: Built based on the contentType and encoding options

sanitizeJSON

1.6

Introduced in Prototype 1.6, this is the companion option to eval-JSON. It controls whether JSON evaluation (be it the *X-JSON* header or the response body) goes through sanity checks before being evaluated. This delegates to String's extended evalJSON() method, shown on page 72.

Ajax.Response and Backward Compatibility

Tobie, who's responsible for the Ajax.Response refactoring, made sure the code remained backward compatible. This is why these objects feature the same crucial properties, such as transport and readyState.

However, there are many more properties designed to help you manipulate the response in a more portable, type-oriented way. You should get familiar with headerJSON and responseJSON, for instance.

Hooking Up Our Code: Ajax Callbacks

Aside from options proper, you can pass, in the options object, callbacks to be called at specific times in the request's life cycle. Prototype defines quite a handful of those, but beware: XHR-level callbacks are not quite "guaranteed," meaning they may not work consistently across browsers, because the W3C specification has not yet been finalized, much less widely implemented. Such callbacks are *emphasized* when listed.

1.6

Note that all callbacks, when defined on an individual requester like this, are called with two arguments: the current state of the Ajax response (an Ajax.Response object) and the evaluation of the *X-JSON* header, if any (this one can be **null**, especially prior to response completion). The onException callback, however, gets different arguments: the requester object and the exception object.

The Ajax.Response object you get lets you access your response's data in a comfortable, portable way, smoothing over some issues with the timing restrictions of calling specific methods on the underlying XHR object (for example, header-related ones) and taking special care of JSON handling (because of its rising popularity). We'll explore it in greater depth later in this chapter.

Callbacks are listed here in chronological order, instead of lexicographical order. I thought you'd like to find both the callback's timing and the definition in the same place.

onCreate

The object was created, with its request about to be prepared and sent.

onUninitialized*(not guaranteed)*

> The XHR was just created.

onLoading*(not guaranteed)*

> The XHR is being set up, with its connection open.

onLoaded*(not guaranteed)*

> The XHR is set up, with its connection open, and is ready to send data.

onInteractive*(not guaranteed)*

> The XHR has sent its request, and it is now receiving parts of the response.

onFailure

> The response was received, its HTTP status code is not considered successful (see next callback), and it doesn't have a dedicated callback in place (see onXYZ).

onSuccess

> The response was received, its HTTP status code is considered successful (it's in the 200–299 range), and it does not have a dedicated callback in place (see the next callback).

onXYZ

> The response was received, and its HTTP status code is *XYZ.* You usually won't define such surgical callbacks for successful codes, but you may want to deal in a special way with, say, codes like 302 or 404....[7]

onComplete

> As you can derive from the three previous callbacks' definitions, they are mutually exclusive. When a request is complete, however, you do end up getting onComplete triggered (this is even shielded against exceptions in the specific callbacks that occur before, for example, onSuccess).

onException

> This can actually happen at just about any point in the request life cycle. When something goes wrong, it's triggered. The second argument is the exception object.

---

7. For further details on the HTTP status codes, see the HTTP/1.1 RFC at http://tools.ietf.org/html/rfc2616.

Other Things Our Ajax.Request Can Do

There are a few more things your requester can do for you, which can be of assistance in your callbacks' code. . . .

Every requester has a success() method that implements the success/failure logic (it returns a boolean) used for callback selection. There's also a getHeader(name) method that lets you grab a response header easily and returns **null** if the header is missing or something borks.

An important feature is *automatic JavaScript evaluation*. When a response consists entirely of JavaScript, the best way for the server to send it is to put the raw script in the response body and advertise the response's content type as JavaScript. Prototype recognizes all accepted values for the response's *Content-Type* header (anything with a main type of *text* or *application* and a subtype of *javascript* or *ecmascript*, possibly prefixed with *x-*).

When such a response is received, the requesters will automatically eval() it. Pay attention to the timing. This occurs *after* specific callbacks (onSuccess, onFailure, and onXYZ), but *before* the generic onComplete. The evaluation logic is wrapped in the evalResponse() method.

This is a very powerful mechanism and easy to leverage from the server side. Rails has RJS templates, for instance, but any good server technology, as long as it has the ability to encode objects to JSON, can quickly whip up similar plumbing. For instance, a recent Rails app of mine features the following template:

```
page["fee_price_#{@att.id}"].update(format_price(@att.fee_price)).
  highlight
page['total_price'].update(format_price(@att.registration.total_price)).
  highlight
```

This can result in the following JavaScript code being returned to the server (with the proper JavaScript MIME type, which is key to automatic evaluation):

```
$('fee_price_42').update('100€').highlight();
$('total_price').update('250€').highlight();
```

Dealing with Ajax.Response

Starting with Prototype 1.6, the first argument to all callbacks (save for onException) is an Ajax.Response object that represents, well, your Ajax response. This object exhibits the following properties and methods, which make it at once backward compatible, safer to use (read: better dealing with exceptions and timing constraints), and more powerful:

getAllHeaders( )

> This is an exception-safe version of getAllResponseHeaders( ). It will return **null** instead of propagating the exception.

getAllResponseHeaders( )

> This forwards to the native method of the same name on the underlying XHR object. It returns all the response headers as a single, protocol-extracted string. But if you're not yet far along enough (in other words, you didn't receive all the response headers over the wire yet), this raises an INVALID_STATE_ERR exception.

getHeader(name)

> This is the same method as available on Ajax requesters, which I described in the previous section.

getResponseHeader(name)

> This forwards to the native method of the same name on the underlying XHR object. It returns the value for the given header or **null** if the header doesn't exist in the response. However, if you're not far along in receiving the response yet, you'll get an INVALID_STATE_ERR exception (as opposed to getHeader( ), which will swallow the exception and return a **null**).

headerJSON

> This is a new property introduced in 1.6. It contains the evaluation of the *X-JSON* header, if any (otherwise it is either **undefined** or **null**, depending on how far along the response reception you are). I advise you to rely on this property instead of the second argument to most callbacks, because the latter is likely to be deprecated in later versions of Prototype.

readyState

> This mirrors the native property of the same name on the underlying XHR object. Just remember that 4 means we're done receiving the response.

responseJSON

> This is a new property introduced in 1.6. Based on the JSON-related options (refer to on page 190), this interprets a JSON response *body*. This is a distinct thing from the *X-JSON* header,

and it was one of the prominent JSON-related feature requests for Prototype.

responseText

This is a safe version of the native property of the same name. It starts out **undefined**, then gets read at every state change until completion, and is guaranteed non-**null**. If it's not there yet on the underlying XHR object, you will see an empty string. This saves you from special-casing your code.

responseXML

This is available only once the response completes. This property is either a valid XML document or **null**. Whether it's interpreted from the response's body is decided by the underlying XHR object according to spec (which essentially means you'll have to send a response with a valid XML MIME type[8]).

status

This returns the underlying XHR object's property of the same name (or zero if it's unavailable just yet), which is the HTTP response code.

statusText

This is the status text going with the HTTP response status code or the empty string if this text is unavailable yet.

transport

This is the underlying XHR object. This is mostly provided for backward compatibility of your scripts, but I advise you strongly to migrate your code so it uses the response object's methods and properties instead of going raw like this. They're more portable, less exception-prone, and overall smarter.

9.3 Streamlining: Ajax.Updater

OK, that was for the common ground and the simple requests. Yet a common need for Ajax requests is to get some XHTML fragment back and inject it into our page. This fragment either replaces existing contents or is inserted somewhere. That's the whole idea of Ajax.Updater. The creation takes one more argument, which actually appears first—the container element(s) for the returned fragment.

---

8. This is essentially a type ending with either /xml or +xml. . . .

```
new Ajax.Updater(container, url [, options])
```

We'll demonstrate this through a search example that will use two new options, specific to updaters.

Get It: Ajax Search

We're going to put together an Ajax-based search. Because I don't want you to have to set up a data source to search through, we'll just use the libraries available to your Ruby server script. As an added perk, that means you have a decent shot at getting exactly the results you see in the book (or close enough, anyway).

The idea is simple: our page has a search field, we type a little text in it, and we hit the Search button, which sends an Ajax request. The server returns an XHTML fragment holding the search results (say, a simple <ul> list), which we display in a predefined "search results" element.

First, we need a search page:

`prototype/ajax/search1/index.html`

```html
<!DOCTYPE html PUBLIC "-//W3C//DTD XHTML 1.0 Strict//EN"
 "http://www.w3.org/TR/xhtml1/DTD/xhtml1-strict.dtd">
<html xmlns="http://www.w3.org/1999/xhtml" lang="en" xml:lang="en">
<head>
  <meta http-equiv="Content-Type" content="text/html; charset=utf-8" />
  <title>Ruby library AJAX search</title>
  <link rel="stylesheet" type="text/css" href="search.css" />
  <script type="text/javascript" src="prototype.js"></script>
  <script type="text/javascript" src="effects.js"></script>
  <script type="text/javascript" src="search.js"></script>
</head>
<body>
  <h1>Ruby library AJAX search</h1>

  <form id="searchForm" method="get" action="/search">
    <fieldset>
      <legend>Your search</legend>
      <p>
        <label for="edtSearch" accesskey="S">Your search</label>
        <input type="text" id="edtSearch" name="q" />
      </p>
      <p><input type="submit" value="Search!" /></p>
    </fieldset>
  </form>

  <div id="results"></div>
</body>
</html>
```

A pinch of CSS will help:

`prototype/ajax/search1/search.css`

```css
#searchForm fieldset, #results {
  width: 30em; margin: 1em auto; padding: 0.5em;
}
#searchForm fieldset { background: #ddd; }
#edtSearch { width: 20em; padding: 0 0.2ex; }
#edtSearch:active, #edtSearch:focus {
  background: #ffd; border: 2px solid black;
}
#results {
  border: 1px solid green; background: #dfd; color: #040;
}
#results ul { margin: 0; padding-left: 1em; }
#results li { font-family: monospace; }
```

Now the server script and our stage will be ready for the star, Java-Script, to make its entrance:

`prototype/ajax/search1/server.rb`

```ruby
#! /usr/bin/env ruby

require 'cgi'
require 'erb'
require 'webrick'
include WEBrick

template_text = File.read('results.rhtml')
template = ERB.new(template_text)

server = HTTPServer.new(:Port => 8042)
server.mount('/', HTTPServlet::FileHandler, '.')

def get_search_results(q)
  suffix = "/*#{Regexp.escape(q)}*.rb"
  $LOAD_PATH.map { |dir|
    Dir.glob(dir + suffix, File::FNM_CASEFOLD).map { |f|
      File.basename(f, '.rb')
    }
  }.flatten.sort.uniq
end

server.mount_proc('/search') do |request, response|
  q = request.query['q'] || ''
  results = get_search_results(q)
  response['Content-Type'] = 'text/html'
  response.body = template.result(binding)
end

trap('INT') { server.shutdown }

server.start
```

The get_search_results() method warrants some explanation. In these very few lines, we explore all the directories in which Ruby loads its standard libraries, grabbing for each one the list of Ruby files containing our query text, regardless of case. The filenames are purged of their path part, leaving only the basename, with no extension.

The preliminary result is an array of arrays of names (one array per library directory). We flatten it, sort, and remove potential duplicates. Our library name list is ready to be served!

There is, indeed, one last touch—the results template file, which is simple enough:

`prototype/ajax/search1/results.rhtml`

```
<% if results.empty? %>
<p>No result found.  Sorry!</p>
<% else %>
<ul>
<% results.each do |lib| %>
  <li><%= lib %></li>
<% end %>
</ul>
<% end %>
```

OK, now for the script. The idea is simple: intercept regular form submission to route it through Ajax instead, and dump the response text (the XHTML fragment produced by our template) into the results section. Here it is:

`prototype/ajax/search1/search.js`

```
function bindForm() {
  $('searchForm').observe('submit', function(e) {
    e.stop();
    new Ajax.Updater('results', this.action, {
      method: 'get', parameters: this.serialize()
    });
  });
} // bindForm

document.observe('dom:loaded', bindForm);
```

Yes, that's all there is to it. You'll have to find another excuse to suck your client's wallet dry. Now run the server script, and navigate to http://localhost:8042. You should see the initial page, as in Figure 9.4, on the following page.

Type in a query—say, "el"—and hit Return or activate the submission button. The page does not reload, but you should see results (or a

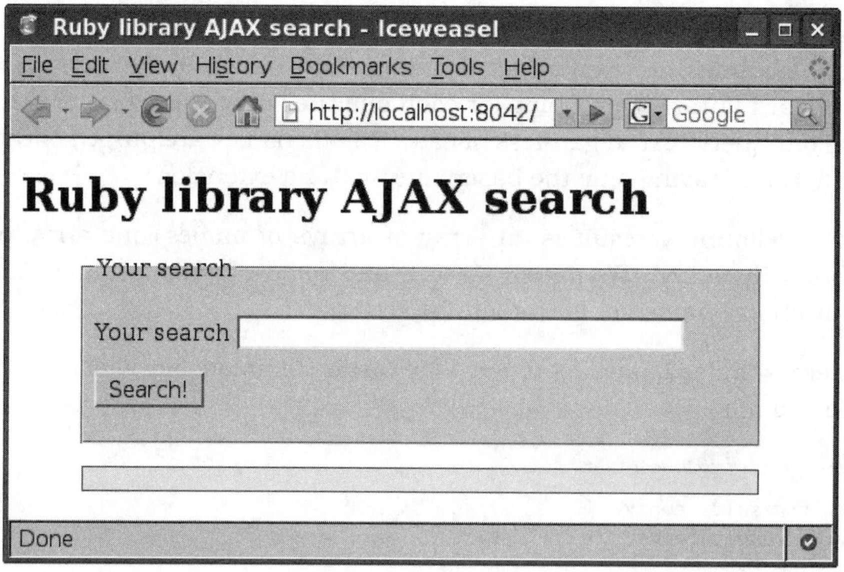

Figure 9.4: OUR INITIAL VIEW. READY TO SEARCH?

no-results message, depending on your query) appear in the results zone, as in Figure 9.5, on the next page.

That's nice, isn't it? I know, I know, you'll want to play with it for a while. Suit yourself. Call the colleagues over and boast (wait a minute, didn't you do that an hour ago with the geometry thing?). Rejoice. Prototype is here, and life is good. Try submitting an empty search if you want to see *all* the libraries.

It's time we look at the two new options Ajax.Updater has over Ajax. Requester yet. One of them is called evalScripts. Set to **true**, it will make sure any <*script*> tag in your returned fragment gets evaluated (once the rest of the fragment is present in the DOM). You see, by default, inline scripts are excised from your fragment, just in case. To make sure they're evaluated, just turn on evalScripts. Note they will be run as JavaScript through eval() (but you weren't planning on burping out VBScript stuff, were you?).

Let's add a bit of spice to our search view by initially hiding the search zone and have it roll down on the first results display, shall we?

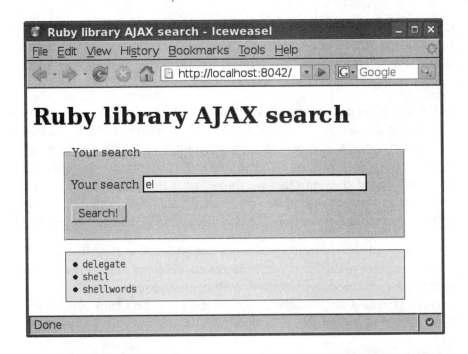

Figure 9.5: SEARCH RESULTS FOR "EL"

We'll just need to fix the initial view so the results area has an inline style effectively masking it:

```
<div id="results" style="display: none;"></div>
```

We also need to alter our template so that it now features, at the tail end of it, the inline script:

```
<script type="text/javascript">
var results = $('results');
if (!results.visible())
  new Effect.BlindDown(results);
</script>
```

And finally, we need to adjust the options set for our request so that scripts are evaluated:

```
new Ajax.Updater('results', this.action, {
  method: 'get', parameters: this.serialize(), evalScripts: true
});
```

OK, stop your server, and then run it again (it needs to load the update template for the results). Refresh the view. You'll note the results area is invisible at first. Type a query, and trigger the search: the results appear using a "blind down" effect. Isn't it nice?

There's another option we can use now, the last one for updaters: insertion. So far, our fragments have replaced the contents of their container (using Element.update(), which we saw on page 128). What if we need to *aggregate* successive fragments instead? For instance, we could want to keep a log of the searches we make, with the latest one on top. To do this, the insertion option lets you specify one of the Insertion objects, which we explored in Section 7.2, *Inserting New Contents*, on page 144.

It's easy as pie. Let's first update our template so it now includes our query (because we'll have multiple result sets, we might need to see which query yielded the results). We'll also adjust the final script so it triggers an effect on the whole results zone the first time and then on the inserted fragment the next time:

`prototype/ajax/search3/results.rhtml`

```
<% id = "results_#{Time.now.to_i}_#{rand 42}" %>
<div id="<%= id %>" style="display: none;">
  <h2>Results for &laquo;<%= q %>&raquo;:</h2>
<% if results.empty? %>
  <p>No result found.  Sorry!</p>
<% else %>
  <ul>
<% results.each do |lib| %>
    <li><%= lib %></li>
<% end %>
  </ul>
<% end %>
</div>
<script type="text/javascript">
var results = $('results');
if (!results.visible()) {
  $('<%= id %>').show();
  new Effect.BlindDown(results);
} else
  new Effect.BlindDown('<%= id %>');
</script>
```

Then we just need to adjust our script to use the proper option. We'll go for latest on top, so we'll use Insertion.Top:

```
new Ajax.Updater('results', this.action, {
  method: 'get', parameters: this.serialize(), evalScripts: true,
  insertion: 'top'
});
```

Again, stop and then restart your server and refresh your page. Then start making a few queries.... Does this *rock* or what? I mean, come on, we wrote a grand total of 110 lines of source code, including CSS and static HTML!

As a final note, there is another nice feature I haven't mentioned yet: the container option can be more than just an ID or DOM reference. Sometimes you need to differentiate between success and failure. You want to put the result somewhere in one case and somewhere else in the other case. Or maybe you don't want to update anything on failure. You just care about success. For both these situations, you can use an object for the container option, with *at least* a success property (identifying the container for successful requests) and possibly a failure property, too. This saves you the trouble of reverting to an Ajax.Request with a custom, tedious onComplete handler, for instance.

9.4 Polling: Ajax.PeriodicalUpdater

If you need periodical updating, the easiest way is to go with Ajax. PeriodicalUpdater. It's not, properly speaking, a specialized version of Ajax.Updater, though. It's a convenience object that uses a fresh Ajax. Updater periodically to save you the bother. And it also has a few more tricks.

Get It: Live Logged-In List

To demonstrate this one, we'll implement a simple application feature: a logged-in user list. You know, like the kind of list you'd want on a community portal's home page or next to the transcript of a chat room. The server maintains a list of the active, or logged-in, users. The client page polls it now and then keeps the displayed list current. To keep things simple and DRY,[9] we'll use the same template for the list when it's part of the full page and when it's sent as an XHTML fragment.

Our server side will simulate a frequently changing user list. It features two URLs, one for the full page and one for the updated list only:

> prototype/ajax/live_users/server.rb

```ruby
#! /usr/bin/env ruby

require 'cgi'
require 'erb'
```

---

9. So you Don't Repeat Yourself...

```ruby
require 'webrick'
include WEBrick

full_template = ERB.new(File.read('index.rhtml'))
list_template = ERB.new(File.read('users.rhtml'))

server = HTTPServer.new(:Port => 8042)
server.mount('/', HTTPServlet::FileHandler, '.')

ALL_USERS = [
  'Dan Webb', 'Élodie Jaubert', 'Justin Palmer', 'Mislav Marohnic',
  'Scott Raymond', 'Andrew Dupont', 'Seth Dillingham'
]

$users = ALL_USERS.select { rand(4) == 0 }.sort

server.mount_proc('/home') do |request, response|
  response['Content-Type'] = 'text/html; charset=UTF-8'
  users_list = list_template.result(binding)
  response.body = full_template.result(binding)
end

server.mount_proc('/users') do |request, response|
  $users.reject! { rand(4) == 0 }
  $users.concat(ALL_USERS.select { rand(4) == 0 }).sort!.uniq!
  response['Content-Type'] = 'text/html; charset=UTF-8'
  response.body = list_template.result(binding)
end

trap('INT') { server.shutdown }

server.start
```

Because default updating will use Element.update() and because we do
not fall prey to *divitis* (putting unnecessary <*div*> tags in the page), we'll
keep the <*ul*> element there all the time and update only its contents.
So, the main template goes like this:

```
prototype/ajax/live_users/index.rhtml
```

```html
<!DOCTYPE html PUBLIC "-//W3C//DTD XHTML 1.0 Strict//EN"
  "http://www.w3.org/TR/xhtml1/DTD/xhtml1-strict.dtd">
<html xmlns="http://www.w3.org/1999/xhtml" lang="en" xml:lang="en">
<head>
  <meta http-equiv="Content-Type" content="text/html; charset=utf-8" />
  <title>Live logged-in users list</title>
  <link rel="stylesheet" type="text/css" href="live.css" />
  <script type="text/javascript" src="prototype.js"></script>
  <script type="text/javascript" src="live.js"></script>
</head>
```

```
<body>
  <h1>Live logged-in users list</h1>

  <ul id="userList">
<%= users_list %>
  </ul>
</body>
</html>
```

And the list template goes like this:

prototype/ajax/live_users/users.rhtml

```
<% $users.each do |user| %>
  <li><%= user %></li>
<% end %>
```

The styling is very minimal, just so our example doesn't look too bad:

prototype/ajax/live_users/live.css

```
#userList {
  width: 15em; margin: 1em 0; padding: 0.25em;
  border: 1px solid navy; background: #ddf; color: navy;
  list-style-type: none;
}
```

And because Ajax.PeriodicalUpdater fits our need so well, the script remains concise:

prototype/ajax/live_users/live.js

```
document.observe('dom:loaded', function() {
  new Ajax.PeriodicalUpdater('userList', '/users',
    { method: 'get', frequency: 3 });
});
```

Because getting an updated list does not modify the application state (well, in our simulation it does, but in a real application it wouldn't) and because we believe in REST and proper HTTP verb usage, we make sure to use a *get* request. We also use a new option, frequency, which states the interval, in seconds, between two updates.[10]

The default interval is two seconds, but I used three here as an example of using the option. Floating-point values are allowed, naturally. Remember that we use seconds here, not milliseconds.

---

10. Yes, it should have been called interval or, for the purists, period, because it's actually the *opposite* of a frequency. I know.

OK, run the server, navigate to http://localhost:8042/home, and keep looking. If you want to look under the hood, use Firefox and Firebug's XHR monitoring. It just works!

Pure JavaScript? Consider the Alternative

When you return only pure JavaScript, having to provide a container that you will update with exactly zero text, since the script you wrapped in a <script> tag got stripped out for separate eval() processing, can sound a bit overkill, not to say cumbersome.

On the other hand, it's very easy to do. Just put a dummy hidden <span> somewhere, or whatever. Still, for those of you who, like me, feel it's not the right way to do, consider the marriage of a PeriodicalExecuter and an Ajax.Request, when you'd send the raw script back with the proper Content-Type header. There's no noticeable workload difference, but it's certainly less roundabout.

A Few More Tricks Up Your Sleeve

Besides its frequency option, Ajax.PeriodicalUpdater also features a rather advanced option called decay. Sometimes, the longer a result stays unchanged, the less often you want to check. In such situations, setting decay to values greater than 1 (its default) will do the trick nicely.

Here is the idea: whenever the response text changes from the last time (which obviously happens on the first request, at any rate), the next request is scheduled frequency seconds later. But every time the response comes back unchanged, the scheduling is multiplied by decay. Incidentally, this means decay values less than 1 result in ever-quickening checks, which will quickly saturate the browser (ouch!).

The official API page at http://prototypejs.org/api/ajax/periodicalUpdater has a nice table illustrating how decay impacts the scheduling of successive requests. Check it out for further details. But remember, this is for slightly edge cases. Most of the time, you're good to go without needing it.

Also know that you can stop, and later resume, the scheduling of requests. The methods stop() and start() are there just for this. This comes in handy when you provide your user with a way to toggle a particular periodical behavior on the fly. By the way, the onComplete callback has different semantics here. It doesn't fire on every Ajax request, but when the periodical update system "completes," which means it stops, it will get called only, therefore, when/if you call stop() (which you may call from within the update function to terminate periodical update based on "internal," business-oriented rules).

9.5 Monitoring Ajax Activity: Ajax.Responders

When doing Ajax, something we often need to do is monitor Ajax activity globally for all requests happening in our page. The most common reason for this is to maintain a status indicator (often the famous "spinner") that is visible while at least one Ajax request is going on, hiding it when the last live one is over. Such indicators are helpful in setting the user's expectations.

The easiest way to go about this is to use the global Ajax.Responders object. This object gets notified about every life cycle event of every request made by the Ajax.* objects. It has all the usual callbacks.

The two methods you'll be interested in are register() and unregister() (mostly the first one). You simply pass a listener object—something with all the callbacks you need. Prototype uses such a listener to maintain Ajax.activeRequestCount, which, nicely enough, tells you how many requests are going on at any given time.

Assuming you have something in your page like this (along with proper styling, probably):

```
<img id="spinner" src="spinner.gif" style="display: none;" />
```

...making this indicator systematically visible while Ajax is going on would be as simple as this:

```
Ajax.Responders.register({
  onCreate: function() { $('spinner').show(); },
  onComplete: function() {
    if (0 == Ajax.activeRequestCount)
      $('spinner').hide();
  }
});
```

Nice and easy. . . .

9.6 Debugging Ajax

When you're doing Ajax work, it can quickly become frustrating not to see what's sent and what's received as a response. The tiniest glitch can ruin the proper behavior of your app, and with no peek into the Ajax exchange, you're left waving your hands in the dark.

Some people take out the pile hammer and fire up network sniffers like Ethereal (renamed Wireshark in 2006). I find this approach extremely cumbersome, not to mention that it slows the whole thing down. Tools such as these are so powerful that they become quite unwieldy, and we're more the agile crowd anyway.

Once again, Firebug to the rescue! It features a *Show XMLHttpRequests* option for its console that lets you track what's going on. We already saw such tracking in action on Figure 9.3, on page 191, for instance. This is, really, your best bet. Of course, if your Ajax works just fine on Firefox but is buggy on another browser, you'll have to find something else.

As far as I know, easy Ajax tracing is not in tools such as the Internet Explorer Developer Toolbar, and it is not featured by Opera or Safari, to name only those. So, selective network sniffing might be your only choice. But remember that if you get your Ajax request right on one browser (say, Firefox), chances are breakage in other browsers is more of a JavaScript or DOM issue. Standard debugging tools, especially JavaScript debuggers, are likely to be the help you need then.

9.7 Ajax Considered Harmful? Thinking About Accessibility and Ergonomy

Before we move ahead, I would very much like to talk a bit about accessibility, not only pertaining to Ajax but also to JavaScript more generally. This falls a bit outside the scope of this book, so I'll try to be concise yet useful.

Most people think accessibility and scripting (especially Ajax) are intrinsically not reconcilable. This is patently untrue. As with most things, best practices go a long way toward having your cake and eating it. There is no titanic effort here—just proper habits to make yours.

Not Using JavaScript? No Problem!

Unless you are working on an intranet-style application where you have control over the browsers, you cannot always afford to require JavaScript. Except perhaps for applications where JavaScript-powered features are key to your product's value (such as most 37signals applications, one could argue), JavaScript should always be used to *improve* usability, not to *implement* it. A classic example is providing navigation (or other important actions) only through clicks over otherwise passive elements (such as images or *<div>* elements). With no JavaScript, your elements are inert. Functionality is lost.

Having no JavaScript at hand is more frequent than you think. A lot of mobile users (using phones, PDAs, and so on) or those equipped with alternative browsing systems (such as a screen reader) still have no JavaScript or have a very limited implementation of it. JavaScript could also be technically available but be disabled by a stringent system administrator.

Even if JavaScript is there and enabled, requiring complex manipulations from your users is inaccessible. Many cannot use a pointing device (for example, a mouse) with good precision, or cannot wield one at all, because of some motor handicap; they may also find it difficult to press complex keyboard shortcuts. Even with no handicap, many may use a browsing device with a limited or absent keyboard (think mobile phones or PDAs) and possibly no efficient pointing mechanism. On the whole, people with one form of handicap or another (cognitive, visual, motor, and so on) make up more than 15% of web users, which means tens of millions of people worldwide. You can't just exclude them.

The key to better accessibility here is to embrace *unobtrusive Java-Script*. Have your page work (even if not too fabulously from a usability standpoint) with no script whatsoever (ideally, with no CSS whatsoever!), and then use separate scripting to hook into regular events (for example, form submission, link activation) to make it behave in a more comfortable way, saving the user's time and effort. Starting with bare-bones stuff and progressively applying feature augmentations through JavaScript and Ajax, in an unobtrusive way, is referred to as *progressive enhancement*.

Ergonomical Ajax: Taking the Right Approach

What's true for JavaScript obviously still stands for Ajax. Jeremy Keith, of DOM Scripting fame, refers to progressive enhancement through Ajax as *Hijax*.[11] Yet Ajax accessibility is not just about technical availability and graceful degradation. On the Web, *users have a different set of expectations* than they do on "desktop" applications.

Most people still expect a web page not to behave quite like a regular application screen. They're not quite alert to your page doing requests

---

11. http://domscripting.com/blog/display/41

in the background, changing fragments of its contents on the fly, allowing drag and drop of elements, and the like. You'll have to make all this very explicit for them so they don't get confused.

Sometimes using Ajax doesn't make sense at all from an ergonomical standpoint. It messes with browser history, and most users are very fond of their Back buttons. Using Ajax to go from one step of a process to another does not alter the history, and improper usage of the Back feature can yield all sorts of issues, not to mention such states are not automatically bookmarkable. You'd need to provide custom URLs for those (think Google Maps). Another common mistake is to autosend forms as they're filled in, which is not always proper. Some forms *should* wait for manual submission, if only to let the user change their mind, go back and finish later, cancel the process, and so on.

Here are a few ground rules, tips, and tricks you can use to make your shiny, wizardy pages more accessible:

- If your site is public-facing, state clearly right from the home page that you use Ajax and JavaScript. Link to a small page that describes, in simple, clear copy, why you use them and what ergonomical expectations the user should have because of this. Setting expectations is a simple but critical thing.

- Doing Ajax? Make sure there's a visible indicator of it (for example, the famous spinner[12]). If this means the user should not manipulate parts of your UI, don't let them try. Disable the relevant parts during the Ajax processing.

- Using drag and drop? Make it obvious! Use a small text hint or perhaps small icons when the mouse is over a draggable element. For instance, to-do lists in 37signals' products use the second approach, as illustrated in Figure 9.6, on the next page.

- Reloading a small part of a page? Make sure the user notices: use a highlight effect, and perhaps play a sound. The fragment might not be visible at this moment because of its viewport size and scrolling issues.

- Doing periodical updates? The extra mile would be to let users turn that into manual triggering, which helps people with screen readers or cognitive handicaps. In the same vein, letting such users request an actual message box (think alert(), which screen

---

12. Need one? Check out http://www.napyfab.com/ajax-indicators/, or quickly get a tailored one at http://www.ajaxload.info/.

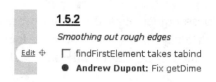

Figure 9.6: ACCESSIBLE DRAG AND DROP (BASECAMP): MAKE IT OBVIOUS!

readers will properly react to, as opposed to pseudo-windows) when content is updated on the page can be very helpful. The extreme case here is to let them toggle Ajax off entirely for your page, reverting to vanilla, manual, full-page reloading.

What We Just Learned

Ajax is a core skill for Web 2.0 development, and Prototype provides a hell of a lot in this regard. Let's briefly review what we saw in this chapter:

- First, we saw how Ajax was not always the best solution for the problem: it could degrade ease of use instead of improving it. Ajax-ifying a page should always be done with great care and be thoroughly tested in various performance and accessibility contexts.
- Prototype's Ajax features are entirely based on a single class: Ajax.Request. Make sure you understand it well and know all its features.
- Synchronous requests (sometimes dubbed SJAX) should be avoided at all costs. They're most likely to freeze the browser, effectively defeating, in a big way, the purpose of Ajax.
- JSON should be your preferred format for data-only exchanges. Just forget XML. It's too much of a bother to parse on the client side, and it's verbose and hence bandwidth-heavy.
- Whenever possible, prefer the hash form of the parameters option to its predigested query string variant. The object form is easier to tweak and maintain.
- Prototype emulates HTTP verbs outside of *get* and *post* by reverting to *post* and using an extra _method field in the request.
- You should not depend on nonguaranteed, intermediate-state callbacks.

- The Ajax.Response object passed as the first argument to the callbacks is the gateway to all the response lookups and examination you might need. It automatically parses JavaScript and JSON results.

- Ajax.Updater is perfect for the common use case of an Ajax request returning a document fragment and can handle different updated locations depending on the response's error state (based on HTTP response codes). It can also insert the new fragment instead of replacing an existing one with it.

- When your periodical Ajax requests do not return a fragment but pure JavaScript, you'll probably be better off with a PeriodicalExecuter over regular Ajax.Request objects.

- Ajax.Responders lets you implement global callbacks that are triggered for all your requests. It's especially useful for global visual indicators and centralized processing (such as logging and error reporting).

Neuron Workout

Ready to gear up? Start with these small assignments:

- What's the best way to return a document fragment on which scripting must be applied?

- Say you use Ajax to add items to a task list. Each task item contains a checkbox, and you need to react to that checkbox being clicked to put the item in the "pending" or "done" list. The easiest solution does *not* use inline <script> tags in your Ajax responses and is more efficient to boot. What is it?

- Create a sign-up form that reacts to the user typing a login by live-checking whether that login is available; if it's not, it styles the field accordingly, displays a message, and disables the submit button. If it is available, it does the opposite. Use a simple server-side script in whatever language you like, with a static list of already-taken logins, to help you test it. Also make sure the lookup interval is not so small it hogs the browser.

More Useful Helper Objects

Prototype dazzles with all the shiny new stuff we saw, but there's more yet to marvel at. Hashes, value ranges, periodical yet nonreentrant code execution, string templating, and browser features—these may be less important than, say, collections, DOM manipulation, events handling, and Ajax, but they sure can come in handy.

10.1 Storing Values in a Hash

Hash was completely rewritten for Prototype 1.6. If you used it in previous versions, pay special attention!

Many languages feature an associative array type. You know, it has some unique keys, which can be just about anything and are associated with values. It's common (and just about indispensable) in scripting languages such as PHP, Perl, or Ruby, and it can also be found in libraries tied to more static languages such as Java (think java.util.Map) or C++ (think std::map). Prototype just calls them *hashes* and offers a Hash type.

JavaScript makes hashes really easy. Any object can be treated as a hash. It is inherently possible to iterate through an object's properties (using the **for. . . in** loop), add and remove properties to an object, change property values, and so on. Properties are also intrinsically unique. But then, you may ask, if objects make such great hashes as it is, why would we need a specific Hash type? Good question, my dear, astute reader.

Well, Hash exists to wrap this basic behavior with a few layers of nice features, such as being able to mix Enumerable in, easily fetching keys or values, merging hashes, and converting to a query string (which comes in handy more often than you may think).

Creating a Hash

```
$H([obj]) → Hash
new Hash([obj]) → Hash
```

We already saw one way to create a hash: the $H() utility function, described in Section 3.7, *$H Makes a Hash of Things*, on page 39. The other way is to use a vanilla class creation syntax such as new Hash() or, if you need to start with a given set of properties and values, new Hash(basicObject). Both syntaxes are absolutely equivalent and always return a fresh, new object.

Hash Maintenance: Tinkering with Keys and Values

Now that we have a hash in our hands, what can we do with it? Well, we want to store, fetch, and remove associations in there. That's what the accessor methods are for.

```
get(propName) → propValue
set(propName, propValue) → samePropValue
unset(propName) → propValue
```

The names of these methods are rather self-explanatory: set() lets you create or replace an association in the hash, get() lets you fetch it (and returns, quite naturally, **undefined** if the association does not exist), and unset() makes sure an association is not there anymore, returning the former association's value, if any.

Note that set() returns the *new* value, not the old one (in the same spirit as JavaScript assignment). This lets you reuse the call in an assignment or method call, as in if (h.set('blah', value)) or v = h.set('blah', value) + 42....

If you need to do more powerful stuff, it's either Prototype's way or the hard way. Here's what becomes available with our beloved library:

```
each(iterator) → Hash
index(value) → firstKey
keys() → Array
merge(obj) → newHash
update(obj) → Hash
values() → Array
```

Before we explore these, remember that Hash mixes Enumerable in. Beware, though—the results you'll get are, still, expressed as arrays, not "subhashes." In this regard, this is not exactly like mixins in Ruby.

I mentioned the each() method in the method list because you may want to know in what order the iteration proceeds. The answer is, quite simply, *that depends*. It relies on JavaScript's native for...in loop, which means the iteration order is mostly browser-dependent (ECMA-262 clearly states that "an Object is an unordered collection of properties"). So, you should not rely on a specific order for your algorithms to work.

Also note that the first argument to your iterator is actually a pair object, with two properties: key and value. It also behaves as an array, with the name at index 0 and the value at index 1, exposing it to all native and extra methods for Array. You thus iterate on map entries, not on map keys.

Here's a short example:

```
prototype/new/hash_each.js
```
```
var lib = $H({ version: 1.5, author: 'Sam Stephenson' });
lib.each(function(pair) {
  alert(pair.key + ' = "' + pair.value + '"');
});
// Alerts, in non-guaranteed order, 'version = "1.5"' and
// 'author = "Sam Stephenson"'.
```

Hashes let you get a list of the keys or values, also ordered based on the native for...in loop. Since these are returned as arrays, they're enumerable as well, which is rather handy.

You can decide to *merge* two hashes by using merge(). The idea is that the hash you're calling merge() on has lower priority than the one passed as an argument. When the merge is done, you get a new hash that has all properties from both, with the argument's values when there is a property name conflict.

Note that the argument doesn't need to be a Hash. It will get passed to $H() prior to use. If you do not want a new hash object but want to update the original hash, use update() instead of merge().

Finally, you can get the first key (in native iteration order) associated with a given value by using the index() method.

A combined example should help:

`prototype/new/hash_tinkering.js`

```
var lib = $H({ name: 'Prototype', version: 1.5 });
lib.keys().sort()
// -> ['name', 'version']
lib.values().sort()
// -> [1.5, 'Prototype']

lib.update({ version: '1.5.1', author: 'sam' });
lib.invoke('join', ' = ').sort().join(', ')
// -> 'author = sam, name = Prototype, version = 1.5.1'

lib.index('sam')
// -> 'author'

lib.unset('author')
// -> 'sam'

lib.keys().sort()
// -> ['name',' version']

$H().keys()
// -> []
```

You may be puzzled by the nifty trick on line 8:

```
lib.invoke('join', ' = ').sort().join(', ')
```

Here's how it works:

1. First, remember that on hashes, each() iterates over key/value pairs, which are, first and foremost, arrays. The first element is the key name, and the second is the value.
2. So when we call invoke() here, we actually produce an array based on the hash, with one string representation per original key/value pair, which has the form *key = value.*
3. Next, we sort the resulting array and produce a unique string out of it with the native join() method, using a comma and a space between each property representation.

This is the kind of line that makes me love Prototype. It just makes me feel warm and fuzzy. JavaScript is cool again.

Looking at Our Hash and Turning It into Something Else

There's little left to say about Hash. It's mostly about converting hashes to string representations. We've got two of those: debug-oriented form and URL-like serialization.

```
inspect() → String
toObject/toTemplateReplacements() → Object
toQueryString() → String
```

We already covered inspect() many times. In the case of Hash, it provides a fully custom representation, as shown in the next code example, a few paragraphs down.

If you need raw access to the storage container for the associations, you can use the toObject() converter. It will likely mostly be used through its toTemplateReplacements() alias in order to use a Hash as any regular object in the context of templating, which we'll discuss in Section 10.4, *Templating Made Easy*, on page 223.

Another common use of hashes is to structure parameters later used for an HTTP request (either directly or, more often, through Ajax). We then need to serialize these properties as parameters in a URI-encoded way (indeed, be it a GET or a POST request, the default format for data is URL-encoding). You can do this on existing Hash instances by simply invoking toQueryString() on them or reuse the algorithm for any Java-Script object by passing them as arguments to Object.toQueryString().

Here are a few details on the serialization process: properties whose value is **undefined** are serialized without value (just their name), properties with value **null** are deemed empty, properties with Array values get serialized once per array element, and all names and values obviously get encoded using JavaScript's native encodeURIComponent() method. The order is, as always with Hash, dependent on the native for...in loop.

Incidentally, note that toQueryString() is essentially reciprocal to String's parseQuery() method, which we covered earlier in Section 4.5, *Converting and Extracting: toQueryParams, parseQuery, toArray, and inspect*, on page 63.

It's time for an example, wouldn't you say?

`prototype/new/hash_strings.js`

```
$H({ name: 'Prototype', version: 1.5 }).inspect()
// -> "<#Hash:{name: 'Prototype', version: 1.5}>" // Order not guaranteed

$H({ action: 'ship', order_id: 123, fees: ['f1', 'f2'],
  'label': 'a demo' }).toQueryString()
// -> 'action=ship&order_id=123&fees=f1&fees=f2&label=a%20demo'

$H().toQueryString()
// -> ''
```

```
// "Class method" variant on any object: use the Object namespace instead.
Object.toQueryString({ foo:'bar' })
// -> 'foo=bar'
```

And that's it for hashes. Simple fellas, really. They're nifty without too much overhead. You've got to like them.

10.2 Expressing Ranges of. . . Well, Anything You Want!

Talking about nice simple guys, meet ObjectRange. This is the class behind the $R() utility function, which we saw in Section 3.8, *Handling Ranges with $R*, on page 39. This class simply represents a range of values, which can be of any type amenable to ranges. OK, so what exactly makes a type amenable to ranges?

Well, in short, it just has to have a succ() method. When you call it on a value, you get the next value. That's it. Prototype puts such a method in Number and String, so out of the box, you can have number ranges and string ranges. The former is actually much more used (and useful) than the latter.

Ranges mix in Enumerable, which is the salient point about them. It lets you iterate easily, slap them on existing sequences with methods such as zip(), or easily convert them to an array (since Enumerable provides ranges with a generic implementation of toArray()).

Creating Ranges

Oh, that's a walk in the park:

```
$R(start, end [, exclusive = false])
new ObjectRange(start, end [, exclusive = false])
```

For once, there is absolutely no distinction whatsoever between the utility function and its vanilla constructor counterpart. They share the same semantics.

Range Iteration

Ranges iterate from the start value to the end value, calling succ() on the current value to get the next one. If the exclusive parameter is set to **true**, the end value is skipped; the iteration will stop right before it.

Have a look at this:

`prototype/new/range_combined.js`

```
$A($R(1, 5)).join(', ')
// -> '1, 2, 3, 4, 5'

$R(1, 5).zip(['one', 'two', 'three', 'four', 'five'], function(tuple) {
  return tuple.join(' = ');
})
// -> ['1 = one', '2 = two', '3 = three', '4 = four', '5 = five']

$A($R('a', 'e'))
// -> ['a', 'b', 'c', 'd', 'e'], no surprise there

$A($R('ax', 'ba'))
// -> Ouch!  Humongous array, starting as
//     ['ax', 'ay', 'az', 'a{', 'a|', 'a}', 'a~'...]
```

Beware of String-based ranges. As described on page 58, the succ()
method does not stop with alphabetical boundaries (which would be
infeasible in an internationalized context) but goes all the way across
the character table, which, in JavaScript, is Unicode.

Range Inclusion

Ranges come with only one specific method:

`include(value) → Boolean`

This is pretty self-explanatory. It tells you whether the value is included
in the range (taking the exclusive initialization parameter into account,
obviously). Note, however, that this relies on the existence of a < operator between values of the range. This is likely not to work so well on
custom value objects that feature just the succ() method. . . .

10.3 Periodical Execution Without Risk of Reentrance

Sometimes you need to periodically call a function. Maybe you need to
poll the server for updates, maybe you're doing some autosave feature,
or maybe you're dealing with some time-related UI effect and haven't
found a suitable treat in libraries such as script.aculo.us or the Prototype Window Class.[1] You just want the periodical call thing.

---

1. http://prototype-window.xilinus.com

This could easily be achieved with the native setInterval() and clearInterval() methods on the window object, but this has several drawbacks:

- This requires you to take care of the nitty-gritty details of timer handles yourself, which essentially means you're going to either pollute the global namespace or create your own namespace-like object to hold it.
- This does not prevent you from getting your callback function called while its prior call is still processing, which can be annoying if it deals with UI interaction (for example, a prompt(), confirm(), or custom dialog call for the user to deal with).

With PeriodicalUpdater, you get the following benefits:

- Your callback function never gets called again while it is still processing; there's an internal flag preventing double calling.
- It encapsulates the timer-handling mechanism into a neat object.
- You can stop the periodical execution at any time by calling the stop() method on the periodical executer object.

```
new PeriodicalExecuter(callback, intervalInSecs) → PeriodicalExecuter
pe.stop()
```

Note that your callback will get called with the PeriodicalExecuter object as its argument (letting you stop it from inside the function) and that the interval is expressed in *seconds* (obviously, you can use a floating-point value, such as 0.75).

Just look at this example code:

prototype/new/periodicalExecuter.js

```
// Campfire style :-)
new PeriodicalExecuter(pollChatRoom, 3);

new PeriodicalExecuter(function(pe) {
  if (!confirm('Want me to annoy you again later?'))
    pe.stop();
}, 5);
// Note that there won't be a stack of such messages if the user takes
// too long answering to the question...

var gCallCount = 0;
new PeriodicalExecuter(function(pe) {
  if (++gCallCount > 3)
    pe.stop();
  else
    alert(gCallCount);
}, 1);
// Will only alert 1, 2 and 3, then the PE stops.
```

10.4 Templating Made Easy

Prototype 1.5 introduced a new object dedicated to template-based string creation: Template. It lets you pluck properties from an object and insert them in a template string. It's also useful when you have a group of similar objects and you need to produce formatted output for these objects, maybe inside a loop.

You would then typically resort to concatenating string literals with the object's fields. There's nothing wrong with the previous approach, except that it is hard to visualize the output immediately just by glancing at the concatenation expression.

The Template class provides a much nicer and clearer way of achieving this formatting:

```
new Template(templateText [, pattern = Template.Pattern]) → Template
template.evaluate(scopeObject) → String
```

By default, the template syntax used by Template is akin to Ruby's string syntax. You can embed fields from the scope object with a #{field-Name} fragment. Because arrays have numerical properties, you can use this syntax for vanilla arrays as well, using #{0} for the first element, #{1} for the second one, and so forth. Here's a first example:

prototype/new/template_simple.js

```
var people = [
  { name: 'Élodie Jaubert', field: 'Heritage management',
    role: 'my fiancée' },
  { name: 'Seth Dillingham', field: 'Web development',
    role: 'a fellow Core' }
];
var tpl = new Template('#{name} works in #{field} and is #{role}.');

people.each(function(person) {
  alert(tpl.evaluate(person));
}
// Alerts
// "Seth Dillingham works in Web development and is a fellow Core.",
// then "Élodie Jaubert works in Heritage management and is my fiancée."
```

Since Prototype 1.6, you can actually use more advanced syntax in expansion blocks (the #{...} thing). You're not limited to a field name anymore but can walk down the properties using dot notation (a.b) or square bracket indexing (a[b]). In this second case, however, quotes for the key are not only unnecessary but will be handled literally.

Here are a few examples:

`prototype/new/template_advanced.js`

```
var people = [
  { name: 'Élodie Jaubert',
    interests: [ 'heritage', 'culture', 'music' ] },
  { name: 'Seth Dillingham' }
];
var tpl = new Template(
  '#{length} people.  #{0.name} likes #{0.interests[2]}, ' +
  'among other things.');
tpl.evaluate(people)
// => '2 people.  Élodie likes music, among other things.'
// You can use [] or . indifferently, except when the prop name is
// empty or contains a dot: then you need the square brackets.
```

Prototype also caters to the few use cases where the scope object for your templating is not exactly what you'd like. Perhaps it provides some information you need through a method instead of a property, for instance. For these cases, you can equip your object with a to-TemplateReplacements() method, which should return an alternate representation of your object, that will be used for the templating. Consider the following:

`prototype/new/template_ttr.js`

```
var student = {
  name: 'John',
  grades: [10, 12, 13.5, 8, 16],

  average: function() {
    return this.grades.inject(0, function(acc, g) { return acc + g }) /
      this.grades.length;
  },
  highest: function() { return this.grades.max(); },
  lowest: function() { return this.grades.min(); },

  toTemplateReplacements: function() {
    var result = Object.clone(this), student = this;
    ['average', 'highest', 'lowest'].each(function(methodName) {
      result[methodName] = student[methodName]();
    });
    return result;
  }
};

var tpl = new Template(
  '#{name} averages at #{average} (lowest: #{lowest})');
tpl.evaluate(student);
// => 'John averages at 11.9 (lowest: 8)'
```

Finally, note that you can use the reserved #{...} syntax as a literal by simply escaping the first character: \#{...}. This is actually not an absolute truth, because it depends on the template pattern being properly defined.

Indeed, if you look closely at the syntax block I used for the Template constructor, you notice that there is a second, optional pattern argument, which defaults to Template.Pattern. What is that? Well, quite simply, this is a regular expression used to search the template text for dynamic fragments and "parse" those fragments in order to provide the templating engine with proper information.

The default pattern, Template.Pattern, looks like this:

```
/(^|.|\r|\n)(#\{(.*?)\})/
```

To better understand it, you need to know that a valid template pattern must identify *at least three groups*, which is done by using paired parentheses:

- The character, or anchor, positioned immediately *before* the dynamic fragment. This is used to detect backslash escaping (yes, it has to be a backslash). This part of the template never needs to change. It's (^|.|\r|\n).

- The full dynamic fragment, including its opening and closing delimiters; the default pattern uses (#\{(.*?)\}) (recall that curly braces, square brackets, and parentheses, among other characters, are special characters in JavaScript's regular expressions. To use them as literals, you must escape them, which is why we use \{ and \} here).

- The property name part, which is the dynamic fragment stripped of its delimiters. This part seldom changes and is generally (.*?).

So if you insist on using another template syntax, you can provide your own pattern. Say you've sloshed too long in the swamps of ASP to easily shed the <%=...%> syntax. You can cater to this sorry need by using the appropriate pattern:

```
prototype/new/template_custom.js
var people = [
  { name: 'Bill Gates', style: 'ASP' },
  { name: 'Andrew Dupont', style: 'Ruby' }
];

var ASP_SYNTAX = /(^|.|\r|\n)(<%=\s*(\w+)\s*=>)/;
```

```
►  var tpl = new Template('<%= name %> prefers <%= style %> syntax.',
►    ASP_SYNTAX);
  people.each(function(person) {
    alert(tpl.evaluate(person));
  });
  // Alerts "Bill Gates prefers ASP syntax.",
  // then "Andrew Dupont prefers Ruby syntax."
```

10.5 Examining the Current Browser and Prototype Library

Before taking on the real gem (Enumerable), let's start at an easy loping pace with Prototype. This is actually a *namespace*. Remember namespaces? We discussed them in Section 2.4, *Objects, Namespaces, and Modules*, on page 25. Quite simply, Prototype is not for instantiation. It is just a named repository for several methods and pseudoconstants. This is where you get information about the version of your Prototype library, details about browser support for specific features, and generic iterators that might come in handy now and then.

Version Information

Any Prototype library lets you access its exact version through Prototype.Version. It is a full version string, such as *1.5.1* or *1.6.0_pre0*. It is especially useful when you are writing a library based on Prototype and need to test for dependency upon a specific minimum version.

For instance, script.aculo.us (which we will explore in the next part of this book) checks that it is run based upon a sufficiently recent version of Prototype (on which it depends entirely) in its scriptaculous.js file with code like this:

```
prototype/new/prototype_version.js
```

```
// Extracted from script.aculo.us 1.8.0
if((typeof Prototype=='undefined') ||
   (typeof Element == 'undefined') ||
   (typeof Element.Methods=='undefined') ||
►  (convertVersionString(Prototype.Version) <
►    convertVersionString(Scriptaculous.REQUIRED_PROTOTYPE)))
    throw("script.aculo.us requires the Prototype JavaScript framework >= " +
      Scriptaculous.REQUIRED_PROTOTYPE);
```

Incidentally, know that Prototype follows a rather usual version naming scheme:

- The earliest stages of a given version are *preversions* and use an incremental *_pre* suffix (for example, *_pre0*).

- Getting close to release, we go *Release Candidate*, with incremental *_rc* suffixes. For instance, the last stage of Prototype before 1.5 was *1.5.0_rc2*.

- Finally, public releases have no suffix (but three numbers still).

So far, prereleases and release candidates were available only through the Subversion repository (and embedded in script.aculo.us). This strategy may well change now that the official site has been fully revamped, though. Keep an eye on the download page,[2] but remember, such releases are mostly for testing and playing around with upcoming features. They can have failing tests, performance issues, unstable parts, and the like.

Browser Features

Whenever Prototype finds itself in repetitive need of a given browser feature detection, it ends up detecting it once and for all and putting the result in the Prototype.BrowserFeatures namespace. There are currently three aspects in there, all of which are booleans:

XPath
> Whether the browser supports DOM Level 3 XPath, which is used for tremendously boosting several DOM retrievals (such as $$() and select()).

ElementExtensions
> Whether the browser provides JavaScript prototypes for DOM elements, enabling direct extension. This speeds up the whole DOM extension mechanism and therefore speeds up Prototype code in general. See Chapter 7, *Playing with the DOM Is Finally Fun!*, on page 119 for the whole story.

SpecificElementExtensions
> Whether the browser uses a common prototype for all DOM elements (as Safari seems to do at the time of this writing). When this is the case, the DOM extension mechanism compensates accordingly to perform direct extension anyway.

Browsers (Firefox, Safari, and So On)

You will also find a Prototype.Browser namespace, which holds boolean constants for most major browsers or rendering engines, letting your

---

2. http://prototypejs.org/download

script detect the current browser in a legible, concise way. At this point, the following booleans are defined in it: IE, Opera, WebKitMobileSafari (which basically means the iPhone or the iPod Touch), and Gecko.

As you can see, this is so far pretty much for internal use, although I can certainly imagine Prototype "add-ons" leveraging this information for better integration. At any rate, more browser-related information may well come up in later releases, such as browser identification, SVG support, and <canvas> support.... So keep a sharp eye out!

Querying the Current Viewport

Sometimes we need to get the dimensions of the viewport itself, not the browser window. The viewport, as you probably know, is the rendering surface for the document. It is what's left in the window once we put in the menus, toolbars, scroll bars, status bars, and so on. This surface is much more interesting to us, for our scripts, than the window's dimensions, especially since the relation between viewport size and window size varies depending on the amount of "chrome" (UI components) present.

1.6

Starting with Prototype 1.6, a new object is maintained, called document.viewport, equipped with four neat methods:

```
document.viewport.getDimensions() → { width: Number, height: Number }
document.viewport.getHeight() → Number
document.viewport.getWidth() → Number
document.viewport.getScrollOffsets() → { left: Number, top: Number }
```

The signatures are pretty much self-explanatory. As a reminder, *scroll offsets* are the shifting operated by the scroll bars (which means, incidentally, that they're never negative).

Boilerplate Functions

To make most iterator arguments optional in Enumerable's methods, Prototype defines an "identity" iterator, which is a function that simply returns its first argument, untouched. It's called Prototype.K(). Take the min() method, for instance; you can call it either with no argument (in which case it will compare the elements directly) or with an iterator of yours (which will be used to compute the values then being compared). Thanks to Prototype.K(), the code for this alternative is pretty simple:

```
value = (iterator || Prototype.K)(value, index);
```

Another area for boilerplate functions is Prototype's Ajax requesters. These offer a variety of callback hooks to let your code react to the many phases of an Ajax communication (including errors and specific types of successful responses). In order not to bother with an **if** test of the presence of a given callback, the code just reverts to an empty function (a function that, literally, does nothing at all): Prototype.emptyFunction() (note the lowercase *e*). Here is a line from Prototype's Ajax state-handling code:

```
(this.options['on' + state] || Prototype.emptyFunction)(transport, json);
```

You might find yourself needing such functions to simplify your code or allow for optional function-typed arguments in your methods.

What We Just Learned

Although less prominent, the features in this chapter do help make our code efforts easier. We should especially remember that...

- Hash provides a few methods to explicitly process a regular object as a hash, mostly by looking at its keys and values as datasets and enumerating on them. It also features a nice inspect(), when regular objects would spew out some unusable string such as "[Object]."

- Hashes also provide the URL-encoding and decoding facilities in Prototype.

- Ranges are mostly used to represent integer ranges, such as $R(1, 100), and are useful in conjunction with many Enumerable operations (for instance, we can use them to index items in another enumeration, perhaps using a zip() call). But essentially anything with a succ() method is range-compatible, so there can be some pretty creative uses out there.

- The Template class provides a robust, simple templating mechanism to inject object properties, however complex, into a text pattern. Remember that one-shot templating is easier to do with a call to String's interpolate(), too.

- The Prototype library itself can be "inspected" by using the Prototype namespace to get the library's version and look at the running browser's type and behavioral capabilities (such as XPath support).

- With Prototype 1.6, you now get support for viewport information, letting you know how big it is and how far it's being scrolled.

Neuron Workout

Here are a few suggestions for bite-size code snippets to fiddle with:

- Produce a sorted list of all the properties in an object.

- Reduce it to methods only.

- Reduce it instead to nonmethod properties that are strings and whose names begin with a vowel.

- Change String#succ() so it wraps at the end of the ASCII alphabet; for example, "wiz".succ() yields "wja" instead of "wi{". Check out $A($R('abc', 'bzz')) then.

- If necessary, adjust it to wrap over from 9 to 0, and from Z to A, too.

And that's a wrap! We've gone through all that Prototype has to offer. Before moving over to script.aculo.us, I'll just remind you of a few performance issues in the next chapter, just so you don't fall prey to unexpected sluggishness.

There is nothing so useless as doing efficiently that which should not be done at all.
► Peter F. Drucker

Chapter 11

Performance Considerations

11.1 Element Extension and the $ Function

If you're running on a browser that does not feature native DOM element prototypes (for example, Internet Explorer), extending elements unnecessarily can have some performance impact. Such extensions are not always easy to spot in your code. A lot of Prototype methods automatically extend their arguments, for instance, or the elements they return. Just look at all the calls to $() in the source.

Still, in most cases this is not a real issue. Here are the two main reasons why:

- Element extension happens at most once per element. Attempting to extend an already extended element has a much lower cost (basically, just the function call cost).

- Element extension is, in itself, not a complex process. It mostly means copying a bunch of properties from one object to the element. To become noticeable from the perspective of a user, it would have to operate on hundreds, if not thousands, of unextended elements.

If you really need to work over a vast amount of elements without extending all of them, you can still revert to a regular loop over these elements and either use a namespaced syntax when calling "extended" methods on them (for example, Element.hide(elt)) or extend only those you're interested in (by manually calling Element.extend() on them).

On the other hand, many Prototype features will automatically extend their element-based results. Most notably, the almighty $$(), which is so helpful in extracting elements from the DOM based on complex criteria, systematically extends the elements it returns. Most element-returning methods added by DOM extension (for example, up()) return extended elements. So, you had better think about how you use descendants().

11.2 Iterations vs. Regular Loops

Using iterator methods (methods that will take a function as an argument and invoke this function for some or all of a collection of elements) basically means that at some point the collection's _each() method is called, and it will call your iterator. That, already, has a slight cost (double function call, with the maintenance of the closures). But the wrapper each() also needs to maintain a **try/catch** block to deal with the $break exception, which has a significant impact.

Generally, you shouldn't worry too much about loop performance using iterators. Unless you're iterating over an exceptionally large collection, you're in the clear. However, sometimes you do need to squeeze every last bit of speed you can get. There is, then, no other alternative than writing your iteration code by hand. Make sure you do it right, then. Cache the collection length, avoid declaring too many variables in the loop block, and so on. Here's a typical "fast" loop:

```
var item;
for (var i = 0, l = data.length; i != l; ++i) {
  item = data[i];
  // Process item
}
```

First, it declares item outside the loop scope, so there's no allocation/release cost for every iteration. Second, it caches the collection's length, which avoids evaluating it at every turn. Third (and least important), it uses the prefix ++ operator, which avoids cloning its operand.

It would appear that another approach, grabbing length and then using something like a while (l--) loop, can squeeze even more juice out of an array iteration. But the aesthetics of it just make me nauseous. Still, it's worth a mention—maybe it does shave off more than a few nanoseconds off the **for** version, should you need it.

11.3 Obsolete Event Handlers

A frequent concern is about the memory cost of large amounts of event observers. When you navigate outside the page, you may risk memory leakage on Internet Explorer, if Prototype did not take special care of this browser by manually detaching all the observers previously defined by the library. On the other hand, you may have registered numerous observers on a page fragment that gets replaced or removed. What then?

Indeed, you would need to do some manual bookkeeping over your observers, because there currently is no simple way to decommission all the observers on a DOM fragment (although you can now easily decommission all those on a single element). This is tedious, not to mention that it's very impractical. Many observers are internal to Prototype objects, and your user code has no easy means of accessing those references.

One thing you can do is minimize the amount of observers you have. I often see people write code that creates tons of elements (say, a tree representation) and attach individual observers on each, for the same event. That's just ludicrous. Event bubbling lets us define a single handler at the container level and use the event's source element concept to handle the specific item we're dealing with. This goes a long way toward dramatically reducing the observer count. For a detailed example of this, look at how we did it with the staff tree on page 138.

11.4 Recent Speed Boosts You Should Know About

Every release of Prototype brings with it a handful of speed improvements that can sometimes be quite dramatic. Warnings that were once good advice become obsolete. Here are a few speed boosts in 1.5.1 that you should know about:

Selectors are blazing fast!

Andrew Dupont (and, to a lesser degree, yours truly) did a full rewrite of the Selector class, with some heavy inspiration from Jack Slocum's DomQuery and a healthy dose of XPath-fu.

Because of this, everything based on Selector (most notably $$() and the DOM traversal extensions) is now blazing fast. Really, at the time of this writing, it's eating everyone's lunch. Andrew maintains a comparison bench on his website[1] for you to check this out.

Iterators are faster.

The $continue thing is not supported anymore in iterations. Use a simple **return** in your callback instead. Not only is it faster than throwing an exception, but this strips one level of exception handling from the iterator, which results in a significant boost of all iterator methods.

Array's uniq() is much faster.

It used to rely on concat(), which meant it had a quadratic cost. It has been rewritten to use a single array and work in linear time if the array is already sorted.

Style manipulations are faster.

The element methods getStyle() and setStyle() are getting faster with just about every release.

HTML escaping is much faster.

String's escapeHTML() method is now significantly faster, because it does not create DOM nodes anymore.

11.5 Small Is Beautiful

Stay lean, stay lithe. Don't churn out megabytes of markup, and don't pre-include all the scripts you'll ever need. Use Ajax for on-demand replacements, content loading, and so on. Improve your mastery of semantic markup and CSS to trim the fat off your DOMs. Quicker to load, quicker to run, quicker to script!

---

1. http://andrewdupont.net/test/double-dollar/

Wrapping Up

Before we close this Prototype part and move on to script.aculo.us, I'd like to take you through a consolidated example that brings together quite a few of the features we've seen so far. Instead of a pure-text conclusion paragraph, I think this will serve better as an executive summary of sorts.

12.1 Building a Fancy Task List

Let's say we need to create a small web page that lets us add to a small task list by entering short task descriptions. The page is designed to use Ajax when JavaScript is enabled, dynamically retrieving XHTML fragments representing the new task and adding it to the current task list. There should also be, for the hell of it, two links that let us select, or deselect, all current task list items. The page would look like this:

`prototype/fireworks/fireworks.html`

```
<!DOCTYPE html PUBLIC "-//W3C//DTD XHTML 1.0 Strict//EN"
 "http://www.w3.org/TR/xhtml1/DTD/xhtml1-strict.dtd">
<html xmlns="http://www.w3.org/1999/xhtml" lang="en-US" xml:lang="en-US">
<head>
    <meta http-equiv="Content-Type" content="text/html; charset=utf-8" />
    <title>A combined example of using Prototype&#8230;</title>
    <link rel="stylesheet" type="text/css" href="fireworks.css" />
    <script type="text/javascript" src="prototype.js"></script>
    <script type="text/javascript" src="fireworks.js"></script>
</head>
<body>

<h1>A combined example of using Prototype</h1>
```

```html
<form id="addForm" method="post" action="/tasks">
  <fieldset>
    <legend>Add task</legend>
    <p>
      <label for="taskText" accesskey="T">Text:</label>
      <input type="text" id="taskText" name="text" />
    </p>
    <p><input type="submit" value="New task!" /></p>
  </fieldset>
</form>

<p id="progress" style="display: none;">Adding task&#8230;</p>

<h2>Task list</h2>

<p id="selectors">
  <a href="#" id="selectAll">Select all</a> &middot;
  <a href="#" id="deselectAll">Deselect all</a>
</p>

<ul id="tasks">
</ul>

</body>
</html>
```

With a tiny bit of CSS, this would look like Figure 12.1, on the facing page.

12.2 Laying the Groundwork

Let's whip up a small Ruby script to act as server. For the sake of brevity, we will not have it handle both Ajax and non-Ajax cases. We'll assume the POST requests come through Ajax and return only the relevant page fragment:

prototype/fireworks/fireworks.rb

```ruby
#! /usr/bin/env ruby

require 'cgi'
require 'erb'
require 'webrick'
include WEBrick

template_text = File.read('task.rhtml')
task = ERB.new(template_text)
taskId = 0

server = HTTPServer.new(:Port => 8042)
```

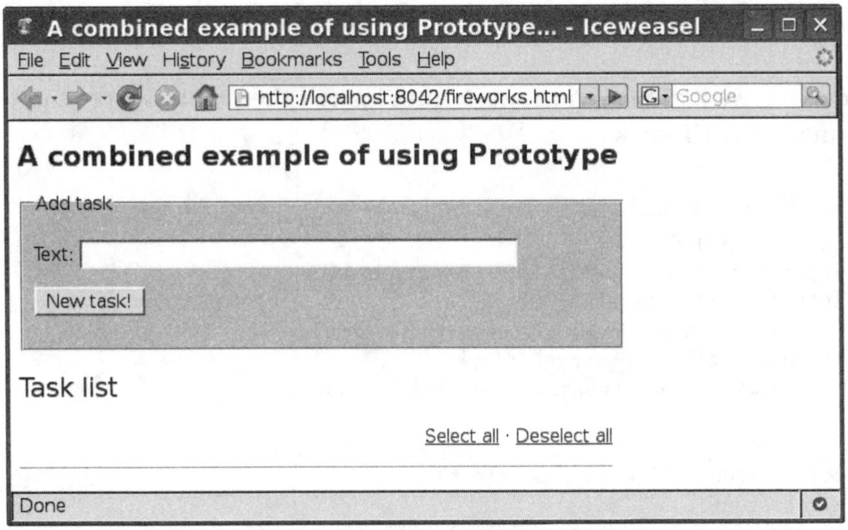

Figure 12.1: AN EMPTY TASK LIST

```
server.mount('/', HTTPServlet::FileHandler, '.')

server.mount_proc('/tasks') do |request, response|
  params = CGI::parse(request.body)
  text = CGI::escapeHTML(params['text'][0])
  taskId += 1
  # Simulate random processing time (0-2 seconds)
  sleep 2*rand
  # Return XHTML fragment
  response['Content-Type'] = 'text/html'
  response.body = task.result(binding)
end

trap('INT') { server.shutdown }

server.start
```

The fragment template is short and to the point:

prototype/fireworks/task.rhtml

```
<li>
  <input type="checkbox" id="chk<%= taskId %>" />
  <label for="chk<%= taskId %>"><%= text %></label>
</li>
```

12.3 It Takes Only 40 Lines: The JavaScript Code

Now that we laid the groundwork, just look at the *whole* script required to make the UI work:

```
prototype/fireworks/fireworks.js
```

```
Line 1   function bindUI() {
   -       $('addForm').observe('submit', routeToAJAX);
   -       $('selectAll').observe('click',
   -         toggleAll.bindAsEventListener(this, true));
   5       $('deselectAll').observe('click',
   -         toggleAll.bindAsEventListener(this, false));
   -     } // bindUI
   -
   -     function toggleAll(event, doSelect) {
  10       event.stop();
   -       $('tasks').select('input[type=checkbox]').each(function(box) {
   -         box.checked = doSelect;
   -       });
   -     } // toggleAll
  15
   -     Ajax.Responders.register({
   -       onCreate: function() {
   -         $('progress').show();
   -       },
  20       onComplete: function() {
   -         if (0 == Ajax.activeRequestCount)
   -           $('progress').hide();
   -       }
   -     });
  25
   -     function routeToAJAX(event) {
   -       event.stop();
   -       var form = event.element();
   -       new Ajax.Updater('tasks', form.action, {
  30         parameters: Form.serialize(form),
   -         insertion: 'bottom',
   -         onLoading: function() { $('addForm').disable(); },
   -         onComplete: function() {
   -           $('addForm').enable();
  35           $('taskText').clear().focus();
   -         }
   -       });
   -     } // routeToAJAX
   -
  40   document.observe('dom:loaded', bindUI);
```

That's it! That's all there is.

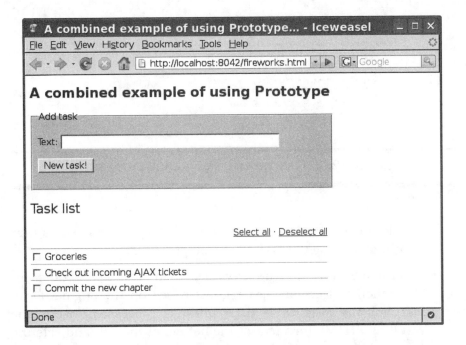

Figure 12.2: OUR LIST AFTER TYPING THREE ITEMS

When using Firefox, Firebug lets us easily track Ajax exchanges in its console, as you can see in Figure 12.3, on the next page.

I'll just give you a few quick comments in case you need to brush up on some of the features we learned:

- The bindUI() function on line 1 registers event handlers on form submission (to route the call through Ajax) and for clicks on the toggler links.

- Thanks to binding methods as in line 4, we can pass predefined arguments to the unique handler: **true** for the selection link and **false** for the deselection one. This is looked up by the toggler function through its doSelect argument.

- Thanks to the select() utility function (see line 11), grabbing elements based on CSS selectors is easy. It is, definitely, one of the most useful (and most used) utility functions in Prototype.

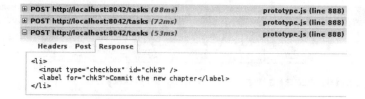

Figure 12.3: AJAX TRACING IN FIREBUG'S CONSOLE

- Thanks to Ajax.Responders, we can register global listeners over Ajax, maintaining the display of a progress indicator.

- From line 29 on, the true fireworks begin. This Ajax.Updater instantiation triggers an Ajax request based on the original form, disabling the form while the request is processed; inserts the resulting XHTML fragment at the bottom of the list; and sets the input field back up for the next input!

Let's try this. If you had a running WEBrick server, stop it by hitting Ctrl+C in its console, and then go to our current example directory and run the server for this example the usual way. For instance, on Windows use something like this:

C:\Spinoffs\prototype\fireworks> **ruby fireworks.rb**

Then navigate to the proper URL: http://localhost:8042/fireworks.html.

And indeed, this works! Typing a few texts and submitting the form triggers Ajax communications that return XHTML fragments then added to the list, as shown in Figure 12.2, on the preceding page.

Thanks to our server script simulating processing delays, we can actually see the progress indicator being toggled on and off by our global responder. This is illustrated by Figure 12.4, on the next page.

This is nontrivial stuff, and yet look how *concise* this code is! It's portable, it's maintainable, it's rather readable, and it does all that work.... There's only one question left really: when do you leverage what you learned in this part of the book to apply the same scripting-fu to *your* projects?

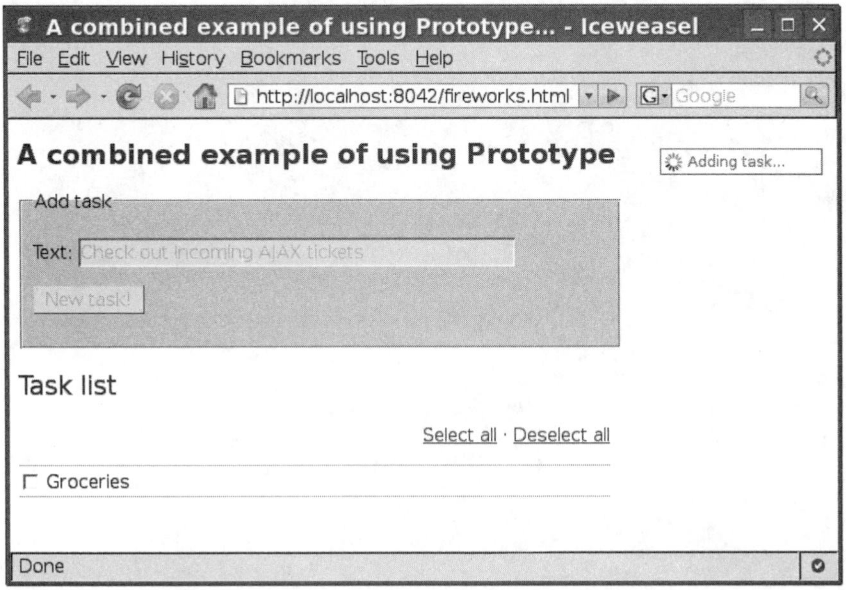

Figure 12.4: THE PROGRESS INDICATOR AND THE DISABLED FORM

Part II

script.aculo.us

It's about the user interface, baby!
  ► script.aculo.us tag line

Chapter 13

Discovering script.aculo.us

We now have some serious Prototype knowledge under our belts. We are ready to write excellent web-based user interfaces. There are two more things that would probably help:

- Generic visual features, such as animated effects (for example, fades, moves, resizes) and drag and drop. Those are relevant in most user interfaces, whether they remain "web-style" or try to mimic a "desktop-like" look.
- Controls! Reusable visual components for your application screens. Most widgets come with one or more predefined look-and-feels, which means you would probably have to use their library throughout your user interface.

We can go widget shopping later, but we'll find that script.aculo.us provides us with a great array of visual features with a few widgets thrown in for good measure. Originally part of Prototype itself, it split off pretty quickly and took on a life of its own. Still, Thomas Fuchs, its Vienna-based creator, has been extremely active in Prototype too and shares the commit rights with Sam.

13.1   The Modules of script.aculo.us

Unlike Prototype, script.aculo.us is divided into modules, each with its own JavaScript file. The modules are arranged by theme. Don't be overwhelmed. Most script.aculo.us users use only the first two of these modules:

Animated effects
    This is the mother lode. The *effects* module comes with more than twenty-five visual effects, seven transition modes (that alter how

> **Which Version of script.aculo.us?**
>
> This book documents script.aculo.us 1.8, the last version in the 1.*x* tree, which was released in sync with Prototype 1.6. The next version of script.aculo.us, 2.0, is currently scheduled for a complete rewrite of the *effects* and *dragdrop* modules; however, fear not—the external API will likely be similar, and if it changes too much, you can expect an update (or new edition) of this book to release quickly on its heels.

the effect goes from start to finish over time), and effect queues (which let you create advanced effect sequences), enough to cover most of your needs. Even if you found it lacking, adding new effects is easy enough.

Drag and drop

You will use the *dragdrop* module to make any element draggable, turn it into a drop zone, or even make entire series of elements sortable so you can rearrange them by dragging and dropping—a killer improvement on list sorting.

Autocompleters and in-place editing

This module makes it easy to slap an autocompletion facility over regular text fields, which can come from the server side (through Ajax) or from a preloaded set of possibilities. You can also make just about any text or collection of items editable in-place by simply clicking it. A specific UI will appear and notify the server side when the editing is done so it can be persisted.

Sliders

A slider is a sort of small rail, or track, along which you can slide a handle. It translates into a numerical value. With script.aculo.us, you can create such sliders with a lot of control: define boundaries, restrict possible positions to specific values, use multiple handles (for instance, to define ranges), and so on.

On the other hand, customizing the aspect of your sliders will be possible only to a certain extent, which is a necessary limitation with such complex UI elements, when they are created using XHTML.

DOM builder

> This is a developer tool that eases DOM creation considerably. When building DOM fragments, not only are the raw W3C interfaces rather bland and unwieldy, they are not flawlessly supported across browsers! There are issues with *<select>* tags or their contents, with table-related elements, with name= attributes on specific tags, with attribute whose names are JavaScript keywords, and so on.

> This object lets you specify DOM fragments in a simple way, smoothing over such discrepancies and issues.

Sound!

> Version 1.7.1 introduced a sound system that lets you play sounds easily, queue them up, use multiple tracks, and so on. It does not require Flash and relies on your browser's native audio capabilities, usually provided through widely spread plug-ins.

> Efficient use of short sounds can be a really nice feature for applications that need to grab the user's attention even when the page is not visible (moved aside, hidden behind another window, reduced to the task bar, or simply not the active tab).

13.2 Using script.aculo.us in Your Pages

First, you'll need to download a recent version. Thomas keeps pushing new releases pretty frequently on the official website, so just head to http://script.aculo.us/ and grab the latest archive. It includes the minimal version of Prototype that this particular release relies on. If you have an earlier Prototype release, either use the one that comes with script.aculo.us or update your copy to a more recent one.

You will need to load Prototype first and script.aculo.us second. The shortest way to do this uses two *<script>* elements, like this:

```
<script type="text/javascript" src=".../prototype.js"></script>
<script type="text/javascript" src=".../scriptaculous.js"></script>
```

However, this will end up loading *all* the modules, which need to be available in the same directory as scriptaculous.js. This is uselessly wasteful. Most of the time, you need only a couple modules. So, be nice on your bandwidth, your users, and everyone by just loading the modules you need.

There is a special syntax you can use for this when loading script.aculo.us—just list the modules you need in the load parameter:

```
<script type="text/javascript" src=".../prototype.js"></script>
<script type="text/javascript"
 src=".../scriptaculous.js?load=effects,dragdrop"></script>
```

The module names are the base names of the additional .js files provided with script.aculo.us. Order might sometimes be significant. Just look inside scriptaculous.js for the order it uses when loading them all by default.

Thomas advises that in production you should include all the separate files directly, in proper order, and leave scriptaculous.js alone, because it's just a convenience loader. The most efficient delivery would be a concatenated .js file sent with gzipping enabled.

Chapter 14

Visual Effects

Animated effects are a huge part of why people use script.aculo.us. They are split in two groups: the *core* effects and the *combined* ones. Combined effects usually rely on the parallel, synchronized execution of other effects. Because such an execution is readily available, creating your own combined effects is very easy.

We'll start with core effects and list the options that are part of the core effect machinery (which means they are available to all effects). Then we'll list the combined effects and their specific options. We will then spend some time on the important topic of *effect queues*, currently far too underknown and underused, which makes all the difference between a newbie and an effects master. Finally, we'll show how to create your own effects.

To use the effects capabilities of script.aculo.us, you'll need to load the *effects* module. So, your minimum loading for script.aculo.us will look like this:

```
<script type="text/javascript" src="effects.js"></script>
```

Note that script.aculo.us relies *heavily* on Prototype, so you would go something like this:

```
<script type="text/javascript" src="prototype.js"></script>
<script type="text/javascript" src="effects.js"></script>
```

14.1 What Are Those Effects, and Why Should We Use Them?

Well, there are plenty of reasons to use effects.

Sometimes you need to bring part of your web page to the user's attention, and visual cues, such as background fade-overs, opacity pulses, growing or shrinking, might be nice. Other times, you're just trying to fine-tune the introduction, or removal, of content; gradually revealing or hiding it (be it by adjusting opacity or by sliding in or out of view) looks and feels better than abruptly displaying or stripping it. You may also want to help users perceive a relocation by gradually moving content from its origin to its destination.

Effects let you do this, and much more, in a uniform, straightforward way. They offer a wide range of standard options and callbacks to help you tailor their execution to your needs. Each specific effect usually provides even more options (for instance, Effect.Highlight, being all about gradually changing the background's color, lets you specify the colors to begin and finish with).

Using effects appropriately can give your web applications a whole new degree of polish and can contribute to the ergonomy of Ajax-powered pages, where there may be minute changes to the contents in locations the user is not necessarily focusing on just then.

Before diving into the myriad options, callbacks, and tweaks surrounding the effects system, I'll introduce you to the core effects so you can get a feel of it quickly. However, we first need to learn how to start an effect.

Starting an Effect

A lot of people get this wrong, so pay attention. The proper way to start a core effect is usually with the **new** operator. This is because otherwise you're using the effect as a function, called in your main code flow, which will prevent multiple effects from properly running in parallel.

Depending on your preferences, you can use one of two syntaxes:

```
new Effect.EffectName(element [, requiredArgs] [, options]) → Effect
extElement.visualEffect('EffectName' [, requiredArgs] [, options]) → extElement
```

These two syntaxes are technically equivalent. Choosing between the two is mostly about your personal sense of code aesthetics. If you look at effect triggering as an external action over an element, you'll probably find the former syntax more intuitive. On the other hand, if we regard effects as extra capabilities of elements, then using the visualEffect() may feel more natural.

Here are two equivalent calls, so you can see how the syntaxes are related, which are very much interchangeable:

```
new Effect.Scale('title', 200, { scaleY: false, scaleContent: false });
$('title').visualEffect('Scale', 200,
  { scaleY: false, scaleContent: false });
```

14.2 Core Effects

Let's start by looking at the core effects. I know we haven't yet looked into the generic options, common to all effects, but there are so many, plus callbacks, that you would be drowned in details without having seen actual effects yet!

So when you see a reference to a common option, such as from, to, or duration, don't worry—it's usually not important enough to disrupt your understanding of the effect, and if you need details, just look inside Section 14.3, *Diving into Effects*, on page 257 for details on the options and callbacks you're wondering about.

Effect.Highlight

Widely known as the Yellow Fade Technique (YFT) effect. This lets you have a background color fade-over, with customizable starting and ending colors. It's ideal to bring the user's attention to a freshly updated fragment of the page (for example, by an Ajax.Updater).

Its specific options include startcolor, endcolor, and revertcolor. The two last ones default to the element's background color (if it can be determined) or, failing that, white. The starting color defaults to *#ffff99*, equivalent to *#ff9*, which is a light yellow. The color fade-over will go from startcolor to endcolor, and once the effect is done, the background color will be reset to revertcolor.

By default, the background image, if any, will be removed during the effect. If you want to have it persist, set the keepBackgroundImage option to **true**.

Because this is such a commonly used effect, there is a special convenience shortcut that lets you trigger this effect on elements with a shorter syntax than the two usual ones:

```
extElement.highlight([options]) → extElement
```

So, triggering it with all the defaults can be as simple as this:

```
$('resultMessage').highlight();
```

Effect.Move

Slides an element to a new position (expressed either as absolute coordinates or as relative offsets), both vertically and horizontally.

Its specific options are x and y, both defaulting to zero, which are either absolute coordinates or relative offsets from the current position. You can tell which by setting the mode option to either *absolute* or *relative* (its default).

Effect.Opacity

Gradually changes an element's opacity to a given level. This relies on Prototype's opacity-related methods to work around the numerous cross-browser kinks.

This effect starts with the element's current opacity unless the from option is defined and ends with an opacity defined by the to option, defaulting to 1.0.

Effect.Parallel

The mechanism for running effects in synchronized parallel mode. If you don't need synchronization (effects starting and ending at the same time), simply run them independently.

You specify the effects as a first argument to the constructor, passing in an array of the effects to be run synchronously. Those effect objects *must* have been created with their sync option set to **true**. The call goes like this:

```
new Effect.Parallel([
  new Effect.Opacity('notice', { sync: true }),
  new Effect.Scale('notice', 100, { sync: true, scaleFrom: 50 })
], { duration: 2 });
```

Note that the effects do not necessarily pertain to the same element; however, there is only one duration (or fps rate, for that matter)—the one set at the Effect.Parallel level; synchronized effects will all step ahead in unison.

Effect.Scale

Gradually scales an element up or down, possibly on only one axis (horizontal or vertical). It features a number of specific options:

- scaleX and scaleY, defaulting to **true**, determine whether scaling occurs in the given direction.

- scaleContent defaults to **true** and activates scaling of the element's content, not just its container box.

- scaleFromCenter lets you rescale not from the top-left corner but from the center (so the element appears to grow outward or shrink inward). This is disabled by default.

- scaleFrom lets you start with the element scaled already at a specific percentage of its original size. This defaults to 100, obviously.

You noticed, I'm sure, there is no scaleTo option. This is because Effect.Scale uses a required argument to obtain its target size, expressed, like the scaleFrom option, as a percentage of its original size. The call goes like this:

```
new Effect.Scale('greeter', 200, { scaleFromCenter: true });
```

Here is a small example combining Effect.Opacity and Effect.Scale through an Effect.Parallel. The result is illustrated through the montage in Figure 14.1, on the next page.

scriptaculous/effects/parallel1/demo.js

```
new Effect.Parallel([
  new Effect.Opacity('demo', { sync: true, from: 1, to: 0.33 }),
  new Effect.Scale('demo', 150, { sync: true,
    scaleFromCenter: true })
], { duration: 2 });
```

We could make the element hide once shrunk, for example by using afterFinish, which is rather intuitive:

scriptaculous/effects/parallel2/demo.js

```
new Effect.Parallel([
  new Effect.Opacity('demo', { sync: true, from: 1, to: 0.33 }),
  new Effect.Scale('demo', 150, { sync: true,
    scaleFromCenter: true })
], { duration: 2, afterFinish: function() {
  $('demo').hide();
}});
```

Effect.Tween

Introduced in version 1.8, this effect encapsulates any progressive series of settings, be it by assigning a property, calling a method, or even calling a callback function you would provide. It

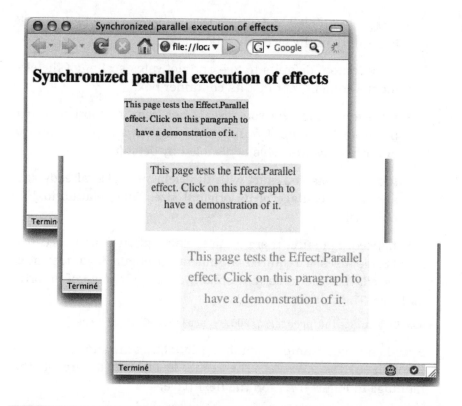

Figure 14.1: SYNCHRONIZED PARALLEL USE OF OPACITY AND SCALE

is a generic machinery that will become more prominently used in version 2.0 (and already powers the combined effect Effect.ScrollTo). Its syntax is rather custom:

```
new Effect.Tween(obj, from, to[, options], propertyOrMethodName)
new Effect.Tween(obj, from, to[, options], callback)
```

The idea is simple: at periodical intervals (for each "frame" of the effect), it will use intermediate values (somewhere between from and to), in sequence, for assigning a property, calling a method, or calling your callback function.

It's sort of PeriodicalExecuter on steroids.

Let's consider a few examples:

```
new Effect.Tween('edtGain', 1, 20, 'value');
```

Assuming the element with an id= of *edtGain* is some form field, its value property will be set from 1 to 20 using default effect parameters (up to 100 frames, or steps, in 1 second).

```
new Effect.Tween('edtGain', 1, 20, { fps: 10, duration: 2 }, 'value');
```

This call features the option hash (do note that it appears *before* the final argument), which makes it here so that there are exactly twenty frames over two seconds (therefore using only integer values during the effect).

```
new Effect.Tween('notice', 30, 120, 'setHeight');
```

Because setHeight is a method on the DOM element, the method will be called (instead of a property assignment).

```
var notice = $('notice'), color = notice.getStyle('backgroundColor');
var blue = parseInt((color.match(/\d+/) || '')[2], 10) || 0;
var rgb;
new Effect.Tween(notice, 0, 255, function(rg) {
  rgb = [rg, rg, blue].inject('#', function(acc, comp) {
    return acc + comp.toColorPart();
  });
  notice.setStyle({ backgroundColor: rgb });
});
```

And this last one quickly ramps up the yellow tone of the element's background (from absent to full bright). As you can see, Tween is pretty generic and versatile.

Effect.Morph

Quite the big gun, introduced in version 1.7. This takes a set of CSS properties and gradually migrates the element's relevant style values to these targets. Mighty!

This effect takes a single specific option, named style. For the sake of convenience, you can express your target style definition in three ways:

- As a CSS class name. The element will then morph toward the style specification for this class name.

- As an inline style specification (think style= attribute values).

- As a hash of CSS properties. Both official (hyphen-based) and camelized (for example, borderStyle) syntaxes are allowed for the property names.

And that's not all there is about convenience! Thomas anticipates so much use of this effect that extended elements get a specific

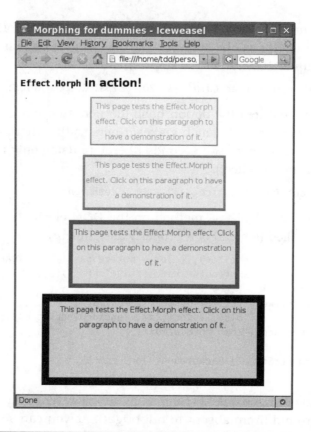

Figure 14.2: THE ALMIGHTY EFFECT.MORPH IN ACTION

morph() method, with the style as the first argument and possible options as the second. Here are examples of all three argument syntaxes:

```
extElement.morph('erroneous'); // CSS class name
extElement.morph(
  'color: maroon; background: #fdd; border-color: maroon;');
extElement.morph({
  width: '50ex', height: '10em',
  backgroundColor: '#ddf', color: '#009',
  borderWidth: '1em', borderColor: '#009',
  opacity: '1'
}, { duration: 2 });
```

You can see a montage of how the last call behaves in Figure 14.2. It may not render too well on the black-and-white paper version of this book, but check out the source code archive!

This works best for color- and length-related properties (as well as opacity) but can be used for just about anything. Color target properties cannot use color names but must use a *rgb(r, g, b)*, *#rgb*, or *#rrggbb* form. However, properties that cannot be gradually modified (for example, font-style or text-decoration) will be set to their target value only when the morph terminates. In a more general manner, not all CSS shorthands are allowed. It will in the end depend on your browser's level of support for DOM Level 2 Style. Test carefully.

A note of warning, though: at the time of this writing, if properties are specified through CSS rules instead of inline styles (CSS rules being best practice), they will be retrieved as computed values, thus in pixels. Such values will be used as the starting point of your effect, *but they will use your target values' units* (indeed, there is no simple way to convert this alternate-unit value to a pixel-based value). So when you morph length values (for example, marginTop or borderLeftWidth), either put the initial values in inline style= attributes or use pixel units. Thomas may have figured out some DOM Style–fu by the time this book is released, but better safe than sorry. Try it to be sure. A similar warning goes for property values, which need to be strings at this time. Note how we set opacity to '1' instead of just 1.

As you can see, with these building blocks available, just about anything can be done. Once you can change an element's position, size, and opacity and then run such changes in synchronized parallel mode, you're all set!

14.3 Diving into Effects

Before going ahead with combined effects, we need to review generic options and callbacks that are available on all effects. Many of those were alluded to in the prior section, so it's time you get the nitty-gritty details.

Common Effect Options

Effects come with a number of standard options. Knowing them is one of the keys to successful effects usage (and something too few developers take the time to learn).

When: delay and queue

The rule of thumb is this: an effect starts as soon as it is created. You can delay it by using the delay option, which is in seconds and which defaults to 0.0. As we'll see later in Section 14.5, *Unlocking the Cool Factor: Effect Queues*, on page 264, effects are put in queues upon creation. The default value for queue, *parallel*, has them start as soon as the delay expires; there are, however, several other possible values, as well as the ability to create custom queues, too.

How Fast: duration, fps, sync, and transition

Effects are animated through a series of steps, or *frames*, spread over a given duration. By default, they run over a duration of 1.0 second, at a rate of up to 100 frames per second (fps). The effect engine adjusts depending on the performance of the user's computer. Note that 25 fps is fast enough for the human eye to see a fluid animation.

Frames are not necessarily spread evenly across the duration of the effect. For most effects, a linear distribution would actually not look too good. As we will see in a moment, script.aculo.us lets you specify, through the transition option, one of eight possible "transitions," which are simple functions determining how to get from one position (in the time window of the effect) to the next. The default transition is Effect.Transitions.sinoidal, which basically makes the effect start up slowly, quicken, and then slow back down at the end. It's usually the best setting.

Finally, sync is both related to effect start and effect progress. In order to run effects in synchronized parallel mode (inside an Effect.Parallel, as we'll see in a moment), you need to make sure all synchronized effects have their sync option set to **true**.

Cutting Corners: from and to

By default, an effect goes from a starting position of zero to a final position of one. You can have it start ahead or stop short by adjusting its from and to options. This is mostly used for effects where these options represent extreme points of the effect's action. For instance, with Effect.Opacity, position zero is full transparence, and position one is full opacity.

Note that from can also be greater than to. The effect will then run "backward," so to speak.

Common Effect Callbacks

All effects provide seven standard callbacks that we can use to hook custom behavior into the effect's processing. They are usually arranged in before/after pairs, and their names contain the name of the effect's method that is wrapped between the two callbacks.

1. beforeStart occurs right before the effect is scheduled to start (right before it is queued up for execution). At this point, all of the effect's internal properties have been defined but not yet adjusted by queue control. This is mostly useful when writing custom effects. Note that there is no *after* variant, because no useful case for it has emerged yet.

2. beforeSetup and afterSetup occur around the setup() call, which happens when the effect *renders for the first time*, after any delay or queue-caused wait has expired. Effect creators use this method to perform whatever element alterations they need for their effect to work (for example, make the element positioned, give it a layout container, and so on). Using beforeSetup is often handy.

3. beforeUpdate and afterUpdate are triggered around every single frame rendering, including the first one.

4. beforeFinish and afterFinish occur around effect finalization; afterFinish is often used instead of a custom queue when there are only two effects to queue or when you need an effect to complete before running some more code.

Bouncy or Smooth? Effect "Transitions"

Most script.aculo.us users don't realize that effects are equipped with a *transition mode*. As I mentioned earlier, a transition is a function that gets the effect from one step to the next, by turning a time position (from zero to one) into another one, used by update(), which does the actual rendering. By tweaking transition functions, we can obtain pretty funky visual variants over any effect.

The transition option is usually assigned one of the eight transition functions in the Effect.Transitions namespace. It defaults to the sinoidal() function. As a special alias, setting it to **false** is equivalent to selecting the linear() function.

Understanding the code of these functions may sometimes be rather daunting, especially if you always hated trigonometry. To save you the trouble, here's a quick rundown on what impact the functions have on the series of rendering positions for the effect:

Function	Impact
flicker	Randomly picks from the 25% last frames, thus flickering.
full	Effect disabler of sorts—sticks with the final frame. This is used in synchronized parallel effects to ensure one of them is fully effective immediately. It's also handy, at debug time, to quickly "enable" the result of an effect.
linear	Goes from start to finish at a steady pace. For most animations (especially moving and scaling), this is actually not too aesthetic. It doesn't feel natural; it feels rather dull.
none	The other effect disabler—sticks with the first frame. Technically, the same effect can be achieved with a full transition over swapped values for the from and to options; it's very much a question of personal aesthetics and logic whether you use full or none. During debugging, it's handy to leave an effect in code while disabling it for a while.
pulse	Accelerates the effect so it runs fully more than one time in its lifetime. By default, it uses five pulses, but you can use bind() to pass it another count. For instance, the combined Effect.Pulsate essentially relies on Effect.Opacity with a rather crafty use of this transition.
reverse	Reverses the effect. This has it go from its final frame to its first one.
sinoidal	The default transition. This has the effect start and finish slowly but accelerate in between. This is aesthetically more pleasing for most effects, such as movements and scalings.
spring	The latest addition. Specifically targeted at effects such as Effect.Move, this lets the effect "overshoot" a bit and then bounce back and forth around the final position, finally stabilizing on it. This is especially nice for giving a slightly bouncy feel to reverting a drag and drop, for instance.

For examples of custom, third-party transitions, see Ken Snyder's script.aculo.us port of Robert Penner's easing library, as reported at http://giancarlo.dimassa.net/2007/07/11.

14.4   Combined Effects

Based on core effects, script.aculo.us provides a number of combined effects, which cater to most common needs. We won't show examples of these, but you'll see combined demos on the documentation site.[1] I'll just list them as they stand at the time of this writing, with a few notes about specific options they may have.

Triggering a Combined Effect

Unlike core effects, the **new** operator is superfluous here. The functions for combined effects are not constructors. On the other hand, they all benefit from a shortcut syntax that makes them available as methods on extended elements (starting with script.aculo.us 1.7.1). So, you can use any of the two following syntaxes:

```
Effect.CombinedEffectName(element [, options])
extElement.combinedEffectName([options]) → extElement
```

Do note that a few combined effects are left out of this latter shortcut syntax because they would conflict with existing extended methods or were deemed irrelevant for this shortcut use. These are Event, ScrollTo, and Transform.

Smooth Operators

Effect.Fade/Effect.Appear

> These make an element fade away or fade in, respectively. Fading out will start, by default, with the element's current opacity; when the effect is over, the element is hidden, and its original opacity is restored. Fading in starts by making sure that the element is displayed and starts with its original opacity if it already was. These effects obviously rely on the Opacity core effect.

Sliding In and Out

Effect.BlindUp/Effect.BlindDown

> These roll up (or down, respectively) a surface on which the element is supposed to be displayed. The element's contents are left untouched and do not move. Only its surface shrinks upward or expands downward. Note that using BlindDown will work even if the element is not "rolled up" then, and the other way around.

---

1. http://wiki.script.aculo.us/scriptaculous/show/CombinationEffectsDemo

Effect.SlideUp/Effect.SlideDown

> These are content-sliding variants of the "blind" effects. These look like the blinds are being slid down or up, so the contents move along. However, this requires that the element's contents are wrapped in an additional container, say, a <div>. You can't just put the contents in the element affected by the effect, as you would on, for instance, BlindDown.

Effect.DropOut

> This opens a trap under the element, in which it falls while fading out. That's a nasty way to die (especially because the trap, being invisible, leaves no evidence whatsoever).

Creative In and Outs

Most of these are based on the Scale core effect.

Effect.Grow/Effect.Shrink

> These make the element expand in (from size zero) or shrivel away (and stay hidden, although with restored properties, as usual). This relies on several core effects, most importantly Scale and Move. There is a specific option, called direction, that defines in which direction the expansion or contraction takes place. It defaults to *center* but can also be any of the box corners: *top-left*, *top-right*, *bottom-right*, and *bottom-left*.

Effect.Puff

> This taps a magical wand and has the element disappear in a cloud of smoke. Well, almost—it expands to twice its size while fading away, which is just as good.

Effect.SwitchOff

> So, your element is on a good ol' TV, and you're switching it off. It'll shrink away much like things did back then—with a flickering, quick contraction toward the center.

Effect.Squish

> This has the element shrivel away with no specific positioning. For most elements for which the point of reference is their top-left corner, it'll contract toward that point.

Effect.Fold

> This is a two-phase shrink. First it shrinks vertically, until only a tiny, 5-pixel bar is left, and then left-wise. Content is not scaled along. Think of it as folding a napkin. Sort of.

Attention Getters

Effect.Pulsate

"It is alive!" Your element will fade out and then in several times (customize with the pulses option, defaulting to 5) over two seconds. This is one of the favorites, along with the simpler Highlight.

Effect.Shake

This one feels a tad more toyish. It shakes the element right and left three times over half a second. It's a nice way to highlight a form field that doesn't pass validation. Starting with version 1.8, it now features extra duration and distance options.

Effect.ScrollTo

This is the animated equivalent of Element.scrollTo(). It gradually scrolls the viewport so the element comes into view. You can add an extra scrolling with the offset option (expressed in pixels).

Miscellanea

Effect.Event

This is just a code placeholder. You would use its afterFinish callback to plug in some code. This is mostly useful in complex effect queues to lace actual effects with custom code.

Effect.Transform

Dreaming about Effect.Morph heavy lifting? This one lets you define multiple morph-related effects (called *tracks*), which will be run *in parallel*. The good thing is that it's reusable! Here's an example, pulled straight out of script.aculo.us's change log (although slightly simplified):

```
// set up transformation
var transformation = new Effect.Transform([
  { 'div.morphing': 'font-size: 20px; padding-left: 40em' },
  { 'blah'         : 'warning' }
], { duration: 0.5 });
// play transformation (can be called more than once)
transformation.play();
```

Three More Things You Should Know...

- Remember that because of reliance on methods such as Element.hide() and Element.show(), you will have to style initially hidden elements with an *inline style="display: none" attribute*. Using a CSS rule will not work. The element will remain hidden.

- A lot of effects will have trouble with table-related elements (mostly <tr>, <th>, and <td>) on Internet Explorer. More often than not, making sure your rows are properly wrapped in a <tbody> (or <thead> or <tfoot>) will help.

- If you hit performance issues (typically frame drops), it's usually a symptom that your DOM trees are way too complex and/or that you're relying on a lot of opacity play. Several browsers (most notably, on Macs, Firefox, and Safari 2) get sluggish in such situations. Reducing opacity-based effects, or the amount of effects running at the same time, usually helps a lot.

14.5 Unlocking the Cool Factor: Effect Queues

Chaining effects is a common need; maybe you want an element to fade in, and then you want to highlight it. Or perhaps it should pulsate and finally fade out. Such cases can be well enough handled by manually defining the afterFinish callback.

However, consider more advanced cases. One question that keeps popping up on the support mailing list sounds like this: "I have this list of items, and when I mouse over them, I'd like their picture to change with a fade-out + fade-in (*not* a crossfade)."

Although the requirements seem difficult, the code for it is quite simple. Sure, it doesn't rely on manually chaining effects using afterFinish. That works mostly when you know the effect list in advance and doesn't scale very well from a readability standpoint.

No, the answer lies with *effect queues*. Effect queues let you define multiple queues in which to put effects. You don't have to put them at the end of the queue, either. You can ask them to zip all the way to the front, for instance.

Using the Global Queue

So far, we haven't used the queue option in our effects. It defaults to 'parallel'. When its value is a string, it is assumed to be a position specification in the global queue (quite simply, the queue whose name is 'global').

Queues are stored in the Effect.Queues repository and are accessed through its get() method, passing in the queue name. When adding an effect to a queue, you can specify a position, which will be interpreted as follows:

- *parallel* will have the effect start the next time the queue processes its effects.
- *front* puts the effect before any pending effect in the queue, delaying them accordingly.
- *end* puts the effect at the end of the queue, obviously. It will trigger after all the effects currently in the queue are done.
- *with-last* schedules the effect to start with the last pending effect currently in the queue, if any (if there is no pending effect, it will start after all running effects in the queue are over).

Queues process their effects at a rather high frequency, currently up to 100Hz, which is, in my humble opinion, faster than needed. The human eye is tricked into seeing continuity from 25Hz, and even the sharpest eyes cannot detect frames faster than 50Hz (although I'm quite certain I'll find hardcore gamers[2] who will swear they need more). This does mean you need to watch the order in which you queue stuff up. It should be the intended order of execution, whenever possible.

So when you specify any of these values for the queue option (once again, *parallel* is the default), you use the global queue, which is fitting for most purposes. For instance, maybe we want to react to an Ajax update in failure mode by morphing the updated panel to a given CSS class and then pulsating it:

```
var updater = new Ajax.Updater('feedback', '/user/update', {
  parameters: $('userForm').serialize(),
  onComplete: function() {
    if (!updater.success()) {
      $('feedback').morph('errors').pulsate({ queue: 'end' });
    }
  }
});
```

Custom Queues: Shifting Gears

This is all well and good, but it won't quite cut it when you need to deal with independent queues for several objects. For instance, the fade-change-fade sequence we mentioned earlier, which is a common use

---

2. Especially first-person-shooter gamers (which is ironic, because the abbreviation also spells FPS. Um. . . .)

case, won't work with a global queue for all the items in the list. Each item needs its own queue.

The solution is to use *scoped queues*. Instead of just using a position string for your queue option, provide an object with two properties: scope, which identifies your queue, and position, which is your position string.

How about a nice example? Let's take this item list we mentioned:

```
<ul id="topics" class="topics">
  <li id="item_js"><span>JavaScript</span></li>
  <li id="item_proto"><span>Prototype</span></li>
  <li id="item_scripty"><span>script.aculo.us</span></li>
</ul>
```

OK, now if we provide some mouseover/mouseout machinery so that going in triggers a black-and-white image and going out goes back to the normal version of the image, the core code for implementing the transition looks like this:

scriptaculous/effects/queues/demo.js

```
var queue = { scope: element.id, position: 'end' };
element.visualEffect('Opacity', { to: 0.1, duration: FADE_DURATION,
  queue: queue });
new Effect.Event({ queue: queue, afterFinish: function() {
  element.setStyle({backgroundImage: url});
}});
element.visualEffect('Opacity', { from: 0.1, to: 1,
  duration: FADE_DURATION, queue: queue });
```

Note the queue definition. It uses a unique scope, based on the suffix of the source element's ID; all effects defined are stored in that queue by using their queue option. Since queues are separate, we can trigger parallel sequences on multiple items while retaining sequential execution for the effects at the item level.

Finally, note that you can enforce a limit to the events in a queue at any given time by using an extra property for your queue option object: limit. This can be useful to prevent rapid-fire clicking from queuing up a huge amount of Ajax requests, for instance, when only a few ones make sense from an ergonomical standpoint.

14.6 Effect Helpers

Thomas acknowledges very common use cases now and then, swooping in with a nice little helper. Over time, the following surfaced:

Effect.toggle()

When hiding elements, you often show them back. And hide them again. And so forth. Because you often toggle visibility, usually with one of the Fade/Appear, BlindUp/BlindDown, or SlideUp/SlideDown sets, the convenience Effect.toggle() is here to make it shorter. Calling it on an element will check whether it's hidden (read: its display CSS property is set to *none*) and call the appropriate effect based on that.

```
Effect.toggle(elt [, family = 'appear'])
```

The allowed families are, logically enough, *appear*, *blind*, and *slide*. Note you don't have to actually use these in pairs. An element toggled off using the *slide* family, for instance, can perfectly be brought back using *blind*.

Effect.multiple()

This is one Flash killer. It applies any effect, in delayed sequence, over a series of elements. For instance, you could use it with Effect.Fade over the items in a list, to have them fade away progressively, from first to last, each beginning to fade out shortly after the previous one. This is governed by the generic delay option, plus the specific (though ill-named) speed option, which expresses the internal delay between two consecutive elements, in seconds. It defaults to 0.1".

You can pass elements in a variety of ways:

```
Effect.multiple(element, effect [, options])
Effect.multiple([ element, ... ], effect [, options])
Effect.multiple(NodeList, effect [, options])
```

When a single element is passed, its childNodes property is used.

The really neat use of this is when you have text where each character is a separate element (for example, a <span> of its own). You can then pull off awesome progressive text fades, for instance. Of course, marking this up is a bore. That is why we have. . .

Effect.tagifyText()

This one is mostly a support function for multiple(). It takes all the text child nodes of an element and replaces them with the proper <span> (taking care of a few styling issues). Making regular text ready for multiple() magic becomes a snap. Here's a short example:

```
Effect.tagifyText('heading'); // just once
Effect.multiple('heading', Effect.Highlight); // any time
```

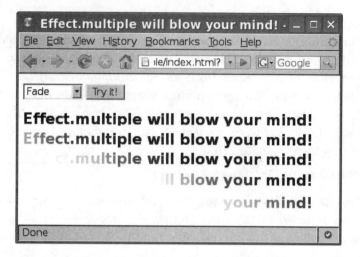

Figure 14.3: WHO NEEDS FLASH ANYWAY?

Beware: many effects end up with actually hiding the element. When applied in sequence over the characters of an element, this can result in weird, left-shifting behavior. You may then want to short-circuit the internal finalizer of these effects. Make sure this has no undesirable side effect, but when you're ready, it should look something like this:

```
Effect.multiple('heading', Effect.Fade, {
  speed: 0.05, afterFinishInternal: Prototype.emptyFunction });
```

The source code for this book comes with a detailed example that lets you pick among five effects and try it. Figure 14.3 shows a montage of how this looks with Fade.

There are also several helpers that are more targeted at effect authors. We'll discover that now.

14.7 How to Create Our Own Effects

Writing custom effects is a skill that can range from simple combinations to aping the code of existing combined effects to truly displaying some script.aculo.us-fu. Covering all of it is beyond the scope of this chapter, but I'd like to give you a few pointers anyway so that you can start on a clear trail.

Before digging in, understand the dependencies for your custom effects. As script.aculo.us changes, you will need to test your work against the new releases. As a matter of fact, script.aculo.us 2.0 will have a completely rewritten effects engine, which should not, however, stop the 1.8 version from working.

What's an Effect to Do?

Most effects are supposed to derive from the Effect.Base class. They can then use this base to hook up their specific logic for initialization, rendering, and finalization.

An effect has a number of properties, mostly for internal use, that constitute its state. Many of them are going to be very useful to you when writing your own effects, especially for the rendering logic, so let me quickly describe them:

Property	Description
currentFrame	As we saw in Section 14.3, *How Fast: duration, fps, sync, and transition*, on page 258, an effect's animation is divided into *frames*. Every frame gets rendered at most once (frames may be skipped because of CPU hogging or debugging breakpoints, for instance). The amount of frames depends on the duration of the effect (duration option, defaults to 1) and its frames per second ratio (fps option). The first actual frame is 1.
finishOn	The moment (expressed in milliseconds since the epoch, the usual numerical form of times) at which the effect should finish (based on delay and duration options).
fromToDelta	The difference between the to and from options. You normally never have to deal with it yourself; render() uses it to create a proper evolution of your rendering positions.
options	The options passed at construction time, possibly adjusted by the initialize() method.
position	Your current rendering position, as a floating-point number between 0 and 1[3] (same scale as the from and to options). It's automatically adjusted by render(), prior to triggering *update* callbacks.

---

3. Although on a few transitions, such as Spring, it may exceed 1 at some point.

Property	Description
startOn	The moment (expressed in milliseconds since the epoch, the usual numerical form of times) at which the effect should start (based on the delay option).
state	A string that tells where your effect stands in its life cycle. The possible values are *idle* (not started yet), *running*, and *finished*.
totalFrames	The total amount of frames for the effect, based on its duration and fps options. By way of consequence, this is the maximum amount of calls to your update() method.
totalTime	The duration of your effect, in milliseconds. It's based on the duration option.

Note that it is possible to short-circuit an effect, abruptly stopping it where it stands, by calling its cancel() method. This does not trigger the *finish* callbacks.

Speaking of callbacks, in order to let users of your shiny new effect use them, you will not hook them up for internal processing. The effect machinery lets you define identical callbacks with the *Internal* prefix (for example, afterFinishInternal()), which are called right before the "public" ones. This is where you should put code that doesn't fit in the clear-cut methods you can redefine.

The execution of an effect is sequenced as follows, codewise:

1. The usual initialize() method is called. It's all yours. You *must* end it with a call to start(), passing it the options hash.
2. start() takes care of all the boilerplate setup. Before scheduling your effect in the proper queue, it triggers the beforeStart() callback.
3. As soon as the effect is scheduled for execution, its loop() method kicks in, which verifies that it should still run (it might be overdue) and, if not, takes it straight to the finish line. Otherwise, it computes its regular position and frame number and delegates to render().
4. render() takes care of the *setup* callbacks on the first rendering, calling your optional setup() method between the two, and then delegates to the effect's chosen transition to adjust the rendering position. It then calls your optional update() method with it.
5. The effect has reached its end time. It renders its final position, it gets decommissioned from the effect queue, and your optional finish() method is called between the two *finish* callbacks.

The following methods are an integral part of the effect system, so you never override them: start(), loop(), render() (it would, anyway, be redefined dynamically by start()), and cancel().

On the other hand, the following methods are undefined by default and are designed for you to define according to your effect's logic. They are all optional, because their usefulness entirely depends on your effect's nature:

1. setup() is called before the first actual rendering.
2. update(pos) is called for every rendering, with a position adjusted by the transition function. It's where you put the actual frame-creating code. For instance, if you look at this method for the core Effect.Opacity, it simply goes like this:

```
update: function(position) {
        this.element.setOpacity(position);
}
```

3. finish() is called after the last rendering and after the effect has been decommissioned from its queue. You'll mostly use it when your effect is supposed to restore some state on its element(s). For instance, numerous official effects that end up hiding an element they transformed do hide it and then restore its original style.

Helpers for the Effect Author

You'll find many helper methods in effects.js that take care of several little tricks you might need to pull off when writing effects (after all, Thomas did). First, element extensions gain more methods still:

- getInlineOpacity() returns the CSS opacity property from the element's inline style= attribute or the empty string if there is no such property.
- forceRerendering() forces the browser to render the element again by doing a flash DOM update and revert on its contents, which can be useful to circumvent the occasional odd browser-rendering bug.
- setContentZoom(percent) alters the element's font size by the given factor (expressed as percents, for example, 120 to zoom up 20%).

Our beloved String also gets a couple helpers:

- parseColor((default)) turns the string representation of a CSS color into the six-digit CSS form (#rrggbb). This can start from the same form, the three-digit form, or the developed form (rgb(r, g, b)). If the string is not deemed valid, it will return the method's argument or, failing one, will return itself.

- parseStyle() takes a CSS property list (for example, the value of an inline style= attribute) and turns it into a hash object with the corresponding properties.

An Example: Effect.Wave

Thomas demonstrated custom effects creation at RailsConf US 2007 with this Effect.Wave class. It makes the characters in an element's text slide up and down to create a wave effect. This is a nice example because it relies only on the two critical methods, setup() and update(), with no internal callbacks or other extra tricks.

scriptaculous/effects/wave/demo.js

```
Line 1    Effect.Wave = Class.create(Effect.Base, {
   -        initialize: function(element) {
   -          this.element = $(element);
   -          this.start(arguments[1] || {});
   5        },
   -
   -        setup: function(){
   -          Effect.tagifyText(this.element);
   -          this.chars = this.element.childElements();
  10        },
   -
   -        update: function(position) {
   -          var factor = position < 0.5 ? position * 2 : (1 - position) * 2;
   -          var topPos;
  15          this.chars.each(function(character, index) {
   -            topPos = Math.sin(position * ((index % 20) + 1)) * 30 * factor;
   -            character.setStyle({ top: Math.round(topPos) + 'px' });
   -          });
   -        }
  20    });
```

This code illustrates a number of common practices in writing your own effect:

- On line 3, we extend the element we're supposed to operate on and cache this in a property. This way, we can use extended methods on it throughout our code without wondering whether we need to extend it on the fly.
- It is essential to remember passing our options argument, if any, to the start() method, as on line 4. If we fail to, all the generic options (for example, to or duration) will stop working! Of course,

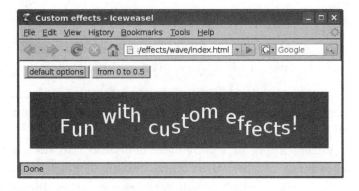

Figure 14.4: Effect.Wave in action

if no options argument was passed, we substitute an empty hash instead.

- Right when the effect is about to render its first frame, on line 8, we replace its text with individual, per-character <span> elements using tagifyText() (which we know from on page 267). This lets us grab all these <span>s on line 9. We might as well cache the result of this DOM exploration, because we don't much care whether it changes while the effect takes place.

Then it's just a matter of playing with a sine function to compute the vertical positions of each letter, one frame after another. There are a lot of magic numbers in this function, but don't be put off. This is just the result of tweaking and adjusting until it feels cool; there's nothing mandatory or mission critical in there. . . .

The effect at work can be seen in Figure 14.4.

Where to Start?

First, you'll find many user contributions (of varying quality) on the official site in the script.aculo.us "Treasure Chest": http://wiki.script.aculo.us/scriptaculous/show/EffectsTreasureChest. You'll find several nice additions in there, such as Effect.DropIn, Effect.Bounce, extra transition functions, and more.

Second, a good idea is to go through the source code of effects.js. By studying the code for official effects, you can understand a lot and get inspired by the wizardry Thomas pulls off now and then.

What We Just Learned

Effects are a prominent part of script.aculo.us and a rather rich API. Let's quickly summarize what we covered in this chapter:

- There are two kinds of effects: *core* and *combined*. The seven core effects are created using the **new** operator, but combined ones are called like regular functions.
- Most effects apply to a single element and can take a hash of options, many of which are common to all effects.
- By default, effects run immediately upon creation; therefore, they execute in parallel, although not necessarily in sync.
- To run multiple effects in perfect sync, we need to wrap them in an Effect.Parallel call and set their individual sync options to **true**.
- Effects can also be arranged in queues, with the queue option.
- Transitions control the variation of speed across the effect's duration. The default transition, Effect.Transitions.sinoidal, has a "natural" feel to it by accelerating slightly after the beginning and decelerating again shortly before the end.
- A few effect helpers facilitate common usage patterns, such as applying the same effect on multiple elements with a small delay between each trigger.
- We can create our own effects and add them to the library.

Neuron Workout

Here are a few questions to ponder and suggestions for code practice:

- Say we have half a dozen items (effects and custom code snippets) we want to queue up like pearls on a string. What's the best option here? afterFinish callbacks or a custom queue? Why?
- How would you queue two effects with a two-second pause between the end of the first effect and the beginning of the second one?
- Write horizontal blind effects (Effect.BlindLeft and Effect.BlindRight).
- How could we turn any effect into a permanent loop?

And that's it for effects. It's a fascinating thing, no doubt, and one of the main reasons people use script.aculo.us. The other main developer magnet is the support for drag and drop, including its use to reorder elements on the page. That's what we'll dive into next.

Drag and Drop

A huge part of what people envision when they think "Web 2.0 interface" is drag and drop. Moving blocks around in a customizable portal page, resizing elements, putting items in a shopping cart, and reordering items in a list—it all comes down to dragging and dropping. Fortunately, script.aculo.us comes with strong support for this capability, easing integration into our own web applications.

To use script.aculo.us's dragging capabilities, you'll need to load the *dragdrop* module, which requires the *effects* module. So, your minimum loading for script.aculo.us will look like this:

```
<script type="text/javascript"
 src="scriptaculous.js?load=effects,dragdrop"></script>
```

15.1 Dragging Stuff Around

Let's start with the basics: making an element draggable and dragging it around. We'll then see how we can react to various stages of the drag and look at the numerous aspects that can be customized.

Also, remember that we did use simple drag and drop in Section 9.2, *Get It: Geometry Persistence*, on page 184, so you'll find example code there as well.

Making an Element Draggable

OK, first things first: making an element draggable. It can be as simple as instantiating a Draggable object over it (or its ID, as usual):

```
new Draggable(element);
```

If you need to remove the dragging capability later, you'll have to keep the reference tucked somewhere and call its destroy() method when its time has come.

Let's create an example that we'll build upon as we discover new options. We'll draw a small checkerboard and put a nice, spiffy Tux (you know, the Linux mascot) on it. (This particular Tux looks lovely but a bit overweight, so dragging sounds appropriate.)

Create a new directory, and then copy the usual prototype.js, scriptaculous.js, and effects.js files, plus dragdrop.js. Here's our HTML page:

`scriptaculous/dragdrop/board/step1/index.html`

```
<!DOCTYPE html PUBLIC "-//W3C//DTD XHTML 1.0 Strict//EN"
 "http://www.w3.org/TR/xhtml11/DTD/xhtml11-strict.dtd">
<html xmlns="http://www.w3.org/1999/xhtml" lang="en-US" xml:lang="en-US">
<head>
    <meta http-equiv="Content-Type" content="text/html; charset=utf-8" />
    <title>Playing with draggables</title>
    <link rel="stylesheet" type="text/css" href="demo.css" />
    <script type="text/javascript" src="prototype.js"></script>
    <script type="text/javascript"
     src="scriptaculous.js?load=effects,dragdrop"></script>
    <script type="text/javascript" src="demo.js"></script>
</head>
<body>

<h1>Playing with Draggables</h1>

<div id="board">
    <span id="piece"></span>
</div>

<form>
    <p>
        <input type="checkbox" id="chkDraggable" checked="checked" />
        <label for="chkDraggable" accesskey="D">Tux is draggable</label>
    </p>
</form>

</body>
</html>
```

We'll create the board cells dynamically. First, this spares us from tedious markup in the board element; second, this opens the door to custom event handling and other scripting tricks later, should we feel like it. Every cell will be a <span> element in the board's <div>, with an id= attribute containing the *cell* class and, alternatively, the *white* or *black* class.

We'll also want to demonstrate how to cancel dragging functionality by destroying the Draggable object. That's what our bottom checkbox is for. Here's the whole script:

scriptaculous/dragdrop/board/step1/demo.js

```
Line 1  var gTux;

        function drawBoard(cols, rows) {
          var board = $('board');
    5     for (var row = 0; row < rows; ++row)
            for (var col = 0; col < cols; ++col) {
              var cell = new Element('span', {
                'class': 'cell ' + (1 == (row + col) % 2 ? 'white' : 'black') });
              board.appendChild(cell);
   10       }
        } // drawBoard

        function toggleTux() {
          if (gTux) {
   15       gTux.element.setStyle({ cursor: 'default' });
            gTux.destroy();
            gTux = null;
            return;
          }
   20     gTux = new Draggable('piece');
          gTux.element.setStyle({ cursor: '' });
        } // toggleTux

        document.observe('dom:loaded', function() {
   25     $('chkDraggable').observe('click', toggleTux);
          drawBoard(3, 3);
          toggleTux();
        });
```

The drawBoard() function, starting on line 3, takes care of creating the cell elements and putting them in the board's <div>. Notice how it uses Element's constructor syntax (on line 7) to easily build the DOM node.

The toggleTux() function is responsible for either making the Tux draggable or removing draggability. It stores the reference in the gTux variable. We're going for the most basic creation here. Just look at line 20. Disabling draggability is as easy as a destroy() call, which you can see on line 16.

Figure 15.1, on the next page, shows a montage of various dragging stages of this first implementation.

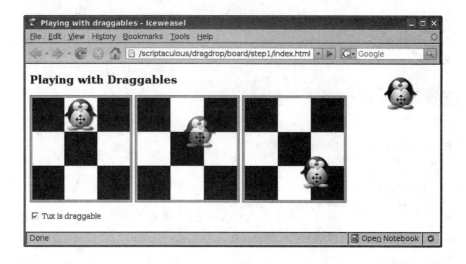

Figure 15.1: TUX DRAGGING ABOUT

Try unchecking the box. You will now notice the cursor no longer indicates dragging capability, and attempting to drag Tux is rewarded by resonant failure. Checking the box again restores the penguin's fleetness of feet.

As basic usage goes, here are a few things you should know:

- You can always interrupt a drag by pressing the [Esc] key.
- During drag, the element's opacity moves to 70%. Its original opacity is restored when the drag ends.
- By default, the whole element is made draggable. Holding the "left" (that is, main) mouse button over any part of it will trigger the drag. You can restrict this to part of the element's contents through the handle option, which we'll discuss in a moment. It's commonly used to drag through a title bar or a corner, for instance.
- If your element needs to be both draggable and clickable, triggering drag as soon as the mouse button is down can be a problem and result in disruptive ergonomy. You can use the delay option, discussed later, to require the button to stay down for a given time before the drag actually happens (it will catch up on the mouse movement in the meantime, if necessary).

Interacting with the Drag: Callbacks

Draggables come with a few callbacks, some of which are reserved for local use (being passed in the draggable object's options) and are marked in the next table with an asterisk (*). We'll see "global" use in Section 15.5, *Monitoring Drags*, on page 293.

When used locally, all callbacks take the Draggable object as the first argument and the event object as the second argument. Also note that when you have a Draggable reference in hand, you can get the element itself using its element property.

Callback	Description
onStart	The drag starts. The start effect, if any, has not been applied yet, but any other preliminary work (cloning, position adjustments, and so on) was performed already.
onDrag	The drag is going on. While in drag state, the element is about to be moved in order to reflect mouse movement.
change*	This occurs immediately *after* having moved the element in response to mouse movement.
onDropped*	The element was just successfully dropped on a defined drop zone somewhere. We'll talk more about drop zones starting on page 293.
onEnd	The drag is freshly over. Finalization (revert effect, reverting, and end effect, if any) is about to start.

Let's demonstrate callbacks by adding a highlight CSS class to our board while the drag is going on and by building a position log of our Tux as it gets dropped on cells. We'll use the chess notation of cells: rows numbered from A, top to bottom, and columns numbered from 1, left to right. Tux is deemed to be on the cell where its top-left corner stands.

First, we need to add an element for the log. An ordered list seems pretty appropriate from a semantic standpoint:

scriptaculous/dragdrop/board/step2/index.html

```
<div id="board">
    <span id="piece"></span>
    <ol id="log"></ol>
</div>
```

The style sheet needs the corresponding adjustments:

`scriptaculous/dragdrop/board/step2/demo.css`

```css
#board.tuxMoving { background-color: #f77; }

#log {
  position: absolute; left: 212px; top: 0; height: 202px; width: 10em;
  font-family: sans-serif; font-size: smaller; color: #555;
  overflow: auto;
}
```

Finally, we'll rework part of our script:

`scriptaculous/dragdrop/board/step2/demo.js`

```js
Line 1  function getTuxCell(tux) {
   -      var pos = tux.positionedOffset();
   -      return [(pos.left / 64).floor(), (pos.top / 64).floor()];
   -    } // getTuxCell
   5
   -    function toggleTux() {
   -      if (gTux) {
   -        gTux.element.setStyle({ cursor: 'default' });
   -        gTux.destroy();
  10        gTux = null;
   -        return;
   -      };
   -      gTux = new Draggable('piece', {
   -        onStart: function() {
  15          $('board').addClassName('tuxMoving');
   -        },
   -        onEnd: function(d) {
   -          $('board').removeClassName('tuxMoving');
   -          var pos = getTuxCell(d.element);
  20          pos = 'ABC'.charAt(pos[1]) + (pos[0] + 1);
   -          $('log').insert('<li>Tux to ' + pos + '</li>');
   -        }
   -      });
   -      gTux.element.setStyle({ cursor: '' });
  25    } // toggleTux
```

The getTuxCell() function converts our Tux's position within the confines of the board (which includes the padding) to a cell number. It's not *entirely* accurate but will do until we rework it later for better movement constraints.

Starting on line 14, notice how our creation call has grown, with its two new callbacks: onStart (which turns on the board highlighting) and onEnd (which turns the highlighting off, computes the cell's name, and adds it to the log).

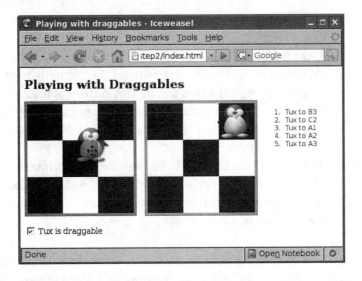

Figure 15.2: CALLBACKS: HIGHLIGHTING AND LOGGING

Figure 15.2 shows the highlighted board (showing a red background around the cells) during a drag and the state of the right-side log after a few movements.

15.2 Controlling How It Starts, Where It Goes, & How It Ends

Drags use effects at three points: starting, ending, and reverting—if there is one. We'll consider reverting first, which can be interesting for our examples.

A reverting draggable element will move to its original position when released. By default, draggable elements do not revert, but you can enable this systematically or based on custom condition code. You can also customize the default reverting movement.

In our example, we'd like our Tux to revert whenever it's dropped outside the board. We'd also want this revert to last a bit longer than the default movement, and to add an extra twist, we'll use the bouncy spring transition for the reverting movement so that Tux overshoots its original location and bounces back and forth around it for a short time before stabilizing.

The two options governing revert are as follows:

Option	Description
revert	Whether to revert the drag (bring the element back to its original position) when the mouse button is released. This can be a boolean, a function, or the special value 'failure', which reverts when there was no successful drop. This defaults to **false**.
reverteffect	The effect to be used for the revert animation. This defaults to a properly defined Effect.Move. It takes three arguments: the dragged element and the dragging's horizontal and vertical offsets.

We'll equip our Tux element with an expando isOut() function. This will serve us well as a value for the revert option and will help us prevent logging of the movement if we decided to revert it.

This leaves our markup and styling untouched. The creation of our Draggable object, however, features two more options:

scriptaculous/dragdrop/board/step3/demo.js

```
Line 1   var range = $R(0, 2);
    -    $('piece').isOut = function() {
    -      var pos = getTuxCell(this);
    -      return !(range.include(pos[0]) && range.include(pos[1]));
    5    };
    -    gTux = new Draggable('piece', {
    -      revert: $('piece').isOut.bind($('piece')),
    -      reverteffect: function(tux, top_offset, left_offset) {
    -        var secs = Math.sqrt((top_offset^2).abs() +
   10          (left_offset^2).abs()) * 0.06;
    -        new Effect.Move(tux, {
    -          x: -left_offset, y: -top_offset, duration: secs,
    -          queue: { scope: '_draggable', position: 'end' },
    -          transition: Effect.Transitions.spring
   15        });
    -      },
    -      onStart: function() {
    -        $('board').addClassName('tuxMoving');
    -      },
   20      onEnd: function(d) {
    -        $('board').removeClassName('tuxMoving');
    -        if (d.element.isOut()) return;
    -        var pos = getTuxCell(d.element);
    -        pos = 'ABC'.charAt(pos[1]) + (pos[0] + 1);
   25        $('log').insert('<li>Tux to ' + pos + '</li>');
    -      }
    -    });
```

The isOut() method takes advantage of an ObjectRange instance to easily check that the computed cell for Tux is within board boundaries (0 to 2 on both axes).

Notice how we take care to *bind* it on line 7. If we didn't do that and simply passed $('piece').isOut, we'd lose the binding, and once invoked, its **this** would evaluate to the calling context (in this particular case, certainly not our Tux element). The revert function is actually passed the dragged element, but that would make for less elegant calling in the onEnd callback, so explicit binding it is!

The code for the reverteffect callback, starting on line 8, is fairly complex, but it's actually lifted straight from the default code in dragdrop.js. Only its duration is altered (using a factor of 0.06 instead of 0.02, giving us more time to savor the effect) and its transition (instead of relying on the default sinoidal one, it uses spring).

Finally, note how we reuse isOut() within onEnd, on line 22, to avoid logging an invalid, reverted movement. Because we're calling the method directly on the proper object, there's no need to bind. Its **this** reference will match the object it's called on.

I'd be hard-pressed to illustrate the resulting effect on a printed snapshot. Just save, reload (make sure you bypass your cache if necessary), and try dragging Tux onto the board and then outside (far outside, be bold!) the board. Observe the spring. Love it. Play for a while, and call your buddies over to your desk. Then on to more options!

I mentioned effects were allowed for revert, but they're also allowed at drag start and drag end. As we saw, those default to playing with opacity (what's too bad is they also maintain an internal state to avoid multiple drag initiations on the same object, which should never occur anyway). The two options for these callbacks are as follows:

Option	Description
endeffect	The visual effect to apply on the element when the drag is completely done. This defaults to bringing its opacity back to its original value in 0.2".
starteffect	The visual effect to apply to the element when the drag starts. If the default end effect applies, this defaults to bringing the element's opacity to 70% in 0.2".

If you need to keep full opacity, for instance, just set the endeffect property to something equivalent to **false** (for example, **false** indeed, or **null**). This will automatically disable the default start effect, too.

On drag start, the element is also pushed "up," from a 3D perspective, to be "closer" to the eye of the user; this is done by adjusting its CSS z-index property, according to the zindex option. The end of drag restores the original setting.

Option	Description
zindex	The z-index ("layer") of the element while being dragged. This defaults to 1,000 in order to be sure it's above anything else. When manually dealing with such layer ordering, you may want to set it to **false**, as we did in Section 9.2, *Get It: Geometry Persistence*, on page 184.

Finally, in certain circumstances, you may not want the drag to be initiated immediately (that is, as soon as the main mouse button is pressed). Perhaps your element is also clickable, and you don't want a regular click to trigger a drag as well. To this end, the delay option lets you specify a duration, in milliseconds,[1] for the main mouse button to remain pressed before the drag is triggered. Naturally, this defaults to zero, but setting it to values as small as 500 can make all the difference in the world.

Option	Description
delay	How long the button should be down before we actually start dragging. This is in seconds, and it defaults to zero. The drag will align on the mouse pointer when the delay expires. If the button is released before the delay is over, no drag is attempted.

Controlling How the Draggable Element Moves

By default, the user can drag your element all over the place. This is fine for many situations, but there are cases where you'd like to constrain how the element moves. There are basically two needs you may have, perhaps combined, too:

- The element must not move on a pixel basis but by larger increments (say, by 10-pixel steps). These increments are not necessarily the same horizontally and vertically.

- The element must not move outside a given bounding box (its container element, for instance, or some arbitrary box you defined).

---

1. This is actually the *only* duration-related option in all of Prototype and script.aculo.us that is in milliseconds, not in seconds.

Both these needs are addressed with the snap option, which defaults to **false**, meaning there is no constraint.

Option   Description

snap   Governs the smoothness and boundaries of the drag. By default, the drag is pixel-fine and roams freely all over the place. You may need to specify a "resolution" for the drag (for example, moving by 25-pixel steps), limit the drag to a specific screen region (for example, the container element), or both.

Sticking to a Grid

By setting snap to a positive integer value, you'll make your element move only by steps of this size, both vertically and horizontally. Prototype will monitor actual mouse movements to determine just when to update the element's actual position. For instance, the following code makes the element with id="item1" draggable by 15-pixel steps:

```
new Draggable('item1', { snap: 15 });
```

Should you need a different "grid size" for horizontal and vertical movement, just specify two pixel sizes in an array. The following example uses 15-pixel horizontal steps but 5-pixel vertical ones:

```
new Draggable('item1', { snap: [15, 5] });
```

This could force our Tux to move on a cell-by-cell basis, staying cleanly aligned. However, that doesn't prevent it from venturing outside the board (at which point it would revert, granted).

Limiting the Movement to a Given Area

However, the real power of snap is revealed only when assigning to it a function that adjusts raw coordinates according to your needs. Such a function takes three arguments: the x and y positions and the Draggable object itself (in case you need to share it across draggable items).

Using such a function is the only way to apply boundaries to the drag's movement. For instance, here's a code snippet that makes sure the element with id="item1" does not stray outside a (0,0)-(100,50) box:

```
new Draggable('item1', {
  snap: function(x, y) {
    return [
      x < 0 ? 0 : (x > 100 ? 100 : x ),
      y < 0 ? 0 : (y > 50 ? 50 : y)];
  }
});
```

And here's a more advanced example forcing it to remain within its container object:

```
new Draggable('item1', {
  snap: function(x, y, draggable) {
    function constrain(n, lower, upper) {
      if (n > upper) return upper;
      return (n < lower ? lower : n);
    };
    elementDims = draggable.element.getDimensions();
    parentDims = Element.getDimensions(draggable.element.parentNode);
    return [
      constrain(x, 0, parentDims.width - elementDims.width),
      constrain(y, 0, parentDims.height - elementDims.height)];
  }
});
```

The possibilities are numerous, but these two cases cover most of them (and, I like to think, provide inspiration for your custom needs).

When it comes to our Tux, what we'd like is a combined snap. It would prevent it from straying outside the board (which we can do simply by checking that it's not "out") and force it to stay aligned on cells. As an added benefit (although whether that *is* a benefit is very much a subjective call), because Tux will stay penned on the board, we can get rid of the revert code!

As before, our markup and styling remains untouched. Only the scripting evolves—to the following creation call:

scriptaculous/dragdrop/board/step4/demo.js

```
Line 1  gTux = new Draggable('piece', {
          snap: function(x, y) {
            return [x, y].map(function(coord) {
              coord = ((coord - 4) / 64).round();
      5       return (coord < 0 ? 0 : (coord > 2 ? 2 : coord)) * 64 + 4;
            });
          },
          onStart: function() {
            $('board').addClassName('tuxMoving');
     10   },
          onEnd: function(d) {
            $('board').removeClassName('tuxMoving');
            var pos = getTuxCell(d.element);
            pos = 'ABC'.charAt(pos[1]) + (pos[0] + 1);
     15     $('log').insert('<li>Tux to ' + pos + '</li>');
          }
        });
```

Notice a creative use of map() on line 3, which applies the same transform to both our coordinates. This time we do adjust accurately, taking into account the 4-pixel padding of the board and using round() to align on the nearest cell, not necessarily the one to the left and top of Tux. You'll probably recognize the double-ternary code for value bounding we used earlier in Section 15.2, *Limiting the Movement to a Given Area*, on page 285.

Once again, snapshots would be useless. Save, refresh, and play with Tux. You'll see it's now nicely constrained to stay aligned over cells and stick within the board.

There is a final movement-related option, which comes in handy when all you need is to restrict movement to a single axis (something that is done implicitly by many script.aculo.us features, such as reorderable containers or sliders, which we'll discover in later chapters).

Option	Description
constraint	Whether to limit how the element is moved by dragging or not. This defaults to **false** but can also be 'horizontal' or 'vertical'. This is cumulative to more fine-grained control with snap. It's handy when you just need to restrict the movement axis.

Drag Handles

Often enough, you won't want the whole surface of the element to trigger the drag. Common UI conventions assign this role to a part of the element, such as a widget's title bar or specific spots along the element's edge. We'll refer to such a part as a *drag handle*.

By default, as we've seen, the whole element is the handle. However, we can change that with the handle option. We can either pass it the DOM reference of the handle element (which is, quite likely, a descendant element of the dragged one) or pass a string. In the latter case, script.-aculo.us will try to use it as a CSS class first, within the context of the dragged element. If that yields no descendant element, it will be used as an id= value. If it still yields nothing, the handle option is silently ignored (so watch out for typos in its value).

Option	Description
handle	Identification of a restricted area of the element to use for initiating drags. Defaults to **false**, which means drag can be initiated from anywhere on the element's surface. This can also be a DOM reference, an ID, or a CSS class name.

The CSS class variant is useful when you're applying the same Drag-gable construction code to multiple elements. You cannot repeat an id=, but you can certainly use the same class in multiple constructs.

Say our Tux doesn't like us grabbing it all over and dragging it around (this guy has its pride, you know). So perhaps we'd drag only its feet (is that any better from a pride standpoint? Hmmm.).

What we need here is to put a transparent element over these feet and make that element the handle. So, let's modify our markup, styling, and scripting quickly:

scriptaculous/dragdrop/board/step5/index.html

```
<span id="piece">
    <span id="pieceHandle"></span>
</span>
```

scriptaculous/dragdrop/board/step5/demo.css

```
#pieceHandle {
  position: absolute; left: 8px; top: 53px; width: 48px; height: 8px;
  cursor: move;
}
```

scriptaculous/dragdrop/board/step5/demo.js

```
function toggleTux() {
  if (gTux) {
    gTux.handle.setStyle({ cursor: 'default' });
    gTux.destroy();
    gTux = null;
    return;
  }
  gTux = new Draggable('piece', {
    handle: 'pieceHandle',
    snap: function(x, y) {
      return [x, y].map(function(coord) {
        coord = ((coord - 4) / 64).round();
        return (coord < 0 ? 0 : (coord > 2 ? 2 : coord)) * 64 + 4;
      });
    },
    onStart: function() {
      $('board').addClassName('tuxMoving');
    },
    onEnd: function(d) {
      $('board').removeClassName('tuxMoving');
      var pos = getTuxCell(d.element);
      pos = 'ABC'.charAt(pos[1]) + (pos[0] + 1);
      $('log').insert('<li>Tux to ' + pos + '</li>');
    }
  });
  gTux.handle.setStyle({ cursor: '' });
} // toggleTux
```

Notice we changed the manual cursor changes so they pertain to the feet-covering *<span>*, not the whole Tux anymore. Save, refresh, and try it. You can't drag Tux anywhere except on its feet anymore!

Naturally, handle is useful in more serious contexts, too. The most common use cases are title bars or resizing handles in widgets and windows for reordering items in a list (à la Ta-da Lists).

15.3 Ghosting

When you're dragging to express an actual movement of data (for example, taking an item out of a "excluded" list into a "included" list), regular drag is fine and proper. In other contexts, dragging may be a means of assigning a specific status to a piece of data. Perhaps you're putting an item in your shopping cart; this doesn't mean the item is not in stock anymore and available for further shopping. Or perhaps the element represents one of a few building blocks for a sequence, and you can drag such elements repeatedly on some sort of sequence container to build the sequence itself.

Or you may just not want the original element to move out of its original position, because this would cause a reflow that you could consider useless until there is an actual drop.

For this kind of situation, you can arrange to drag a temporary clone of the draggable element; this clone is called a *ghost*, so the option for it is ghosting, which defaults to **false**. By simply setting it to **true**, you'll get to drag a ghost of the element instead of the element itself. This doesn't change anything about other aspects of the drag (for example, movement constraints, reverting, or effects). When you're done with the drag, you can use callback hooks to manipulate the original element if need be.

Option	Description
ghosting	Whether to use ghosting, that is, dragging a clone of the element instead of the original one. This defaults to **false**.

Note that ghosting doesn't make a lot of sense unless you're dealing with specific drop locations or drop-related actions. We'll deal with dropping in the next major section. In the meantime, Figure 15.3, on the next page, illustrates what a ghosting-enabled drag looks like. You will find the example in the source code archive for this book in scriptaculous/dragdrop/ghosting.

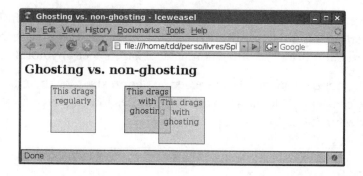

Figure 15.3: A DRAG WITH GHOSTING ENABLED

15.4 Dragging and Scrolling

Option	Description
scroll	Identifies the scroll container, if any. This is used for autoscrolling. If defined and the drag reaches the borders of the container's viewport, it will scroll automatically based on factors defined in the two next options. This can be any element (or its ID) or the window object.
scrollSensitivity	The threshold for autoscrolling, in pixels from the edges of the scroll container. This defaults to 20.
scrollSpeed	The autoscrolling speed, in pixels per second. This is used as a basis for the actual scroll speed, which depends on how close to the edge of the container (or how far over the edge) the mouse cursor is. This defaults to 15.

When ramping up to advanced UIs, you'll sometimes find yourself needing to let the user drag stuff around within scrollable containers. The simplest case is when the web page itself is higher (or wider) than the window's viewport (the part of the window that renders your page) and your user needs to drag somewhere on the page that is not currently visible.

You may also have a scrollable container somewhere within the page (a <div> with overflow="auto", perhaps), in which elements can be dragged.

By default, script.aculo.us's dragging systems will not deal with this. But you can have them detect that your cursor is on the edges of such a container and have it scroll accordingly to let the user reach the intended drop location. This simply requires setting the scroll variable so it references the container element, either by ID or by direct reference. If you're working with the whole viewport, set it to the predefined window object.

However, this also means you cannot have an element drag inside its scrolling container (with autoscrolling) *and* be able to "drag out" of it.

You can adjust edge detection and scroll speed using the two companion options: scrollSensitivity, which determines how close to the container's edges the cursor must get to trigger autoscrolling (defaults to 20 pixels), and scrollSpeed, which states how fast autoscrolling will go, in pixels per second (defaults to 15). This is actually a *basis* for computing the actual speed, which will increase as the cursor gets closer to—or even go over—the edges.

Here's a simple XHTML page to demo this feature:

scriptaculous/dragdrop/autoscroll/index.html

```
<!DOCTYPE html PUBLIC "-//W3C//DTD XHTML 1.0 Strict//EN"
 "http://www.w3.org/TR/xhtml1/DTD/xhtml1-strict.dtd">
<html xmlns="http://www.w3.org/1999/xhtml" lang="en-US" xml:lang="en-US">
<head>
    <meta http-equiv="Content-Type" content="text/html; charset=utf-8" />
    <title>Auto-scrolling in action</title>
    <link rel="stylesheet" type="text/css" href="demo.css" />
    <script type="text/javascript" src="prototype.js"></script>
    <script type="text/javascript"
     src="scriptaculous.js?load=effects,dragdrop"></script>
    <script type="text/javascript" src="demo.js"></script>
</head>
<body>

<h1>Auto-scrolling in action</h1>

<div id="container">
  <p>This is a simple paragraph just so we fill this thing</p>
  <p id="queen">Drag this around!</p>
  <p>This is yet another filler paragraph, just for kicks.</p>
</div>
</body>
</html>
```

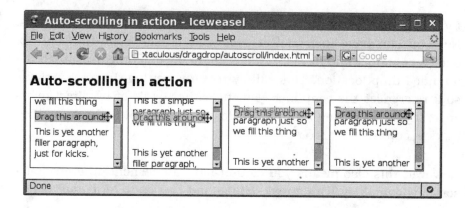

Figure 15.4: AUTOSCROLLING IN ACTION

A dollop of CSS will make it clearer for us to play with:

scriptaculous/dragdrop/autoscroll/demo.css

```
h1 { font-size: 1.5em; }

#container {
  overflow: auto; width: 10em; height: 7em; padding: 0.5em;
  border: 1px solid black;
}

#container p { margin: 0 0 0.5em; }

#queen { background-color: #ddd; cursor: move; }
```

The script for it is very simple:

scriptaculous/dragdrop/autoscroll/demo.js

```
document.observe('dom:loaded', function() {
  new Draggable('queen', { scroll: 'container' });
});
```

Figure 15.4 is a montage attempting to show you this in action.

Autoscrolling can be particularly useful when dealing with sortable lists, which we'll dive deeper into starting at Section 15.8, *Sorting with Drag and Drop*, on page 299.

15.5 Monitoring Drags

Should you need to monitor dragging activity throughout your page, you can use the observer facility provided by the global Draggables object. All drag activity passes through it, and it is always happy to let you know.

All you need to do is register your own observer object by passing it to Draggables.addObserver(). Your observer can implement any of the three callbacks described as available globally in Section 15.1, *Interacting with the Drag: Callbacks*, on page 279: onStart (the drag just started), onDrag (the position is about to change), and onEnd (the drag has just concluded).

All callbacks get passed three arguments: the callback name (in case you share a callback across multiple events), Draggable object (in case you share a callback across multiple elements), and the event object itself.

Astute readers (that's all of you) will have remembered that we used this global monitoring facility in our geometry persistence example, back on on page 188. We used it to monitor drops so we could persist window positions ("geometry") on the server side through Ajax.

15.6 Dropping Stuff

So far we just dragged stuff around with no special place to put them down. Although this can be sufficient for certain applications, most of the time we don't let our users just shuffle the UI. Items are usually supposed to be dropped on specific locations: a task list, a shopping cart, and so on.

Much as you can make elements draggable by creating a Draggable object on them, you can turn elements into drop zones by registering them with Droppables.

A Simple Drop Zone

So, you have this element that should act as a drop zone. Fine. Just call Droppables.add() on it. This can be as simple as the following:

```
Droppables.add('dropZoneId');
```

However, the actual syntax is as follows:

```
Droppables.add(element [, options])
```

There are many options, which we'll discover in a moment. The important thing is, once your element is a drop zone, dragging will interact with it. Your element will get notified when something is dragged over it or dropped on it, for instance. And dropping an element on a drop zone triggers a new callback, onDropped, just before the usual onEnd callback.

By default, your drop zone will accept any element for dropping. It's very liberal about what you drop in its lap. Naturally, we'll be able to tailor all this to your needs, as we'll see in the next section.

15.7 Customizing Drop Behavior

Just as you can take a draggable element and strip its dragging ability, you can take a drop zone and turn it back into a regular element, using the Droppables.remove() method. Just pass it your element.

Not Letting Everybody In

A common need is to be picky about which elements you accept on a particular drop zone. In a nontrivial UI, you may well have several kinds of draggable elements, each category being droppable at specific locations. You can specify this with two options: accept and containment.

- accept takes a CSS class name and requires any draggable element to have it among its CSS classes in order to be "cleared for landing." This offers maximum flexibility for your dropping policy, and it lets you flag any element, regardless of its tag name or origin in the document. You can also pass in an array of CSS class names.

- containment spares you manual CSS class assignment when all acceptable elements come from the same container (which is very frequently). Just specify the id= of their container element, and only they will be allowed to drop. Like with accept, you can pass either a single value or an array of values. Because the values here are elements, you can pass, as always, either id= values or direct DOM references.

Naturally, you can further refine your dropping policy by mixing both options together.

To demonstrate this, we'll build a simple shopping cart. To keep things simple, we'll stay on the client side, but notifying the server is as simple as creating an Ajax.Request in the drop zone's onDrop callback.

Our simple shopping cart will feature several items we can put (as many times as we'd like) in our shopping cart. We can also decide to put stuff out of the shopping cart by dropping them into the trash can. Obviously, there would be no point in dragging buyable items directly to the trash, and we won't let the user drag cart items back onto buyable items.

So, let's mock up a massively discounted (and massively reduced) version of the Pragmatic Bookshelf's online store. The XHTML page looks like this:

```
scriptaculous/dragdrop/cart1/index.html
```
```
<!DOCTYPE html PUBLIC "-//W3C//DTD XHTML 1.0 Strict//EN"
  "http://www.w3.org/TR/xhtml1/DTD/xhtml1-strict.dtd">
<html xmlns="http://www.w3.org/1999/xhtml" lang="en-US" xml:lang="en-US">
<head>
    <meta http-equiv="Content-Type" content="text/html; charset=utf-8" />
    <title>Discount bookshelf</title>
    <link rel="stylesheet" type="text/css" href="demo.css" />
    <script type="text/javascript" src="prototype.js"></script>
    <script type="text/javascript"
     src="scriptaculous.js?load=effects,dragdrop"></script>
    <script type="text/javascript" src="demo.js"></script>
</head>
<body>

<h1>Discount bookshelf</h1>

<div id="products">
  <img src="rails2.jpg" id="rails2" alt="Great book #1" class="product" />
  <img src="svn2.jpg" id="svn2" alt="Great book #2" class="product" />
</div>

<h2>Your cart:</h2>

<div id="cart"></div>
<p id="trash"><img src="trash.png" alt="Trashcan" /></p>
</body>
</html>
```

We'll need a bit of CSS for this to work:

scriptaculous/dragdrop/cart1/demo.css

```
h1 { font-size: 1.5em; }

#products { margin-bottom: 20px; height: 180px; }

.product, #cart img { cursor: move; }

#cart {
  width: 350px; height: 100px; padding: 1ex;
  border: 1px solid #fa0;
  font-family: sans-serif; color: gray;
}

#trash {
  width: 64px; margin: 0; padding: 1ex;
  border: 2px dotted white;
  /* Internet Explorer doesn't know transparent... */
}
```

Now for the script. It's actually rather concise:

scriptaculous/dragdrop/cart1/demo.js

```
Line 1  document.observe('dom:loaded', function() {
     -    $$('.product').each(function(book) {
     -      new Draggable(book, { revert: true });
     -    });
     5    Droppables.add('cart', { //
     -      accept: 'product', onDrop: function(book) {
     -        var bought = new Element('img');
     -        bought.src = book.readAttribute('src').replace('.', '_tiny.');
     -        new Draggable(bought, { revert: true });
    10        $('cart').appendChild(bought);
     -      }
     -    });
     -    Droppables.add('trash', {
     -      containment: 'cart', onDrop: function(bought) {
    15        bought.remove();
     -      }
     -    });
     -  });
```

We start by making all elements with the *product* CSS class draggable, on line 3. Then we proceed to create two drop zones. The first one is the cart, which accepts only those elements with a *product* CSS class, as required by the accept option on line 6. The second one is the trash can, which accepts only those elements originating from the shopping cart. This is what the containment option says on line 14.

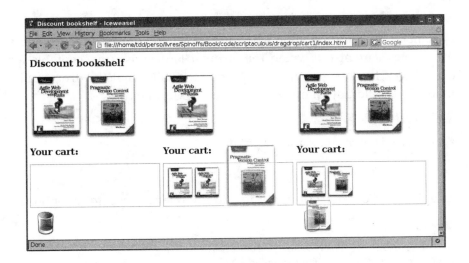

Figure 15.5: SEVERAL STEPS OF OUR CART WORKING

Note how we create small, draggable *<img>* elements to populate the cart but still let the user take them away to the trash can. On line 9, we create Draggable objects for them, with the revert option, which will have them slide back into place unless they're properly dropped. In such a case, we'll simply remove them from the DOM.

If you were to implement this with a server notification, the server side would probably compute the new representation of the whole cart, and you'd use Ajax.Updater over the *cart* container.

Figure 15.5 shows a montage of our shopping cart on load (empty), during cart addition, and during trashing (a few additions and trashings in between were skipped).

If you're using multiple drop zones and they happen to overlap, you must be careful about the order in which you're creating them. Check out Section 15.9, *Creating Droppables in the Right Order*, on page 312 for details.

Reacting to Drag

A few options let you exert finer control over how the drop zone reacts to dragged elements hovering over it.

A useful one is hoverclass, which lets you specify an extra CSS class that is slapped on the drop zone when it is hovered over by an acceptable draggable element (*not* when the element is deemed unacceptable for dropping). This lets you make it obvious, visually, that the drop can be made. We could adjust our shopping cart CSS like this:

`scriptaculous/dragdrop/cart2/demo.css`

```
#cart.dropAllowed { background: #ffd; }

#trash.readyToTrash { border-color: red; }
```

And then, we change our script to add the relevant hoverclass options:

`scriptaculous/dragdrop/cart2/demo.js`

```
document.observe('dom:loaded', function() {
  $$('.product').each(function(book) {
    new Draggable(book, { revert: true });
  });
  Droppables.add('cart', {
    accept: 'product', hoverclass: 'dropAllowed',
    onDrop: function(book) {
      var bought = new Element('img');
      bought.src = book.readAttribute('src').replace('.', '_tiny.');
      new Draggable(bought, { revert: true });
      $('cart').appendChild(bought);
    }
  });
  Droppables.add('trash', {
    containment: 'cart', hoverclass: 'readyToTrash',
    onDrop: function(bought) {
      bought.remove();
    }
  });
});
```

Figure 15.6, on the facing page, shows these options in action, both for the cart and the trash can.

By the way, in addition to the onDrop callback, there's also a onHover callback that gets fired on a drop zone, with three arguments: the dragged element, the drop zone element, and an overlap factor. (You can safely ignore this last one, though. It's mostly for Sortable purposes.)

Also remember that Draggable elements can have a onDropped callback, as I mentioned on page 279, which is fired whenever the draggable element is released on a drop zone that had accepted it. This takes the draggable element as its sole argument and triggers *after* the zone's onDrop callback.

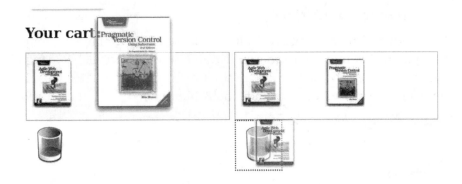

Figure 15.6: HOVERCLASS ON DROP ZONES

Finally, I'd like to mention this little-used option you can put on Draggable when you intend to work with drop zones:

Option	Description
quiet	Whether to wait until drop to check whether dropping is allowed and work with the drop zone. This defaults to **false**, so drop zones interact with the drag on the fly. If you have a truckload of drop zones, enabling it can help improve performance.

15.8 Sorting with Drag and Drop

By using Draggable and Droppables, you can achieve just about any drag-and-drop need you may have.

One of the most common needs is to provide the user with the ability to reorder elements (such as items in a list) by dragging them. Without drag and drop, reordering can be a nightmare of clicking arrow glyphs or similar buttons and can take a while to go through. For users, it does seem to take *forever*, which is a sure sign your reordering is not going to be used much. Mouse support is a big help here, letting users simply drag items in their final position. However, this particular feature calls for quite a hefty amount of advanced code (if you want to make it reusable), which is why script.aculo.us provides extended reordering support out of the box through the Sortable class.

I Want a Sortable List, Now!

Yes, I can feel it from where I sit. So, let's go for a simple example. We'll just define a regular ordered list and make it sortable, leaving all options (for they are numerous) to their defaults. Our XHTML page has the usual structure, and the body looks like this:

`scriptaculous/dragdrop/sortable1/index.html`

```
<h1>You ought to love these guys</h1>

<ol id="guys">
    <li id="guy_1">Arnaud Berthomier</li>
    <li id="guy_2">Élodie Jaubert</li>
    <li id="guy_3">Justin Palmer</li>
    <li id="guy_4">Rick Olson</li>
    <li id="guy_5">Thomas Fuchs</li>
</ol>
```

We'll keep the styling to almost nothing:

`scriptaculous/dragdrop/sortable1/demo.css`

```
h1 { font-size: 1.5em; }
li { cursor: move; }
```

We'll just need a pinch of scripting, based on the following method:

```
Sortable.create(element [, options])
```

The scripting goes like this:

`scriptaculous/dragdrop/sortable1/demo.js`

```
document.observe('dom:loaded', function() {
  Sortable.create('guys');
});
```

That's it. Honest! Figure 15.7, on the facing page, shows various stages of toying around with the list through drag and drop.

And it's not just for <ul> or <ol> containers, either. You'll be able to use this for just about any elements within a given container. We'll see how to customize this in a few moments with the options.

Getting the Items' Order

As the user reorders the elements in your sortable container, you'll probably want to get the current ordering now and then, perhaps to store it on the server.

```
Sortable.serialize(element [, options]) → URLEncodedString
```

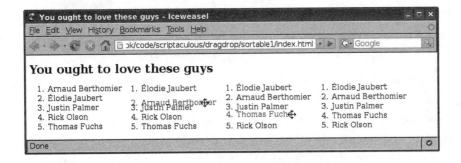

Figure 15.7: DEAD-SIMPLE LIST SORTING

It produces a URL-encoded representation of the current ordering, based on the id= attributes for the container and the ordered elements. The default rule is as follows:

- The container's id= attribute is used as field name, suffixed with [] (this makes things easy on server layers based on PHP or Rails, for instance, and poses no discomfort to other technologies). If that's unsatisfactory to you, you can override this by passing a name option (it will still be suffixed with square brackets).

- The id= attributes for the ordered elements (Sortable uses <li> children by default) are used to extract field values. They are analyzed using a regular expression, which defaults to Sortable. SERIALIZE_RULE; I'll spare you the details, but this means your id= attributes need to be of the form *xxx_yyy*, and the second part (everything after the first underscore) will be used as a value.

So, let's take our previous example. We had the following list:

```
scriptaculous/dragdrop/sortable1/index.html
```

```html
<h1>You ought to love these guys</h1>

<ol id="guys">
    <li id="guy_1">Arnaud Berthomier</li>
    <li id="guy_2">Élodie Jaubert</li>
    <li id="guy_3">Justin Palmer</li>
    <li id="guy_4">Rick Olson</li>
    <li id="guy_5">Thomas Fuchs</li>
</ol>
```

Now let's assume the user moved Élodie in first position and Thomas in fourth, as shown on Figure 15.7.

Here are a couple serialization calls and their results:

```
Sortable.serialize('guys')
// -> 'guys[]=2&guys[]=1&guys[]=3&guys[]=5&guys[]=4'

Sortable.serialize('guys', { name: 'users' })
// -> 'users[]=2&users[]=1&users[]=3&users[]=5&users[]=4'
```

The default requirement for id= structure is usually just fine, but you might need to cater to other formats. Perhaps you need to use hyphens instead of underscores or take the whole id= instead of just a part?

You can do this by providing a custom format option, which must be a regular expression object isolating the desired part as the first captured group.[2] Note that you can define this option once and for all when creating the Sortable object, too. It doesn't have to be defined every time you call serialize().

Let's suppose we have the following list:

```
<ol id="subs">
    <li id="sub123">Wired</li>
    <li id="sub456">456 Berea St.</li>
    <li id="sub789">A List Apart</li>
</ol>
```

These id= attributes do not match the default format option, and we would end up with a useless result: *subs[]=&subs[]=&subs[]=*. But we can provide a custom format, either at creation time or, as in the following script, when serializing:

```
Sortable.serialize('subs', { format: /^sub(\d+)/ })
// -> 'subs[]=123&subs[]=456&subs[]=789'
```

Keeping Posted with Two Callbacks

When you let your users reorder elements, you want to be notified when they do. There are actually two distinct situations here:

- An element is being dragged and gets into a new position; it's not being dropped yet, so it might end up being dropped in its original position eventually. Still, the onChange callback is notified, with the dragged element as an argument.

---

2. In regexes, a captured group is a group of characters delimited by parentheses (unless the opening parenthesis is immediately followed by ?:, in which case the group is noncapturing). They are numbered starting from 1 and are useful to individually grab parts of the matched string, perhaps to reuse them later in the search pattern or in a replacement pattern.

- An element was dragged and dropped, and the ordering actually changed compared to before the drag. The onUpdate callback is fired, with the container element as argument.

A small note about just *when* an element "changes position" in the list while being dragged: it requires the mouse cursor itself to be dragged beyond half the hovered element, in the dragging direction (for instance, if you're dragging vertically, the mouse cursor must go beyond half the height of the hovered element). That's pretty intuitive behavior for most users.

Let's augment our previous example to get the hang of just when these callbacks get called. We'll just add two notification zones below the <ol> element, like this:

scriptaculous/dragdrop/sortable2/index.html

```
<p id="changeNotification"></p>
<p id="updateNotification"></p>
```

Now let's change our Sortable creation to register two callbacks:

scriptaculous/dragdrop/sortable2/demo.js

```
Line 1  document.observe('dom:loaded', function() {
     -    var changeEffect;
     -    Sortable.create('guys', {
     -      onChange: function(item) {
     5        var list = Sortable.options(item).element;
     -        $('changeNotification').update(Sortable.serialize(list).escapeHTML());
     -        if (changeEffect) changeEffect.cancel();
     -        changeEffect = new Effect.Highlight('changeNotification',
     -          { restorecolor: 'transparent' });
    10      },
     -      onUpdate: function(list) {
     -        $('updateNotification').update(Sortable.serialize(list).escapeHTML());
     -        $('updateNotification').highlight({ startcolor: '#99ff99' });
     -      }
    15    });
     -  });
```

Notice the trick on line 5. The argument we receive is the dragged element that just changed position, but we cannot use this on Sortable. serialize(). We need the container on which we called Sortable.create(). Naturally, we could just pass the id= of the container, or the reference to it, but the code here is more generic and dynamically retrieves the container for the element we pass.

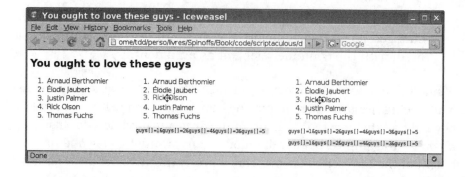

Figure 15.8: ONCHANGE AND ONUPDATE IN ACTION

We also avoid multiple highlight effects going on concurrently when the user drags too fast across the list, and we make sure any highlight finishes with a transparency instead of whatever degree of yellowness was current (because of a previous highlight going on) when the latest onChange() callback happened.

Figure 15.8 shows various states of the page as we drag an item around and finally release it. Releasing it on its original position does *not* fire onUpdate, because the final order is unchanged.

Binding to Ajax

Of course, onUpdate is a prime candidate for triggering Ajax notifications to the server, for instance when the user reorders a to-do list or some other data set. Combining Ajax.Request and Sortable.serialize makes live persistence simple enough:

```
Sortable.create('tasks', {
  onUpdate: function(list) {
    new Ajax.Request('/tasklist/1', {
      parameters: Sortable.serialize(list)
    });
  }
});
```

Note that if your server side is RESTful, you'll probably want to add the method: 'put' option, because you're updating data, not creating it.

Reordering with Horizontal Layouts

So far we've used list reordering in a vertical layout, and you may have noticed, when trying our examples, that the dragging won't let you move items horizontally; only vertical movement is rendered.

This behavior is controlled by the constraint option, which defaults here to *vertical*. And indeed, for most cases, it's a reasonable constraint.

But your list might be horizontally displayed, in which case you'll need to constrain movement accordingly. You may even have multiple lists and need to swap elements between them, a frequent use case we'll illustrate later in this chapter, at which point you'll need to remove movement constraints altogether.

To address all three cases, constraint has three possible values, which we already listed back when looking at Draggable options: 'vertical' (the default), 'horizontal', and **false** (no constraint at all).

Also note that Sortable relies on its overlap option to determine whether a dragged element should change position in the list. When using a constrained layout (that is, a constraint option that is not **false**), overlap should use a matching value.

Let's see a quick example of a horizontal layout. We'll take the following XHTML list:

`scriptaculous/dragdrop/sortable3/index.html`

```
<ol id="guys">
    <li id="guy_1">Alexis Toulotte</li>
    <li id="guy_2">Amir Jaballah</li>
    <li id="guy_3">Anne-Julie Peschaud</li>
    <li id="guy_4">Élodie Jaubert</li>
    <li id="guy_5">Erin Odenweller</li>
</ol>
```

Then we'll style it so as to obtain a horizontality:

`scriptaculous/dragdrop/sortable3/demo.css`

```
h1 { font-size: 1.5em; }
#guys {
  list-style-type: none;
  padding: 0;
}
#guys li {
  float: left; cursor: move;
  margin-left: 1em; padding: 0.2em; width: 10em;
  border: 0.05em solid gray; background: #ddd;
  text-align: center;
}
```

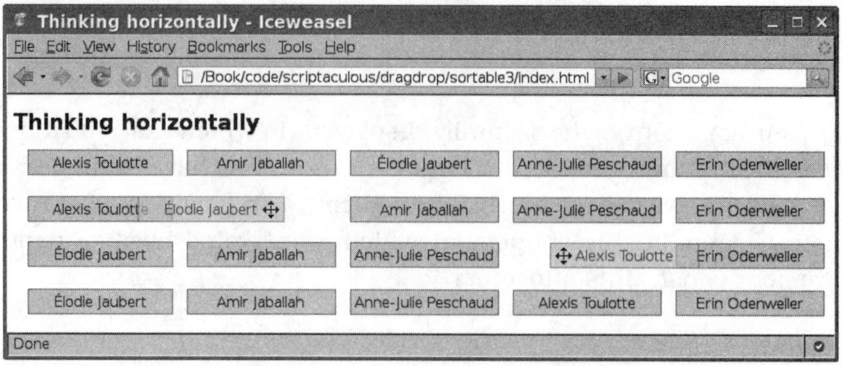

Figure 15.9: HORIZONTAL REORDERING

Finally, we'll adjust our scripting so it takes horizontality into account:

scriptaculous/dragdrop/sortable3/demo.js
```
document.observe('dom:loaded', function() {
  Sortable.create('guys', { constraint: 'horizontal',
    overlap: 'horizontal' });
});
```

Notice how we take care to synchronize the constraint and overlap options in a single-direction reordering like this? Figure 15.9 uses a montage to illustrate reordering in action on such a list.

Sorting More Than Regular Lists

You're absolutely not required to use list markup (that is, <ul>, <ol>, and <li>) in order to get reordering capabilities. Sortable lets you specify the tag identifying which child elements of your container are up for dragging.

You can express this primarily with the tag option, which defaults to 'li'. All child elements with the tag name you provide are then taken into account. For instance, say you have the following markup:

```
<div id="avatars">
  <img src="/avatars/john_1.jpg" alt="John (favorite)" />
  <img src="/avatars/john_2.jpg" alt="John (regular)" />
  <img src="/avatars/john_3.jpg" alt="John (wacky)" />
</div>
```

To let your users reorder the elements in your *<div>* container, you'd need code like this:

```
Sortable.create('avatars', { tag: 'img' });
```

Perhaps you need to restrict this, however, to only a subset of these children, in which case you can also define the only option. It defaults to **false**, which disables it. You can set it to either a single CSS class name or an array of CSS class names to precisely select which children elements are to be used.

We can try this easily; let's take our previous page and change the list definition to the following markup:

scriptaculous/dragdrop/sortable4/index.html

```html
<div id="chapter">
    <p>This stays on top.</p>
    <p class="orderable">This can, on the other hand.</p>
    <p class="orderable">And this too!</p>
    <p class="moveIt">You can reorder this one.</p>
    <p>This stays at bottom.</p>
</div>
```

Now all we need to do is change our Sortable creation to this:

scriptaculous/dragdrop/sortable4/demo.js

```javascript
document.observe('dom:loaded', function() {
  Sortable.create('chapter', { tag: 'p', only: ['orderable', 'moveIt'] });
});
```

There! We can drag all but the two outermost paragraphs, because they do not match any of the CSS classes we specified for the only option.

Version 1.7.2 introduced a new option, called elements, which lets you specify exactly which child elements you want to reorder, and only those will be taken into account. When you do know, beforehand, which elements will need to be draggable for reordering, this is by far the fastest way to initialize your Sortable object. It skips any sort of DOM traversal or CSS-based selection.

The elements option is originally disabled (by being set to **false**), so you would enable it by assigning it with an array of elements (for example, the result of a $$() call). As usual, any item in this array can be either a string with the element's id= value or the element's DOM reference.

Naturally, if this option is enabled, it supersedes any other means of defining child elements for reordering.

Reordering Trees!

Sometimes you're not dealing with linear lists (or list equivalents) but element trees, with containers inside items inside containers inside.... In short, these are nested lists.

Dealing with this efficiently and correctly is by no means a simple task; script.aculo.us does provide a tree-handling feature, which is still somewhat experimental, but seems to hold up pretty well to real-world use. You need to create a Sortable object only on the outermost container, but you must pass the proper options, including two specific ones: tree and treeTag.

The tree option is simply a boolean flag used to activate alternative behaviors in the Sortable internals in order to deal with tree-like element structures. Set it to **true** in order to deal with nested containers.

The treeTag option lets you specify which tag you rely on for containers. This assumes all containers, outermost or nested, use the same tag. This defaults to 'ul', but you can change it for your needs (for example, 'ol' or 'div').

To put credit where it's due, I should mention that most of the tree support code was contributed by Sammi Williams.

You can look at a fairly good demonstration of sortable trees at work in the corresponding functional test page within your script.aculo.us distribution: test/functional/sortable_tree_test.html. Also note that the serialized form of a tree is slightly different than for linear lists in order to account for the nesting.

A Classic: Two Lists Mixing It Up

Users often need to drag elements back and forth between multiple lists. This is interesting because it requires a specific setup for several options:

- constraint will likely be set to **false** in order to let our users drag elements in both directions.

- containment, inherited from Droppable options, will probably be used to restrict acceptance of drops from our own list and a few other ones, not just from anywhere.

- dropOnEmpty will be useful if we want a list to still accept items from the outside once we depopulated it entirely. This will implement drop logic but may not be sufficient. If our container has no specific style ensuring it has a nonzero size when empty, there won't be a single pixel to drop on when all items are gone. We'll use onUpdate callbacks to toggle a specific CSS class on empty lists in order to ensure they're visible even when empty and can thus be dropped items on.

Let's take a page similar to our previous examples, but we'll use two lists this time:

scriptaculous/dragdrop/sortable_multiple/index.html

```
<ul id="paris">
    <li>Diane Mellini</li>
    <li>Élodie Jaubert</li>
    <li>Valérie Savalle</li>
</ul>

<ul id="world">
    <li>Dan Webb</li>
    <li>Justin Palmer</li>
    <li>Scott Raymond</li>
</ul>
```

We'll throw in some styling to make it easier on the eyes:

scriptaculous/dragdrop/sortable_multiple/demo.css

```
h1 { font-size: 1.5em; }

ul {
  position: absolute; top: 4em; padding: 0;
  list-style-type: none; width: 10em;
}

li {
  height: 2em; cursor: move;
  line-height: 2em; text-align: center;
  margin-bottom: 0.5em;
  border: 1px solid gray;
  background: #ff9;
}

ul.empty { height: 2em; border: 1px solid silver; background: #ddd; }

#paris { left: 2em; }

#world { left: 18em; }

#world li { background: #9f9; }
```

Finally, we just need a few lines of script:

```
scriptaculous/dragdrop/sortable_multiple/demo.js
document.observe('dom:loaded', function() {
  var options = {
    constraint: false, containment: ['paris', 'world'],
    dropOnEmpty: true, onUpdate: function(list) {
      var methodStart = list.down('li') ? 'remove' : 'add';
      list[methodStart + 'ClassName']('empty');
    }
  };
  Sortable.create('paris', options);
  Sortable.create('world', options);
});
```

Figure 15.10, on the next page shows a montage of several stages in using these lists. Play with it, and notice how items change containers past a certain overlap threshold and what happens when a list becomes empty (or goes from empty to one element). Isn't it cool?

Using Regular Drag-and-Drop Options with Sortable

Internally, Sortable works with the two core objects: Draggable and Droppables. It astutely combines both features to achieve this reordering capability. From a developer perspective, this means you can customize a lot of things by using options you would normally pass to new Draggable or Droppables.add.

Of course, Sortable may need to ensure certain options have specific values, but most of them are passed untouched to the underlying objects. Here's a quick rundown. Refer to the description of these options earlier in this chapter for further details.

- Underlying Draggable objects take the following options into account: constraint, delay, ghosting, handle, scroll, scrollSpeed, and scrollSensitivity. In addition, effects (starteffect, reverteffect, and endeffect) are used if you do provide a function (if you attempt to disable them by using false, for instance, that will be ignored). In the same spirit, a non-null zindex option will be used.

- Underlying Droppable objects take the following options into account: containment, hoverclass, and overlap.

Version 1.7.2 introduced a special optimization with regard to the handle option, though. It is similar to the new elements option. When you know exactly which elements should serve as handles, you can pass an array of these elements through the handles option. They will be used in

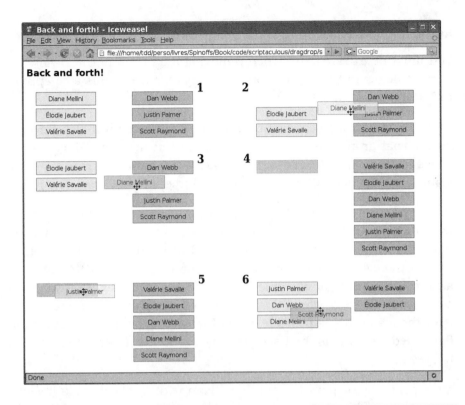

Figure 15.10: MULTIPLE LISTS AT VARIOUS STAGES

ascending order on whatever elements are deemed eligible for reordering (see Section 15.8, *Sorting More Than Regular Lists*, on page 306 for details on that).

As usual, you can pass in the array either id= values or direct DOM references. The handles option defaults to **false**, which effectively disables it. When enabled, it supersedes the regular handle option.

15.9 Common Pitfalls

Drag and drop generally works just fine, but you should be on the lookout for a few common issues. It's quite possible to inadvertently misuse it.

Removing or Replacing a DOM Fragment

You must be extra careful when removing fragments of the DOM containing elements that were drop zones (by extension, this also applies to Sortable elements).

Whenever you drag elements around, script.aculo.us will loop through its internal drop zone list to find geographical matches. Having drop zones in this list that are not in the DOM anymore can cause several issues, but the dominant one is a painful freeze of the browser.

Prototype Core is currently working on implementing custom events, which would let Thomas jump in and make sure script.aculo.us automatically mops up relevant drop zones, but for now you have to take care of the cleanup yourself. So, be on the lookout for DOM removals and replacements (for example, Ajax.Updater processing) that wipe out sections of the DOM where drop zones are registered. Be sure to unregister them as soon as possible (it's OK to do this after the replacement happened, as long as the user didn't get a chance to initiate a drag in between).

More generally, it pays to try to stay lean with the Draggable objects, Droppables-registered elements, and Sortable objects you keep around. For instance, if you have a very large set of items that are *potentially* draggable, use lazy initialization over those that the user appears to want to drag. Only make those draggable, on the fly. You'll notice a significant speedup! For further details, search through the archives of the Spinoffs mailing list.[3]

The cleanup methods are as follows:

```
draggable.destroy()
Droppables.remove(element)
Sortable.destroy(element)
```

Creating Droppables in the Right Order

A common mistake is to create drop zones in the inappropriate order. When a draggable element hovers the document, it will iterate through the drop zone list in registration order, and the first one to match will be used, regardless of layering (the z-index property).

---

3. http://groups.google.com/group/rubyonrails-spinoffs

So if you have a drop zone B that is located "inside" a drop zone A but A was registered *before* B, you're in trouble, because B will never get a hold on your element; only A will.

There is actually one case where script.aculo.us will still behave properly despite this—when B is a descendant element of A in the DOM. But if you're playing with unrelated elements put where they are through specific positioning, you need to tread carefully.

The rule of thumb to avoid this is simple. Always register your drop zones from the inside outward, instead of the other way around. It may appear counterintuitive, because we're used to the outside-inward order because of DOM creation, but we need to think about it from a layering standpoint: the foremost zone first and then working away toward the background.

What We Just Learned

As you can see, in barely 30KB of uncompressed JavaScript, script.aculo.us provides an incredible wealth of features for dragging and dropping, thanks to a few core objects and a wealth of options that cater to just about every need. This part of the library truly opens the doors to significant improvements of the user experience in our web applications.

Let's recap what we just saw:

- Making an element draggable is as simple as doing a new Draggable over it.

- Draggable supports a wealth of options to control movement and behavior.

- Any element can become a *drop zone*, that is, a surface that reacts to a dragging operation hovering over it and dropping onto it. We just need to do a Droppables.add over the element. Options let us filter out unwanted drops.

- An observer mechanism lets us globally monitor drag and drops in our page.

- Because drag and drop is a great way to sort items and sorting is a common need, we have the Sortable class, which enables drag-based reordering of any series of elements.

- We need to look out for DOM removal of elements that were made draggable or droppable and to be cautious about the order of creation of our drop zones.

Neuron Workout

Here are some issues we should think about...

- What happens when we dynamically add an item to an already sortable list? Does it participate in the reordering? Why?

- How can we fix this? In general, how should we react to the contents of a sortable sequence being changed?

- When should we use constraint instead of going all the way with snap?

- What kind of optimizations can you imagine for situations where a sortable list has a very large set of elements (say, thousands)?

script.aculo.us doesn't stop there. It goes on to provide autocompletion for text zones, in-place editing, and even sliders, as we'll see in the following chapters.

Autocompletion

Autocompletion is one of those features that suddenly popped up on a popular site and soon became an obvious one to have. It's immensely useful to help your users zero in on existing values, which reduces their time to task completion (no multiple round-trips for the whole page in order to get the spelling right or refine the search, for instance), alleviates your need to process such suboptimal submissions, and generally makes everyone happier.

So, how do we use it in our apps? Thanks to script.aculo.us's built-in autocompletion facility, making any text field autocompletable is a snap, be it from a client-side data source or through Ajax.

You'll need the controls.js module, which contains the autocompletion classes but also effects.js (the default behavior for showing and hiding the autocompletion list relies on quick appear/fade effects). So, your script.aculo.us loading will look, at minimum, like this:

```
<script type="text/javascript"
 src="scriptaculous?load=effects,controls"></script>
```

16.1 The Basics

By default, script.aculo.us supports two sources for autocompletion:

- Local sources (string arrays in your web page's scripts)
- Remote sources (obtained through Ajax)

Depending on the source you're planning to use, you'll instantiate Autocompleter.Local or Ajax.Autocompleter, respectively. Although equipped with specific options, these two objects share a large feature set and provide a uniform user experience.

There are four things you'll always pass to these objects when building them:

- The text field you want to make autocompletable. As usual, you can pass the field itself or the value of its id= attribute.

- The container for autocompletion choices, which will end up holding a <ul>/<li> list of options to pick from. Again, pass the element directly or its id=. This element is most often a simple <div>.

- The data source, which will be expressed, depending on the source type, as a JavaScript array of strings or as a URL to the remote source.

- Finally, the options. As always, they're provided as a hash of sorts, and both autocompletion objects can make do with no custom option; there are suitable defaults for everything.

The shared feature set and behavior is put in the base object for everything autocomplete-related: Autocompleter.Base. You'll probably never need to use it in your code, even if you're building a custom autocompletion widget (you'll more likely extend one of the specific objects).

Built-in Behaviors

Autocompleter.Base goes to great lengths to make it as easy as possible on you by providing a lot of proper default behaviors. Note in particular the following:

Automatic container configuration

You don't need to do anything special to your container for autocompletion choices. You'll usually just put a <div> in the markup, with an id= and, likely, a dedicated CSS class.

When you build your autocompletion object, this container will automatically be hidden; when it's time to display choices in it, it will automatically be positioned absolutely if need be and then aligned and resized below the text field (it will retain any height you may have specified, however). It then fades in quickly (0.15"). When a choice is selected or the completion is aborted, it automatically fades out just as fast.

In the same spirit, your text field's autocomplete= attribute will be turned off automatically to prevent conflict between the browser's native autocompletion feature and script.aculo.us's.

Using the keyboard and mouse

Once a list of choices is displayed, it automatically reacts to the keyboard and mouse to help you pick an option as easily as possible:

- The up and down arrow keys change the selected option (and wrap at the limits of the list). Hovering the mouse over options automatically changes the selected option to the one below the cursor.

- Pressing Tab or Return, or clicking an option, confirms its selection and completes the text field accordingly. The list is then hidden.

- Pressing Esc or moving the focus away from the text field cancels completion, hiding the list.

Options You'll Get No Matter What

Whatever the source mode, you'll always get at least the following three options:

autoSelect

Determines whether to automatically accept the autocompletion choice when it's the only one. Defaults to **false** (indeed, in many situations, this can be confusing to the user).

frequency

This option lets you specify the interval, in seconds, between two attempts at autocompleting the input. It defaults to 0.4, which is reasonably fast from a user's standpoint.

minChars

Determines how many characters need to be typed before auto-completion kicks in. This is useful when relying on a data source that has so many values that choices would be too numerous based on only a few characters. Still, it defaults to 1.

16.2 Local Autocompletion

Let's start here with the simplest setup: a data source provided by a JavaScript array in our own script. Create a directory for this, and put the necessary JavaScript files in it—prototype.js and scriptaculous.js, of course, but also effects.js and controls.js, which we will need for our demonstration.

Our XHTML page is simple enough:

```
scriptaculous/autocomplete/local/index.html
```

```html
<!DOCTYPE html PUBLIC "-//W3C//DTD XHTML 1.0 Strict//EN"
 "http://www.w3.org/TR/xhtml1/DTD/xhtml1-strict.dtd">
<html xmlns="http://www.w3.org/1999/xhtml" lang="en-US" xml:lang="en-US">
<head>
    <meta http-equiv="Content-Type" content="text/html; charset=utf-8" />
    <title>Local autocompletion</title>
    <link rel="stylesheet" type="text/css" href="demo.css" />
    <script type="text/javascript" src="prototype.js"></script>
    <script type="text/javascript"
     src="scriptaculous.js?load=effects,controls"></script>
    <script type="text/javascript" src="demo.js"></script>
</head>
<body>

<h1>Local autocompletion</h1>

<form>
    <p>
        <label for="edtContact" accesskey="C">Contact</label>
        <input type="text" id="edtContact" name="contact" />
        <div id="contactChoices" class="autocomplete"></div>
    </p>
</form>

</body>
</html>
```

Note how we just need to provide a bare-bones *<div>* as a container for
the choice list. We do provide a CSS class name for it, though, because
we plan to add custom styling later; for now, however, we don't need
any special styling in demo.css.

On to the scripting:

```
scriptaculous/autocomplete/local/demo.js
```

```javascript
var girls = [
  'Anne-Julie Peschaud', 'Audrey Guillemenot', 'Aurore Jaballah',
  'Clotilde Michel',     'Corinne Dillingham', 'Diane Mellini',
  'Élodie Jaubert',      'Erin Odenweller',    'Jes "Canllaith" Hall',
  'Laurie Fatoux',       'Sandrine Daspet',    'Serpil Uren',
  'Valérie Savalle'
];

document.observe('dom:loaded', function() {
  new Autocompleter.Local('edtContact', 'contactChoices', girls);
});
```

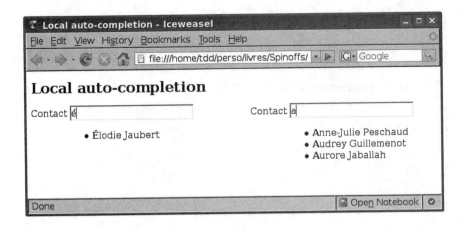

Figure 16.1: TWO AUTOCOMPLETIONS, NO STYLING

There! No options, no fluff—just the input field, its completion container, and the data source. The whole construction syntax is actually as follows:

```
new Autocompleter.Local(field, container, dataSource [, options])
```

Let's fire up our trusty browser and open the page. Figure 16.1 shows various stages of completion as we type initials. You'll notice that despite the matched typing being conveniently set apart with a <strong> tag, the whole thing looks rather bare. The local completion process builds a nice, semantically correct unordered list (<ul>), but the lack of styling makes us look pretty dumb. So, let's fix this:

scriptaculous/autocomplete/local/demo.css

```css
h1 { font-size: 1.5em; }

div.autocomplete {
  position: absolute;
  width: 250px; /* will be adjusted by script.aculo.us */
  background-color: white; border: 1px solid #888;
  margin: 0px; padding: 0px;
}
div.autocomplete ul {
  list-style-type: none; margin: 0px; padding: 0px;
}
div.autocomplete ul li.selected { background-color:  #ff9;}
div.autocomplete ul li {
  list-style-type: none; display: block;
  font-family: sans-serif; font-size: smaller; color: #444;
  margin: 0; padding: 0.1em; height: 1.5em; line-height: 1.5em;
  cursor: pointer;
}
```

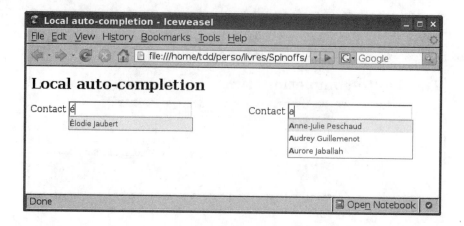

Figure 16.2: SAME VIEWS, WITH "STANDARD" STYLING

A couple notes about this:

- The *autocomplete* class is not a mandatory name. You can use whatever class name you like on the *<div>* element in your markup (the element that will act as a container for your suggestions).

- On the other hand, the *selected* class is a "magic" name. script.-aculo.us will apply this class automatically to the currently selected suggestion (and update this as the user moves the selection, obviously).

Refresh the page and try again. It should look more like Figure 16.2. That's *much* better indeed!

Customizing Local Completion

The first thing you can adjust is the maximum amount of visible choices (above which you'd have to scroll). It defaults to 10, but you can adjust this with the choices option.

The focus of local-completion options is the completion algorithm itself. By default, the search will be as follows:

- *Partial*: it searches for the typed text at the beginning of any *word* in the completion choices. You can search only at the beginning of the whole choice *text* by setting the partialSearch option to **false.**

  Also note that partial search will trigger only once a given amount of characters has been typed. This defaults to 2, which you can adjust with the partialChars option. Do not confuse partialChars with minChars. The latter has precedence, given that no completion whatsoever will trigger below its value. However, when the amount of typed characters is greater than or equal to minChars but below partialChars, you'll get a nonpartial search (beginning of full-choice text only).

- *Prefix-only*: only beginnings (of words or full texts) will be looked up. It's generally the better way, but should you want to search *anywhere* in the choice text, set the fullSearch option to **true**.

- *Case-insensitive*: you can change by setting the ignoreCase option to **false**.

I should also mention that the actual completion algorithm is performed by a method reference by the selector option. Such a method gets passed the current Autocompleter.Local instance and is responsible for building the appropriate <*ul*>/<*li*> markup and returning it. The default value for this option implements all the options discussed in this section, and you should generally not need to implement your own.

Changing the List of Completions

Every so often, someone will pop up on the mailing list asking how they can change the list of completions for a local autocompleter without destroying it and constructing it anew.

There's no official support for this, but so far the reference to your JavaScript array has always been stored in an array option in the Autocompleter.Local object. Changing this property to reference your new array of choices does the trick:

```
var ac = new Autocompleter.Local('edtContact', 'contactChoices', girls);
// ...
// And when you'd want to switch to another list of choices:
ac.options.array = guys;
```

Once again, this is not officially supported, because array is not intended to be part of a "public" API, but it has been untouched since the object first appeared in script.aculo.us and certainly works well enough.

16.3 Getting Ajaxy

The other data source mode available is, of course, Ajax, which lets you get completion choices from a remote source (your server side). The construction syntax is similar to the local variant, except the data source is not specified as a JavaScript array anymore but as the URL to your server-side completion logic:

```
new Ajax.Autocompleter(element, container, url [, options])
```

Your server side gets passed one parameter, which defaults to the input field's name= attribute and holds the typed characters. The server code is then responsible for producing a list of completion choices using the same format built internally by local completion: an unordered list of choices, expressed as a *<ul>* element with its *<li>* items.

Automatically Displaying an Indicator

Because we're going through Ajax and having a round-trip to the server side, completion might not be instantaneous. As always, letting the user know processing is going on behind the scenes is a good idea. When dealing manually with such objects as Ajax.Updater, we had to manually show and hide an indicator element on our page from the onCreate and onComplete callbacks. This indicator element was usually an *<img>* somewhere, holding a spinner or progress bar of some sort.

Autocompleter.Base acknowledges this common need with a custom indicator option that holds the DOM reference or ID of our indicator element and will automatically show and hide it appropriately. The option is originally undefined, and whenever it is **false**-equivalent, it is simply ignored. It's available to all autocompleters, but local completion rarely needs it, being usually fast enough. . . .

A First Example

Let's work up a simple Ajax example. We'll need all the stuff from our local demo, but we'll adjust the web page's title and heading and the demo script. The new web page says this:

scriptaculous/autocomplete/ajax/index.html

```
<!DOCTYPE html PUBLIC "-//W3C//DTD XHTML 1.0 Strict//EN"
 "http://www.w3.org/TR/xhtml1/DTD/xhtml1-strict.dtd">
<html xmlns="http://www.w3.org/1999/xhtml" lang="en-US" xml:lang="en-US">
<head>
    <meta http-equiv="Content-Type" content="text/html; charset=utf-8" />
    <title>AJAX autocompletion</title>
```

```html
<link rel="stylesheet" type="text/css" href="demo.css" />
<script type="text/javascript" src="prototype.js"></script>
<script type="text/javascript"
 src="scriptaculous.js?load=effects,controls"></script>
<script type="text/javascript" src="demo.js"></script>
</head>
<body>

<h1>AJAX autocompletion</h1>

<form>
    <p>
        <label for="edtLibName" accesskey="L">Ruby library</label>
        <input type="text" id="edtLibName" name="libName" />
        <div id="libChoices" class="autocomplete"></div>
    </p>
</form>

</body>
</html>
```

And the script simply goes like this:

`scriptaculous/autocomplete/ajax/demo.js`

```javascript
document.observe('dom:loaded', function() {
  new Ajax.Autocompleter('edtLibName', 'libChoices', '/completions');
});
```

Now we need a server side to access this page and serve the data source URL (/completions). As always, we'll get by with a short Ruby script. To give it some appeal, I suggest we have it complete on all installed Ruby libraries:

`scriptaculous/autocomplete/ajax/server.rb`

```ruby
Line 1   #! /usr/bin/env ruby
   -
   -     require 'cgi'
   -     require 'erb'
   5     require 'webrick'
   -     include WEBrick
   -
   -     template_text = File.read('suggestions.rhtml')
   -     suggestions = ERB.new(template_text)
   10
   -     server = HTTPServer.new(:Port => 8042)
   -     server.mount('/', HTTPServlet::FileHandler, '.')
   -
   -     server.mount_proc('/completions') do |request, response|
   15      name_start = request.query['libName']
   -       suffix = "/#{Regexp.escape(name_start)}*.rb"
```

```
        libs = $LOAD_PATH.map { |dir|
          Dir.glob(dir + suffix, File::FNM_CASEFOLD).map { |f|
              File.basename(f, '.rb')
20        }
      }.flatten.sort.uniq
      response['Content-Type'] = 'text/html'
      response.body = suggestions.result(binding)
    end
25
    trap('INT') { server.shutdown }

    server.start
```

For the non-Rubyists among you, this code probably calls for a few explanations:

- The escaping on line 16 lets us type any character that would hold a special meaning for filename globbing (such as *?* or ***) without messing up the file-searching algorithm.
- In Ruby, the $LOAD_PATH variable (used on line 17) holds all the directories in the file system where Ruby libraries are known to be found. We'll take each such directory and produce a list of libraries based on the Ruby files each contains.
- The per-directory file search actually happens on line 18, with the Dir.glob() method. It produces a list of filenames, which our map() strips of their directory and extension, leaving only the base library name.
- In the end we get an array of arrays of strings, which we want to turn into a flat, sorted array with no duplicates. That's what the chained calls on line 21 do.

This is one of these small code pieces that makes me love Ruby. If you're a Java, .NET, or PHP person (just to name a few prevalent technologies), just compare it to the equivalent code in your language. . . . I mean, this is *expressive* (that is, both concise and very readable)!

The suggestions.rhtml template file is rather concise, too:

scriptaculous/autocomplete/ajax/suggestions.rhtml

```
<ul>
<% libs.each do |lib| %>
    <li><%= lib %></li>
<% end %>
</ul>
```

Time to try it. Shut down any running server script you may still have, and run this one (the usual ruby server.rb command line). Then navigate

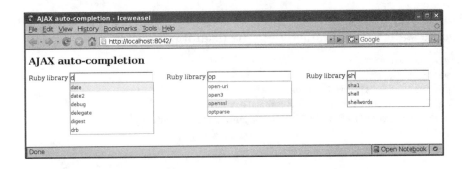

Figure 16.3: AJAX COMPLETION OVER RUBY LIBRARIES

to http://localhost:8042/, and type a letter. You'll get something like the results in Figure 16.3.

I'll let you play around a bit with all of the alphabet. I know, you can't help it; I *know* the libraries, and I still couldn't refrain from trying it out myself.

Customizing the Request Parameters

You can specify a method option for the underlying Ajax.Request object. It does default to 'post', as usual, but you may want to make that a 'get'. After all, you're only fetching data.

You can tweak the parameters sent to the server side in a variety of ways:

- A single parameter contains the currently typed text; its name defaults to the input field's name= attribute. You can change this parameter's name with the paramName option.
- If you want to dynamically craft the passed parameters, you can provide a callback method with the callback (ahem) option. It will get passed both the input field and the current parameter text. It returns the new parameter text (properly encoded, like any query string in a URL).
- You can specify static parameters to be passed no matter what (cumulative to the result of a potential callback result) with the parameters option, which must be a properly encoded query string fragment.

For instance, here's a call that would pass a dynamic timestamp and a couple static extra parameters to the default parameter:

```
new Ajax.Autocompleter('edtLibName', 'libChoices', '/completions', {
  method: 'get',
  parameters: 'static1=value1',
  callback: function(editor, paramText) {
    return paramText + '&stamp=' + new Date().getTime();
  }
});
```

Assuming an input field with name="libName", completion on typing "ab" would issue a request URL something like the following:

```
GET /completions?libName=ab&stamp=1178039580757&static1=value1
```

As you can see, you can tailor the underlying request to your needs with no hassle.

16.4 Using Rich-Markup Choices

So far we've stayed basic in our content model. Our options used only raw text within the confines of their <*li*> element. Often enough, however, we'll want to provide the user with more than just one text; additional details could be useful, such as images, dates, and whatnot.

The trouble is, autocompletion will collect all text nodes within the selected <*li*>. As an example, the following markup:

```
<li>
  <img src="/i/mugshots/ejaubert.png" alt="[Mugshot]"/>
  <span class="contactName">Élodie Jaubert</span><br />
  <span class="job">Heritage consultant</span>
</li>
```

...would produce the completion text "Élodie JaubertHeritage consultant." Damn. What is a web developer to do? Well, you have two options to deal with rich contents in your list items.

The first option is that you can embrace conventions and mark any accessory text with the CSS class *informal*. Any element with this class will automatically get ignored. The previous markup could be adjusted easily:

```
<li>
  <img src="/i/mugshots/ejaubert.png" alt="[Mugshot]"/>
  <span class="contactName">Élodie Jaubert</span><br />
  <span class="job informal">Heritage consultant</span>
</li>
```

That was easy. However, this quickly gets ugly when your content model gets rich enough. All elements but the one with your intended completion text are marked with this CSS class, which feels bloated. So, you can turn the idea on its head and specify a CSS class to identify the elements you *want to include*. This is done with the select option. The markup could go like this:

```
<li>
  <img src="/i/mugshots/ejaubert.png" alt="[Mugshot]"/>
  <span class="contactName">Élodie Jaubert</span>
  <div class="job">Heritage consultant</div>
  <div class="email">heritage@example.com</div>
  <div class="cell">Cell: (478) 555-1234</div>
</li>
```

The autocompleter construction would then just need to state (here for Ajax completion) the following:

```
new Ajax.Autocompleter('edtContact', 'contactChoices', '/completions', {
  select: 'contactName'
});
```

We'll go through a combined example in a moment.

Note that both ways of selecting completion contents are mutually exclusive. If you specify a select option, *informal* classes won't be taken into account, and the elements they tag will still be included if within a selected container element. For instance, with the previous completion constructor call, the following markup:

```
<li>
  <div class="contactName">
    Élodie Jaubert
    <span class="informal"> Oops!</span>
  </div>
</li>
```

... would indeed produce "Élodie Jaubert Oops!"

16.5 Autocompleting Multiple Values in One Field

Autocompleting needs not be restricted to only one value per field. You may very well let the user type multiple values, usually separated by one or more characters among a predefined list of separators (for example, commas, spaces, or line breaks). Perhaps you're offering to free-type a list of tags for an article or image or want to help with the typing of keywords for a search.

The option that lets you deal with this is tokens. You just need to set it to an array of delimiter characters, and the completion mechanism will automatically work with the latest token (text part)—either the only one or the one past the latest delimiter. It's especially useful when you're working with a multiple-line field and want to work on a per-line basis, because you need to put only the newline character ('\n') in the allowed separators.

tokens defaults to an empty array, effectively disabling the multiple-value mode. If you need only one delimiter character, you can set it to a single string; you don't have to bother with a single-element array.

Let's adapt our Ajax completion example to use a few more options, including tokens. We'll adjust our web page to use a multiline input field, that is, a *<textarea>*:

scriptaculous/autocomplete/advanced/index.html

```html
<!DOCTYPE html PUBLIC "-//W3C//DTD XHTML 1.0 Strict//EN"
 "http://www.w3.org/TR/xhtml1/DTD/xhtml1-strict.dtd">
<html xmlns="http://www.w3.org/1999/xhtml" lang="en-US" xml:lang="en-US">
<head>
    <meta http-equiv="Content-Type" content="text/html; charset=utf-8" />
    <title>Advanced autocompletion</title>
    <link rel="stylesheet" type="text/css" href="demo.css" />
    <script type="text/javascript" src="prototype.js"></script>
    <script type="text/javascript"
     src="scriptaculous.js?load=effects,controls"></script>
    <script type="text/javascript" src="demo.js"></script>
</head>
<body>

<h1>Advanced autocompletion</h1>

<form>
  <p>
    <label for="edtLibNames" accesskey="L">Ruby libraries</label><br/>
    <textarea type="text" id="edtLibNames" name="libNames"></textarea>
    <div id="libChoices" class="autocomplete"></div>
  </p>
</form>

</body>
</html>
```

Notice that we adjusted the id= and name= attributes accordingly. On the server side, we'd like to provide richer content, with not only library names but, for each one, its last modification time and its file size in bytes. To store all these data, we'll create a simple LibInfo class and use its constructor to extract all the necessary information from the original File object:

```
scriptaculous/autocomplete/advanced/server.rb
```

```ruby
#! /usr/bin/env ruby

require 'cgi'
require 'erb'
require 'webrick'
include WEBrick

class LibInfo
  attr_reader :name, :mtime, :size

  def initialize(name)
    @name = File.basename(name, '.rb')
    @mtime = File.mtime(name)
    @size = File.size(name)
  end

  def <=>(other)
    self.name <=> other.name
  end
end

template_text = File.read('suggestions.rhtml')
suggestions = ERB.new(template_text)

server = HTTPServer.new(:Port => 8042)
server.mount('/', HTTPServlet::FileHandler, '.')

server.mount_proc('/completions') do |request, response|
  name_start = request.query['libName']
  suffix = "/#{Regexp.escape(name_start)}*.rb"
  libs = $LOAD_PATH.map { |dir|
    Dir.glob(dir + suffix, File::FNM_CASEFOLD).map { |f| LibInfo.new(f) }
  }.flatten.sort.uniq
  response['Content-Type'] = 'text/html'
  response.body = suggestions.result(binding)
end

trap('INT') { server.shutdown }

server.start
```

The <=>() method on line 17 is probably very weird-looking to the non-Rubyists among you. We call it the "Tie Fighter" operator. It's used for sorting, as a comparator between two LibInfo objects. It simply makes sure they're sorted by name. On line 32, notice that we simply map every File object we get to a new LibInfo object.

The new suggestions template is adjusted accordingly:

scriptaculous/autocomplete/advanced/suggestions.rhtml

```
<ul>
<% libs.each do |lib| %>
    <li>
        <div class="libName"><%= lib.name %></div>
        <div class="libMTime"><%= lib.mtime.strftime(
          '%m/%d/%Y %H:%M:%S') %></div>
        <div class="libSize"><%= lib.size %> bytes</div>
    </li>
<% end %>
</ul>
```

We rely on the usual strftime() method (well known to C and PHP developers, for instance) to format the modification time. Of course, these new CSS classes call for custom styling, and the container *<li>* needs a bit of revamping to comfortably host this extra information:

scriptaculous/autocomplete/advanced/demo.css

```
h1 { font-size: 1.5em; }

div.autocomplete {
  position: absolute;
  width: 250px; /* will be adjusted by script.aculo.us */
  background-color: white; border: 1px solid #888;
  margin: 0px; padding: 0px;
}
div.autocomplete ul {
  list-style-type: none; margin: 0px; padding: 0px;
}
div.autocomplete ul li.selected { background-color:  #ff9;}
div.autocomplete ul li {
  list-style-type: none; display: block;
  font-family: sans-serif; font-size: smaller; color: #444;
  margin: 0; padding: 0.1em; height: 3.5em;
  cursor: pointer;
}
#edtLibNames {
  border: 0.1em solid gray; padding: 0.1em; height: 4em;
}
div.libMTime, div.libSize {
  font-size: 80%;
  color: #444;
}

div.libMTime {
  margin: 0.2ex 0 0 2ex;
}
```

```
div.libName {
  font-weight: bold;
}

div.libSize {
  margin: 0 0 0.5em 2ex;
}
```

Finally, we need to adjust our Ajax.Autocompleter call to make use of these new options. It's still fairly concise:

```
scriptaculous/autocomplete/advanced/demo.js
document.observe('dom:loaded', function() {
  new Ajax.Autocompleter('edtLibNames', 'libChoices', '/completions', {
    method: 'get', paramName: 'libName',
    tokens: [',', '\n'], select: 'libName'
  });
});
```

Notice that this time, we make a cleaner use of HTTP methods by using a GET, which is more appropriate to data fetching. Because our input field's original name (its name= attribute) is now a plural, but we're completing a single name, we also override the parameter name used in the Ajax completion calls.

To allow multiple values both on a per-line basis and on the same line (by using commas), we define a two-element tokens option. And to only use the library's name (not its details) for the completion, we specify a CSS class name for the content fragment holding the data we're interested in.

Well, how about testing it? Stop any running server script, run this one, load it up with no cache in your browser (still http://localhost:8042/), and start typing values, accepting completions, going multiline, or using commas.... In the end, you should get results like the montage in Figure 16.4, on the following page.

16.6 Reacting to Completion with Callbacks

Autocompleters come with a few callbacks that let you customize how the completion list is revealed or hidden, get notified once a completion gets used, or even replace the standard text extraction mechanism when a completion is selected.

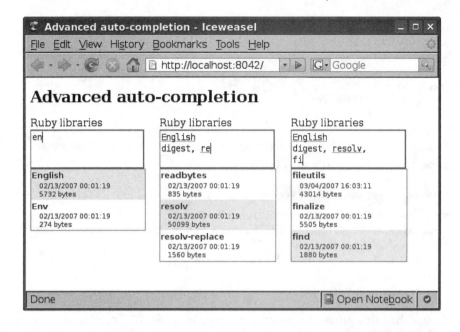

Figure 16.4: ADVANCED COMPLETION: TOKENS AND RICH CONTENTS

Here's a quick rundown, in chronological (triggering) order:

onShow

> In charge of positioning and revealing the choice list. You should rarely need to change it. The default behavior positions the completion container under the input field, aligns its width, and makes it fade in pretty fast (0.15″) with a Effect.Appear. This takes two arguments: the input field and the completion container (the two first arguments you passed at construction time).

updateElement

> In charge of reacting to a <*li*> completion choice being accepted in order to actually complete the input field's value. This is very seldom overridden, because it *replaces* the default behavior, which is responsible for a hell of a lot—dealing with richly structured contents (the *informal* class and the select option), handling tokenization (tokens option), actually updating the input field's value, and eventually calling the afterUpdateElement callback.

If you define this, you're very much on your own. Most options and behaviors are dealt with by the default processing, which your callback replaces entirely. You would get only one argument: the accepted <*li*> element (but you would run bound to the auto-completer object, so you could access, say, this.options and this.element).

In short, be careful with this!

afterUpdateElement

Undoubtedly the most-often used callback. It is triggered by the default updateElement behavior once the value was completed by an accepted choice. It takes two arguments: the input field and the accepted <*li*> element. This is what lets you react to completions in the easiest manner.

onHide

In charge of taking the choice list away. Just like onShow, it's rarely overridden. The default behavior just fades out in 0.15 second. It takes the same arguments as onShow.

What We Just Learned

Providing dynamic completion of text input, be it from a page-local or, more often, remote data source through Ajax, is a breeze with script.-aculo.us. Our completion items can be content-rich, and we can hook onto the completion extraction process when an item is picked so as to complete more than just the visible editor. Use cases for completion-assisted input are numerous and sometimes unexpected. Be on the lookout for situations where they can help your users!

Here's a quick recap:

- The most common form of autocompletion is through Ajax, thanks to Ajax.Autocompleter. However, a local variant, based on Java-Script arrays embedded in our code, is also possible.

- We can easily tune when and how the completion process triggers by adjusting a few options, such as minChars and frequency.

- Ajax-based completion requires a <*ul*>/<*li*> structure as a response, but the contents of the list items can be as rich as we need. Options let us easily extract only part of the selected item for the actual text completion.

- Callbacks let us augment the basic completion process. For example, we can grab hidden data from the selected element to populate both visual and hidden form fields.

- It is possible to complete not just one but multiple values in a single field, thanks to the tokens option.

Neuron Workout

Time to think harder!

- When is it more practical to rely on the *informal* CSS class as opposed to specifying a select option?

- What situations can you see where local completion is a good fit?

- How could we tweak an Ajax.Autocompleter call so that it can deal with a resultset that is not a <*ul*>/<*li*> structure? For example, how could we complete based on an Atom feed or an XML export of a MySQL schema?

Chapter 17

Building DOM Fragments the Easy Way: Builder

Frequently, you need to inject some new content into your page's document. Depending on the complexity of the content and potential browser quirks, you'll choose between three ways to do this:

- If producing the markup text for your contents is easy enough, you'll usually want to go with Element extension methods such as insert(), replace(), or update(). We covered these back in Section 7.2, *Replacing vs. Inserting*, on page 145.

  However, because such methods internally rely (most of the time) on the innerHTML property, which is currently not quite standardized/normative and has a few issues on Firefox (prior to version 2, if I'm not mistaken), you may hit browser inconsistencies once in a while (especially when dealing with <*select*> and <*option*> in my humble experience). In some cases, you may also find it easier (or more natural) to manually build the DOM elements instead of composing XHTML markup.

- When manual element construction is what you're going for, simple needs can be addressed by the new Element(...) syntax we discussed in Section 7.2, *Lightweight DOM Element Creation*, on page 145. Unfortunately, this facility currently will not let you specify text or nested elements as content for the element you are creating. You are limited to the element's tag name and its attribute list.

- That leaves us with a large array of use cases, where we need to create actual DOM trees (or just hit a snag with innerHTML-based ways and need to revert to good ol' DOM interfaces under the hood).

This is what Builder is for.

It lets you quickly specify the construction of DOM fragments, to any depth and degree of complexity you'd need, with a rather concise, expressive syntax.

You'll need the builder.js module. So, your script.aculo.us loading will look, at minimum, like this:

```
<script type="text/javascript" src="builder.js"></script>
```

17.1 Building Explicitly

Let's start with the fundamental building block: Builder.node(). You can call it in a variety of ways, but using a single statement block requires some thinking to decipher it, so I'll use one line per variant:

```
Builder.node(tagName) → Element
Builder.node(tagName, attributes) → Element
Builder.node(tagName, text | child | [ child, ... ]) → Element
Builder.node(tagName, attributes, text | child | [ child, ... ]) → Element
```

Starting Easy: Just One Element

This is the safest way and lets you explicitly specify every tag name, attribute, and parent-child relationship. You always start by passing a tag name. If you stop there, you'll get a rather raw element, but this is, in many subtle ways, superior to the usual document.createElement() call you would normally do with the DOM. Indeed, there are stealthy bugs across browsers when you attempt to create, out of the blue, certain HTML elements this way.

Builder.node() tries a variety of approaches, based on the innerHTML property and synthetic parent nodes, using document.createElement() only as a fallback. This results in maximum portability, with one exception. In Firefox prior to version 1.5, you will not be able to create *<optgroup>* and *<option>* elements this way, because of an acknowledged Firefox bug. But then, Firefox users usually have at least version 1.5. . . .

Of course, Builder.node() does not stop at the tag name but lets you specify attributes, simple text as element contents, or one or more children elements (which can, naturally, be Builder.node() calls themselves).

Attributes are provided as a hash, usually an anonymous object. When the property name is a JavaScript reserved word (two cases come to mind: class= and for=), you will have to use the DOM property name instead (respectively className and htmlFor). Otherwise, use the attribute names in the case mandated by your document's DTD (for example, lowercase for XHTML). There are a number of issues with native attribute manipulation, which are smoothed over, once again, by the method's algorithm.

With attributes available, Builder.node() is already way more interesting than document.createElement(), which does not support shorthand attribute creation in its official syntax. Here are a few example calls:

```
Builder.node('a', { href: 'http://script.aculo.us' })
Builder.node('label', { htmlFor: 'edtLogin', accesskey: 'L' })
Builder.node('p', { className: 'intro' })
```

When you create a nonempty element that has a textual content, you just need to pass the text as the last argument:

```
// Text child
Builder.node('h1', 'Builder rules')
// Attributes, text child
Builder.node('a', { href: 'http://prototypejs.org' }, 'Prototype!')
```

Elements Within Elements

Textual contents are nice, but you may very well want to quickly create a small DOM fragment, with nested elements and all. If there's only one child node, just pass it directly, be it text or another element; if there are many, pass an array. A few examples will be clearer than further explanations, I guess:

```
// Element child
Builder.node('h1', Builder.node('code', 'Builder'))
// Multiple children
Builder.node('h1', [Builder.node('code', 'Builder'), ' rules'])
// Attributes, element child
Builder.node('p', { className: 'submission' },
  Builder.node('input', { type: 'submit', value: 'Sign in' }))
// Attributes, multiple children
Builder.node('a',
  { href: 'http://prototypejs.org/api/ajax/update' },
  [Builder.node('code', 'Ajax.Updater'), ' documentation'])
```

In the source code archive for this book, you'll find a demo page that lets you dynamically try all these example calls. You'll find it in the code/scriptaculous/builder directory in the archive. By using a DOM inspector such as Firebug's, you'll be able to inspect the DOM for the resulting elements easily enough.

Method Dumping: Still Explicit, But Shorter

If you feel like shortening your code and if your personal sense of code aesthetics tolerates it, you can equip any object, including the global scope (that is, the window object) with convenience methods for just about every XHTML tag. These convenience methods are really just wrappers around Builder.node(), with the first argument prefilled.

For instance, instead of doing this:

```
Builder.node('h1', Builder.node('code', 'Builder'))
```

. . . you would do this:

```
H1(CODE('Builder'))
```

In the same vein, the following snippet:

```
Builder.node('h1', [Builder.node('code', 'Builder'), ' rules'])
```

. . . would become this:

```
H1([CODE('Builder'), ' rules'])
```

As a final example, the two following calls:

```
Builder.node('p', { className: 'submission' },
  Builder.node('input', { type: 'submit', value: 'Sign in' }))
Builder.node('a',
  { href: 'http://prototypejs.org/api/ajax/update' },
  [Builder.node('code', 'Ajax.Updater'), ' documentation' ])
```

. . . would be turned into this:

```
P({ className: 'submission' }, INPUT({ type: 'submit',
  value: 'Sign in'}))
A({ href: 'http://prototypejs.org/api/ajax/update' },
  [CODE('Ajax.Updater'), 'documentation'])
```

So, how do we achieve this? Simply by calling Builder.dump()—just once, at some point before we start using these shortcuts. The method takes an optional scope argument:

```
Builder.build([scope = window])
```

So, calling it with no argument sprinkles the global scope with those uppercase methods. Uppercase was chosen so the risk of conflict with existing methods would be lower; indeed, if a method exists in the scope with one of the "dumped" names, it will be overridden by the node-building one.

But you can refrain from polluting the global namespace and still gain some concision by using an object of your choice as the namespace. Just look at the following code:

```
var B = {}
Builder.dump(B);
B.H1(B.CODE('Builder'))
```

When using dump(), I certainly prefer this way. . . . You can even simply alias to Builder so as to keep a uniform interface:

```
var B = Builder;
Builder.dump(B);
B.H1('Builder') // <=> B.node('h1', 'Builder')
```

17.2 Using an (X)HTML Representation

I personally like the structured way of Builder.node(), which is retained by the shortcuts you can get through Builder.dump(), but sometimes the fragment you're looking to build is way shorter to express using XHTML syntax. For instance, consider the following simple fragment:

```
<h1 id="intro">Introduction to the <code>Builder</code> object</h1>
```

Then look at its building, either with node() or convenience methods:

```
Builder.node('h1', { id: 'intro' }, [
  'Introduction to the ', Builder.node('code', 'Builder'), ' object'])
// or...
H1({ id: 'intro' }, ['Introduction to the ', CODE('Builder'), ' object'])
```

Sure, anyone can argue about the relative merits of each variant, but when you do find yourself needing—or wanting—to work based on an XHTML fragment, you can use Builder.build():

```
Builder.build(html) → Element
```

There's one gotcha: the fragment you pass must use an overall container element. If it has many top-level elements, you'll get only the first one. Here's an example:

```
// Single container element: OK
Builder.build(
  '<h1 id="intro">Introduction to the <code>Builder</code> object</h1>')
// Multiple top-level elements: woops!  We'll only get the <h1> back!
Builder.build('<h1>Intro</h1><p>So the story goes&#8230;</p>')
```

Builder.build() works very much like Element.update(), which we discussed on page 128, except it doesn't need an element to work inside of. Indeed, it *does* entirely rely on Element.update(), which it uses on a temporary <*div*> it creates outside the page's DOM. So, whatever Element.update() can deal with, Builder.build() can.

Wow, after the power tools we covered in the previous chapters, this one was quick enough to walk through. Refreshing, wouldn't you say? Just the right length for a public-transport commute. . . . The next chapter is about in-place editing, which lets us take just about any text on our pages, edit it on the fly, and save it through Ajax. It's so Web 2.0!

In-Place Editing

18.1 What's In-Place Editing Exactly?

In-place editing is about taking noneditable content, such as a *<p>*, *<h1>*, or *<div>*, and letting the user edit its contents by simply clicking it. This turns the static element into an editable zone (either single-line or multiline) and pops up submit and cancel buttons (or links, depending on your options) for the user to commit or roll back the modification. It then synchronizes the edit on the server side through Ajax and makes the element noneditable again.

In-place editing is one of the hallmarks of Web 2.0–style applications, which aim to make the user more and more participative in the contents and reduce the barrier to contribution and writing. You could use it for customizing the title of a per-user portal page, editing "notes" sprinkled throughout the screen space by the user, and so on.

What script.aculo.us Brings to the Table

Two classes focus on in-place editing: Ajax.InPlaceEditor and Ajax. InPlaceCollectionEditor. The former one is the most commonly used and relies on free-typing text fields for content modification. The latter one, which specializes the former, limits the options by using a drop-down list from which our users can pick the value they want.

As their names imply, both use Ajax to synchronize the new content on the server. Both come with a wealth of options that give you fine-grained control over the look and feel of the resulting UI. We'll tackle these capabilities by theme in the following sections.

Careful About Versions: Code Refactoring

In version 1.8, the two classes responsible for in-place editing underwent massive refactoring, and their public API changed a bit, especially where available options and callbacks are concerned.

The former code was mostly a third-party contribution, which so far had worked well enough. Unfortunately, the code had then grown organically and had not kept very well in sync with new, better Prototypish ways. It had become a rather haphazard collection of methods with more than a few inconsistencies and odd behaviors under specific circumstances. Hence, it was refactored; it was close to a full rewrite.

Step by Step with In-Place Editors

Before diving in with examples and the numerous features, I think it's better if we take a moment to stand back and get the big picture. Here's a surface rundown on the successive stages of an in-place editor's life:

1. First, you make an element in-place editable. As always when using script.aculo.us, it is the job of a single call, in our case the construction of the proper wrapper object based on the relevant element.

2. From then on, when users hover over our element with the mouse, a few features mark this element as in-place editable. All of these are customizable to your needs, but here are the defaults:
   - Hovering in immediately highlights the element.
   - Lingering will display the element's title= in a tooltip, which is set by default to *Click to edit*.
   - Hovering out dehighlights with a quick fade-out (aesthetics, my friend, aesthetics...).

3. Clicking the element enters *edit mode*. A proper <form> is created on the fly, with an appropriate editor UI (for example, a single-line text field, a drop-down list of possible choices, submission and cancellation buttons or links, and so on). Although rarely used, an option exists to bind click and hovering listeners to another element instead of the content-containing element, if you want to dissociate them.

If you use an alternate form of the contents on the server side and just generate its XHTML representation to produce this content, you can elect to load the "source" text through Ajax and have the user edit this original content (for example, Textile[1] or Markdown[2] text instead of actual XHTML).

4. Editing takes place. In regular mode, hitting `Return` (on single-line editors) or triggering the submission control (button or link) commits it; conversely, hitting `Esc` or triggering the cancellation control reverts it.

   However, you may elect not to have any OK/cancel controls. Submitting takes place when hitting `Return` or getting out of the field (for example, by clicking elsewhere or hitting `Tab`), and reverting is still bound to `Esc`. This is a popular behavior, because it unclutters the editing area.

5. If the editing is canceled, the original content is restored. If it's committed, the editing UI goes away and is replaced by a message stating that the modification is being saved; when the modification *is* saved, the original element reappears, with updated content. If you used an alternate syntax for the edited content, the server will have sent the XHTML conversion for your static element to use instead of the "source" text.

6. The element undergoes a quick highlight effect to state its recent modification.

We'll explore these steps, and the various options and callbacks available for our customizing pleasure, in the following sections.

Using in-Place Editors in Our Code

You'll need the controls.js module, which also contains, as you'll no doubt recall, the autocompletion stuff. Because default behaviors for in-place editing heavily rely on the Effect.Highlight object, you'll also need to include effects.js. So, your script.aculo.us loading will look, at minimum, like this:

```
<script type="text/javascript"
 src="scriptaculous.js?load=effects,controls"></script>
```

---

1. http://www.textism.com/tools/textile/
2. http://daringfireball.net/projects/markdown/

18.2 A Simple Example

It's time we start playing with this. We'll need the usual files: Prototype, the required script.aculo.us modules and the loader, and our custom CSS and JavaScript files. Because we are talking about in-place editing, that means we expect the user to be able to modify content that will later be served again. So, we'll use template files and serve our demo page dynamically, instead of with a static index.html file.

For starters, here is our template file, index.rhtml:

`scriptaculous/ipe/simple/index.rhtml`

```
<!DOCTYPE html PUBLIC "-//W3C//DTD XHTML 1.0 Strict//EN"
 "http://www.w3.org/TR/xhtml1/DTD/xhtml1-strict.dtd">
<html xmlns="http://www.w3.org/1999/xhtml" lang="en-US" xml:lang="en-US">
<head>
    <meta http-equiv="Content-Type" content="text/html; charset=utf-8" />
    <title>Simple in-place editing</title>
    <link rel="stylesheet" type="text/css" href="demo.css" />
    <script type="text/javascript" src="prototype.js"></script>
    <script type="text/javascript"
     src="scriptaculous.js?load=effects,controls"></script>
    <script type="text/javascript" src="demo.js"></script>
</head>
<body>

<h1>Simple in-place editing</h1>

<p id="freeZone"><%= editableHTML %></p>

</body>
</html>
```

The CSS could just as well be missing, because it retains only our usual <h1> downplay:

`scriptaculous/ipe/simple/demo.css`

```
h1 { font-size: 1.5em; }
```

We'll go with all the defaults here, so activating in-place editing will be extremely concise:

`scriptaculous/ipe/simple/demo.js`

```
document.observe('dom:loaded', function() {
  new Ajax.InPlaceEditor('freeZone', '/update');
});
```

Neat, isn't it? It's short and to the point. The constructor syntax is actually the following:

```
new Ajax.InPlaceEditor(element, url [, options])
```

... but we don't use any options yet. The final piece for our puzzle is the server script, of course. Here it is:

scriptaculous/ipe/simple/server.rb

```
Line 1   #! /usr/bin/env ruby

    -    require 'cgi'
    -    require 'erb'
    5    require 'webrick'
    -    include WEBrick

    -    template_text = File.read('index.rhtml')
    -    template = ERB.new(template_text)
    10
    -    server = HTTPServer.new(:Port => 8042)
    -    server.mount('/', HTTPServlet::FileHandler, '.')

    -    editableHTML =
    15     'Click here to edit with <code>Ajax.InPlaceEditor</code>&#8230;'

    -    server.mount_proc('/home') do |request, response|
    -      response['Content-Type'] = 'text/html'
    -      response.body = template.result(binding)
    20   end

    -    server.mount_proc('/update') do |request, response|
    -      editableHTML = request.query['value']
    -      response.body = editableHTML
    25   end

    -    trap('INT') { server.shutdown }

    -    server.start
```

Note the default content, on line 15. More important, note the code on line 24. This round-trip is a bit overkill here, because we do not use any alternative syntax for the content, and the client side could go with the raw content typed in by the user. But we went with all the defaults, which assume the server will return the final content. After all, even with no alternative syntax, we could very well strip specific tags, or limit the length, or whatever. It's your code on the server. You can implement whatever validation logic you want!

Now that we have everything in place, kill any running example server you may still have around, and run this the usual way (ruby server.rb). Figure 18.1, on the following page, is a montage of the successive stages in using our simple in-place editor: basic, hovering, editing, and edited. You won't notice the "saving" stage because we're running against a local server that, not doing anything long, responds too fast for this step to linger at all.

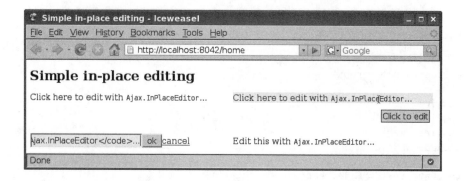

Figure 18.1: SIMPLE IN-PLACE EDITING IN ACTION

18.3 How Can We Tweak the Ajax Persistence?

First, we need to know what the defaults are. Basically, we rely on a call to Ajax.Updater, with our element as the success container, no specific Ajax options (so all the defaults of Ajax.Updater apply; for instance, we're using asynchronous post), and two parameters: a value parameter with our editable field's value and an editorId parameter with the id= of our original element (unless it doesn't have any, in which case this second parameter is absent).

We can customize quite a handful of things here:

- We can change the name of the parameter holding the field's value using the paramName option (defaults to 'value').
- We can change the whole series of parameters (except for the editorId one, which is handled internally) by replacing the default callback, er, callback, with our own. The default one simply goes like this:

```
function(form) {
  return Form.serialize(form);
}
```

We can provide our own logic. It will actually be passed *two* arguments: the synthesized <*form*> element and the editable field's value (as retrieved by the $F() method, which we discussed on page 38). Using this, you could add any extra parameters you need, transform the passed value, and so on.
- You can provide any options you want for the Ajax call with the ajaxOptions option, which defaults to the following simple set: {evalScripts: true}.

- Finally, you can tell the in-place editing mechanism that the server won't return a finalized markup by setting the htmlResponse option to **false** (defaults to **true**). The system will then revert to using an Ajax.Request object, which can still autoevaluate JavaScript-typed results (see Section 9.2, *Other Things Our Ajax.Request Can Do*, on page 196 for more details on this). More generally, you can pass your own callbacks (for example, onComplete to deal with any response text you'd send). Such a callback must be specified at the regular options level, *not* in ajaxOptions.

18.4 Customizing the Appearance

There's a lot you can do to tailor the appearance of in-place editors to your needs: buttons or links (or none!), additional texts, styling, external controls, and callbacks that let you add custom logic, including visual effects, to various stages of the editor's life cycle.

Buttons vs. Links

As you noticed, by default, you get an OK button and a cancel link. This is the original choice, made back when dinosaurs still roamed the earth. You can customize this in a variety of ways:

- The okControl and cancelControl options each can take three values: 'button', 'link', and **false**. The latter choice removes the respective widget, pure and simple. Respective defaults are, obviously enough, 'button' and 'link'.
- You can change the text of the buttons or links with the okText and cancelText options, which default to 'ok' and 'cancel', respectively.
- You can go bare and strip both controls, which leaves you with the keyboard hooks on `Return` and `Esc`. This alone, however, is a risky choice, because plenty of users may not hit any of these keys. So, you can make sure the modification is committed as soon as the focus leaves the editable field (for example, our user clicks elsewhere). Simply set the submitOnBlur option to **true** (defaults to **false**). Of course, if this option is enabled, OK/cancel controls become entirely useless; clicking them would first cause a focus loss, which would immediately trigger submission of the new content anyway.

We'll see variants based on these options, and a few more, in the following section.

Additional Text

In addition to adjusting how submission and cancellation are triggered, you can insert custom text before, between, and after the OK and cancel controls:

- textBeforeControls appears before the first visible control.

- textBetweenControls appears between the OK and cancel controls, but only if both are visible.

- textAfterControls appears after the last visible control.

All three options default to the empty string.

As long as we're talking about text-related options, you can customize the tooltip displayed when the mouse lingers over the static element. Just change the value of the clickToEditText option, which defaults to *Click to edit*.

Finally, you can change the text that appears, however briefly, while the new content is being saved through Ajax. Use the savingText option for this, which defaults to *Saving...*.

Let's test a fair number of these options to see what the results look like. We'll have a number of editors here, so we need to adjust our server script in order to maintain not one, but multiple, contents:

```
scriptaculous/ipe/variants/server.rb
```
```ruby
#! /usr/bin/env ruby

require 'cgi'
require 'erb'
require 'webrick'
include WEBrick

template_text = File.read('index.rhtml')
template = ERB.new(template_text)

server = HTTPServer.new(:Port => 8042)
server.mount('/', HTTPServlet::FileHandler, '.')

editableHTMLs = [
  'Andrew Dupont',
  'Mislav Marohnitextquotesinglec',
  'Thomas Fuchs',
  'Tobie Langel'
]
```

```ruby
server.mount_proc('/home') do |request, response|
  response['Content-Type'] = 'text/html'
  response.body = template.result(binding)
end

server.mount_proc('/update') do |request, response|
  sentContent = request.query['value']
  request.query['editorId'] =~ /^freeZone(\d+)$/
  index = $1.to_i - 1
  editableHTMLs[index] = sentContent
  sleep 2 if index == 3 # Simulate lag so we can see the custom text...
  response.body = sentContent
end

trap('INT') { server.shutdown }

server.start
```

Notice how the automatically added editorId parameter makes it easy to persist multiple contents. We won't have anything special to do in the JavaScript to get that.

The template for our page adjusts accordingly:

`scriptaculous/ipe/variants/index.rhtml`

```html
<!DOCTYPE html PUBLIC "-//W3C//DTD XHTML 1.0 Strict//EN"
  "http://www.w3.org/TR/xhtml1/DTD/xhtml1-strict.dtd">
<html xmlns="http://www.w3.org/1999/xhtml" lang="en-US" xml:lang="en-US">
<head>
    <meta http-equiv="Content-Type" content="text/html; charset=utf-8" />
    <title>Variants on in-place editing</title>
    <link rel="stylesheet" type="text/css" href="demo.css" />
    <script type="text/javascript" src="prototype.js"></script>
    <script type="text/javascript"
     src="scriptaculous.js?load=effects,controls"></script>
    <script type="text/javascript" src="demo.js"></script>
</head>
<body>

<h1>Variants on in-place editing</h1>
<% editableHTMLs.each_with_index do |html, index| %>
<p id="freeZone<%= index + 1 %>" class="editable"><%= html %></p>
<% end %>
</body>
</html>
```

We don't apply any styling yet (that will be the topic of our next section), but we need to adjust the scripting in order to create in-place editors for each paragraph, with various option sets.

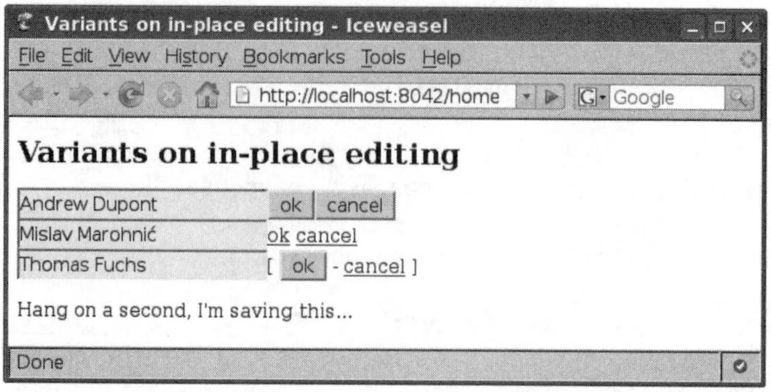

Figure 18.2: FIDDLING WITH CONTROLS AND TEXTS

Here's how we do that:

`scriptaculous/ipe/variants/demo.js`

```
document.observe('dom:loaded', function() {
  new Ajax.InPlaceEditor('freeZone1', '/update', {
    cancelControl: 'button' });
  new Ajax.InPlaceEditor('freeZone2', '/update', {
    okControl: 'link', textBetweenControls: ' '
  });
  new Ajax.InPlaceEditor('freeZone3', '/update', {
    textBeforeControls: '[ ', textBetweenControls: ' - ',
    textAfterControls: ' ]'
  });
  new Ajax.InPlaceEditor('freeZone4', '/update', {
    clickToEditText: 'You\'d better click on this!',
    savingText: 'Hang on a second, I\'m saving this...'
  });
});
```

Figure 18.2 captures the state of our page with all editors enabled, save for the last one, which is saving (the server script simulates a two-second processing for this one, leaving us enough time to notice the custom text).

CSS Classes, Colors, and Other Style Properties

In-place editors are a kind of widget, since they actually produce UI components on the page (the editor, its OK/cancel controls, and so on). And widgets would be no good if they could not properly adapt to your application's visual identity. Fortunately, you can rely on numerous CSS classes and several options to tune the editors' appearance.

The following CSS classes are defined, which you can then define as you want in your style sheet:

- *inplaceeditor-form* applies to the dynamically created forms that wrap the edition controls.
- *editor_ok_button* and *editor_ok_link* are used for OK controls, depending on the type.
- *editor_cancel_button* and *editor_cancel_link* are used for cancel controls.
- *editor_field* is used for the editor itself (in other words, the <*input*> or <*textarea*>).
- *inplaceeditor-saving* is used for the saving message, and we'll see later that *inplaceeditor-loading* is used for the loading message when your editor uses an alternate text.

You can use your own class names for several of these but not all (and at some future point, you won't be able to change these names at all, as I'll discuss in a moment). Currently, the following options are available for specifying custom class names:

- hoverClassName applies to editable elements when the mouse hovers over them in noneditable mode. It has no default value.
- formClassName is for the wrapper forms and defaults to *inplaceeditor-form*.
- loadingClassName is for the loading status message, when you edit alternate text instead of the raw content. It defaults to *inplaceeditor-loading*.
- savingClassName is for the saving status message. It defaults to *inplaceeditor-saving*.

Finally, note that there is a size property, which lets you specify the "size" of the single-line editor field, as per the old size= attribute. Most of the time, you'll resort to CSS instead, which is much more flexible and accurate.

Let's adapt our previous example to use these styles. The CSS file grows a bit to become this:

`scriptaculous/Ipe/styled/demo.css`

```
h1 { font-size: 1.5em; }

.editable.hovered {
  border: 1px dashed #880;
}
```

```
form.first {
  border: 3px solid silver;
  background: #ddd;
  padding: 0.5em;
  margin-bottom: 1em;
}

.inplaceeditor-saving {
  height: 16px; padding-left: 20px;
  background: url(/spinner.gif) no-repeat left center;
  font: italic smaller/16px sans-serif; color: gray;
}
```

Notice how it uses custom CSS classes, such as *hovered* and *first*, along with default ones such as *inplaceeditor-saving*. The script adapts accordingly:

```
scriptaculous/ipe/styled/demo.js
document.observe('dom:loaded', function() {
  new Ajax.InPlaceEditor('freeZone1', '/update', {
    hoverClassName: 'hovered', formClassName: 'first'
  });
  new Ajax.InPlaceEditor('freeZone2', '/update', {
    hoverClassName: 'hovered'
  });
  new Ajax.InPlaceEditor('freeZone3', '/update', {
    hoverClassName: 'hovered'
  });
  new Ajax.InPlaceEditor('freeZone4', '/update', {
    hoverClassName: 'hovered',
    savingText: 'Hang on, I\'m saving this...'
  });
});
```

There's nothing fancy here. And the server side remains unchanged. Now reload the example, making sure to bypass the browser's cache to use the latest script and style sheet (on Firefox and Mozilla browsers, holding Shift while hitting the Refresh button will do that), and you'll notice the new styling when hovering on paragraphs, activating the editor for the first one, or saving the last one. Figure 18.3, on the facing page, shows all these changes in one shot.

How Can We Use Different Styles for Different Editors?

You noticed that not all CSS class names could be customized, and I alluded to the fact that in some future version of script.aculo.us, the custom-class options will be stripped altogether.

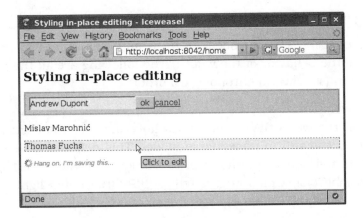

Figure 18.3: STYLING EDITORS

This is because you can achieve full customization results on a per-editor basis without these options. Each editor has its own form, and each form has an id= attribute.

So, you could rely on the same classes but within different ID contexts, which CSS makes easy to specify. The only question is, what's an editor's form ID?

The single "bad case" is the one where your original element has no ID, and the options don't include formId. Then the form won't have an ID, and you won't be able to tell it apart.

Now let's say your original element has an ID, and you didn't specify a formId option (just like we did so far). Then the wrapper form's ID is your element's suffixed by *-inplaceeditor* (for instance, over <p id="freeZone1">, you'll get a <form> with id="freeZone1-inplaceeditor"). Note that if such an element already has the resulting ID, the ID won't be used.

Finally, you can specify your own form ID using the formId option. Just pass whichever form ID you want. Be careful, though—this does not mean the system will build an editor within an existing <form>! You will get a fresh <form> no matter what, right where the original element was.

Pitching In with Callbacks

Ajax.InPlaceEditor lets you hook in at all important times in order to customize the behavior of the widget. The following are all the defined callbacks in (somewhat) chronological order:

onEnterHover

> Triggered when the mouse starts hovering over the element (because it is still in noneditable mode). This defaults to setting its inline style's background color to Ajax.InPlaceEditor.DefaultOptions. highlightColor, which originally is #ffff99 (the usual light yellow). This takes the element as its single argument.

onLeaveHover

> Triggered when the mouse stops hovering over the element (it gets out of the element's "airspace"). This defaults to fading out the highlight color toward Ajax.InPlaceEditor.DefaultOptions. highlightEndColor (which originally is #ffffff, a full white) and finally restoring the original background color, if any. This takes the element as its single argument.

onEnterEditMode

> The editor UI was just created and activated. The semantics changed slightly compared to before the refactoring, where this got triggered *before* the editor UI was created. This takes the element as its single argument.

onFailure

> An error occurred in the saving Ajax call. This defaults to showing an error message that includes the response's text stripped bare of markup tags. This takes at least one argument: the XMLHttpRequest object that was used. If htmlResponse is **true** (its default value), the element will be passed as the second argument.

onComplete

> The saving Ajax call completed, with or without error. This takes at least one argument—the XMLHttpRequest object that was used. If htmlResponse is **true** (its default value), the element will be passed as the second argument.

onLeaveEditMode

> The element is visible again and updated if no error came up. This takes the element as its single argument.

As a minor note, before the recent refactoring of Ajax.InPlaceEditor, background images in the various CSS classes (especially the loading- and saving-related ones) got ignored after the first use. This was because of a tiny misconfiguration of internal Effect.Highlight objects, which is now fixed. You can provide background images again, as our latest CSS file and as Figure 18.3 demonstrate.

Using an External Control

Perhaps you want to provide an obvious means of editing. Indeed, for most users, it is not at all self-evident that your element is editable in-place: titles, paragraphs, and their lot are usually fairly static. By default, only the element itself reacts to hovering and clicking, but you may want to use "sidekicks" such as an associated *Edit* link or button, which will loudly (and proudly) proclaim to your users that something can be edited here.

If you want to use such associated controls, you'll be happy with the externalControl option. Just have it reference the element (directly or by ID, as usual) that's supposed to react to hovering and clicks. The element itself still reacts, but so does your associated component.

You may also want to require the user to click this external control in order to trigger the editing mode. By default, both the original element *and* the external control would work. You can use the external-ControlOnly option to limit triggering to the external control.

Changing Default Options

There are a lot of defaults, and they may just not suit you all that well. For instance, perhaps all your failure callbacks should behave the same way...just not the default one. Or you'd like to get rid of highlights entirely. Or something.

To let you change these defaults, they are all centralized in the Ajax. InPlaceEditor.DefaultOptions object. You can alter them, and whenever you create a new Ajax.InPlaceEditor, it will use the current state of this object as defaults. Of course, the specific options you pass for this construction override the current defaults, as usual.

18.5 Dealing with Multiple Lines

So far we've used single-line editor fields. But sometimes the element you make in-place editable holds quite a lot of markup, and multiple-line editing would be preferable. How can we do this?

Well, it all hinges on two things: the rows option and whether there are line breaks (\r or \n: carriage returns or linefeed characters) in the content to edit.

If rows is at its default of 1 and there are no line breaks, you'll get a single-line editor (an *<input>* element with type="text"). But if there are line breaks or rows is set to greater than 1, you'll get multiple-line editing. If rows is 1, it is ignored in favor of the value stored in Ajax.InPlaceEditor.DefaultOptions.rowsAuto, which originally is 3.

The rows option governs the height of multiple-line editors; their width is governed by the cols option, which, lacking a default, is assumed to be 40 if missing. The reason there is no default value is that if there is no size option to set the width of single-line editors but there is a cols option, it will be used for single-line editors too. This is intended to help homogenize the width of a given editor over time, whether the content has multiple lines or not.

You should also know that when a multiple-line editor (technically a *<textarea>*) is used, OK and cancel controls will appear below it, not next to it; a *
* element will be added right after the editor.

In a general manner, the logic for deciding when to use single- or multiple-line editors, along with how the content was transformed prior to putting it in the editors, has changed significantly during the refactoring. The new behavior is not entirely backward compatible but is thought to be much more useful and flexible.

18.6 Editing Alternative Text

OK, now for a very cool moment—you can actually have your users edit alternate content, instead of the raw markup inside the element. For instance, perhaps you're building some sort of wiki; although it's rendered as XHTML, you're using some simpler markup, such as Textile or Markdown, for the source text of articles and sections. The server side renders these into the XHTML seen on your pages but stores content using the simpler syntax.

You can do this all the way by having your in-place editors load the alternate—"source"—content when being activated and benefit from the default htmlResponse mode in order to get the corresponding XHTML from the server side when saving to it.

All you need to do is use the loadTextURL option to specify the URL required to load the alternate content. It will automatically be passed an extra editorId parameter, just like the saving operation detailed in Section 18.3, *How Can We Tweak the Ajax Persistence?*, on page 346. However, it will use a GET method by default, instead of POST (as opposed to the behavior prior to the recent refactoring), unless your ajaxOptions option explicitly contains a method option that says otherwise.

When loading alternate text, the editor's content is temporarily set to the text specified in the loadingText option, which defaults to *Loading...*, and the editor and submission systems ($\boxed{\text{Return}}$ key, OK control) are disabled. The whole form can be styled, during loading, with the CSS class specified in loadingClassName, which defaults to *inplaceeditor-loading*.[3]

As soon as the alternate content is retrieved, it is put in the editor, and the whole editor UI is enabled again.

This certainly calls for an example. Textile and Markdown are both readily available as gems (Ruby packages) but are not part of the standard Ruby library, and I do not want to take you through the steps of gem installation for this example, so we'll make do without these neat markup libraries. We'll just assume that empty lines delimit paragraphs and that triple percent signs (%%%) are to be interpreted as explicit line breaks (which will become *
* tags followed by a line break).

So, let's copy over our original example, with only one simple in-place editor. We'll need three actions: one to serve the full page, one to serve the source markup for the editable element, and one to save it and return the XHTML equivalent. The resulting server script is as follows:

`scriptaculous/ipe/alternate/server.rb`

```
Line 1   #! /usr/bin/env ruby
    -
    -    require 'cgi'
    -    require 'erb'
    5    require 'webrick'
    -    include WEBrick
    -
    -    template_text = File.read('index.rhtml')
    -    template = ERB.new(template_text)
   10
```

---

3. Beware of the difference of targets between loadingClassName, which applies to the whole editing form, and savingClassName, which applies only to your original element whose content is, at this point, only the saving message.

```
     server = HTTPServer.new(:Port => 8042)
     server.mount('/', HTTPServlet::FileHandler, '.')

     source = 'Some basic text'
15
     def xhtml_convert(text)
       '<p>' +
       text.gsub(/(?:\r|\n){2,}/, "</p>\n<p>").gsub('%%%', "<br/>\n") +
       '</p>'
20   end

     server.mount_proc('/home') do |request, response|
       response['Content-Type'] = 'text/html'
       xhtmlVersion = xhtml_convert(source)
25     response.body = template.result(binding)
     end

     server.mount_proc('/source') do |request, response|
       sleep 2 # Darn we're slow...
30     response['Content-Type'] = 'text/plain'
       response.body = source
     end

     server.mount_proc('/update') do |request, response|
35     sleep 2 # Darn we're slow...
       source = request.query['value']
       response.body = xhtml_convert(source)
     end

40   trap('INT') { server.shutdown }

     server.start
```

Note how we simulate loading and saving times, so you can easily see these steps in the browser. The tiny xhtml_convert() method starting on line 16 implements our small conversion algorithm.

The CSS will also change to use some styling for the loading and saving messages:

`scriptaculous/ipe/alternate/demo.css`

```css
h1 { font-size: 1.5em; }

.inplaceeditor-loading { background: #ddd; color: gray; }

.inplaceeditor-saving {
  height: 16px; padding-left: 20px;
  background: url(/spinner.gif) no-repeat left center;
  font: italic smaller/16px sans-serif; color: gray;
}
```

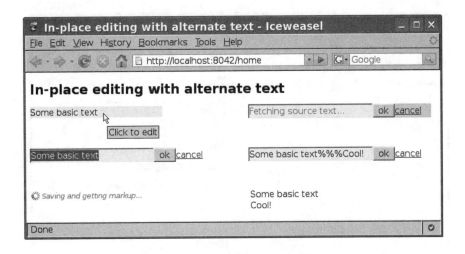

Figure 18.4: USING ALTERNATE TEXT

Finally, we'll adjust the script so it relies on alternate text:

scriptaculous/ipe/alternate/demo.js

```
document.observe('dom:loaded', function() {
  new Ajax.InPlaceEditor('freeZone', '/update', {
    loadingText: 'Fetching source text...',
    savingText: 'Saving and getting markup...',
    loadTextURL: '/source'
  });
});
```

Now let's kill any running server, launch this one, and reload our page (with a healthy cache bypass). Figure 18.4 shows a montage of the various stages for the first edition.

The stages are represented from left to right and from top to bottom. Note that because we now have line breaks in the final content, next time we edit we'll end up using a multiple-line editor. And because we did not specify an explicit rows option, we'll get the default 3, as explained earlier. Figure 18.5, on the next page, shows the stages of a second editing attempt, with line breaks in the original content.

18.7 Disabling In-Place Editing

As usual, script.aculo.us provides you with the means to stop using a feature over an element. In this case, you can strip in-place editing

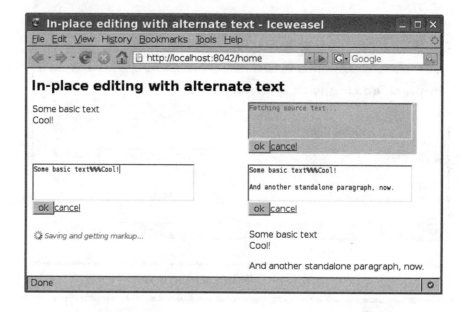

Figure 18.5: EDITING CONTENT WITH LINE BREAKS

capabilities from an element by simply calling the destroy() method on the Ajax.InPlaceEditor object:

```
ipe.destroy()
```

The former name for this method, dispose(), is still available as an alias but is deprecated.

18.8 Offering a List of Values Instead of Text Typing

There are situations where we'd like to let our users change an element's content, but they should select among a series of possibilities. These choices would be presented as a single-selection drop-down list, based on a *<select>* tag.

To let you do this easily, script.aculo.us comes with a special subclass of Ajax.InPlaceEditor, called Ajax.InPlaceCollectionEditor. It builds exactly the same way:

```
new Ajax.InPlaceCollectionEditor(element, savingURL [, options])
```

It's otherwise used in an identical manner as Ajax.InPlaceEditor, except you get a few more options.

collection

> A list of options to pick from. This means you're statically defining these options in the script (perhaps you're generating the script dynamically, but mostly you won't). This has to be an array, or something convertible through an array (as defined in Section 3.5, *$A, the Collection Unifier,* on page 36).
>
> The array can contain simple values, which will be used as both the *<option>* tag's value= attribute and its textual content, or two-item arrays, where the first item is the value= attribute and the second item is the textual content. We'll see examples in a minute.

loadCollectionURL

> In many cases you'll either have a static, client-side list definition (through the collection option) or fetch it dynamically from the server. You can do this with loadCollectionURL, which points to a URL that will be called with the usual automatic editorId parameter and must return a JavaScript array that fits the description for the collection option. This array will then be evaluated and used as if it had been passed directly.

loadCollectionText

> The text to be shown in the pending drop-down while the list of choices is being fetched. This is similar to the role of loadingText for loadTextURL. This defaults to *Loading choices....*

The former value option was deprecated, because it basically makes no sense. Either the content (alternate or direct, depending on your settings) matches one of the option values, and that option will be selected; or there is no match, and the first option will be selected.

Let's look at a simple example that fetches its list of options dynamically from the server. The styling is as minimalistic as ever:

scriptaculous/ipe/collection/demo.css

```
h1 { font-size: 1.5em; }
```

The scripting is also very brief:

scriptaculous/ipe/collection/demo.js

```
document.observe('dom:loaded', function() {
  new Ajax.InPlaceCollectionEditor('name', '/update', {
    loadCollectionURL: '/names'
  });
});
```

Now, our server must provide the /names action for the choice list, which is expressed like the collection option, as a JavaScript array. We'll artificially delay the loading of options and the saving of the edited content so as to be able to see these steps.

scriptaculous/ipe/collection/server.rb

```ruby
#! /usr/bin/env ruby

require 'cgi'
require 'erb'
require 'webrick'
include WEBrick

template_text = File.read('index.rhtml')
template = ERB.new(template_text)

server = HTTPServer.new(:Port => 8042)
server.mount('/', HTTPServlet::FileHandler, '.')

options = %w(Seth Corinne Lauren)
content = options[0]

server.mount_proc('/home') do |request, response|
  response['Content-Type'] = 'text/html'
  response.body = template.result(binding)
end

server.mount_proc('/names') do |request, response|
  sleep 1 # Simulate slow option fetching...
  response['Content-Type'] = 'text/plain' # No need for auto JS eval...
  response.body = '[' + options.map { |s| s.inspect() }.join(', ') + ']'
end

server.mount_proc('/update') do |request, response|
  sleep 1 # Simulate slow option saving...
  content = request.query['value']
  response.body = content
end

trap('INT') { server.shutdown }

server.start
```

Firing up this new server and refreshing our browser on http://localhost: 8042/home (bypassing the cache, as always), we can now use list-assisted content choice, as demonstrated by the montage in Figure 18.6, on the next page.

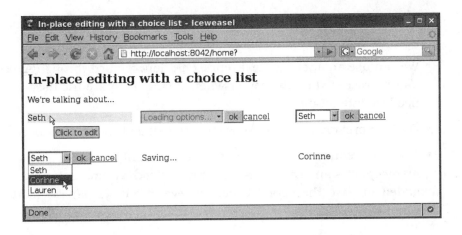

Figure 18.6: Editing with a choice list

This class was massively overhauled in the recent refactoring, because the former implementation suffered from quite a number of issues. The API has changed a bit, especially regarding option names, the processing of alternate content, and the dynamic fetching of the option list (something that was simply not possible before).

Well, that's about it for in-place editing. If you used it in the past, do remember that it got through a complete rewrite for script.aculo.us 1.8, and the API changed a bit. Ajax.InPlaceCollectionEditor, in particular, became much more usable, and latent holes were plugged, making the whole thing more robust.

What We Just Learned

Despite the numerous features and possible tweaks, in-place editing is not a very complex subject. It boils down to these key points:

- In-place editing is mostly about the Ajax.InPlaceEditor class. There is also a dropbox-based, predefined-values variant using Ajax. InPlaceCollectionEditor.

- Both were rewritten in 2007 to clean up their code base and add functionality. This rewrite changed parts of the API, especially the options.

- Editing mode is triggered by clicking, either on the editable zone itself (by default) or on a specified external control.

- We can use an alternate text representation, fetched through Ajax and reprocessed by the server when saving, to spare the user the need to understand HTML.

- Options provide fine control over every detail of the appearance.

- The Ajax requests sent to the server are highly customizable via many options and callbacks. An extra editorId parameter is always added in case the server code for several editors can be made generic.

Neuron Workout

- What set of options would let us implement "unobtrusive in-place editing," where clicking, say, titles would make them editable with no visual clutter and just clicking outside it or pressing the Return key would save to the server and revert to noneditable mode?

- Let's consider the following scenario:

  - We have a site with a home page that features one of the articles among those we have stored away in the News section.

  - We're viewing the home page in "design mode," which lets us click a small Edit link or icon next to the featured article's title.

  - When that control is clicked, the current article is replaced by a drop-down list of the available article titles.

  - We pick a title, we click a OK button or something, and the newly selected article comes in.

  How would we go about using our in-place editing capabilities to achieve this?

Chapter 19

Sliders

Sliders are thin tracks with one or more handles on them that the user can drag along the track. The goal of a slider is to provide an alternative input method for defining a numerical value; the slider represents a range, and sliding a handle along the track defines a value within this range.

Figure 19.1 provides an overview of what sliders can look like, with a rather simple look. Internally, they are implemented by *<div>* and *<span>* elements that *we* define, so the styling is entirely up to us. It will easily fit whatever design our page already uses.

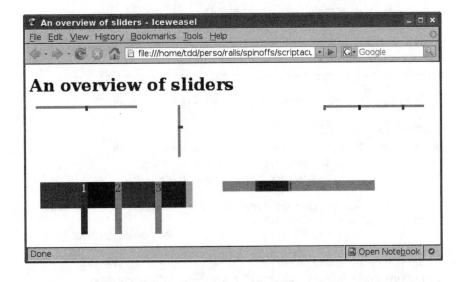

Figure 19.1: A VARIETY OF POSSIBLE SLIDERS

We'll need the slider.js module, which contains the Control.Slider class. There is no dependency on other script.aculo.us modules. So, our script.aculo.us loading will look, at minimum, like this:

```
<script type="text/javascript" src="slider.js"></script>
```

19.1 Creating a Simple Slider

Let's start with a slider somewhere that lets the user define a numerical value within a given range.

Creating a slider is, as usual, a matter of constructing a custom object over a few existing elements in your page's DOM. You'll need two elements here: one for the *handle* and one for the *track*.

```
new Control.Slider(handle, track [, options])
```

The track element is usually a *<div>*, and the handle element is a *<div>* or *<span>* within the track element. Both can be passed either by their id= or by direct DOM references, as usual.

Let's imagine the following XHTML fragment:

```
<div id="track1" class="track" style="width: 20em;">
  <div id="handle1" class="handle" style="width: 0.5em;"></div>
</div>
```

Creating a basic, all-defaults slider would simply require this:

```
new Control.Slider('handle1', 'track1');
```

To try this, we'll create a simple demonstration that will let us experiment with the orientation of the slider (its *axis*, horizontal or vertical), the definition of a preset value, and range customization.

Our "test bench," index.html, will look like this:

```
scriptaculous/slider/simple/index.html
```

```
<!DOCTYPE html PUBLIC "-//W3C//DTD XHTML 1.0 Strict//EN"
 "http://www.w3.org/TR/xhtml1/DTD/xhtml1-strict.dtd">
<html xmlns="http://www.w3.org/1999/xhtml" lang="en-US" xml:lang="en-US">
<head>
    <meta http-equiv="Content-Type" content="text/html; charset=utf-8" />
    <title>Simple sliders</title>
    <link rel="stylesheet" type="text/css" href="demo.css" />
    <script type="text/javascript" src="prototype.js"></script>
    <script type="text/javascript" src="slider.js"></script>
    <script type="text/javascript" src="demo.js"></script>
</head>
<body>
```

```html
<h1>Simple sliders</h1>
<div id="track1" class="track" style="width: 20em;">
  <div id="handle1" class="handle" style="width: 0.5em;"></div>
</div>

<p id="sliding"></p>
<p id="changed"></p>

<div id="track2" class="track vertical"
 style="position: absolute; left: 25em; top: 3em;">
  <div id="handle2" class="handle" style="height: 0.5em;"></div>
</div>
</body>
</html>
```

Notice we'll need to bring in prototype.js, scriptaculous.js (unless you prefer loading individual script.aculo.us modules individually, as we could very well do here), and slider.js.

You can also see we put two <p> elements, which will provide us with feedback on the operation of the sliders, and indeed we put *two sliders* in there, one horizontal and one vertical.

We'll also define a rather all-purpose style sheet for our sliders, which will use font-size-based dimensions, letting our UI adjust to the user's zooming in or out:

scriptaculous/slider/simple/demo.css

```css
h1 { font-size: 1.5em; }

.track {
  background-color: #aaa;
  position: relative;
  height: 0.5em; width: 10em;
  cursor: pointer; z-index: 0;
}
.handle {
  background-color: red;
  position: absolute;
  height: 1em; width: 0.25em; top: -0.25em;
  cursor: move; z-index: 2;
}
.track.vertical { width: 0.5em; height: 10em; }
.track.vertical .handle {
  width: 1em; height: 0.25em; top: 0; left: -0.25em; }
```

These styles are fairly reusable. Notice how we offset the handles slightly in the proper direction (using either left or top) so that they appear "centered" on the track, not tacked to one side of it.

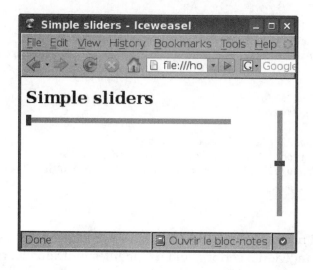

Figure 19.2: INITIAL STATE OF OUR SIMPLE SLIDERS

19.2 Customizing the Basics

We'll start playing with two options that let us change the slider's orientation and its initial value:

axis

> This lets us define whether the slider is *horizontal* (default) or *vertical*. This setting constrains the dragging movement of the handle on the proper axis.

sliderValue

> This determines the initial position of the handle, which defaults to the beginning of the range. This range defaults to [0;1], meaning we start at zero. Our vertical slider will start in the middle, therefore at 0.5.

So here's our current slider creation code:

```
document.observe('dom:loaded', function() {
  new Control.Slider('handle1', 'track1');
  new Control.Slider('handle2', 'track2', {
    axis: 'vertical', sliderValue: 0.5 });
});
```

Figure 19.2, shows the initial state of our sliders. Go ahead, drag the handles! Don't forget to release the dragging *within* the document, lest it not be detected and, when you'd hover the mouse again, keep dragging your handle (this won't happen in all browsers but still is an issue). Now, when we're dragging handles around, we'd like to know which position that is; after all, we generally use sliders as an alternate input method for numerical values. It's only fair that our users *know* which value they're setting. This can be done with the two available callbacks:

onSlide

> Triggered whenever the handle is moved

onChange

> Triggered when the mouse button is finally released, ending the dragging of the handle

Both callbacks take two arguments: the value of the slider (expressed as a value within the range, so by default it will be between zero and one) and the slider object itself (the Control.Slider instance, not the track or handle element).

Do note that you can access such properties of the slider object as track and handle, which refer to the extended DOM elements for these two parts of the UI.

To demonstrate callbacks at work, we'll define two simple functions that update each of our two feedback paragraphs, and then we'll use these callbacks in our two sliders. To avoid defining these functions twice, we'll put them in a local object and reuse them in our Control.Slider definitions. Here's the new script:

```
document.observe('dom:loaded', function() {
  var callbacks = {
    onSlide: function(value, slider) {
      $('sliding').update(slider.track.id + ' sliding to ' +
        value.toFixed(3));
    },
    onChange: function(value, slider) {
      $('changed').update(slider.track.id + '\'s value changed to ' +
        value.toFixed(3));
    }
  };
  new Control.Slider('handle1', 'track1', {
    onSlide: callbacks.onSlide, onChange: callbacks.onChange
  });
  new Control.Slider('handle2', 'track2', {
    axis: 'vertical', sliderValue: 0.5,
    onSlide: callbacks.onSlide, onChange: callbacks.onChange
  });
});
```

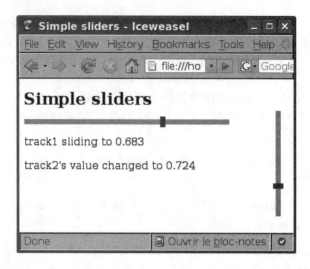

Figure 19.3: FEEDBACK MESSAGES THANKS TO CALLBACKS

Notice how we can access slider.track.id from our callback to differentiate the messages depending on which slider was manipulated.

Reload the page and start sliding around. It should look something like Figure 19.3. You may wonder how it is that on this snapshot, the second message refers to *track2* but the first one still refers to *track1*. Isn't sliding supposed to happen before finally setting a value? Well, not quite. You see, sliders let you click *directly on the track* to bring the handle right where you clicked. It's a convenient trick. In such a case, the handle was not dragged and there was no sliding, but the value was changed.

19.3 Restricting Range or Allowed Values

Most of the time, you'll probably need to work on a different range that holds some business meaning in the context of your page. Perhaps it's a percentage and should go from 0 to 100. Perhaps it's a minimum age, which should start around 3 and not exceed 21. Whatever the reason, you may need to customize the range, which is done with the range option.

range

>   Expressed as an ObjectRange object (the result of a $R() call), defines the range of acceptable values from one end of the slider to the other. This defaults to $R(0, 1).

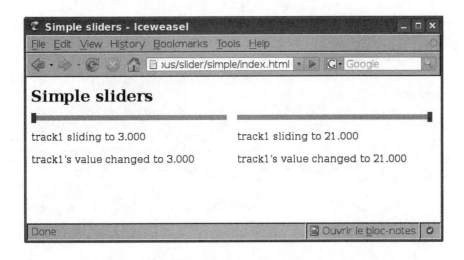

Figure 19.4: A CUSTOM RANGE ON OUR FIRST SLIDER

Let's adjust our script so that the first slider (the horizontal one) works on a range from 3 to 21, for instance:

scriptaculous/slider/simple/demo.js
```
new Control.Slider('handle1', 'track1', {
  range: $R(3, 21),
  onSlide: callbacks.onSlide, onChange: callbacks.onChange
});
```

Reload and play with this first slider. The boundaries should be clearly expressed in the feedback paragraphs, as shown in the montage in Figure 19.4.

That's it for the ranges, but this doesn't always cut it. Sometimes you need to allow only a discrete series of values, not a quasilinear progression from one boundary to the other.

Say you're dealing with integers only, perhaps for the difficulty level of an online game, or the zoom factor of an image viewer, or the amount of tiles to a side you want for a map display. Letting the user free-range between boundary values won't do. You need specific values only! This is done with the values option:

values

An Enumerable of allowed values, which is ignored if **false**-equivalent (and it does default to **false**)

> ### Warning: Always Sync range with values!
>
> At the time of this writing, the computing of handle positions is entirely based on the range option. When using values, if you leave range to its default (zero to one), your handles may very well appear way off the track.
>
> Conversely, if you use a range larger than the extreme values you're allowing, portions of the track won't be accessible to your handles.
>
> So when using values, I recommend you make sure range uses the two extreme values. For instance:
>
> ```
> new Control.Slider('handle1', 'track1', {
>   range: $R(3, 10), values: $R(3, 10) // other options here...
> });
> ```

So, let's say we want to use a slider to let our users choose an integer from 3 to 10, inclusive. We could do this with the following call:

```
new Control.Slider('handle1', 'track1', {
  values: $R(3, 10), range: $R(3, 10)
});
```

Keep in mind the difference between these options' behaviors: values uses the range's *enumerated values*, which will be apart from each other by exactly one (as Number#succ() uses an increment of one), and only these values will be allowed. On the other hand, range cares only about the minimum and maximum values, which Control.Slider uses to compute handle positions over the track.

When values is defined, sliding the handles will "stick" to the nearest allowed positions as you're dragging.

Of course, you don't have to use a regular series of values. It can be much more... personal:

```
new Control.Slider('handle1', 'track1', { values: [1, 5, 38, 46] });
```

Still, this may be a bit unwieldy for the user. It's better then to use a regular series and map the raw values to those you need by using, for instance, one-to-one mapping between both arrays.

19.4 Tweaking an Existing Slider and Adding Controls

There are a few things you can do to a slider once it's up and running. For instance, you can disable it and enable it later (which is useful when you use it as part of a form, because it won't be disabled automatically by Form#disable(), for instance). The methods for this are simply setEnabled() and setDisabled(). You can check whether it's disabled by looking at the value for its disabled property.

You can also programmatically change the value of a slider by using setValue(value). If you need to specify a delta instead of an actually value, use setValueBy(delta). This lets you easily implement external controls, such as arrow links or buttons. You'll find an example of this in script.-aculo.us's sliders functional test in test/functional/slider_test.html.

Finally, as always with script.aculo.us controls, you can take back their features by destroying the control object. The method for this here is dispose().

19.5 Defining Multiple Values

A great feature of sliders lets you use multiple handles on a single track, which allows your users to define multiple values on a single slider.

The trick is to provide an alternative syntax for the sliderValue and handle options. They can take arrays, too. Each handle will be preset to the original value that matches it, on a one-to-one basis, in sliderValue.

The value-setting methods, setValue and setValueBy, also take an optional second argument that is the index (starting at zero) of the handle whose value is being assigned. Instead of the single value property, you would use the values property, an array indexed in the same order as the handles.

Your slider control maintains two properties for this: activeHandle and activeHandleIdx. The latest used handle (be it by clicking, dragging, or programmatic value setting) is the only one featuring a *selected* CSS class, which lets you set it visually apart.

Finally, note that you can prevent handles from crossing each other (when dragging, you could prevent a handle from moving across another one). This is enabled with the restricted option, which you just need to set to **true**.

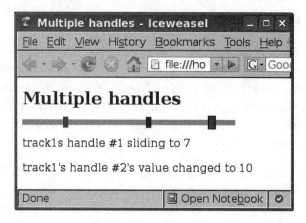

Figure 19.5: MULTIPLE HANDLES AND VALUES

Here's an example XHTML fragment:

```
scriptaculous/slider/multiple/index.html
```

```
<div id="track1" class="track" style="width: 20em;">
  <div id="handle1" class="handle" style="width: 0.5em;"></div>
  <div id="handle2" class="handle"
   style="width: 0.5em; background: blue;"></div>
  <div id="handle3" class="handle"
   style="width: 0.5em; background: green;"></div>
</div>
```

And here's the corresponding construction call:

```
scriptaculous/slider/multiple/demo.js
```

```
new Control.Slider(['handle1', 'handle2', 'handle3'],
  'track1', {
  range: $R(1, 11), values: $R(1, 11),
  sliderValue: [3, 6, 9],
  onSlide: callbacks.onSlide, onChange: callbacks.onChange
});
```

In code/scriptaculous/slider/multiple, the source code archive contains an example page that is visible, after a couple clicks and drags, in Figure 19.5. You'll find more examples in script.aculo.us's sliders functional test page, located in the archive at test/functional/slider_test.html.

There's a last feature I'd like to mention, which lets you add a visual hint that you're using sliders to define ranges (generally adjacent ones): *spans*. By styling these elements (usually <*span*> ones), you give a visual cue as to the ranges being defined, instead of relying on the uniform color of the track.

> ### Advanced Sliders and Opera
>
> When you get advanced with sliders, you may end up having minor visual quirks running on Opera. Opera is not, after all, officially supported yet, and although just about every code in this book runs just fine on it, sliders may get a bit quirky here and there.

By interleaving span elements with your handle elements (all of this within your track's *<div>*), you can ask Control.Slider to adjust their positions and dimensions so they stick to surrounding handles. This is most often used in conjunction with "restricted" handle movement (in which handle order is preserved over time, because handles cannot be dragged across each other).

Three properties are involved here:

spans

> An array of elements (or their id= values, as always), usually *<span>*s, in ascending range order (that is, the first *<span>* is between the first and second handle, the second *<span>* lies between the second and third handle, and so on). This defaults to **false**, which disables the feature.

startSpan

> Optional initial range, appearing between the beginning of the track and the first handle. This defaults to **null**.

endSpan

> Optional final range, appearing between the last track and the end of the track. This defaults to **null**.

Here's an example XHTML fragment:

`scriptaculous/slider/spans/index.html`

```
<div id="track1" class="track" style="width: 20em;">
  <div id="handle1" class="handle" style="width: 0.5em;"></div>
  <span id="range1" class="range" style="background: black;"></span>
  <div id="handle2" class="handle"
   style="width: 0.5em; background: blue;"></div>
  <span id="range2" class="range" style="background: #666;"></span>
  <div id="handle3" class="handle"
   style="width: 0.5em; background: green;"></div>
</div>
```

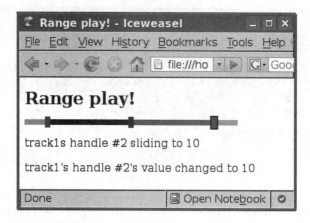

Figure 19.6: MULTIPLE HANDLES AND SPANS

And here's the corresponding construction call:

`scriptaculous/slider/spans/demo.js`

```
new Control.Slider(['handle1', 'handle2', 'handle3'],
  'track1', {
  range: $R(1, 11), values: $R(1, 11),
  sliderValue: [3, 6, 9],
  spans: ['range1', 'range2'], restricted: true,
  onSlide: callbacks.onSlide, onChange: callbacks.onChange
});
```

This will require an extra dollop of CSS:

`scriptaculous/slider/spans/demo.css`

```
.handle.selected { outline: 2px solid black; z-index: 3; }
.track .range {
  position: absolute; height: 0.5em; width: 0.5em; z-index: 1; }
```

See code/scriptaculous/slider/spans for an example page; playing with it can yield something like Figure 19.6. You'll find more examples, yet again, in script.aculo.us's sliders functional test page.

Neuron Workout

How about a pop quiz?

- We're building a shopping site for home appliances (for example, fridges, ovens, and washing machines) for a client. She tells us she would like to offer users the possibility of quickly specifying a minimum and maximum price they're willing to pay as an extra criterion in the form they're using to sift through the catalog. How could we use a single slider to implement this? Think about the details of price feedback (showing the range being created) and integrating with the form that's going to be sent to the server.

- Say we have a thumbnail gallery of photographs. How could we use a slider to dynamically set thumbnail size?

- Create a small function that, given a hash of (value × label) pairs, creates a fixed-size slider that uses only those values and displays the matching label in an associated element as the user moves the handle along.

Chapter 20

Sound Without Flash

Version 1.7 of script.aculo.us introduced a new tiny module that lets you play sounds in your web pages without having to resort to an embedded, Flash-based player. The upshot is, well, you don't need Flash. That means you do not need to load a Flash sound-playing object in addition to your sound file(s). The potential issue, however, is that this module assumes your browser can natively process the sound file (for example, a MP3 file).

20.1 Where Does It Work?

This module works wherever your browser has native (or plug-in-based) support for the sound files you're using, which are assumed to be based on the MPEG audio layer (the most common variant nowadays being MP3). This essentially means the following situations:

- On OS X, you're good to go. Every browser on OS X benefits from the platform's QuickTime support for sound files. It Just Works.

- On Windows, it works natively on Internet Explorer; otherwise, you usually need the QuickTime plug-in installed; it has pretty good market penetration (especially since, recently, it has been bundled with Windows versions of iTunes and Safari), although it's perhaps not quite as ubiquitous as Flash.

- On Linux, as always, it all depends on which packages were installed by the system's administrator. But then, it's as true for QuickTime as it is for Flash, and all major distributions have packages for both.

20.2 How Do We Play Sounds?

First, you need to load the sound module, just like you would load any other script.aculo.us module, for instance, using the loader system:

```
<script type="text/javascript" src="sound.js"></script>
```

Then, all you need to do in your code is something as simple as this:

```
Sound.play('sounds/myeffect.mp3');
```

That's it! This alone plays your sound now (the module does not support looping). As you might expect, there can be a bit more to it, though. The full syntax goes like this:

```
Sound.disable()
Sound.enable()
Sound.play(url [, options])
```

The disable() and enable() methods globally toggle whether play() calls are actually processed. They do not impact previously made calls; any ongoing sound keeps going. They impact only future calls to play(). They're the obvious way to implement a user-togglable Mute feature.

The core method is, expectedly, play(). At the minimum, you provide the URL of your sound file. The module will assume your file format is related to MPEG audio, so you should use MP3, for instance. The options parameter is a hash of options, as usual, and Sound supports two of those: track and replace. We'll explore them now.

20.3 Playing Multiple Sounds on Multiple Tracks

The sound module lets you play multiple sounds in parallel and group them as *tracks*. Whenever you ask for a new sound to play, you can put it into a specific group (or track), and either add it to the currently playing sounds of that track or make it replace the whole track.

The track Option

By default, sounds are added to the default track, named *global*. They also add to the track, which means they do not replace the currently running sounds. They start playing *over* whatever sound is currently playing.

To specify sound groups, use the track option. You can use whatever names you want for the tracks, as long as you observe XHTML's id= syntax requirements. This is because your track name will become part of the id= for the DOM element responsible for playing the sound. You would likely use such names as *effects*, *notifications*, *music*, or *ambience*.

Note that, currently, grouping sounds in tracks is useful only when you need to replace them with another sound, as described in the next section.

The replace Option

Sometimes you may want a new sound to replace any currently running sound in its track. Perhaps you're signaling the end of a process and that process was made "audible" through the use of a little tune or something; or perhaps you have "ambient" sounds that reflect the current visual theme or universe, and the user just switched to another theme, which you need to reflect not only visually but also audibly. In this case, you can use the replace option and set it to **true** (it defaults to **false**). All currently running sounds in the track will then be stopped, and your new sound will start.

In the source code archive for this book, you will find a few free sound effect files in the code/scriptaculous/sound directory:

effect_crowd_....mp3
> Crowd sound effects: applause, excitement, and three laughs

ambience_....mp3
> Ambient sounds: an outdoor café, a simple tune, rain falling and surf crashing on the shore

Let's quickly put together a simple demo that'll let us play any ambience sound *one at a time* and layer as many sound effects as we need on top of that. Create a directory for the demo, and then whip up the following HTML file:

scriptaculous/sound/index.html

```
<!DOCTYPE html PUBLIC "-//W3C//DTD XHTML 1.0 Strict//EN"
 "http://www.w3.org/TR/xhtml1/DTD/xhtml1-strict.dtd">
<html xmlns="http://www.w3.org/1999/xhtml" lang="en-US" xml:lang="en-US">
<head>
    <meta http-equiv="Content-Type" content="text/html; charset=utf-8" />
    <title>Sounding out</title>
    <script type="text/javascript" src="prototype.js"></script>
    <script type="text/javascript" src="sound.js"></script>
    <script type="text/javascript" src="demo.js"></script>
</head>
<body>
```

```
<h1>Sounding out with script.aculo.us</h1>

<h2>Sound effects</h2>

<ul id="effects">
    <li><a href="effect_crowd_applause.mp3">Applause</a></li>
    <li><a href="effect_crowd_excited.mp3">Excitement</a></li>
    <li><a href="effect_crowd_laugh1.mp3">Laugh #1</a></li>
    <li><a href="effect_crowd_laugh2.mp3">Laugh #2</a></li>
    <li><a href="effect_crowd_laugh3.mp3">Laugh #3</a></li>
</ul>

<h2>Ambience</h2>

<ul id="ambience">
    <li><a href="ambience_cafe.mp3">Outdoor café</a></li>
    <li><a href="ambience_music.mp3">A simple tune</a></li>
    <li><a href="ambience_rain.mp3">Rainfall</a></li>
    <li><a href="ambience_seasurf.mp3">Surf crashing on the
        shore</a></li>
</ul>
</body>
</html>
```

Don't forget to put prototype.js and sound.js in there, too. Finally, we'll put the script together. It's very simple indeed:

scriptaculous/sound/demo.js

```
function playAmbience(e) {
  e.stop();
  Sound.play(e.findElement('a').href, { track: 'ambience',
    replace: true });
}

function playEffect(e) {
  e.stop();
  Sound.play(e.findElement('a').href, { track: 'effects' });
}

document.observe('dom:loaded', function() {
  $('effects').select('a').invoke('observe', 'click', playEffect);
  $('ambience').select('a').invoke('observe', 'click', playAmbience);
});
```

Technically, we could have left the ambience sounds on the default, global track, but it's always best to put special-purpose sounds in their own track so we can manipulate them separately.

OK, now start by clicking an ambience sound, say, the simple tune (it stands out better than the other ambience sounds once we start layering effects over it). Then start clicking a short effect, perhaps the first laugh. When it's done, try a longer one (for example, the applause), and start heavy-clicking to layer multiple effects. Once we're all sounded up, change the ambience. Because we specified replace: true, the tune stops and gets replaced by the new ambience.

And that's all there is to the sound module for now. It's really simple, as you can plainly see from our script. But it sure can help to complement your UI with appropriate, well-used audio feedback (think chat windows, event dashboards, and the like). Be careful not to clutter the audio space with too much sound, though. . . .

Extending and Contributing

It doesn't take long before you end up with complicated scripts providing complex functionality. You might very well need to complement Prototype's features with your own, either in separate objects or by extending existing ones. In this appendix, you'll see how to extend Prototype objects and how to contribute back.

A.1 Building Over: Classes, Inheritance, and DOM Extension

First you need to understand the object system in Prototype. As you may know, JavaScript is not a class-based language, with the usual class/object dichotomy and the usual class inheritance reflexes and habits. No. JavaScript is a *prototype-based* language.

Getting into the details of how this actually works would be way beyond the scope of this appendix, or even this book. You'll find excellent articles about prototypes and other JavaScript OO issues (such as how to encode public, private, and "privileged" methods, as well as "static" members) on the websites of several JavaScript gurus, such as Douglas Crockford and Dean Edwards:

- http://javascript.crockford.com/prototypal.html
- http://javascript.crockford.com/private.html
- http://www.litotes.demon.co.uk/js_info/private_static.html
- http://dean.edwards.name/base/

However, we can *simulate* the traditional OO concepts, such as the class/object dichotomy, inheritance, mixins, and so on, using regular JavaScript and a healthy dose of syntactic sugar provided by Prototype.

What "Classes" Actually Are in JavaScript

The main point to remember is that there are no classes *per se*, only objects. Every object is created based on a *constructor function* (which most people call a class so as not to lose their sanity too quickly). Functions are objects, too (like numbers and regular expressions, by the way). Every object has a *prototype*, which defines properties (including methods) shared by all instances of this object—yes, I actually said "instances of this object." Get a grip.

So when you're defining methods in a constructor function's prototype, for instance, you're defining methods for all the instances obtained by using the **new** operator on this function (for example, new String (or string literals) and new Array (or array literals). This is exactly what Prototype does to existing constructor functions to extend the capabilities of native JavaScript objects.

The reason I'm not diving more into the details is that Prototype does most of it its own way, which is much simpler and feels more like traditional OO programming. It has been profoundly redesigned in version 1.6 and now features more convenient syntax and properly simulates inheritance and mixins.

Defining a New Class

The Prototype way of creating a class still relies on Class.create(), although the syntax has been enriched. The full syntax, which lets you define a superclass when you want to, is as follows:

Class.create([*superclass*] [, *Module...*]> [, { *instanceMethod<ldots/>* }]) → Class

Because all arguments are optional, you can indeed call it with no argument, as you used to do in, say, Prototype 1.5. You would then add the instance methods later. However, why keep with the old, two-phase, kludgy way when we can now put the instance methods right in the call? Here's an example class creation:

prototype/classes/creation.js

```
var Animal = Class.create({
  initialize: function(name) {
    this.name = name;
  },
  eat: function(food) {
    return this.say('Yum!');
  },
  say: function(msg) {
    return this.name + ': ' + msg;
  }
});
```

Class Mechanism: 1.6 Changed Everything!

If you had already created your own classes in versions of Prototype prior to 1.6, your code should still work in this new version. However, to fully leverage the new capabilities (such as inheritance), you'll need to migrate your code to the new, extended syntaxes. The former dichotomy (Class.create() / Object.extend()) is not the way to go anymore.

The following pattern:

```
var Loader = Class.create();
Object.extend(Loader.prototype, {
        initialize: ...,
        otherInstanceMethod: ...
});
Object.extend(Loader, {
        staticMethod1: ...,
        staticMethod2: ...
});
```

... would still work but should now read as follows:

```
var Loader = Class.create({
        initialize: ...,
        otherInstanceMethod: ...
});
Object.extend(Loader, {
        staticMethod1: ...,
        staticMethod2: ...
});
```

Note that the initialize() method is not mandatory anymore. If you don't have construction-time behavior in your class, you can now skip it (it will be stubbed out by Prototype.emptyFunction).

Our simple class can now be used in a straightforward manner:

prototype/classes/creation.js

```
var fido = new Animal('Fido');
fido.name
// => 'Fido'
fido.say('Hi')
// => 'Fido: Hi'
fido.eat('bone');
// => 'Fido: Yum!'
```

Modules are also sets of instance methods, so you can specify modules to mix in, not just a literal set of custom methods for your class:

```
var Dequeue = Class.create(Enumerable, {
  // dequeue methods
});
```

Naturally, you can combine both a parent class and modules:

```
var ChildClass = Class.create(ParentClass, Enumerable, MyCoolModule, {
  // child's instance methods
});
```

Inheriting from Another Class

This was a sore point of the former versions. "Traditional" inheritance in JavaScript is implemented in a rather disturbing fashion—by reassigning the prototype of the constructor function for the subclass. This can quickly lead to headaches for the nonexpert, so Prototype hides all this complexity from you. When you want to define a class as a subclass of another one, you simply pass the superclass as the first argument to Class.create(), before the mixins and set of instance methods.

Let's look at an example:

prototype/classes/extend.js

```
var Cat = Class.create(Animal, {
  eat: function($super, food) {
    if (food instanceof Mouse) return $super(food);
    return this.say('Yuck!  I only eat mice.');
  }
});

var Mouse = Class.create(Animal); // Dumb subclass
```

And that's all there is to it! Note how we didn't even need to declare initialize() this time. We automatically inherit it from Animal, and because we do not need to augment the inherited behavior for it, we don't need to override it.

Overriding a Method and Calling the Inherited One

I'm sure you noticed the $super first parameter to eat(). This is a specific name that Prototype detects. When you prepend your method's signature with it, you'll get passed the inherited version of the method as an argument, which you can then call when you need it. If you don't need to invoke the inherited version, just don't declare this first argument.

Here's an example use:

`prototype/classes/extend.js`

```
var fido = new Animal('Fido');
var tom = new Cat('Tom');
var jerry = new Mouse('Jerry');
tom.say('Hi')
// => 'Tom: Hi'
jerry.eat('cheese')
// => 'Jerry: Yum!'
tom.eat(fido)
// => 'Tom: Yuck!  I only eat mice.'
tom.eat('bone')
// => 'Tom: Yuck!  I only eat mice.'
tom.eat(jerry)
// => 'Tom: Yum!'
```

Isn't life beautiful now? As a final note on inheritance, I'd like to give due credit, on behalf of the Prototype Core team, to those whose work and research inspired the API and implementation; prominently, we benefited from the excellent works by Dean Edwards and Alex Arnell. As for Core, this new goodness is mostly the work of Mislav and Andrew, with Sam shooting them a withering glare whenever their suggested names and syntaxes were too outlandish.

Adding More Instance Properties and Methods

```
klass.addMethods({ instanceMethod<ldots/> }) → klass
```

Once a class is created, it is possible to add more instance properties (including methods) to it using its addMethods() class method. Here's an example:

`prototype/classes/extend.js`

```
Cat.addMethods({
        purr: function() { return this.say('Rrrrrr...'); }
});
tom.purr();
// => 'Tom: Rrrrrr...'
```

Incidentally, this lets you mix modules in, too, because modules are just sets of instance methods (and possibly other properties). Still, you'll generally mix modules in at creation time.

Adding Static Properties and Methods

```
Object.extend(klass, { staticMethod<ldots/> }) → klass
```

Adding static properties (and thus methods) to a class is just one case of adding properties to an object (remember that in JavaScript, classes are functions, and functions are objects), so we can use the regular Object.extend() mechanism.

You could use it like this, for instance:

```
prototype/classes/extend.js
```

```
var Animal = Class.create({
  initialize: function(name) {
        Animal.newInstance();
    this.name = name;
  },
  eat: function(food) {
    return this.say('Yum!');
  },
  say: function(msg) {
    return this.name + ': ' + msg;
  }
});

Object.extend(Animal, {
        instanceCount: 0,
        newInstance: function() { ++this.instanceCount; }
});
```

It is likely that Prototype 1.6.1 will provide a more integrated mechanism for specifying class methods and properties, though, especially at creation time.

Automatic Class Properties

Prototype maintains three properties for you that open the door to powerful introspection:

```
obj.constructor → Class
class.superclass → Class
class.subclasses → [ Class, ... ]
```

Theoretically, every object has a native constructor property that refers to its constructor function, which basically means its class. However, there are a few issues across browsers with this property, so Prototype overwrites it to guarantee its value is correct.

Prototype also adds two new properties. First, every class features a superclass property, which refers to its parent class (or **null** if there is no parent class, which means the class was created with no parent class first argument passed to Class.create()).

Second, every class also features a subclasses property, which is an array of references to the classes that extend the current class. This property is never **null**, much less **undefined**. At worst, it's an empty array. Whenever a class is created by extension of another, it registers itself in its parent's subclasses property. Using these two properties, you can see it's fairly easy to walk a class hierarchy.

Here's a series of expressions based on our previous code:

```
prototype/classes/extend.js
tom.constructor == Cat                      // => true
tom.constructor.superclass == Animal        // => true
Cat.superclass == Animal                    // => true
Animal.superclass                           // => null
Animal.subclasses.length                    // => 2
Animal.subclasses.first() == Cat            // => true
Animal.subclasses.last() == Mouse           // => true
Cat.subclasses                              // => []
```

Extending DOM Elements

If you want to equip DOM elements with even more methods than Prototype already does, you need to work with Element.addMethods(). It lets you add methods to all elements or elements with specific tag names (say, <form> or <input> elements alone).

```
Element.addMethods([tagNameOrNames,] methods)
```

The first, optional argument is a single tag name or an array of tag names. The mandatory argument is a hash-like object with the methods inside.

Each method you define must take the element as its first argument. It does not have the guarantee that **this** will be bound to the element. The extension mechanism will let you invoke these methods without that first argument, right on the extended elements. But you can also invoke them directly, passing an unextended element to them.

I advise you against directly hacking Prototype's original method repositories (such as Element.Methods). Use your own repositories, and perform the addMethods() call with it.

Say you want to add a convenience pulsate() shortcut that would basically be a prefilled call on script.aculo.us's generic addition, visualEffect(). You'd go like this:

```
YourLib.Element.Methods = {
  pulsate: function(element, options) {
    return $(element).pulsate(options);
  }
};

Element.addMethods(YourLib.Element.Methods);
```

That would be a generic extension. Now suppose you need to add a markAsRequired() method to form fields. It would be more like this:

```
YourLib.Field.Methods = {
  markAsRequired: function(element) {
    element = $(element);
    element.addClassName('required');
    var lbl = $$('label[for="' + element.id + '"]').reduce();
    if (lbl) lbl.addClassName('required');
  }
}

Element.addMethods($w('input textarea select'), YourLib.Field.Methods);
```

Do not confuse Element.addMethods() with the addMethods() facility you get on custom classes. They share the same name but are otherwise unrelated.

A.2 Contributing!

You'll find a quick rundown on the official site, written by our enthusiast Prototype Core member Mislav Marohnić: http://prototypejs.org/contribute. This section has a lot in common with it but tries to get into slightly deeper detail now and then.

So, Prototype changed your life, uh? I know, I can relate.

Whenever you code with Prototype, a warm fuzzy feeling comes over you, and you think "Life is so much better now. Those guys rule. I wish I could give something back to the community."

There you go.

There are a lot of ways you can help and share your (however newly acquired) Prototype skills. Here are the main ones:

- Subscribe to the support list,[1] and start answering questions. Avoid guessing too wildly, but you don't need to be absolutely authoritative either. If you miss a detail when replying, someone will likely chime in with a quick fix.

- Start browsing the Trac, which is where everybody files bug reports and enhancement requests. You can start with hunting down duplicate or invalid tickets. If you do notice as-yet unreported issues that you can easily reproduce, feel free to submit bug reports, too.

- Learn to use the Subversion repository, so as to play with "Prototype Edge," the latest state of the library. This is important in order to know what's cooking and to help close incoming tickets when they're now fixed, for instance.

- Shift into third gear, and start writing patches! This will require mastering the unit test library that Prototype relies on, because patches need to come with a full complement of tests to be accepted. You'll have to test on as many browsers as you can, too. But once your patches start making it in, you'll likely find it addictive (and contributor glory is at hand!).

Because Trac and Subversion are the two pivotal tools of contributing to Prototype, I'll spend a few pages giving you as many useful pointers as I can about how we expect contributors to use them. This should help you contribute in the most efficient (and appreciated) manner.

Staying on Top of Things: Trac

Trac is a tracking system that lets people file bug reports and enhancement requests. It also has a lot of nice features, such as document sharing, reports (custom queries over the ticket database that can be saved and reused at will), and a wonderful integration with version control systems such as Subversion.

Prototype shares a Trac (and a Subversion server, actually) with Ruby on Rails (remember that although backend-agnostic, Prototype and script.aculo.us *are*, originally, Rails spin-offs). The basic URL is http://dev.rubyonrails.org.

---

1. http://groups.google.com/group/rubyonrails-spinoffs

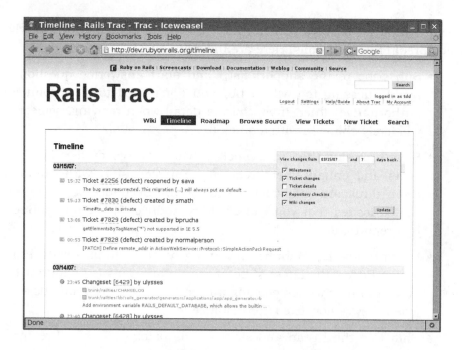

Figure A.1: THE TRAC TIMELINE

Anybody can browse tickets, do searches, and the like. However, only authenticated users can modify tickets (for example, add a comment, attach a file, close the ticket, reopen it) and create new ones. Getting a user account is simple enough. Use the Register link on the top-right corner of the Trac's home page, and sign up. When you come to Trac later, don't forget to log in first (there's a Login link in the same area).

Browsing the Trac

The Trac is mostly tickets, plus terse information about past and up-coming milestones. Those are Rails milestones, so they're not directly related to Prototype.

You can see the latest ticket activity by looking at the *timeline* (http://dev.rubyonrails.org/timeline), which displays everything that happened in a given timeframe. By default, it lists just about everything (changes to tickets and milestones, Subversion commits—called *changesets*) in the past seven days, but you can customize this thanks to a little pad on the right side, as displayed in Figure A.1.

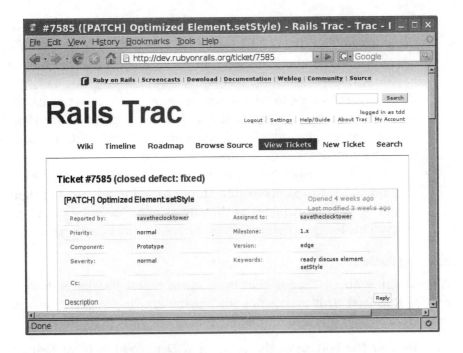

Figure A.2: A TRAC TICKET

You can also zero in on tickets that fall within a specific category. In Trac, categories are mostly represented by reports, which are predefined search criteria. Our Trac features a bunch of such reports, accessible through the *View Tickets* link. For instance, report #22 contains all the pending patches for Prototype and script.aculo.us. They're usually in need of further review or complementary tests. That's a great place to start helping.

A Trac ticket looks like Figure A.2. It features a summary, a description, comments, attached files, and a whole bunch of properties. The most important ones are the *Type* (for example, defect or enhancement), the *Component* (which in our case will always be *Prototype* or *script.aculo.us*), and the *Severity*.

Searching the Trac

Sometimes you just need to find specific tickets in the Trac. There are several ways to do that quickly:

- If you're looking for a specific ticket, you can just type its number, preceded by a hash sign (#), in the top-right search box. That will take you right to it. Übergeeks actually use their browser history to bring up a recent ticket URL (something like http://dev.rubyonrails. org/ticket/7417) and replace the number in it so as to avoid having to load a Trac page before.

- If you're just looking to filter down on reports, just load the appropriate report, either by first going to their list page (the View Tickets link) or by playing it hard and using a direct URL, such as http://dev.rubyonrails.org/report/22.

- Advanced searches with complex criteria will need to use the "Custom query" feature, accessible through a link in the top-right corner of the report pages or directly at http://dev.rubyonrails.org/ query. This lets you define custom filters on any ticket property.

Keeping Posted

A great thing about Trac is that most of its report-like pages have a related RSS feed. This is true not only for the timeline, reports, or even individual tickets but also for any custom query you could create!

Just look at the bottom of the page for a *Download in other formats* section. You can get several variants in there and always an RSS feed. By putting it in your favorite aggregator, you're certain not to miss a thing!

A word of caution about this, though, when it comes to the Timeline feed. By default, it is configured to load a maximum of 50 items, going at most 90 days back. The URL you'll get for it is simple enough to customize, in case you want it to be more (or less) comprehensive than the default settings.

Pragmatic Tickets

OK, so the next step is to contribute to the tickets. There are two things you can do here: file new stuff and help with the triage of existing stuff. Both are helpful, although maybe the second task is easier and perhaps a smooth way of warming up to using Trac.

Hunting Down Invalid Tickets and Duplicates

A significant part of the work over Prototype and script.aculo.us tickets in Trac is hunting down duplicate or invalid tickets. Helping with this is easy enough and very useful to Prototype Core. Common cases where tickets are invalid include the following:

- The current stable version does not exhibit the reported issue.

- The ticket requests an enhancement that is far too user-specific (it does not look like it is generally useful and should be implemented in the library).
- The ticket is obviously a spam of some kind.

Detecting duplicates is a bit harder, because it requires a good knowledge of the existing tickets, which means you spend time now and then keeping up-to-date on the open tickets and knowing enough of the code base that you can determine two issues are actually the same one. For instance, after Prototype 1.5.0 released, tickets started coming in hard about Ajax being broken and Hash#toQueryString() not behaving properly. The two issues were actually very much related. Duplicate hunting meant understanding this and closing all but the first such report as duplicates.

A final note about good manners: when you do close a ticket because you deem it a duplicate, be sure to add a comment that states which ticket it is a duplicate of!

Completing or Creating Tickets

If you're at all interested in contributing to Prototype and script.aculo.us, this section is important. It defines what a *good ticket* is.

A good ticket should satisfy the following requirements (most of which are detailed later):

- It's not a duplicate, and it is valid against the current trunk.
- Its summary is concise yet explicit and features the proper prefixes.
- The description (and comments) uses proper markup, especially for code fragments (either inline or blocks).
- The key properties (Type, Component, Severity, and to a slightly lesser degree Priority) are properly set.
- It makes efficient use of the normalized keywords.
- It comes with a clean patch, made against the current trunk (or a reasonably close version), provided as an attached file.
- The patch includes all relevant unit tests (and possibly functional tests). The trunk fails these tests without the patch and passes them, on all supported browsers, with the patch applied.

I already talked about what duplicates were and what was a sure flag for an invalid one.

Now about the rest:

Summaries

A summary needs to be as expressive as possible. By "expressive," I mean both concise and informational enough. For instance, "The Back button clears out autocompleter fields in Mozilla-based browsers" is pretty good, but "Ajax doesn't work" is as lame as it gets.

Another very important part of summaries is the informal standards in place for their prefixes. You should always prefix a ticket that comes with a patch using *[PATCH]*. If this patch comes with tests, you should add *[TEST]*. This helps triage a lot for Prototype Core.

Descriptions

Always use clear descriptions. Classic copy advice holds true—simple sentences, clear punctuation, and so on. Also make sure you use proper markup for code, be it inline (for example, variable or method names) or as a separate block (code samples). The trick is to wrap code between triple curly braces, like this:

```
The following code:
```

```
{{{
var obj = HumongousLib.dom.util.short.get('someID');
HumongousLib.effects.visual.simple.hide(obj);
}}}
```

```
...was OK, but I realized {{{$('someID').hide()}}} just rules.
Do you get a lot of switchers?
```

This makes it easier on the eyes of everybody.

If you're reporting a bug or editing an existing bug report, be sure to include clear steps for reproducing it. You may have put up a minimalistic reproducible case online (aww, aren't you great!), in which case the description is an ideal place to put a link to it. URLs get linked automatically. By the way, Trac's automatic number formats get detected and linked. Most notably, you can use *#ticketId*, *[changeSetId]*, and *{reportId}*. Use the *WikiFormatting* link above the description zone for the full details of the available syntax.

Properties

Be sure to set all key properties with care. *Type* will usually be *defect* (bug report) or *enhancement*. *Component* will be either *Prototype* or *script.aculo.us*. *Priority* determines how urgent the ticket is, while *Severity* determines its impact (how bad the bug is and how deeply the enhancement impacts the code base).

Leave fields such as *Milestone* and *Version* alone; those are decisions by Those Who Commit To Trunk. Also refrain from manually assigning the ticket to someone in particular.

Keywords

Spin-offs teams have agreed on a series of normalized keywords to use in the *Keywords* field that let them sort through incoming stuff. When a ticket requires only a tiny patch (for example, a trivial one-liner), use the keyword *tiny*. When the patch is well-tested and deemed ready (possibly after multiple revisions and a consensus in the comments) for application to the trunk, add the *ready* keyword.

Patches and tests

Whatever the ticket, good patches are paramount. To have a decent chance at being processed quickly, a ticket has to come with a clean patch and a full complement of tests. The art of producing such things is what we'll discuss in the next section.

Edge Spin-offs: The Subversion Repository

Prototype, script.aculo.us, and everything in the Rails universe use Subversion for version control (keeping track of all the history for all files in the source tree). You don't need to be a Subversion guru to contribute code to Prototype and script.aculo.us, but you'll need, at the very least, to be able to get Prototype Edge from it.

If you know CVS, you'll be right at home with Subversion. The basic usage is identical. If you don't know any of those, the website is http://subversion.tigris.org, where you'll find, among other things, a link to the excellent Subversion book,[2] available in many formats, including PDF and online HTML. Chapters 1 and 2 should get you up and running in no time.

---

2. http://svnbook.red-bean.com/

Getting the Latest Source Code

Prototype and script.aculo.us live in a branch of Rails' Subversion repository, located at http://svn.rubyonrails.org/rails/spinoffs/.

At the time of this writing, script.aculo.us has no branches, but Prototype uses the classical trunk/tags/branches split:

- The trunk is where the next version is being cooked up. It's the home of Prototype Edge.
- Branches provide separate areas for Prototype Core members to tweak stuff. For instance, the selector branch is where Andrew Dupont and I play around when pushing Selector (and therefore $$()) forward; event is the playground for new ideas being tossed around toward a full rewrite of the event management system; and so on. . . .
- Tags are frozen states of the trunk that represent specific versions. You'll find every released version of Prototype in there, from 1.5.0 onward.

To contribute, the only thing you really need to do is check out the trunk and later update it. To do this, you just need to grab a Subversion client program and point it to the URL of the trunk (or higher up the repository tree, perhaps all the way to spinoffs).

There are client programs for all tastes, from TortoiseSVN (which integrates with the Windows Explorer) to the classic command-line client. This is the one we are going to use in this chapter. Look at what is available for your specific platform at http://subversion.tigris.org/project_packages.html, and download and install it.

The first time, you'll need to check out the part of the repository you need. For instance, to check out the trunk, just open a command prompt, go to the directory you want to check it out to, and then simply type this:

```
$ svn co http://svn.rubyonrails.org/rails/spinoffs/prototype/trunk/
A    trunk/test
A    trunk/test/unit
A    trunk/test/unit/range.html
...
A    trunk/src/ajax.js
A    trunk/src/form.js
A    trunk/src/hash.js
A    trunk/README
Checked out revision 6390.
$
```

Of course, you'll get a higher version number (it rises with every commit operation). You now have a trunk directory, which is bound to the Subversion repository. To update it to the latest version, you just need to get in there and type this:

```
$ svn up
U    test/unit/selector.html
U    Rakefile
U    CHANGELOG
U    src/selector.js
Updated to revision 6435.
$
```

There! You're all set to work with the latest sources.

The last thing you need is a Ruby setup, with Ruby and Rake executables. You can learn how to do that in Appendix C, on page 409.

Road to Glory: Creating Patches

Writing a patch is as simple as getting into the trunk's src directory and changing the appropriate .js file. Once this is done, you need to rebuild the consolidated prototype.js file. To do this, from somewhere in the trunk's directory tree, just type rake dist. This will build the library file in the trunk's dist directory. This file is used by the tests.

Working with Tests

When you're done with a patch, make sure you run the proper test files. Simply open them in the browsers you have handy. Passing tests go green, and failing ones go red. This can actually be a way to contribute. Run all the tests, find the failing ones, and go figure out what's wrong and fix them!

To see tests in action, just do this:

1. Fire up your trusty browser. Have it open the test/unit/array.html file. The page loads, runs all its tests, and is done. If everything is groovy, they all pass, as in Figure A.3, on the next page.

2. Now open src/array.js and break something! For instance, change first() to return **null** instead of this[0]. Rebuild the library (rake dist, remember?), and refresh the test page in your browser. It should look like Figure A.4, on the following page.

3. OK, you just ruined this file. Undo by hand and rebuild, or just use Subversion to revert to the latest checked-out version: svn revert src/array.js.

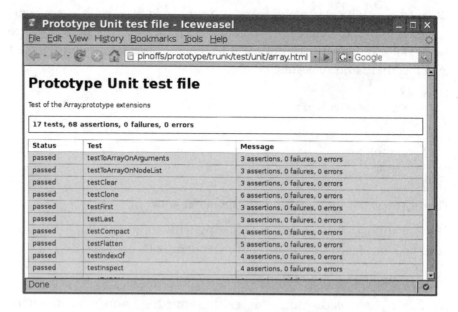

Figure A.3: A FLURRY OF PASSING TESTS

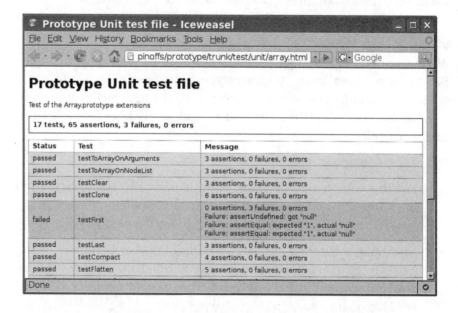

Figure A.4: OOPS! WE BROKE SOMETHING!

When your patch is done, *make sure you provide good test coverage.* Figure out as many things as you can that seem to need tests, and then write those tests in a way that will *fail* without your patch. Test with and without your patch applied. You can even run all tests automatically by using rake test. It runs all the tests on all the available browsers (which some tests, like Ajax ones, require so they get a valid server side). You can restrict it by using its BROWSERS and TESTS variables.

The test files are located in the test subdirectory, with the unit tests in test/unit. Just look at the large inline scripts in there for inspiration on how to add tests to the suites.

Packaging, Submitting, and Cleaning Up

All set? Then package your patch as a Subversion *diff file.* It's easy, really. Just go to the trunk's base directory, and do something like this:

```
$ svn diff > good_patch_name.diff
$
```

You might want to put these files outside the trunk directory. Then go to the Trac, edit or create the proper ticket, and attach your patch to it. Add a comment to add whatever explanations are required about this patch. Update the summary if need be.

Also, don't forget to revert your trunk directory to its normal state before tackling any other work or updating it once again. Just go the trunk's base directory, and do this:

```
$ svn revert -R .
Reverted 'src/array.js'
$
```

Code Style Guidelines

- Indent with two spaces, *not* tabs. Make sure your editor of choice doesn't use some autofill mode that will convert given amounts of spaces to tabs automatically.

- Use expressive variable names; n, e, or ePC won't quite cut it.

- Use semicolons to terminate statements.

- If possible, use Unix line breaks.

- Just look at the existing source code for inspiration about general code architecture and layout. Avoid polluting the global namespace as much as possible; put function-specific constants, variables, and subfunctions in the calling function's prototype; and so on.

- Notice some low-hanging fruit (trivial fix about performance or cleanliness)? Pick it!

Common Pitfalls

- First, don't go writing a patch that will end up being considered invalid (see earlier in this chapter about such cases). Also make sure you're not duplicating an existing effort.

- Make sure you revert your local repository before starting up on a new patch so you don't aggregate it with prior patching work.

- Make sure you update your local repository, too, so you do patch against the latest trunk (revert *before* updating).

- The tests keep failing? Are you sure you rebuilt the library (rake dist) after saving the source file?

- Make sure you test in at least two browsers, one of which must be Firefox. If you're on Linux, try testing on Firefox and Konqueror, at least. If you're on Mac OS X, use Firefox, Safari (ideally 2 and 3), and perhaps Opera. If you're on Windows, go crazy and use Firefox, Internet Explorer (ideally both versions 6 and 7), Opera 9 or later, and perhaps even Safari 3!

We're looking forward to your contributions!

Appendix B

Further Reading

B.1 Official Websites

Prototype..http://prototypejs.org
This holds the reference API documentation, replete with examples and cross-references. You'll also find various tutorials and get to know Prototype Core members. New sections open from time to time, such as a recommended books list, a centralized listing of third-party add-ons and libraries, and so on.

script.aculo.us...http://script.aculo.us
Although the documentation part is currently lackluster in comparison with Prototype's, it still holds a lot of information and a large number of demos. A documentation effort should assemble late in 2007 to try to bring it up to par with Prototype's, so keep your fingers crossed.

B.2 Useful Blogs by Prototype Core Members

Andrew Dupont: Painfully Obvious ....http://andrewdupont.net/
Andrew has been an extremely active contributor, being the driving force behind 1.5.1's Selector rewrite and helping with countless other topics such as style manipulation, DOM tweaks, or the future inheritance scheme. His blog talks not only of Prototype but also other frameworks, JavaScript, and web development in general.

Dan Webb..http://www.danwebb.net/
The man behind so many cool things: Dan has his fingers in such acclaimed pies as Prototype, LowPro, the JavaScript CodeHighlighter library, and the Unobtrusive JavaScript (UJS) plug-in for Rails, just to name a few. He's very active in everything related to JavaScript events and speaks at a number of top-notch conferences.

Justin Palmer: Encytemedia .... http://www.encytemedia.com/
Justin spear-headed Prototype's documentation effort around Christmas 2006 and has been an active voice in promoting the framework for a long time. When he's not over his head with client work, he dumps little golden nuggets of healthy Prototype usage in his blog.

Thomas Fuchs: mir.aculo.us .... http://mir.aculo.us/
The gifted creator of script.aculo.us keeps tabs on releases and release candidates for both his and Sam's framework and looks at books and other resources, too.

Tobie Langel .... http://tobielangel.com/
One of the most active Core members, Tobie posts regularly about everything Prototype and JavaScript: tips, books, new versions, other frameworks, cool features, tutorial articles—you name it.

Yours truly: The Bungee Blog .... http://thebungeebook.net
So Prototype and script.aculo.us kept moving ahead after this book released? I sure hope they did! But fear not—this book is, very likely, still very, very much up-to-date and useful, and you can catch up on all the new tricks on this blog. . . while waiting for the next edition!

B.3 JavaScript Masters

Dean Edwards .... http://dean.edwards.name/
He Who Writes Dazzling JavaScript. Dean is revered throughout the JavaScript world and keeps coming up with code that pushes the envelope of what the rest of us thought possible. . . with code that sometimes makes other ninjas' heads hurt. This is a must-read for serious, advanced scripters.

Douglas Crockford .... http://www.crockford.com/
The man behind JSON (and so much more) provides a great site chock-full with useful information, tricks, advanced scripting, and nifty tools.

Jack Slocum .... http://www.jackslocum.com/blog/index.php
Jack's work on YUI-Ext and DomQuery is inspirational, and great ideas keep being exchanged between Prototype Core members and Jack, which have led to major performance boosts and nifty features all around. His blog is full of JavaScript news, framework reviews, and detailed examples.

John Resig .... http://ejohn.org/
John is the creator of the jQuery library. Although most people see it as a competitor to Prototype, I would more gladly say it's great for smaller-scale sites, with a subset of the needs Prototype covers. Still, it's excellent code, and John knows his stuff very well. His site overflows with great articles, blog posts, and technical insights.

B.4 Community and New Sites Around Ajax

Ajaxian . . . . http://ajaxian.com/
Dion Almaer and Ben Galbraith, who authored [JG06], maintain a lively overview of the Ajax/Web 2.0 world, with numerous reviews of frameworks, libraries, books, and articles throughout the Web. This is sort of a one-stop shop to stay up-to-date.

B.5 ECMAScript Intimacy

Official ES4 / JS2 web page . . . . http://www.ecmascript-lang.org/
Official information, details about standard development, downloads of reference implementations, sneak peeks, and soon.

Brendan Eich: Roadmap updates. . .
. . . http://weblogs.mozillazine.org/roadmap/
Brendan, inventor of JavaScript, posts now and then about core developments to the next version of JavaScript. With JavaScript 2.0 currently cooking, it's a whole new world of possibilities that is opening up.

B.6 Bibliography

[JG06]   Dion Almaer Justin Gehtland, Ben Galbraith. *Pragmatic Ajax: A Web 2.0 Primer*. The Pragmatic Programmers, LLC, Raleigh, NC, and Dallas, TX, 2006.

Appendix C

Installing and Using Ruby

Although Prototype and script.aculo.us are totally agnostic about the server side, I chose to use Ruby when writing the small servers for Ajax-based examples. The reasons for this are many:

- Using server layers such as JavaEE, ASP.NET, or PHP requires some serious setup on your machine if it's not already your working environment. Sure, there are tools like EasyPHP for Windows, but that leaves out other platforms.

- JavaEE and ASP.NET require too much groundwork in order to get a working page. There's project creation, server configuration, and more. And with PHP, unless you're using EasyPHP, there's a lot of setup to do as well, binding it to a web server, and so on.

- I just don't like PHP all that much, too.

- Getting the server technology up and running, in the context of this book, should be as unobtrusive as possible. Monitoring the server side should be easy, too, in case you mistype the scripts. This book is about Prototype and script.aculo.us, *not* about server-side technologies.

So, I chose Ruby, because it's simple enough for non-Rubyists to grasp quickly (or at least, get the hang of how the script works), it's simple to install on most platforms (when it's not already there), and there's zero setup groundwork when you need a server with dynamic contents.

To run the examples in this book, you will thus need to have Ruby installed on your machine. This is pretty easy to do, and this appendix will show you how.

C.1 On Windows

The golden way to go for Microsoft Windows is to use the 1-Click Ruby Installer, a package maintained on RubyForge. Its home page is at http://rubyinstaller.rubyforge.org/wiki/wiki.pl?RubyInstaller, with the latest download (Ruby 1.8.6) at the time of this writing being accessible at http://rubyforge.org/frs/download.php/18566/ruby186-25.exe.

This installer does not only contain Ruby but also popular tools, extensions, and documentation files in various formats. If all you need is Ruby itself, you can go with the binary download at ftp://ftp.ruby-lang. org/pub/ruby/binaries/mswin32/ruby-1.8.6-i386-mswin32.zip.

C.2 On Linux

Well, chances are you already have Ruby installed if you're running Linux. It's used by many system tools. Open a console, and try the following command:

```
$ ruby -v
ruby 1.8.6 (2007-03-13 patchlevel 0) [i486-linux]
```

If you get a *Command not found* error, you don't have it yet. But fear not—all you need to do is install the relevant packages. Depending on your distribution, the package system will vary, but the package name is usually *ruby*. There are currently packages for Debian, Mandriva, SuSE, Red Hat Linux, BSDs, and a number of their variants (including Ubuntu, OpenSuSE, Fedora, and more). Slackware also gets packages through LinuxPackages.net, for instance.

If you plan only to run the examples in this book, that is in fact all you need. If you plan to tinker a bit more with Ruby, you will probably want irb (interactive Ruby shell, great to try stuff out) and ri (the help browser), too.

For instance, on Debian and its derivates (for example, Ubuntu), all you need to do is something like this:

```
$ sudo apt-get install ruby irb ri
```

(Note that if you use Ubuntu or its derivatives, you'll have to enable the *universe* repository to get these.)

C.3 On Mac OS X

OS X is now in a love affair with Ruby and Ruby on Rails, which mostly shows in Leopard (OS X 10.5, just released as this book is going to press). Depending on the version of OS X you have, there are a bunch of options for binaries:

- Panther (10.3), Tiger (10.4) and Leopard (10.5) have Ruby 1.8 pre-installed; Leopard features version 1.8.6, which is the latest one at the time of this writing.

- Jaguar (10.2): there's a .dmg package for Ruby 1.8.2 available at http://homepage.mac.com/discord/Ruby.

If you're technically savvy, you can naturally elect to grab the source for the latest version and compile it yourself: ftp://ftp.ruby-lang.org/pub/ruby/ruby-1.8.6.tar.gz. A middle-of-the-road approach would be to use tools such as MacPorts[1] or Fink[2]; for instance, with MacPorts, you can grab Ruby like this:

```
$ port install ruby
```

C.4 Running a Ruby Script

The universal way of running a Ruby script is simply to pass its filename to the ruby interpreter. For instance, you would open a command prompt, move into the script's directory, and invoke the interpreter on it. For instance:

```
$ ruby server.rb
```

In all our server-side examples for this book, we use Ruby's inclusion of the WEBrick module in its standard library to provide us with a working, lightweight HTTP server that can still run Ruby code dynamically. To make things simpler, WEBrick will, by default, do all its logging on the script's standard output, which is your console window. We can make it very easy to stop, too. Just press `Ctrl+C` in the console window once it's running.

This all makes it very easy to run a server, track its logs, and stop it, especially when compared to other server-side solutions.

---

1. http://www.macports.org/
2. http://fink.sourceforge.net/

C.5 "But I Don't Know a Thing About Ruby!"

Have no fear, have no fear. Ruby is the kind of language you can quickly get the basics of; it follows the principle of least surprise. To newcomers, a piece of Ruby code often does *what it seems to be doing*. And the code in this book refrains from using too much Ruby-fu so as not to make your head spin.

At any rate, if you're interested into learning more about this wonderful language, the prime resource to head for is the official website, which links to everything you'll need to quickly get on the saddle, from 20-minute tutorials to book-length material.

The official site is at http://ruby-lang.org.

Here are some great write-ups that will take you less than an hour and equip you with everything you need to comfortably wade through the examples:

http://tryruby.hobix.com/
> An interactive, 15-minute demo. It's entirely online and doesn't require you to install Ruby first! Coming from the infamous Why The Lucky Stiff, it's very funny to walk through, too.

http://www.ruby-lang.org/en/documentation/quickstart/
> A 20-minute intro to Ruby, which is pretty cool to help you dive in. Like a lot of documentation on the Ruby official website, it's available in a variety of languages, usually including English, French, Spanish, and Japanese.

http://www.ruby-lang.org/en/documentation/ruby-from-other-languages/
> Ruby is very cool, but coming from other languages can sometimes inhibit us with bred reflexes as to what is or is not possible and how to achieve certain results. This write-up highlights important points and idioms every newcomer should know in order to take best advantage of Ruby's syntax and possibilities.

You'll find a lot more material, including books (sometimes very offbeat ones, such as "Why's (poignant) guide to Ruby") on the documentation page at http://www.ruby-lang.org/en/documentation/.

Index

Web 2.0

It's not a one-browser world anymore. Are you ready for new portable devices, assistive technologies, and more? Learn what cross-browser compatible *really* means with *Design Accessible Web Sites*.

If you'd like to learn Ajax in greater depth, then a great place to start is *Pragmatic Ajax*.

The Accessible Web

The 2000 U.S. census revealed that 12% of the population is severely disabled. Sometime in the next two decades, one in five Americans will be over 65. Section 508 of the Americans with Disabilities Act requires your web site to provide *equivalent access* to all potential users. But beyond the law, it is both good manners and good business to make your site accessible to everyone. This book shows you how to design sites that excel for all audiences.

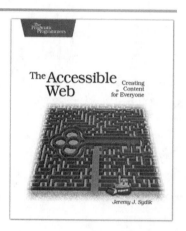

The Accessible Web
Jeremy Sydik
(304 pages) ISBN: 1-934356-02-6. $34.95
http://pragprog.com/titles/jsaccess

Pragmatic Ajax

Ajax redefines the user experience for web applications, providing compelling user interfaces. Now you can dig deeper into Ajax itself as this book shows you how to make Ajax magic. Explore both the fundamental technologies and the emerging frameworks that make it easy.

From Google Maps to Ajaxified Java, .NET, and Ruby on Rails applications, this Pragmatic guide strips away the mystery and shows you the easy way to make Ajax work for you.

Pragmatic Ajax: A Web 2.0 Primer
Justin Gehtland, Ben Galbraith, Dion Almaer
(296 pages) ISBN: 0-9766940-8-5. $29.95
http://pragprog.com/titles/ajax

Pragmatic Projects

See what an agile project is supposed to feel like in the award-winning *Practices of an Agile Developer*.

Have you ever noticed that project retrospectives feel too little, too late? What you need to do is start having *Agile Retrospectives*.

Practices of an Agile Developer

Agility is all about using feedback to respond to change. Learn how to apply the principles of agility throughout the software development process • Establish and maintain an agile working environment • Deliver what users really want • Use personal agile techniques for better coding and debugging • Use effective collaborative techniques for better teamwork • Move to an agile approach

Practices of an Agile Developer: Working in the Real World
Venkat Subramaniam and Andy Hunt
(189 pages) ISBN: 0-9745140-8-X. $29.95
http://pragprog.com/titles/pad

Agile Retrospectives

Mine the experience of your software development team continually throughout the life of the project. Rather than waiting until the end of the project—as with a traditional retrospective, when it's too late to help—agile retrospectives help you adjust to change *today*.

The tools and recipes in this book will help you uncover and solve hidden (and not-so-hidden) problems with your technology, your methodology, and those difficult "people issues" on your team.

Agile Retrospectives: Making Good Teams Great
Esther Derby and Diana Larsen
(170 pages) ISBN: 0-9776166-4-9. $29.95
http://pragprog.com/titles/dlret

Enterprise Ready

Your application is feature complete, but is it ready for the real world? See how to design and deploy production-ready software and *Release It!*

Did you know Ruby could glue together all sorts of enterprise technologies? See how in *Enterprise Integration with Ruby.*

Release It!

Whether it's in Java, .NET, or Ruby on Rails, getting your application ready to ship is only half the battle. Did you design your system to survive a sudden rush of visitors from Digg or Slashdot? Or an influx of real-world customers from 100 different countries? Are you ready for a world filled with flaky networks, tangled databases, and impatient users?

If you're a developer and don't want to be on call at 3 a.m. for the rest of your life, this book will help.

Design and Deploy Production-Ready Software
Michael T. Nygard
(368 pages) ISBN: 0-9787392-1-3. $34.95
http://pragprog.com/titles/mnee

Enterprise Integration with Ruby

See how to use the power of Ruby to integrate all the applications in your environment. Learn how to
• use relational databases directly and via mapping layers such as ActiveRecord • harness the power of directory services • create, validate, and read XML documents for easy information interchange • use both high- and low-level protocols to knit applications together

Enterprise Integration with Ruby
Maik Schmidt
(360 pages) ISBN: 0-9766940-6-9. $32.95
http://pragprog.com/titles/fr_eir

Ruby and Rails

Interested in learning Ruby or in learning how to use a scripting language the right way? Start with *Everyday Scripting with Ruby: For Teams, Testers, and You.*

If you know PHP and are curious about Ruby on Rails, you don't have to start from scratch. Read *Rails for PHP Developers*, and you can catch up to the industry leaders by learning this exciting new technology.

Everyday Scripting with Ruby

Don't waste that computer on your desk. Offload your daily drudgery to where it belongs, and free yourself to do what you should be doing: thinking. All you need is a scripting language (free!), this book (cheap!), and the dedication to work through the examples and exercises. Learn the basics of the Ruby scripting language and see how to create scripts in a steady, controlled way using test-driven design.

Everyday Scripting with Ruby: For Teams, Testers, and You
Brian Marick
(320 pages) ISBN: 0-9776166-1-4. $29.95
http://pragprog.com/titles/bmsft

Rails for PHP Developers

Rails for PHP Developers kick-starts your Rails experience by guiding you through learning both Ruby and Rails from a PHP developer's perspective. Written by developers with deep experience using PHP, Ruby, and Rails, this book leverages your existing knowledge of PHP to learn Rails application development quickly and effectively.

Rails for PHP Developers
Derek DeVries and Mike Naberezny
(375 pages) ISBN: 978-1-9343560-4-3. $34.95
http://pragprog.com/titles/ndphpr

The Pragmatic Bookshelf

The Pragmatic Bookshelf features books written by developers for developers. The titles continue the well-known Pragmatic Programmer style and continue to garner awards and rave reviews. As development gets more and more difficult, the Pragmatic Programmers will be there with more titles and products to help you stay on top of your game.

Visit Us Online

Prototype and script.aculo.us's Home Page
http://pragprog.com/titles/cppsu
Source code from this book, errata, and other resources. Come give us feedback, too!

Register for Updates
http://pragprog.com/updates
Be notified when updates and new books become available.

Join the Community
http://pragprog.com/community
Read our weblogs, join our online discussions, participate in our mailing list, interact with our wiki, and benefit from the experience of other Pragmatic Programmers.

New and Noteworthy
http://pragprog.com/news
Check out the latest pragmatic developments in the news.

Save on the PDF

Save on the PDF version of this book. Owning the paper version of this book entitles you to purchase the PDF version at a terrific discount. The PDF is great for carrying around on your laptop. It's hyperlinked, has color, and is fully searchable.

Buy it now at pragmaticprogrammer.com/coupon.

Contact Us

Phone Orders:	1-800-699-PROG (+1 919 847 3884)
Online Orders:	www.pragmaticprogrammer.com/catalog
Customer Service:	orders@pragmaticprogrammer.com
Non-English Versions:	translations@pragmaticprogrammer.com
Pragmatic Teaching:	academic@pragmaticprogrammer.com
Author Proposals:	proposals@pragmaticprogrammer.com